PARENTAL LEAVE AND BEYOND

Recent international developments, current issues and future directions

Edited by Peter Moss, Ann-Zofie Duvander and Alison Koslowski

P

This paperback edition first published in Great Britain in 2020 by

Policy Press
University of Bristol
1-9 Old Park Hill
Bristol
BS2 8BB
UK
t: +44 (0)117 954 5940
pp-info@bristol.ac.uk
www.policypress.co.uk

British Library Cataloguing in Publication Data
A catalogue record for this book is available from the British Library

978-1-4473-3877-2 hardback
978-1-4473-3878-9 paperback
978-1-4473-3879-6 ePdf
978-1-4473-3880-2 ePub
978-1-4473-3881-9 Mobi

Cover design by Robin Hawes
Front cover image: iStock

Contents

List of figures and tables

Figures

Tables

List of abbreviations

EC	European Commission
ECEC	Early Childhood Education and Care
EEC	European Economic Community
EU	European Union
ILO	International Labour Organisation
OECD	Organisation for Economic Cooperation and Development
TFR	Total Fertility Rate
WHO	World Health Organization

Notes on contributors

Sonja Blum (Germany) is a Researcher and Lecturer at the University of Hagen, Institute of Political Science, Public Policy Chair.

Maria Letizia Bosoni (Italy) is an Associate Professor at the Department of Sociology (Faculty of Education), Catholic University of Milan.

Berit Brandth (Norway) is a Professor Emerita at the Department of Sociology and Political Science, Norwegian University of Science and Technology (NTNU).

Fred Deven (Belgium) is a senior consultant on Family Policies and Social Cohesion.

Ivana Dobrotić (Croatia) is an Assistant Professor at the Department of Social Work (Faculty of Law), University of Zagreb.

Andrea Doucet (Canada) is a Canada Research Chair and Professor, Department of Sociology and Centre for Gender and Women's Studies, Brock University.

Ann-Zofie Duvander (Sweden) is a Professor at the Department of Sociology, Demography Unit, Stockholm University.

Anna Escobedo (Spain) is an Associate Professor at the Department of Sociology, University of Barcelona.

Guðný Björk Eydal (Iceland) is a Professor at the Faculty of Social Work, University of Iceland.

Bernard Fusulier (Belgium) is Research Director at the National Fund for Scientific Research; and Professor of Sociology at the Université catholique de Louvain.

Shirley Gatenio Gabel (United States) is a Professor at the Graduate School of Social Service, Fordham University, New York.

Ingólfur V. Gíslason (Iceland) is an Associate Professor at the Department of Sociology, University of Iceland.

Wen-Jui Han (United States) is a Professor at the Silver School of Social Work, New York University.

Valérie Harvey (Canada) is a doctoral candidate at the Université Laval, Québec.

Gayle Kaufman (United States) is a Professor at the Departments of Sociology and Gender & Sexuality Studies, Davidson College.

Alison Koslowski (United Kingdom) is a Professor at the School of Social and Political Science, University of Edinburgh, Scotland.

Anna Kurowska (Poland) is an Assistant Professor at the Faculty of Political Science and International Studies, University of Warsaw.

Elin Kvande (Norway) is a Professor at the Department of Sociology and Political Science, Norwegian University of Science and Technology (NTNU).

Johanna Lammi-Taskula (Finland) is a Research Manager at the National Institute for Health and Welfare.

Sophie Mathieu (Canada) is a postdoctoral fellow, Brock University.

Sara Mazzucchelli (Italy) is an Associate Professor at the Department of Sociology (Faculty of Psychology), Catholic University of Milan.

Lindsey McKay (Canada) is a Lecturer in the Department of Sociology and Anthropology, Thompson Rivers University, Canada.

Gerardo Meil (Spain) is a Professor at the Department of Sociology, Universidad Autonoma de Madrid.

Laura Merla (Belgium) is a Professor of Sociology at the Interdisciplinary Research Centre on Families and Sexualities, Université catholique de Louvain, Belgium; and Honorary Research Fellow, University of Western Australia.

Peter Moss (United Kingdom) is an Emeritus Professor at the Thomas Coram Research Unit, UCL Institute of Education, University College London.

Hideki Nakazato (Japan) is a Professor at the Department of Sociology, Faculty of Letters, Konan University, Kobe.

Chantal Nicole-Drancourt (France) is Research Director at the National Centre for Scientific Research, LISE-CNAM, Paris.

Margaret O'Brien (United Kingdom) is a Professor at the Thomas Coram Research Unit, UCL Institute of Education, University College London.

Cándido Pérez-Hernández (Mexico) is a doctoral candidate at the Faculty of Economics and Business, Anahuac University and Research Director, Early Institute.

Nadav Perez-Vaisvidovsky (Israel) is a Lecturer at the School of Social Work, Ashkelon Academic College.

Luca Pesenti (Italy) is an Associate Professor at the Department of Sociology (Faculty of Political Science), Catholic University of Milan.

Jesús Rogero-García (Spain) is a Lecturer at the Department of Sociology, Universidad Autonoma de Madrid.

Pedro Romero-Balsas (Spain) is a Lecturer at the Department of Sociology, Universidad Autonoma de Madrid.

Tine Rostgaard (Denmark) is a Professor at VIVE – The Danish Centre for Social Science Research.

Diane-Gabrielle Tremblay (Canada) is a Professor and Director of the CURA research centre on Work Life Articulation over the life course at TÉLUQ University, Québec.

Isabel Valarino (Switzerland) is a Research Officer at the Education Research Unit of the Canton of Geneva (SRED).

Xiaoran Wang (United States) is a doctoral candidate at the Graduate School of Social Service, Fordham University, New York.

Acknowledgements

This book is the product of a collective endeavour by a group of authors sharing a common interest in leave policy as well as membership of the International Network on Leave Policies & Research. During the preparation of the book, authors read and commented on each others' early draft chapters, and all benefited from this process. As editors, we would like to thank all the authors of chapters in this book for freely contributing their expertise, knowledge and work to this common project. We would also like to recognise the collegiality and support of all members of the International Network, who have created a community of scholars conducive to mutual exchange and collaborative working, cutting across national and disciplinary boundaries.

Peter Moss, Ann-Zofie Duvander and Alison Koslowski

ONE

Introduction:
much work still to do

Peter Moss, Alison Koslowski
and Ann-Zofie Duvander

Leave high on the policy agenda

Entitlements for workers to take leave from work for health or welfare reasons have been part of the policy scene for a long time. Maternity Leave for women, to protect their health before and after childbirth and that of their newborn children, was first introduced towards the end of the nineteenth century, and was present in 21 countries by 1914; in 1919, the International Labour Office (ILO) adopted a Maternity Protection Convention, which included minimum leave standards. Maternity Leave continued to spread, to be followed by a second wave of leave policy, starting in Sweden in 1974, which introduced Parental Leave, leave available equally to mothers and fathers to enable both to spend time away from the workplace caring for their young child. This wave of leave has also included some countries adopting Paternity Leave, a provision only for fathers to allow them to spend time in the period immediately after childbirth with their partner, new child and older children; other entitlements, also increasingly to be found, include leave to care for sick children and adult relatives. It could be said that we are on the cusp of a third wave of leave, looking beyond a gendered primary carer model to allow for more diverse family types, including same-sex families.

Today, Parental Leave and other forms of statutory leave are widespread and still spreading; high on the policy agenda, they have become a staple of the modern welfare state, concerned as it is with actively supporting parental employment, child well-being, and (on paper at least) promoting gender equality. According to the ILO, in its 2013 survey of legal provision in 185 countries, all provided some form of statutory leave for pregnant women, and all but two (Papua New Guinea and the United States) included some payment. However, only

> 34 per cent (57 countries) fully meet the requirements of [ILO] Convention No. 183 [2000] on three key aspects [of Maternity Leave]: they provide for at least 14 weeks of leave at a rate of at least two thirds of previous earnings, paid by social insurance or public funds or in a manner determined by national law and practice where the employer is not solely responsible for payment. (ILO, 2014, p.xiii)

The report also acknowledges substantial regional differences, with particularly low provision for leave in Africa and Latin America and the Caribbean, and a mixed picture in Asia and the Middle East.

Widespread leave provision is no longer confined to women. The ILO's 2013 survey found that Paternity Leave was available in 79 out of 167 countries for whom information was available, with payment of some sort in most cases. Parental Leave in some form was present in 66 out of 169 countries supplying information, though only paid in 36 countries. Leave provision for men is found most often in higher income countries.

Yet despite the increasing prominence given to leave across the world, it is also clear that there is much work still to do on the development of this policy field. It remains disorderly and unresolved, with large variations in leave policies, even among high-income countries. This variability is brought home to us each year, when we and colleagues in the International Network on Leave Policies and Research produce a review of leave policies in countries represented in the network; in 2017, this meant 42 countries, mainly in Europe, but also including countries in the Americas, East Asia, Africa and Australasia (the network and its annual review are discussed further below). The country notes in this annual review show how much leave policies differ, on such basics as duration, payment, eligibility and overall design, for example whether or not Maternity Leave is partially transferable to fathers and whether Parental Leave is a family or individual entitlement.

Such variations have led to scholars attempting to impose some order on the confused and confusing picture. At the level of the welfare state, there have been various developments and critiques of typologies, including an increasing emphasis on women's work and the gendering of welfare state studies (Orloff, 2009). The importance of going from a uni-dimensional categorisation of family policies as more or less 'woman friendly' to a multi-dimensional categorisation, which, for example, includes such factors as social class, has been recognised as a necessary step towards a fuller understanding of existing welfare regimes (Korpi et al, 2013). Scholars have also begun to go beyond broader welfare state typologies to propose ideal types specifically designed to aid our understanding of the diversity in leave policies (for example, Ray et al, 2010; Ciccia and Verloo, 2012; Wall and Escobedo, 2013).

Useful as such attempts at ordering leave policies undoubtedly are, helping us to see some pattern within a confused picture, there is still work to be done in explaining the reasons behind the variations that exist, either between ideal leave types or between countries included within the same ideal type – and it is worth emphasising that even among countries often grouped together because of broad similarities in their leave policies or, more broadly, across their whole welfare states, for example the five Nordic states, there remain major differences once policies are studied in greater detail (Duvander and Lammi-Taskula, 2011). To understand more, we must turn to other approaches, in particular the politics of leave policy. For variations are mainly the result of national (or occasionally regional or provincial) politics. As Patricia Boling puts it, when asking 'why the US can't be Sweden',

> [e]very country has a political logic that guides its approach to work–family policy making. While it is important to think about which policies work best, there are also crucial lessons to draw from a comparative study of the political and historical constraints on policy change...
>
> Countries have well-established constellations of political power, political rules and institutions, policy repertoires, ways of governing their markets and value systems. These shape the policy approaches they adopt to deal with particular problems, and, indeed, what they recognize as problems in need of solution in the first place. (2015, pp.204, 208)

It is the politics of leave that maintains existing approaches, even when they are not fit for purpose, or constrains the scope for changing them, what some have termed 'path dependency'; or that may occasionally lead to substantive change as a country diverts on to a new path taking policy in a different direction. Leave policies will often be the product of compromises made between political actors of different persuasions, but also representing different policy areas, for example family, labour market or gender equality. These actors may find some common ground across the political and policy spectrums, but not in all cases.

The politics that lead to policy stasis or policy change do not, of course, occur in a vacuum; they are conditioned and they are symptomatic. They are shaped by the past, 'by early and strategic choices made in a given area of regulation or policy' (Boling, 2015, p.17), choices that set the direction of travel, from which it can prove hard to deviate. They are shaped by many contextual factors: cultural values and widespread beliefs, for example about gender and parenthood; forms of capitalism and the organisation of labour markets; and the many facets of demography. As Robin Alexander writes of education, but equally applicable to social welfare, no 'policy or practice can be properly understood except by reference to the web of inherited ideas and values, habits and customs, institutions and world views, that make one country distinct from another' (Alexander, 2001, p.5). Last but not least, politics are shaped by the interplay of many interests and views, their relative influence and power at any given time, and the institutions and processes through which these interests and views are represented and by which policy decisions are arrived at. We will return to the theme of the politics of leave policy later in this chapter and in the first part of the book.

Leave policy: unfinished business

Parental Leave...

Variations in leave policies and their political causes mean that many issues in this field remain unresolved; there is no international consensus on the why and how of such policies. The issue of gender is perhaps the most contentious. Despite a widespread rhetoric of gender equality, relatively few countries have actually designed leave policies in such a way as to promote this goal (for example, by having substantial periods of well-paid and non-transferable father-only Parental Leave); while some are designed in such a way as to actually undermine it (for example, by having long periods of low paid or unpaid Parental Leave allotted to 'families', for parents to decide how to divide).

But there are other contentious issues in deciding leave policy. For example, how much flexibility (that is, scope to vary the way leave can be taken) should there be for different types of leave? What eligibility conditions should there be, especially in a world with increasing levels of so-called 'atypical' or precarious employment and growing pools of migrant labour? How long should the period of leave last, and what should be the level of payment? How should leave policy relate to other policies (such as entitlement to a place in an early childhood education and care (ECEC) service), which support the same broad aims such as gender equality, support for families with employed parents or child welfare? What should be the respective roles of statutory and workplace policies and how supportive are workplaces of those women and men who take leave? Or, to take a last example, how should the interests of young children in leave policies be represented and should these interests be paramount?

These issues are, of course, inter-connected. In an ideal world, they would be mutually supportive, offering a seamless and coherent whole. But in practice, they can present conflicting positions. For example, some will advocate for a flexible leave system that enables both parents to choose how to divide Parental Leave between themselves and both parents, if they choose, to take leave together; while others will argue that such flexibility undermines progress towards greater equality in childrearing between women and men, and should not be part of leave policy.

Leave policy is not just unresolved; it can also be considered as under-developed from a range of perspectives, adding to a sense of unfinished business. This under-development of leave policy manifests itself in a number of ways. For those who see the promotion of gender equality as a main purpose of leave, it is clear, as already noted, that policies in many countries are not designed (and probably not actually intended) to achieve this. A minority of countries have overly long periods of Maternity Leave that, even if part transferable to fathers with the mother's consent, send a clear signal about women retaining primary responsibility for childrearing. More significantly, few countries have designed Parental Leave so as to maximise use by fathers, that is with a substantial period of well-paid, father-only leave (the six months for fathers in Japan is the longest such period, far ahead of any other country; see Chapter Six). For those who see the best interests of the child as a main purpose of leave, it is clear that a substantial care gap remains in many countries, as leave and ECEC systems are often not aligned. Similarly, those who consider the economic perspective as a main purpose of leave might point to benefit levels that are often not sufficient to reduce maternal and child poverty.

Irrespective of the purposes of leave that are valued and the differences of opinion on this topic, most could agree about the under-development of national data collection around leave take-up. This means, for example, that it is difficult or impossible to know what proportion of women and men having a child are eligible for different types of leave; what proportion of those who are eligible take leave; the duration of leave actually taken; what benefits are received;

and how take-up and use vary according to social and employment background. Tables in the OECD Family Database for 2013 provide some information on the relative use of Parental Leave between women and men, confirming that in most cases this leave is predominantly taken by women, but data for many of OECD's member states are missing.[1] So, despite the policy attention paid to leave policy in recent years, we are left with woefully little basic, reliable and comparable information about how and for whom it works. We can only hope that the mounting pressure, from policy-makers, academics and others, for better statistics and indicators will produce results in the not too distant future, enabling better understanding and evaluation of leave policies.

...and beyond

After more than a hundred years of development, and despite the last 40 years of more intensive development, the field of leave policy is still focused, one might even say fixated, on one relatively short, albeit rather critical, period of the life course: early parenthood. While countries are still struggling to create coherent and effective policies for the earliest years of childrearing, they have, by and large, ignored the rest of the life course, and the caring needs that it may generate, for example for older children and adults with chronic disabilities and for frail older people. With perhaps the exception of the career break system in Belgium (see Chapter Seventeen), the most that has been done, and only in some countries, is to give workers some rights to take some leave, often unpaid, to care for some family members for limited periods when these relatives are sick or disabled.

For these reasons, there has been a longstanding argument for leave policies to broaden their scope to cover the whole of the life course. But the case is getting more urgent. Increasing longevity[2] means increasing numbers of older citizens needing care, which has implications for younger (and employed) family members. Leave, of course, is not the only answer; development of leave policies needs to be matched by development of formal care services as such services

---

[1] www.oecd.org/els/family/PF2-2-Use-childbirth-leave.pdf

[2] More than half of children born in 2007 in the G7 countries are predicted to live for 100 years or longer (www.theguardian.com/business/2017/jun/04/job-opportunities-should-not-wither-as-we-age). In the shorter term, the share of those aged 80 years or above in the EU-28's population is projected to more than double between 2016 and 2080, from 5.4 per cent to 12.7 per cent (http://ec.europa.eu/eurostat/statistics-explained/index.php/Population_structure_and_ageing).

are crucial if care is not to be left an individual family responsibility, which is often highly gendered in practice and puts those without available family at risk.

Caring also needs to be seen not only as long-term, required over the life course, but as a wide-ranging responsibility and activity, covering not only the care of others, but also care for the community (for example, by participation in local democracy and civil society organisations) and for the environment. Leave policies, it can be argued, need to address all these diverse forms of caring. Moreover, caring broadly defined needs to be viewed as attaching equally to men and women, with the assumption – by individuals, families, communities and workplaces – of what Nancy Fraser (2016) has called the 'universal caregiving' model of life (see Chapter Nineteen). Leave policies could have a potentially important role to play in helping all concerned adapt to and implement such a model, in close partnership with complementary public services.

But there are other reasons for thinking beyond Parental Leave. The life course of individuals as workers is also changing. Increasing longevity and pension costs suggest that many members of the workforce will be expected to continue in employment longer, putting back the start of retirement. Yet, at the same time, the future of that employment is increasingly in doubt, with the possibility of the mass eradication of jobs and human employment as the full impact of technological change is felt across our world. In a 2013 publication (*The Future of Employment: How Susceptible are Jobs to Computerisation?*), Frey and Osborne conclude that nearly half of all US jobs are at high risk of disappearing within 20 years. While a recent report on the UK in 2030 concludes that

> 15 million jobs – two-thirds of the total – are at medium to high risk of being automated in the coming decades. Both routine and non-routine work will be displaced... Over time there will be fewer and fewer tasks – and in time, jobs – where humans can outperform machines. Given this, it is likely we are at 'peak human' in terms of human labour being the most important factor of production. (IPPR, 2016, p.28)

To which it can be countered that past production revolutions have destroyed jobs, but also created new ones in at least equal measure. But that argument too is contested. This time round, some contend, such job replacement may not happen; in the latest technological revolution, new work will not fill the gap left by the destruction of current jobs. As Yuval Harari observes:

> [this job replacement] is not a law of nature, and nothing guarantees it will continue to be like that in the future… As long as machines competed with us merely in physical abilities, you could always find cognitive tasks that humans do better. So machines took over purely manual jobs, while humans focused on jobs requiring at least some cognitive skills. Yet what will happen once algorithms outperform us in remembering, analysing and recognising patterns… (so) the crucial problem isn't creating new jobs. The crucial problem is creating new jobs that humans perform better than algorithms. (Harari, 2016, p.326)

This, Yuval Harari suggests, may create a wholly new and disturbing situation: 'The technological bonanza will probably make it feasible to feed and support the useless masses even without any effort on their side. But what will keep them occupied and content? People must do something, or they will go crazy. What will they do all day?' (Harari, 2016, p.326).

Doom-laden scenarios may prove too pessimistic and over dramatic, and are highly contentious. Former patterns of job generation may repeat themselves, a sufficiency of good new jobs may emerge; one potential growth area is employment in education, care and health services, especially if this goes alongside a revaluing of much work in these fields that is currently treated as low paid and low skilled. Humankind may continue to be as busy as ever, with work of some kind continuing to play a central role in life. The problem may continue to be too little free time, not too much.

But whatever happens, there is a strong case for thinking – here and now – more broadly and holistically about leave policies, moving towards a life course approach that can accommodate both certain demographic changes and less certain employment changes; and that can help to create a new, more equal and fulfilling relationship between gender, care and employment, supporting a genuine balance between working life and life outside the workplace, in what the authors of Chapter Eighteen refer to as a 'multi-activity' society. In the face of the changes coming down the tracks – some clearly visible, others shrouded in uncertainty – the current focus on leave for early parenthood seems short-sighted. Important though it is to continue to work on Parental Leave policy to get the details right, there is a pressing need to get beyond Parental Leave and to think deeply about future directions for a broadly conceived leave policy.

Future directions or wishful thinking?

The need to think about future directions for leave policies, which take account both of changing circumstances and more constant desires for human flourishing and the good society, is urgent. Desirability is the starting point, which is about laying out values, ethics and goals. One asks, says Erik Olin Wright: 'what are the moral principles that a given alternative is supposed to serve? This is the domain of pure utopian social theory and much normative political philosophy. Typically, such discussions are institutionally very thin, the emphasis being on the enunciation of abstract principles rather than actual institutional designs' (Wright, 2007, p.27).

Desirability is necessary but by no means sufficient when deciding future directions. There is a need, too, to consider viability, ensuring that envisaged future directions are workable in practice, for example proving accessible to all social groups and capable of achieving policy goals. Viability, Erik Olin Wright argues, represents:

> a response to the perpetual objection to radical egalitarian proposals 'it sounds good on paper, but it will never work'...[The exploration of viability focuses] on the likely dynamics and unintended consequences of the proposal if it were to be implemented. Two kinds of analysis are especially pertinent here: systematic theoretical models of how particular social structures and institutions would work, and empirical studies of cases, both historical and contemporary, where at least some aspects of the proposal have been tried. (Wright, 2007, p.28)

There is a third and final stage in this process of building what Wright terms 'real utopias', a mixture of imagination and what is pragmatically possible. That stage is achievability, which is about the process of transformation and the practical political work of strategies for social change: 'It asks of proposals for social change that have passed the test of desirability and viability, what it would take to actually implement them' (Wright, 2007, p.27). Wright argues that these three criteria are 'nested in a kind of hierarchy: Not all desirable alternatives are viable, and not all viable alternatives are achievable' (Wright, 2006, p.96).

Put another way, desirability without both viability and achievability is mere wishful thinking.

This book addresses issues of desirability and viability. It encourages the reader to think about what might be desirable in leave policies; and it explores viability, through both theoretical models and empirical case studies. But, in particular through its attention to politics, it raises questions about achievability. What are the major obstacles to transforming social policies? And what conditions may favour such fundamental changes, enabling their actual implementation? This will inevitably take us well beyond leave policies or even social policies and into, for example, questions about capitalism, relationships between economic production and social reproduction, and the place of leave policies within a full spectrum of social arrangements 'that could enable people of every class, gender, sexuality and colour to combine social-reproductive activities with safe, interesting and well-remunerated work' (Fraser, 2016, p.116). We will return to consider desirability and viability in the final concluding chapter, but in particular the big issue of achievability, with particular emphasis on the distribution of accessible benefits across the whole population.

The origins and purposes of this book

Much effort is currently going into developing leave policies for early parenthood; the results, though, are variable and uneven, due in large part to the politics of leave policy, with many issues, as we have argued, left unresolved. Moreover, much policy-making energy is narrowly focused. Rather than recent developments in leave representing the final stages of what must be done, it is apparent that our societies are still only in the early stages of appreciating what can be done. With much of the current policy attention focused on leave for parents of young children, we have hardly begun to question what future directions policy should take if it is to respond to the wider changes and challenges that our societies face. In short, the scale of the transformation we need is large, yet only dimly apparent. It is these considerations – both detailed analysis and improvement of existing policies and thinking broadly about possible future directions for leave policy – that have motivated the writing of this book.

The book has other origins, too. First and foremost, it emerges from the shared interests and collaborative ethos of a community of scholars – from a range of disciplinary backgrounds and diverse linguistic and cultural contexts – with a shared interest in leave policies, all members of the International Network on Leave Policies and Research (referred to below as the 'international network'). This originated in a more formal network established by the European Commission (EC) in 1986, the European Childcare Network (ECCN). Consisting of an expert from each of the then member states in the European Economic Community (EEC), later the European Union (EU), this network had a number of interests, including services for children from birth to ten years, men as carers for children (both as workers in services and as fathers), and leave policies. As part of its comparative work, the ECCN produced surveys of leave policies in EU member states.

After the ECCN ended in 1996, two members, its coordinator Peter Moss from the UK and the member for Belgian Flanders, Fred Deven, retained a strong interest in leave policies and convened a European seminar on the subject in Brussels in 1998, which resulted in an edited book (Moss and Deven, 1999), whose title suggested one of the key issues raised by leave policies: *Parental Leave: Progress or Pitfall?*. Then in 2004, they convened a second meeting in Brussels, at which the decision was made to establish a network focused specifically on leave policies and research. The international network was then coordinated by its two founders until handing over this responsibility in 2015, and it continues its work to this day. Indeed, it has not just continued, but has grown and thrived, despite having neither funding nor formal organisation, operating as a self-regulating community of scholars and a forum for the exchange of knowledge.

Today the international network numbers more than 60 members from over 40 countries, mostly in Europe (including representatives from all EU member states except Cyprus, as well as from Iceland, Norway and Switzerland), but also from further afield (including Australia, Brazil, Canada, China, Japan, Korea, Mexico, New Zealand, Russia, South Africa and Uruguay). The network holds an annual international seminar and produces an annual online review of leave policies and research in the countries represented in the network, a publication that over time has established itself as an important source of information for those studying leave policies. Presentations from past seminars and the annual reviews since 2005 can be found at the international network's website (www.leavenetwork.org).

The international network has established itself as a major and widely cited source of information on leave policies and research. It also provides an environment supportive of collaborative work, the output of which includes special journal issues and books. One such book was published in 2009, an edited volume titled *The Politics of Parental Leave Policies: Children, Gender, Parenting and the Labour Market* (Kamerman and Moss, 2009), and was inspired by one of the earliest members of the international network, and one of the leading figures in social policy of her generation, Professor Sheila Kamerman from Columbia University in New York. At successive network seminars, Sheila would raise an important subject: the paucity of work on the politics of leave policies – the who, how and why of leave policies as they emerged and evolved in individual countries (and in international organisations, too, such as the EU). Consequently, while there was an increasing body of work on leave policies themselves, Sheila constantly reminded the network that we knew little about the formation of these policies – why did they differ so much and how change came about (or failed to do so). The eventual result of Sheila's persistent *cri de coeur* was the 2009 volume, with chapters on 15 countries (all but two in Europe), as well as one about the creation of the 1996 EU Directive on Parental Leave.

That volume provided the starting point for the current volume. In proposing a new book, the three of us wanted to build on the earlier one, by further studying the politics of leave policies. This volume therefore looks at and analyses both implemented or attempted but failed policy changes in a range of countries and tries to understand the politics that enabled or obstructed change. The net this time is spread more widely, with only three chapters looking at European countries, the remainder coming from beyond, including China, Israel, Japan, Mexico and the United States. Though not, perhaps, widely enough, with no representation from low-income countries or, indeed, the Southern hemisphere; so while this volume provides a broader and more nunaced understanding of leave policy, much more remains to be done.

The focus of this book has also broadened in other ways, compared with the earlier volume. Rather than only looking at the politics of recent changes to leave policy in individual countries, we have added two new sections. The first explores a number of current issues in leave policy, each chapter illustrated by research on the subject. The second new section moves us from the recent past and the present day to a consideration of possible future directions for leave policies. We hope that this will provoke that wider perspective and deeper thought that we believe essential if leave policies are to fully contribute to human and societal well-being and flourishing.

A brief summary of the contributions found in this volume follows. Part I has eight chapters, which consider the politics of leave policy in a range of countries across the globe, starting with three European countries. In Chapter Two, Gerardo Meil, Pedro Romero-Balsas and Jesús Rogero-García relate the postponement of improvements in Spain's leave policy to the political scene during the economic crisis; the eventual doubling of Paternity Leave in 2017 marked a consensus achieved on the need for such reforms. In Chapter Three, Anna Kurowska explains the introduction of Parental Leave reform in 2013 in Poland with the help of a multiple streams approach; while using a capability approach, she seeks to understand the lack of gender equality in the policy that emerged. In Chapter Four, Peter Moss and Margaret O'Brien investigate the UK as a latecomer to leave policies compared to the rest of Europe, and analyse a recent failed attempt at reform, indicating the difficulty of taking a new direction. The remaining chapters are located outside Europe, starting with two high-income countries. Chapter Five by Nadav Perez-Vaisvidovsky focuses on a decade of attempted reform in Israel, whose leave policies have fallen behind those in Europe, and the limited success achieved, which he ascribes to the neoliberalisation of the Israeli welfare state and its adherence to the 'Austerity of Welfare' principle. Hideki Nakazato, in Chapter Six, plots the development of policy in Japan over 25 years that has led to that country today having 'by far the most generous paid father-specific entitlement in the OECD', while highlighting a continuing low take-up of leave by fathers, arguing that this reflects in part a failure to build a broad and coherent package of work–family policies. Attention then turns to two middle income countries. In Chapter Seven, Shirley Gatenio Gabel, Wen-Jui Han and Xiaoran Wang address leave policy in China, and specifically the development of Maternity and Paternity Leave in response to changing political, socio-economic and demographic goals, most recently changes to the one-child policy. In Chapter Eight, Cándido Pérez-Hernández and Anna Escobedo give an overview of leave policies in Latin American but focus on the situation in Mexico, and a problematic context created by a large informal economy, inadequate funding and fragmented early childcare provision. This first part concludes by considering, in Chapter Nine, the exceptional case of the United States, one of the few countries in the world without any paid statutory leave; Gayle Kaufman considers some possible reasons for such exceptionalism and how, in the absence of federal action, some states are taking a lead in creating their own programmes of paid leave.

Part II of the book considers some current issues in leave policy that go beyond the experience of individual countries, examined and illustrated with a mix of regional, national and cross-national analyses. The starting point, in Chapter Ten, is the issue of what people want from leave policies and how far they get what they want. Isabel Valarino presents a cross-national comparative study of 27 countries using

International Social Survey Programme data, to look at leave policy preferences across populations and how these vary internationally; stark differences exist related to welfare regimes regarding what is considered a 'good' leave. In Chapter Eleven, a Nordic team (Ann-Zofie Duvander, Guđný Björk Eydal, Berit Brandth, Ingólfur V. Gíslason, Johanna Lammi-Taskula and Tine Rostgaard) draw on that region's extensive experience to provide insight into a key issue: the relationship between leave-taking by fathers and gender equality more generally, and different designs for Parental Leave seen across the Nordic countries; they also consider how to conceptualise and measure gender equality in association with Parental Leave. The next two chapters also go into the issue of gender and leave-taking by fathers, as well as issues arising from workplace culture and practice. Chapter Twelve, by Berit Brandth and Elin Kvande, presents evidence from interviews with Norwegian fathers about the potential pitfalls to making Parental Leave more flexible, especially ennabling it to be taken part time. The study is set in Norway, but the issue extends well beyond, as illustrated in Chapter Thirteen, in which Valérie Harvey and Diane-Gabrielle Tremblay draw upon rich interview data to explore both the success of regional policies in Québec Province in Canada, which enable fathers to take time away from the workplace to care for their infants, but also the challenges that these arrangements bring to fathers and their employers. In Chapter Fourteen, Sara Mazzucchelli, Luca Pesenti and M. Letizia Bosoni consider how leave policy is a necessary but by no means sufficient condition for enabling a good relationship between care, employment and gender; we would do well, they argue, to conceptualise statutory Parental Leave policy within a broader framework of care-work policies, drawing upon four countries for illustration (Germany, Italy, Sweden, and the UK). Finally, in this part, in Chapter Fifteen Ivana Dobrotić and Sonja Blum consider the fraught and often hidden issue of eligibility for leave and reflect upon the extent to which leave can be considered a social right rather than being contingent on labour market position. Working with three country case examples (Belgium, Croatia and Germany), they develop a conceptual framework that permits distinctions to be made about whether and how Parental Leave rights are granted (in)dependent of parents' labour market position.

The third part of the book opens up for some possible future directions for leave policy. In Chapter Sixteen, Alison Koslowski considers the gendered implications of a Basic Income, a policy proposal currently receiving much attention, in particular with regards to early parenthood, and whether or not Basic Income could replace parenting leave policy or whether parenting leave would still be needed as a complementary policy. In Chapter Seventeen, Laura Merla and Fred Deven examine a unique experiment in leave policy, the Belgian time credit system that has provided a life course approach over more than 30 years, looking at the use made of the system as well as the growing inequalities in access, while also highlighting the failure to realise its full potential. Developing this theme of a life course approach, Bernard Fusulier and Chantal Nicole-Drancourt in Chapter Eighteen envisage a fundamental transformation in the work/family regime of modern societies, putting forward the scenario of a 'multi-activity society', based on a wide-ranging understanding of contribution, as a way to resolve the current paradox of an improvement in women's condition and an increase in gender inequalities. In Chapter Nineteen, Andrea Doucet, Lindsey McKay and Sophie Mathieu, working with a case study of Canada and concepts including decommodification, defamilialisation, degenderisation and demotherisation, engage in imaginative and utopian thinking to propose a future for leave policy no longer understood and enacted as an employment benefit but rather as a universal right of citizenship to provide and receive care.

Chapter Twenty concludes the volume with a discussion on the themes and developments brought up throughout.

This is an ambitious book in its scope, but it cannot hope to be comprehensive. While the authors come from 18 countries, this still leaves most of the world unrepresented, not least those poorer countries where welfare states, let alone leave policies, are in their infancy. The book does not cover all the issues currently in play concerning leave policy, with notable exclusions, such as many aspects of demography (including the relationship between leave policies and age at childbearing); children (including how their interests can be represented in policy-making); and the inadequacy of statistical information. There is far more to be said about possible future directions, since we are touching here on such fundamental elements of human life and relationships.

Having conceded these limitations, we hope the book will provide food for thought for a wide range of readers and on a broad span of subjects. We hope it will contribute to the current debates about Parental Leave, which remains an important subject. But we hope, too, that it will also contribute to taking those debates beyond Parental Leave towards new and imaginative thinking about what we want for ourselves, our children and our societies both here and now and in the future.

References

Alexander, R.J. (2001) *Culture and Pedagogy: International Comparisons in Primary Education*, Oxford: Blackwell.

Blum, S., Koslowski, A. and Moss, P. (eds) (2017) *International Review of Leave Policies and Research 2017*. Available at www.leavenetwork.org/lp_and_r_reports/

Boling, P. (2015) *The Politics Of Work–Family Policies: Comparing Japan, France, Germany and the United States*, Cambridge: Cambridge University Press.

Ciccia, R. and Verloo, M. (2012) 'Parental leave regulations and the persistence of the male breadwinner model: Using fuzzy-set ideal type analysis to assess gender equality in an enlarged Europe', *Journal of European Social Policy*, 22(5): 507–528.

Duvander, A.-Z. and Lammi-Taskula, J. (2011) 'Parental leave', in I. Gislason and G.B. Eydal (eds) *Parental Leave, Childcare and Gender Equality in the Nordic Countries*, Copenhagen: Nordic Council of Ministers, pp 31–64.

Fraser, N. (2016) 'Contradictions of capital and care', *New Left Review*,100: 99–117.

Frey, C.B. and Osborne, M.A. (2013) *The Future of Employment: How Susceptible are Jobs to Computerisation?*, Oxford: Oxford Martin School, University of Oxford. Available at www.oxfordmartin.ox.ac.uk/downloads/academic/future-of-employment.pdf

Harari, Y.N. (2016) *Homo Deus: A Brief History of Tomorrow*, London: Harvill Sacker.

ILO (International Labour Office) (2014) *Maternity and Paternity at Work Law and Practice Across the World*, Geneva: ILO. Available at www.ilo.org/wcmsp5/groups/public/---dgreports/---dcomm/---publ/documents/publication/wcms_242615.pdf

IPPR (Institute for Public Policy Research) (2016) *Future Proof: Britain in the 20102s*, London: IPPR. Available at www.ippr.org/files/publications/pdf/future-proof_Dec2016.pdf?noredirect=1

Kamerman, S. and Moss, P. (eds) (2009) *The Politics of Parental Leave Policies: Children, Gender, Parenting and the Labour Market*, Bristol: Policy Press.

Korpi, K., Ferrarini, T. and Englund, S. (2013) 'Women's opportunities under different family policy constellations: Gender, class, and inequality tradeoffs in Western countries re-examined', *Social Politics*, 20(1): 1–40.

Moss, P. and Deven, F. (eds) (1999) *Parental Leave, Progress or Pitfall? Research and Policy Issues in Europe*, The Hague and Brussels: NIDI/CBGS.

Orloff, A.S. (2009) 'Gendering the comparative analysis of welfare states: An unfinished agenda', *Sociological Theory*, 27(3): 317–343.

Ray, R., Gornick, R.C. and Schmitt, J. (2010) 'Who cares? Assessing generosity and gender equality in parental leave policy designs in 21 countries', *Journal of European Social Policy*, 20(3): 196–216.

Wall, K. and Escobedo, A. (2013) 'Parental Leave policies, gender equity and family well-being in Europe: A comparative perspective', in A. Moreno Minguez (ed) *Family Well-Being: Social Indicators Research Series*, vol 49, Dordrecht: Springer, pp 103–129.

Wright, E.O. (2006) 'Compass points: Towards a Socialist alternative', *New Left Review*, 41 (September–October): 93–124.

Wright, E.O. (2007) 'Guidelines for envisioning real utopias', *Soundings*, 36 (Summer): 26–39.

PART I

Recent developments
and the politics of leave policy

TWO

Spain: leave policy in times of economic crisis[1]

Gerardo Meil, Pedro Romero-Balsas
and Jesús Rogero-García

Introduction

This chapter analyses developments in leave policy between 2007 and 2017 in Spain, focusing on political debate, legislative measures and take-up rates. Most of this period was characterised by a severe economic crisis that ultimately prompted a political crisis, in which an imperfect two-party system gave way to a multi-party system with no party having a clear parliamentary majority. It was, then, a period of intense economic, political and social change, hence the relevance of analysing the extent to which leave policy occupied a significant place in public policy during this period.

Four objectives, not mutually exclusive, can be identified in leave policy: protection of mothers' health after childbirth; protection of female employment; furtherance of gender equality; and supporting children's physical and educational development. Specific leave-related measures vary depending on the weight given to each of these objectives in political discourse. While according to Borchorst (2009), three factors must be addressed to analyse why a public policy, such as leave, finds its way onto the political agenda: the characteristics and situation of the actors at any given time, opportunity structures, and the convergence between the two (timing). Opportunity structures have an economic dimension, for they depend on the availability of resources, as well as a political dimension, inasmuch as they vary with the discourse present in the public domain. They are also shaped by the direction taken by specific policies and conditioned by prior policy patterns. The opportunity structures in leave policy development in Spain during the period under consideration were clearly defined by

[1] Funding for the project on which this chapter draws was provided by the Spanish Ministry of Economy and Competitiveness (CSO2013-44097-R).

the economic and social consequences of the economic crisis and by political cycles. The key actors were political parties of different persuasion and certain social movements.

The methodological strategy for the study on which this chapter is based consisted in analysing the political discourses of the national parties as expressed in their campaign platforms for the 2008, 2011, 2015 and 2016 elections and in the inter-party agreements after elections, as well as the legislation on leave and take-up rates during this period. The discourse, activity and proposals of the lobby that goes by the name 'Platform for Equal and Non-Transferable Leave for Birth and Adoption' (*Plataforma por Permisos Iguales e Intransferibles de Nacimiento y Adopción* (PPiiNA)) are also addressed, and their possible political implications evaluated. A total of 17 campaign platforms, two bi-party agreements, a number of legal texts and several PPiiNA documents were analysed.

Path-setting moments prior to 2007

Innovative public policy often establishes the direction for future policy (Borchorst, 2009), as was the case in Spain. Three path-setting moments can be defined in Spain's leave policy since the restoration of democracy in 1976. The first was the enactment of the Workers' By-Laws in 1980, after the demise of the Franco dictatorship and the institution of democracy, a true turning point in workers' rights legislation that established workers' fundamental rights and the role of collective bargaining. The Act consolidated the right of all employed women to Maternity Leave, which was extended from 12 to 14 weeks, maintained nursing leave (a reduction in working hours for breastfeeding women workers), introduced part-time Parental Leave and redefined full-time Parental Leave as a family right when both partners were employed (Meil, 2006; Wall and Escobedo, 2009).

The second significant moment was Spain's accession to the EU in 1986. In 1989, with the Socialist Party (*Partido Socialista Obrero Español* (PSOE)) in power, this prompted further measures: the extension of Maternity Leave to 16 weeks, its partial transferability (up to four weeks) to fathers and, when full-time Parental Leave was taken, a guarantee that for the first year the leave-taker would be able to return to the same job (Wall and Escobedo, 2009). The third moment was the Conciliation Act of 1999 adopted under the conservative People's Party (*Partido Popular* (PP)), which extended the transferability of Maternity Leave to fathers from four to ten weeks and introduced full-time leave to care for dependent family members. It also extended the right to return to work to the full three-year duration of Parental Leave, which was now defined as an individual right to which both mothers and fathers were entitled (Meil, 2006); some regional governments subsequently introduced a lump sum payment for mothers or fathers taking Parental Leave (Lapuerta, 2013). In Spain, then, as in other European countries such as France and Austria (Morgan and Zippel, 2003), both social democratic and conservative parties extended and consolidated leave policy.

As Table 2.1 shows, at the beginning of the period under review in this chapter, Spain's leave policy for early parenthood included 16 weeks fully paid Maternity Leave (ten weeks of which could be transferred to the father), two days fully paid Paternity Leave; and

Table 2.1: Leave policy for early parenthood in Spain in 2006 and changes between 2007 and 2017

Type of leave	Situation at 2006	Changes 2007–2017
Maternity Leave	16 weeks, fully paid by Social Security Fund, eligibility conditional on paying social security contributions for 180 days in the five years prior to maternity. Up to ten weeks transferable to the father	2007: Flat-rate benefit for 42 calendar days for mothers who do not meet eligibility criteria. Easing of eligibility criteria for mothers under the age of 27.
		2009: 14 additional days for non-eligible mothers with large families, lone mothers, multiple births and mothers of disabled children.
Paternity Leave	Two days, fully paid by employer	2007: 15 calendar days, fully paid by Social Security Fund, eligibility conditional upon having paid social security contributions for 180 days in the seven years prior to fatherhood.
		2009: 20 calendar days in large families
		2017: 30 calendar days
Full-time Parental Leave	Unpaid leave for each parent for the first three years after childbirth. Job protection for two years (that is, to a job of the same type but not necessarily the job position previously held) and social security credits for up to 15–18 months for large families	2007: Social security credits for up to 24 months (36 in 2011) for all leave takers

(continued)

Table 2.1: Leave policy for early parenthood in Spain in 2006 and changes between 2007 and 2017 (continued)

Type of leave	Situation at 2006	Changes 2007–2017
Part-time Parental Leave	Unpaid part-time leave (one-third to one-half of the working hours) for a child's first six years or to care for a disabled child	2007: Part-time leave (one-eighth to one-half of working hours) for a child's first eight years
Leave for protection from risk during pregnancy	Right to change workplace in the event of risk during pregnancy; or, where not possible, to a 75% paid leave until delivery	2007: The same right for breastfeeding mothers during the first nine months after delivery, but fully paid
Leave to care for sick children	None	2011: Fully paid part-time leave (minimum 50% reduction in working hours) to care for a severely ill child (cancer or similar) for as long as the child needs direct, permanent and continuous care

three years unpaid Parental Leave as an individual right for each parent, which could be taken on a part-time basis.

2007–2011: socialist government and the onset of the crisis

The Gender Equality Act of 2007 (Spanish Official State Journal, 2007), sponsored by the then PSOE government, was another significant event for leave policy. The Act introduced a broad spectrum of measures to further gender equality in the public and private sectors and to foster the harmonisation of working and family life (Wall and Escobedo, 2009). In connection with family leave, it enhanced protection for mothers subject to job vulnerability and introduced incentives for male leave-taking. The conditions for accessing maternity benefits were relaxed[2] and a six weeks' non-contributory flat-rate benefit was introduced for working mothers not eligible for Maternity Leave. A new leave in the event of risk while breastfeeding was also introduced, the maximum duration for taking

---

[2] Eligibility subject to 180 days of social security contributions in the seven years prior to birth, adoption or fostering, was amended to apply only to mothers over the age of 26; mothers under the age of 21 were subject to no eligibility criteria and mothers from age 21 to 26, to 90 days of social security contributions.

part-time Parental Leave was extended until a child's eighth birthday, and provision was made for more flexible use of this option.

The most significant change, however, was the introduction of a non-transferable, fully paid two-week Paternity Leave for fathers, which was to be gradually extended to four weeks over a six-year period. This prioritising of extending male leave-taking derived from an insistence in prior political discourse on the need to promote gender equality at all levels, but particularly in the labour market and in the division on housework. Paternity Leave was designed to be used simultaneously with Maternity Leave and could be taken at any time during the latter. All these measures were to be funded by social security contributions paid by employers and employees, which were not increased when the legislation came into effect.

Paternity Leave was an immediate success. According to a number of surveys, around 75 per cent of eligible fathers made use of the entitlement (Romero-Balsas, 2012; Fernández-Cornejo et al, 2016); however, fathers with temporary jobs, who were self-employed or in executive positions were least likely to take it. Most fathers taking leave also took their full period of leave. This success contrasted with the minimal impact of the earlier extension, in 1999, of (unpaid) Parental Leave as an individual right for fathers (Wall and Escobedo, 2009). According to a 2012 survey, *El uso social de los permisos parentales* (Take up of Parental Leave), only 2 per cent of eligible fathers between the ages of 25 and 60 made use of either part-time or full-time Parental Leave, compared to 26 per cent of mothers (Meil et al, 2017).

The campaign platforms of the political parties for the March 2008 general election took the 2007 Act as a reference point. The ruling PSOE, which retained power after the elections, advocated extending Paternity Leave to four weeks (already envisaged in the Act) and 'other financial incentives' to foster men's use of Parental Leave. The main opposition party, the conservative PP, proposed extending Paternity and Maternity Leave by two weeks and a more flexible use of such leave in the first three years after childbirth. It likewise proposed introducing leave during children's hospitalisation and to attend meetings about children's education. Along similar lines, the minority centrist party, *Unión, Progreso y Democracia* (UPyD), proposed a compulsory four- to six-week Paternity Leave to distribute the career costs of raising a family between the two parents. The parliamentary left, represented by the minority *Izquierda Unida* (IU), made no proposals on leave policy, although they stated a commitment to the overall objective of improving job quality and stability.

Analysis of the parties' platforms reveals the extent to which work–family conciliation discourse had penetrated the entire political spectrum, although with nuanced differences. The PSOE stressed gender equality, co-responsibility and conciliation: 'The Constitutional Act on Effective Equality between Women and Men acknowledges new workers' rights as a way of favouring conciliation between work life and family needs, with innovative measures, such as Paternity Leave, to further co-responsibility, that is, the balanced distribution of family responsibilities between men and women' (PSOE, 2008, p.30). While the PP advocated equality and conciliation, its platform made no mention of co-responsibility or gender, proposing measures to protect 'the right to have children': 'In many families both partners work outside the home and must balance family and work responsibilities... Difficulties in conciliating family and work life limit participation in the labour market and the exercise of the right to have children' (PP, 2008, p.170).

The centrist UPyD referred neither to inequality between men and women nor to the notion of co-responsibility, and their campaign platform was the only one to justify more Maternity Leave on the grounds of 'the opportunity to breast-feed' babies:

> *Introduction of compulsory four- to six-week Paternal Leave* subsequent to the present Parental Leave normally taken by the mother. The aim is to prevent Parental Leave from being identified with a cost for employers who hire women. Maintaining the present 16-week [Maternity] Leave as it stands at this time is deemed necessary to enable mothers to breastfeed their babies. (UPyD, 2008, p.41)

The IU mentioned conciliation but not co-responsibility, the PSOE's political initiative in these years possibly inhibiting, to some extent, left-wing action in this area. Its platform argued for '[t]he approval of collective bargaining agreements in all companies and public bodies in which all benefits granted to married couples are extended to unmarried couples of the same or different sex (permission to marry, Paternity/Maternity leave and so on)' (IU, 2008, p.136).

These election promises on leave policy came at a time of economic slowdown. But it was not until the second half of 2008 that Spanish society and political parties began to become aware of the depth of the country's economic crisis. For a brief period only, the opportunity structure stemming from the 2007 Gender Equality Act, relative political stability and favourable public opinion provided ideal support for a positive view of leave measures. The differences in political discourse are evident in the targets of such measures: both parents, as advocated by the conservative and centrist parties, or fathers, the focus of the socialist party's proposals.

After the 2008 election and with the onset of the crisis, the PSOE, which continued in power, turned its attention essentially to choosing where to cut public spending to tackle rising unemployment and a rapidly growing deficit in the public finances. Such circumstances led to a tacit acceptance by all parties of the need to put leave measures on ice, illustrated by the fate of the proposed extension of Paternity Leave to four weeks. In 2009, the PSOE agreed with the Democratic Convergence of Catalonia (*Convergència Democràtica de Catalunya* (CIU), a Catalan regional party) to enact a law that would implement the extension in 2011, when the worst of the crisis was expected to have passed. Given the intensity of the recession when that time came, however, the measure was postponed year after year (until 2017, when it was finally extended to four weeks since 1st January; in July 2018 it was extended to five weeks).

Nonetheless, a series of low-cost reforms were instituted during the period to favour access to leave by weaker segments of the population and offset the costs to individuals of leave-taking. In 2009, for instance, non-contributory maternity pay was extended by 14 calendar days (in addition to the existing six weeks) for large and lone-parent families, multiple births or mothers of new-borns with disabilities. In 2011, a new leave was introduced to care for children with cancer or other severe diseases calling for hospitalisation: it provided for full income replacement for as long as direct, continuous and permanent care was required or until the child came of age. In the first few years, take-up was around 1,100 per year, with mean duration of slightly less than one year; in the last two years that number has roughly doubled (Seguridad Social, 2017).

As part of the pension reform undertaken in 2011, measures were adopted to neutralise the effects of parenthood on pension and other social security benefits, with the exception of unemployment. All years of full-time Parental Leave (to a maximum of five) were to be treated as contributory. Another provision stipulated that if work was interrupted as a result of pregnancy, childbirth, adoption or foster parenting (for children under the age of six years), up to 270 days were acknowledged as contributory. Either mother or father was eligible for this benefit. No equivalent provision was made, however, for full-time leave to care for dependent family members, with no more than one year treated as contributory, despite the right to two years of such unpaid leave; or for part-time Parental Leave, where two years is the maximum period treated as contributory for social security benefits.

2011–2015: conservative government and accentuation of the crisis

The next general election was brought forward to November 2011 in response to the PSOE's declining popularity due to the economic situation. Because of the severe economic crisis and the deep social spending cuts, conciliation policies and in particular leave policy did not play a significant role in the electoral campaign. After having postponed the extension of Paternity Leave, the PSOE omitted any mention of leave from its campaign platform, although it maintained its discourse around gender equality and co-responsibility: 'Maternity continues to obstruct too many women's careers…Our commitment to co-responsibility, support for families and the extension of the network of nursery schools (0–3) is indispensable to permanently ensure female employability' (PSOE, 2011, p.101).

In contrast, all the opposition parties, irrespective of ideology (left, centre or right), had proposals focused on longer Paternity Leave. The IU proposed extending 'the duration of Maternity and Paternity Leave as a measure to favour conciliation and foster positive parenthood' (IU, 2011, p.49), but made no reference to Parental Leave. The centrist UPyD changed its gender equality and leave policy proposals, without, though, defining any specific measures, speaking in general terms about 'the expansion of Parental Leave, tending to equate Maternity and Paternity Leave to favour the equality of work opportunities for men and women and the right of both parents to participate equally in their children's upbringing' (UPyD, 2011, p.31). But the main discursive innovation was introduced by the conservative PP, with its call to 'favour men's and women's freedom of choice in managing their responsibilities'. Co-responsibility, in this view, was a matter of individual choice and preference, in keeping with the ideological tradition of conservative parties in other European countries, as discussed below (Morgan and Zippel, 2003).

> Our commitment will be to favour men's and women's freedom of choice in managing their responsibilities. Only individuals and families should decide how to organise their time and harmonise their personal, working and family lives: opting for domestic or nursery care of babies, for part- or full-time work for one of the parents, or for sharing

domestic and childcare tasks equally or in keeping with parents' preferences and specialisation. (PP, 2011, p.119)

The 2011 election was won by the PP, in an economic scenario characterised by high unemployment and a deep fiscal crisis at all levels of government. Unemployment grew from 8.2 per cent in 2006 to 24.8 per cent in 2012, peaking at 26.1 per cent in 2013 and declining slowly thereafter. Unemployment grew primarily among men and young people, resulting in approximately equal rates for men and women. Job insecurity rose: around 55 per cent of young people's jobs, and 25 per cent for the total working population, were temporary, with a mean duration of two 63 day contracts (CES, 2012). Related to the decline in job security came a later age for young people to gain independence, a decline in the Total Fertility Rate (from 1.45 in 2009 to 1.27 in 2013) and a rise in mean age at birth of first child (from 29.3 to 30.4). The national budget deficit peaked at 11 per cent of GDP in 2009, dipping to 9 per cent by 2012, after which it began to decline steeply in an attempt to adapt to the eurozone requirement of a 3 per cent maximum. As a result, cutback followed cutback in public spending and, as in the preceding parliament, conciliation and gender equality policies lost priority.

Despite the austerity measures, spending on leave remained untouched, although most of the regional payment supplements disappeared, and Paternity Leave, which had been introduced in the preceding parliament, was not abolished (Lapuerta, 2013; Escobedo et al, 2016). This indicated a general determination to retain the same basic structure for leave policy, the political consensus around the subject being reminiscent of the situation in 1990s' Austria, France and Germany (Morgan and Zippel, 2003). The sole improvement introduced in the 2011–2015 parliament came in 2012, when nursing leave, an entitlement of one hour's absence per day from work during the first nine months after a child's birth, was re-defined as an individual right to be used by either women or men (though only one parent could take the leave). This definition had been in place since 1999, but subject to both parents' having paid employment and with women's right prevailing over men's. In the wake of an adverse European Court of Justice ruling in 2010, which deemed such practice discriminatory, both conditions were abolished. With no other changes in public leave policy, collective bargaining and corporate gender equality plans became the sole vehicles for improvement and development (MSSSI, 2017).

The severity of the economic crisis and legislative inaction did not, however, put an end to the debate on the role of leave policy in conciliation and co-responsibility. As time passed, the arguments put forward by PPiiNA gained influence in social and political debate. This 'Platform' was an association founded in 2005, with a membership including over 150 organisations and individuals, many of them academics, for the sole purpose of reforming the Spanish leave system to make leave for women and men equal, non-transferable and paid at 100 per cent of earnings. The discourse of this increasingly important actor influenced both the traditional parties and the new leftist and centrist political parties emerging at the time (and discussed further in the following section), who played a prominent role in social debate despite their lack of parliamentary representation.

Significantly, a parliamentary sub-commission was created under the Gender Equality Commission to study the rationalisation of working hours, harmonisation of personal, family and professional life and co-responsibility. The sub-commission consulted many civil society experts, including PPiiNA representatives. Created at the request of the centrist, socialist and conservative parties, the sub-commission was mandated to analyse conciliation and flexible working measures and their practical implementation with a view to putting forward proposals to further conciliation, co-responsibility and working time rationalisation. Its recommendations called for collective bargaining to rationalise work schedules and leave. At the same time, the sub-commission levelled criticism against existing measures restricting the individualisation of leave entitlements, such as fathers' use of Maternity Leave being conditional on mothers' agreement: 'The present leave system consolidates the division of work along sex lines and has a negative impact on birth rates...co-responsibility calls for equal and non-transferable leave' (Congreso de los Diputados, 2013, p.81). It also questioned the excessive length of Parental Leave because of its adverse effects on women's careers, given that this measure is primarily used by mothers (though most mothers use it for only short periods of time (Meil et al, 2017)), suggesting the need to modernise this leave. Although some references were made to Spain's low fertility rate, most of the sub-commission's rationale for demanding a reform of the leave system was based on gender equality in work and family life.

Although not directly related to leave, at the end of the Parliament, with the PP facing defeat in the next election, a significant change targeted at mothers was introduced. The government adopted a rule, beginning in 2016, by which women's retirement (including widows') pensions would be raised according to the number of children they have – by 5 per cent for two children, 10 per cent for three and 15 per cent for four or more. The measure was not intended to reward fertility *per se*, but rather to help offset the indirect long-term costs of maternity for retired women.

2015–2017: political instability and initial economic recovery

The most prominent feature of the general election held in late 2015 was the appearance of two new parties, the leftist *Podemos* and the centrist *Ciudadanos*, which respectively won the third and fourth largest number of seats in the new Parliament. The latter occupied the space left vacant when UPyD, the former centrist party, disbanded. The *Podemos* platform directly and explicitly adopted the PPiiNA proposals on Parental Leave: equal and non-transferable leave for each parent paid at 100 per cent of earnings and equal protection of jobs during the exercise of these rights.

> We'll reform the leave system for birth or adoption by establishing a schedule to progressively extend the present Paternity Leave until it equals Maternity Leave. To guarantee effective equality of rights, leave must be non-transferable, fully paid and the same for both parents, while guaranteeing job protection equally for the exercise of maternity and paternity rights. (Podemos, 2015, pp.125–126)

This proposal would extend Paternity Leave from four to 16 weeks and revoke the option to transfer up to ten weeks of Maternity Leave to fathers. *Podemos* staunchly defended gender equality and improvement in working conditions. The impact of the proposals put forward by the traditional leftist party, IU, which were essentially the same and similarly defended, was weakened by the advent of *Podemos*.

The PSOE, now an opposition party, renewed their proposals, including one to extend the six-week non-contributory maternity pay to non-employed women and another to progressively lengthen Paternity Leave to the same duration as Maternity Leave. It continued to defend co-responsibility and gender equality instead of just conciliation, questioning the gender neutrality of leave provisions: '[We will] revise all the rules on Parental Leave to ensure that neutrality in their formulation does not favour leave-taking by women, progressing toward co-responsibility in the assumption of family responsibilities rather than in the mere conciliation of work and family life' (PSOE, 2015, p.123).

Like the PSOE when it faced elections while in government, the ruling PP made no specific proposals about leave in its campaign platform. However, it continued to offer families 'more freedom in their decision-making', explicitly adopting a traditionalist approach to women's role in childcare and extolling 'the social value of motherhood'. It proposed providing 'more specific attention to women during pregnancy and care for young children' by, among other measures, fostering mothers' support groups, comprising healthcare professionals and other mothers, who would hold meetings and talks in out-patient clinics:

> We want to encourage families to re-energise society and we believe that supporting families, particularly those with children, means offering them greater freedom of decision. The conciliation of family, personal and working life is an obvious aim to ensure that no-one is forced to choose between taking a job and taking care of their loved ones. (PP, 2015, p.90)

The new centrist party, *Ciudadanos*, espoused the PP's discourse on flexible working hours to enhance conciliation and proposed 'equalising Paternity and Maternity Leave, which should be non-transferable' (Ciudadanos, 2015), resulting in fully paid leave for 26 weeks, eight for each parent and ten to be shared, and increasing total paid leave by six weeks.

> We'll equate non-transferable Paternity to Maternity Leave, in keeping with the Nordic model. We propose a 26-week leave, eight weeks of which would be reserved to each parent and the remaining ten weeks would be shared. Enhancing parental co-responsibility helps reduce labour market discrimination against women and fosters conciliation with family life by raising the duration of the total leave by around eight weeks (from the mother's present 16 and the father's present two). (Ciudadanos, 2015, p.177)

This rhetoric, which combined freedom and supposedly neutral flexibility while extolling motherhood and homemaker well-being, resembled the discourse characteristic of conservative and centrist parties in European countries such as Germany, France and Austria, which in previous years took a stand in favour of Maternity Leave (Morgan and Zippel, 2003). These ideas justified leave flexibility, normally targeting mothers. They competed for discursive hegemony with the leftist ideas of gender equality and co-responsibility, with their translation into non-transferable leave to guarantee men's participation in childcare (Borchorst, 2009). In spite of this discourse, PP and *Ciudadanos* would eventually support the extension of non-transferable Paternity Leave.

The results of the December 2015 elections led to a period of considerable political instability. Parliamentary fragmentation meant that any new government would need the agreement of three parties. An agreement between the PSOE and the new centrist party, *Ciudadanos*, failed for lack of support from any other party. The agreement did, however, include the thrust of the *Ciudadanos* proposal: to expand non-transferable Maternity Leave from six to eight weeks and non-transferable Paternity Leave to eight weeks, with provision for ten additional shared weeks for which mothers and fathers would be equally eligible. The PSOE proposal to extend the non-contributory maternity benefit to non-employed mothers was also included. This last measure might, however, be seen as discouraging many women from staying in the labour market, reducing the demand for jobs and hence unemployment rates, reminiscent of leave policies fostered by political parties in European countries such as France and Germany during the 1970s' economic crisis (Morgan and Zippel, 2003).

The inconclusive 2015 election and its subsequent impasse led to new elections in June 2016, which once again led to negotiations, since no party won a clear majority. The outcome was an agreement between the PP and *Ciudadanos*, which has enabled the PP to govern since late 2016. In addition to many other proposals, the agreement included 'approving the necessary measures to equalise Paternity and Maternity Leave in the years to come' (PP and Ciudadanos, 2016) and specifying that Paternity Leave would be extended to four weeks in the government's first year and to eight in the second.

One of the new government's first measures, which had high media impact, served to publicly reinforce its willingness to engage in political dialogue: Paternity Leave was extended from two to four weeks starting on 1 January 2017. Besides being one of the measures in the parliamentary agreement, it entailed applying a provision approved by the PSOE when in government in 2009, though systematically postponed. The provisional data available for the first three quarters of 2017 show a rise in the number of fathers using the leave, up by 6.94 percentage points over the same period in 2016; lengthening the duration has not, therefore, translated into lower uptake. However, rather than doubling with the duration of the leave, total spending for this benefit has climbed by just 86 per cent, suggesting that a small number of eligible men did not take all the time to which they were entitled (Seguridad Social, 2017).

Slow economic recovery and the PP's need to reach agreement with more than one party had thus generated a new opportunity structure for expanding Paternity Leave. Whether or not any substantial progress will be made towards a substantial increase of men's leave-taking remains to be seen. In the interim, the notion of 'equal and non-transferable' leave has permeated the media, which more and more frequently echo legal debates and other arguments on the subject, questioning the rationality of the system as a whole.

Conclusions

Leave policy in Spain from 2007 to 2017 has developed against a backdrop of intense economic and political change. Throughout the period, developments in leave policy have been justified essentially on the grounds of protecting women's employment and furthering gender equality, with conservative parties placing more discursive emphasis on the former and leftist parties on the latter. Strikingly, in contrast to countries such as Denmark where pedagogues played an active and significant role in policy discussion (Borchorst, 2009), the degree to which leave measures may benefit children's development has received little attention in public debate in Spain; by contrast, the development of early childhood services in the country has been based on an educational logic (Valiente, 2010). Although Spain has one of the world's lowest fertility rates, this issue has played no role in the leave policy debate.

The period began with a path-setting event: the enactment of the Gender Equality Act (2007), the product of a period of political stability and economic prosperity. Its most significant provisions (the introduction of 15 days Paternity Leave and improvements in Maternity Leave) laid the groundwork for future policy and consolidated the position of leave policy as an item on the political agenda. Proof of this new status can be found in the inclusion by all political parties in their 2008 campaign platforms of a proposal to extend the recently created Paternity Leave to foster equality between fathers and mothers.

The opportunity structure changed radically with the onset of the 2008 economic crisis, although leave policy did not vanish from political discourse. Although in the following years, characterised by austerity in public spending, the PSOE government failed to extend the duration of Paternity Leave, entitlement was consolidated by enhancing access for society's weakest members. The PP's successful bid for power in 2011 did not alter that situation, despite intensified austerity. The absence of new measures in the years when the crisis was most acute contrasted with the progressive consolidation of leave policy into public discourse (for example, in academia, social movements and Parliament), where it became associated with notions of co-responsibility, gender equality and conciliation.

With these elements in place, the opportunity structure changed again in 2015, when the Spanish economy began to show signs of recovery and the composition of Parliament changed radically, with the emergence of new centre and left parties. Leave policy remained on parties' political agendas, although the differences in their respective discourses began to come into sharper focus. On the conservative end of the spectrum, leave was linked more closely to freedom of choice and flexibility, and conceived as a means to offer families more choice in the organisation of childcare, without implying substantial improvements in leave provisions. Although gender equality appeared across the entire political spectrum, the 'family freedom' rhetoric began to challenge the discursive hegemony of co-responsibility between fathers and mothers set by the Gender Equality Act (2007).

By way of summary, in 2007–2017 leave policy was consolidated on political party agendas and discourse. While the economic context curbed the development of leave measures, leave policy has maintained a significant presence in political discourse. The new opportunity structure generated by the political instability following the 2015 general elections, more favourable economic circumstances, and a clearer focus in the stance adopted by the various actors herald further developments to come. The future direction of these developments is unclear, but it will depend on who secures discursive hegemony through the balance of parliamentary power and on the country's economic future. The extension of Paternity Leave duration has nonetheless become an objective shared by all the country's political parties.

References

Borchorst, A. (2009) 'Danish child-care policies within Path–Timing, sequence, actors and opportunity structures', in K. Scheiwe and H. Willekens (eds) *Childcare and Preschool Development in Europe*, Basingstoke: Palgrave Macmillan, pp 126–141.

CES (Consejo Económico y Social) (2012) *Memoria sobre la situación socioeconómica y laboral. España 2011* [*Report on the Socioeconomic and Labour Situation. Spain 2011*]. Available at www.ces.es/memorias

Ciudadanos (2015) *Campaign Platform*. Available at http://servicios. lasprovincias.es/documentos/programa-electoral-ciudadanos-20D-2015.pdf

Congreso de los Diputados (2013) *Informe de la Subcomisión para el estudio de la Racionalización de Horarios, la Conciliación de la Vida Personal, Familiar y Laboral y la Corresponsabilidad* [*Report of the Comission for the Study of the Rationalization of Schedules, Conciliation of Personal, Family and Working Life, and Co-Responsibility*], Boletín Oficial de las Cortes Generales, serie D, nr. 330, 26/09/2016. Available at http://ep00.epimg.net/descargables/2013/09/26/ed87c0772aeb2b9406fa383995b93026.pdf

Escobedo, A., Meil, G. and Lapuerta, I. (2016) 'Spain country note', in A. Koslowski, S. Blum and P. Moss (eds) *International Review of Leave Policies and Research 2016*. Available at www.leavenetwork.org/lp_and_r_reports/

Fernández-Cornejo, J.A., Escot, L., Del-Pozo, E. and Castellanos-Serrano, C. (2016) 'Do fathers who took childbirth leave become more involved in their children's care? The case of Spain', *Journal of Comparative Family Studies*, 47(2): 169–191.

IU (Izquierda Unida) (2008) *Campaign Platform*. Available at www. izquierda-unida.es/sites/default/files/1203936573085.pdf

IU (Izquierda Unida) (2011) *Campaign Platform*. Available at http:// izquierda-unida.es/sites/default/files/doc/Programa_Electoral_IU_2011_0.pdf

Lapuerta, I. (2013) '¿Influyen las políticas autónomicas en la utilización de la excedencia por cuidado de hijos?' [Do regional policies influence the uptake of full-time Parental Leave?], *Revista Española de Investigaciones Sociológicas*, 141: 29–60.

Mahoney, J. (2000) 'Path dependence in historical sociology', *Theory and Society*, 29(4): 507–548.

Meil, G. (2006) 'The Evolution of Family Policy in Spain', *Marriage and Family Review*, 39(3–4): 359–380.

Meil, G., Romero-Balsas, P. and Rogero-García, J. (2017) 'Why parents take unpaid parental leave: Evidence from Spain' in V. Cesnuiytè, D. Lück and E.D. Widmer (eds) *Family Continuity and Change: Comtemporary European Perspectives*, Basingstoke: Palgrave Macmillan Studies in Family and Intimate Life, pp 247–270.

Morgan, K.J. and Zippel, K. (2003) 'Paid to care: The origins and effects of care leave policies in Western Europe', *Social Politics: International Studies in Gender, State and Society*, 10(1): 49–85.

MSSSI (2017) *Buenas prácticas de conciliación y corresponsabilidad en las empresas con distintivo 'igualdad en la empresa'* [*Good Practice on Conciliation and Co-responsibility in Companies with the Distinction 'Workplace equality'*], Madrid: Ministerio de Sanidad, Servicios Sociales e Igualdad, Subdirección General para la Igualdad en la Empresa y la Negociación Colectiva. NIPO: 685-16-036-2.

Podemos (2015) *Campaign Platform*. Available at https://lasonrisadeunpais.es/wp-content/plugins/programa/data/programa-es.pdf

PP (Partido Popular) (2008) *Campaign Platform*. Available at www.pp.es/sites/default/files/documentos/1191-20090909122124.pdf

PP (Partido Popular) (2011) *Campaign Platform*. Available at www.pp.es/sites/default/files/documentos/5751-20111101123811.pdf

PP (Partido Popular) (2015) *Campaign Platform*. Available at www.pp.es/sites/default/files/documentos/programa2015.pdf

PP (Partido Popular) and Ciudadanos (2016) *150 Compromisos para mejorar España*. Available at www.aelpa.org/actualidad/201608/pacto_150medidas.pdf

PSOE (Partido Socialista Obrero Español) (2008) *Campaign Platform*. Available at http://web.psoe.es/source-media/000000118500/000000118784.pdf

PSOE (Partido Socialista Obrero Español) (2011) *Campaign Platform*. Available at www.abc.es/elecciones/20n-2011/programas/programa-psoe.pdf

PSOE (Partido Socialista Obrero Español) (2015) *Campaign Platform*. Available at www.psoe.es/media-content/2015/11/PSOE_Programa_Electoral_2015.pdf

Romero-Balsas, P. (2012) 'Fathers taking paternity leave in Spain: Which characteristics foster and which hamper the use of Paternity Leave?', *Sociologia e Politiche Sociali*, 15: 105–130.

Seguridad Social (2017) *Statistics of the Social Security*. Available at www.seg-social.es/Internet_1/Estadistica/Est/index.htm

Spanish Official State Journal (2007) *Ley Orgánica 3/2007 para la Igualdad Efectiva de Mujeres y Hombres* [*Act 3/2007 on Effective Equality between Women and Men*], BOE, 71, 23/03/2007, pp 12611–12645.

UPyD (Unión, Progreso y Democracia) (2008) *Campaign Platform*. Available at www.archivoelectoral.org/archivo/doc/Programa%20Electoral%202008.pdf

UPyD (Unión, Progreso y Democracia) (2011) *Campaign Platform*. Available at http: //s01.s3c.es/imag3/pdf/elecciones/UPyD.pdf

Valiente, C. (2010) 'The erosion of "familism" in the Spanish welfare state: Childcare policy since 1975', in M. Ajzenstadt and J. Gal (eds) *Children, Gender and Families in Mediterranean Welfare States*, London: Springer, pp 129–142.

Wall, K. and Escobedo, A. (2009) 'Portugal and Spain: Two pathways in Southern Europe', in S.B. Kamerman and P. Moss (eds) *The politics of Parental Leave policies: Children, parenting, gender and the labour market*, Bristol: Policy Press, pp 207–226.

THREE

Poland: leave policy and the process and goals of a major reform[1]

Anna Kurowska

Introduction

The statutory right to a paid Maternity Leave was introduced in communist Poland in 1975. The 16 weeks of leave it initially guaranteed came in just above western standards.[2] From the start, the leave was fully paid, covering 100 per cent of eligible employees' previous (basic) earnings. During the first decade of Poland's political and economic transformation the length of paid Maternity Leave was not changed, as other socio-economic issues dominated the political agenda. It was extended to 20 weeks by a right-wing government in 2000, and to 26 weeks in 2001.[3] However, a social democratic government assumed power later in 2001, and rolled Maternity Leave back to 16 weeks.

From 2006, when another right-wing party came to power, Maternity Leave was incrementally increased by two weeks until it again reached 20 weeks in 2009. From 2010 the centre-left coalition government of Civic Platform (*Platforma Obywatelska* (PO)) and the Polish People's Party (*Polskie Stronnictwo Ludowe* (PSL)) further

---

[1] Funding for the project on which this chapter draws was provided by the National Science Centre, Poland (grant 2014/13/D/HS4/03645).

[2] The number of weeks was increased to 18 weeks for higher-order births and to 26 weeks for multiple births. Parental Leave was introduced in 1968, but remained unpaid until 1981, when a Parental Leave allowance was introduced, which was means-tested and therefore available to a limited share of mothers. Furthermore, it came in at a mere 11 per cent of the average wage (Michoń, 2010).

[3] In this chapter only the basic length of Maternity Leave is refered to, that is, for first and single births. Maternity Leave is usually longer for higher order and multiple births. For more detail, see Poland's country reports in the annual review of the international network at www.leavenetwork.org/.

extended it by means of an 'additional Maternity Leave' designed to grow incrementally by two weeks each two years until 2014, when the total amount of leave available to mothers would again reach 26 weeks. However, in 2013 the same coalition implemented a new, major reform of the leave system that doubled the total length of paid leave by introducing 26 weeks of paid Parental Leave on top of 26 weeks of paid Maternity Leave (see Figure 3.1); Maternity Leave is paid at 100 per cent of previous earnings and Parental Leave at 60 per cent, or these leaves can be combined into a one-year leave paid at 80 per cent. This reform pushed Poland into the group of EU countries with the most generous leave systems (OECD, 2017).

The first aim of this chapter is to explore the political drivers of the sudden, major reform in 2013. This is done using the multiple-streams approach (MSA) proposed originally by Kingdon (1984) and

Figure 3.1: Length of the contributory-based, generous, paid Maternity/ Parental Leave in Poland (1995–2015)

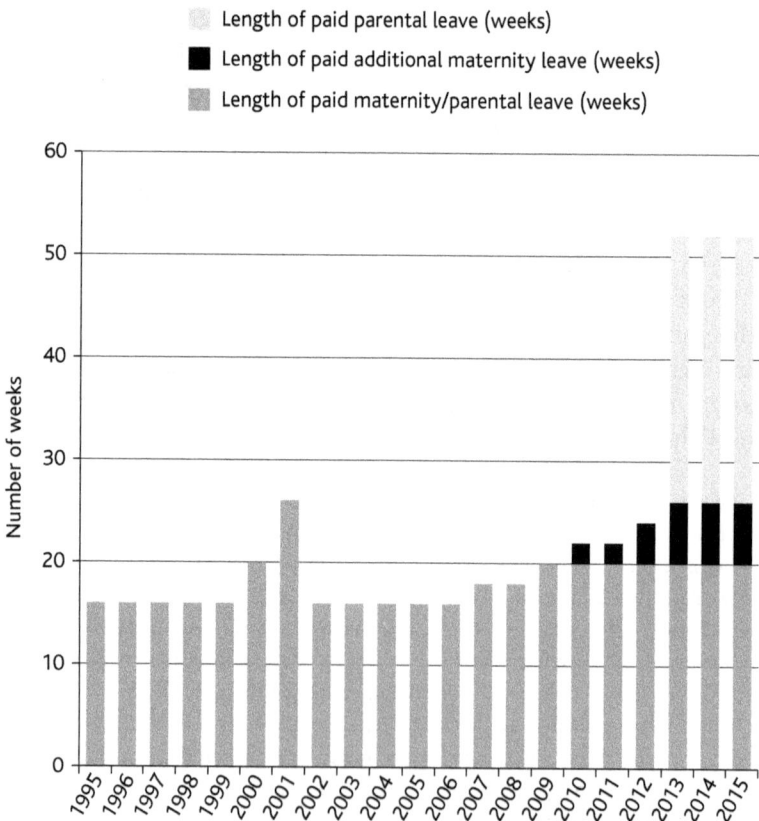

developed further by, among others, Zahariadis (2003; 2014). The MSA is one of the mainstream theoretical approaches used to study political processes. It is particularly useful in studying modern policy making that is characterised by ambiguity and time constraints (see for example, Zohlnhöfer et al, 2015), and also helps in explaining why and how some sudden, major policy decisions are made.

The reform was significant not only for its unprecedented length and generosity, but also for two very ambitious objectives. Apart from boosting fertility, it sought to enable and encourage fathers to engage in childcare to a larger extent than they previously had. The second aim of this chapter is, therefore, to assess the solutions introduced by the reform with regard to the second objective. In order to do so, the capability approach is used, a theoretical perspective that serves to analyse family policies in terms of the real opportunities which they provide to beneficiaries to achieve valued functionings, that is, doings and beings that people have reason to value (Sen, 1999; see also Javornik and Kurowska, 2017; Kurowska, 2018).

Policy process behind the paid Parental Leave in Poland

In the MSA, which provides the theoretical framework for this analysis of the policy process leading to the introduction of the 2013 Parental Leave reform in Poland, three streams are identified as flowing through policy systems: *problems, policies* and *politics* (Zahariadis, 2014, p.25). Each system is conceptualised as largely separate from the others, with its own rules and dynamics. At critical points in time, that is, *policy windows/opportunity windows*, the three streams are combined by policy entrepreneurs into a single package or stream. This dramatically enhances the chances that a specific policy will be adopted (Zahariadis, 2014). In this section, the three streams are examined in the period directly preceding the adoption of the Parental Leave reform as well as how they combined in the 2013 policy window.

The *problem stream* consists of various conditions that policymakers and citizens would like to see addressed. Policymakers find out about these conditions thanks to indicators, focusing events and feedback (Zahariadis, 2014, p.32). In order to identify the focusing indicator or event that could have provided the grounds for proposing the leave reform, the parliamentary debate around the introduction of this reform is analysed. The idea of introducing paid Parental Leave was discussed during the 40th sitting of the *Sejm* (The Lower Chamber of the Polish Parliament) on 14 May 2013 (Sejm, 2013). The full transcripts of this debate have been analysed, as well as the four drafts of the bills that introduced the reform and their justifications[4] (Bill 2012; 2013a; 2013b; 2013c). One social indicator in particular is identified, Poland's low total fertility rate (TFR), which was brought up in the debate repeatedly and had gained the attention of policymakers in the period preceding the reform. It was cited in the bills as the main reason why the policy was implemented.

Poland's TFR had been falling since the 1990s (see Figure 3.2), though low fertility rates as a major social problem only entered the national dialogue and political debate much later, during the second term in office (2011–2015) of the PO-PSL coalition. During the 1990s, the sharp fall in the fertility rate was not accompanied by a significant increase in the old-age dependency ratio (ODR) (see Figure 3.2). As a consequence, the issue of fertility did not draw much attention in the media at the time.

Figure 3.2: Total fertility rate and old-age dependency ratio in Poland (1990–2015)

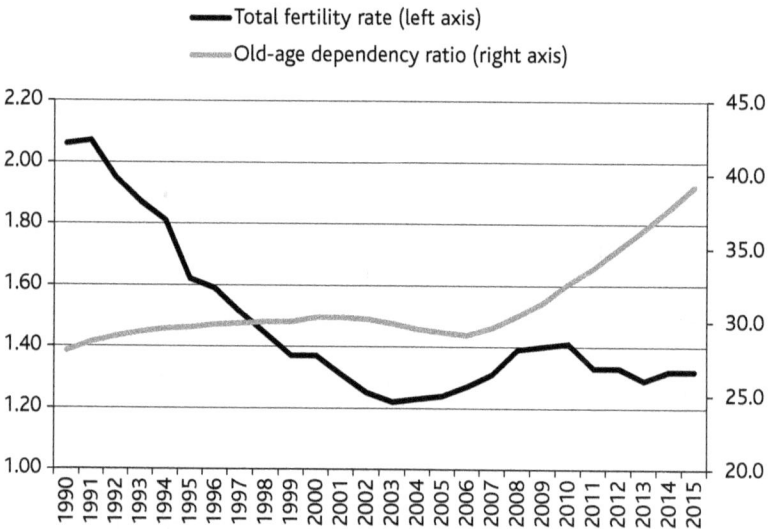

──── Total fertility rate (left axis)

──── Old-age dependency ratio (right axis)

Note: The ODR used here is the ratio of people aged 60+ to people aged 20–59.
Source: Eurostat database

---

[4] Initially four different bills were put forward in parliament by four major parties to introduce the reform; these were combined in a parliamentary commission and turned into the bill that was voted on. A justification is a document attached to the draft of a bill explaining why the bill is needed and how it is expected to affect society, existing law and public finances.

Later, after falling to its lowest level (below 1.3), the TFR began to increase. However, in 2011 it started to fall anew and was accompanied by a continuously and sharply growing share of the retired population, an increasing ODR and a decline in the country's overall population (see Figure 3.2). This created a 'focusing event' (Birkland, 1997) that drew the attention of media and politicians to the problematic demographic conditions that threatened the solvency of public finances (the pension and healthcare systems), economic growth and the reproduction of Poland's population.

In the parliamentary debate around the four draft policy bills proposing the introduction of paid Parental Leave, representatives from all major parties claimed that the most urgent social problem to be solved was declining fertility. Table 3.1 shows some parts of the narratives referencing demography and falling fertility put forward during the 2013 parliamentary debate. However, such references to low TFR were mentioned repeatedly throughout the course of the debate.

During the parliamentary debate around the implementation of the bill, a causal link between the proposed reform and the expected increase in fertility rates was implicitly assumed, but not discussed. This is in line with Kingdon's claim that problems have a 'perceptual, interpretive element' (Kingdon, 1995, p.110), and people define phenomena or conditions as problems by letting their values and beliefs guide their decisions (Zahariadis, 2014, p.32). Poland's long Parental Leave was simply interpreted as a solution to the country's low fertility rate, on the basis of the common belief among Poles that longer Parental Leave is the best instrument to encourage young people to have children (CBOS, 2013). The scientific arguments, however, actually proved the opposite (see, for example, Kurowska, 2012; 2013; for empirical evidence for Poland, see Kurowska and Słotwińska-Rosłanowska, 2013); but these were not considered by politicians. Zahariadis (2003; 2014) argues that the political process is ideological, and that policies are made in the search for a rationale: 'what matters more is the solution to be adopted than the problem to be solved' (Zahariadis, 2003, p.37). While rational choice theory assumes that policymakers attend to problems first and then develop policies to solve them, MSA suggests that opportunities ration our attention. This helps to explain the lack of a sound evidence-based background for the Parental Leave policy solution proposed by politicians in Poland in 2013.

According to MSA, the *policy stream* includes a 'primeval soup' of ideas that compete to win acceptance in policy networks (Zahariadis,

Table 3.1: Parts of the narratives by representatives from the major parties in the Polish parliament referencing falling fertility/demography during the parliamentary debate (2013)

Party representative	Quotations from the political speeches made during parliamentary debate in May 2013
W. K.-K., PSL, ruling coalition	'I remember one of our meetings last year...When we went to discuss the agenda for the next few months...somebody said – I don't remember who – that this is a good idea, but we have to look before we leap. Let's give up this project until our economy runs at a 6 per cent pace. I thought: we cannot wait longer. It is enough to have a look at the numbers. The fertility rate is already one of the lowest in Europe. Demographic projections are irrevocable. We are ageing and there will be less and less of us. Unless we do something. Mr Marshall! The High House! I have the honour of presenting you the government's bill extending paid leave for parents' (p.2)
I.K.M. CO, ruling coalition	'The High House! We often talk today in this hall, that Poland needs changes to fertility rates...In several aspects 2013 is becoming crucial for Polish families' (p.15)
B.Sz., Law and Justice, opposition	'Currently, demography constitutes the biggest challenge and the biggest problem that if not observed and understood by the government, may have painful consequences' (p.6)
A.R., Solidary Poland, opposition	'In the opinion of Solidary Poland, family policy today, in the XXI century, constitutes a crucial element for the future of our country. Obviously, demography will decide Poland's future, as well as Europe and the world. This [the proposed bill] is a crucial solution' (p.6) 'We all realise that the birth rate in Poland is really low. Among 222 countries we rank 209th. This is a catastrophe. The fertility rate in Poland is 1.31...By 2014, from 38 million, only 34 million of us will be left in Poland...This is catastrophic for Poles and the Polish economy' (pp.6–7) 'There were times when 800,000 children were born in Poland... today it is no more than 400,000 children. This is for us, for Poland in the perspective of several years, very bad – very bad records, very bad data, when it comes to the development of our country and our social development' (p.8)

Source: Quotations are taken from the transcripts of the 40th sitting of the Polish Parliament, on 14 May 2013 (Sejm, 2013). Page numbers for each quotation refer to the page of the transcript. Translations from Polish were made by the author.

2014, p.33). While numerous ideas may be discussed, only a few ever receive serious consideration; selection criteria include: technical feasibility, value acceptability and resource adequacy (Zahariadis, 2014). With the Parental Leave introduced in Poland in 2013, the most important of these was value acceptability. This was exemplified in the unprecedented consistency of the four bills proposing the leave reform that were submitted to parliament by four major political parties in 2012/2013: two right-wing parties – Law and

Justice (*Prawo i Sprawiedliwość* (PiS)) and Solidary Poland (created by a group of PiS representatives in the parliament in 2012), the ruling PO–PSL coalition, and the Democratic Left Alliance (*Sojusz Lewicy Demokratycznej* (SLD)). All of the drafts proposed the same 26 weeks' leave. Only the proposal submitted by the SLD additionally proposed a four-week quota for 'the second entitled parent', that is, fathers. However, during the parliamentary debate, this proposal was not discussed at all, the SLD's political power being very weak at the time.

In the MSA, the *politics stream* consists of three elements: national mood, pressure group campaigns and administrative or legislative turnover (Zahariadis, 2014, p.33). The national mood can be monitored through opinion polls, and influences the promotion of certain items in the agenda. Several opinion polls and surveys carried out in and prior to 2013 showed that the majority of Poles hold traditional views on both what is best for small children and the role of the mother in the first year or two after childbirth. According to the European Values Study (2008), over 61 per cent of Polish respondents believe that a pre-school child suffers when his/her mother is employed. Furthermore, over 60 per cent declared that one of the major reasons young people do not have children is that the payments for childcare-related leave are too low (Czapiński and Panek, 2013). Such public attitudes can be interpreted as constituting a national mood that was conducive to introducing reform.

Furthermore, the autumn 2011 elections provided a *political/opportunity window* for the change. Civic Platform, the major party in the ruling coalition between 2007–2011, was elected for a second time and again forged a coalition with the PSL. Reforms undertaken during the coalition's first term (2007–2011), including the incremental extension of Maternity Leave, had been well received. Furthermore, the major opposition party, PiS, would not oppose the reform due to its pro-natalist and pro-family orientation. The coalition and PiS had over 85 per cent of the seats in parliament, while the progressive SLD had only 6 per cent. This led to overwhelming support for the reform. During his second term exposé in October 2012, Prime Minister Donald Tusk promised to double the period of paid leave available to parents after childbirth.

Pressure to solve the problem of very poor access to institutional childcare for children under three years of age (particularly for two-year-olds) further contributed to the political context of Parental Leave; this pressure came not only from the Polish public, but from EU officials as well (Kurowska and Wolniewicz, 2015). In 2011, the ruling coalition had launched a reform intended to increase the supply of institutional childcare. However, in 2013 the availability of nurseries for children under three years remained among the lowest in the EU (Kurowska, 2015). Over 80 per cent of Polish municipalities (*gminas*) had not a single nursery for children under the age of three years, while those that did had long waiting lists, as demand far outstripped the supply of places (Kurowska, 2015). Paid parental care for children under one year of age was expected to free up space for older children and reduce the number of children on waiting lists for nurseries.

This exemplifies Ackrill and Kay's argument that 'if a policy issue occupies multiple institutionally connected arenas, a policy decision taken in one arena may impact directly on policy decisions taken in others' (2011, p.73; see also Zahariadis 2014, p.36). The decision taken in 2011 to invest in childcare for children under three years, and the need to achieve quick results in reducing waiting lists for nurseries, provided an additional impetus to adopt the paid leave extension in 2013. These two reforms constituted major complementary elements in the family policy of the ruling coalition led by Donald Tusk and Civic Platform, which was oriented towards increasing the fertility rate and also enabling work–family reconciliation.

Increasing real opportunities for fathers' engagement in childcare?

In addition to demographic issues and reform as a primary solution to low fertility within the frame of the conservative family model, representatives of both the ruling coalition and the opposition also used a 'gender equality' frame in their narratives. During their speeches in the *Sejm*, emphasis was frequently placed on conferring equal rights and entitlements on both mothers and fathers, thus enabling them to share in the provision of care (see Table 3.2).

What stands out in the political narratives exemplified by the quotations in Table 3.2 is that policymakers interpreted the paid Parental Leave as an opportunity not only for mothers to engage in childcare, but also fathers. However, in order to properly assess whether a policy solution creates a *real* opportunity for people, it is not enough to analyse the formal rights and benefits that a policy provides (Javornik and Kurowska, 2017; Kurowska, 2018). The capability approach perspective applied here underlines the crucial role of the social, economic and institutional contexts of a certain policy. These shape the real opportunities individuals have to transform (convert) their rights and entitlements into valued functionings, that is, doings

Table 3.2: Parts of the narratives by the representatives from the major parties in the Polish parliament referencing gender equality during the parliamentary debate (2013)

Party representative	Quotation from the political speeches made during parliamentary debates in May 2013
W.K.-K., PSL, ruling coalition	'We propose a series of important *amenities* for families. One of them provides both parents the same entitlements to use the additional Maternity Leave...Simultaneously we adopt the rule that when editing all legal regulations about additional Maternity Leave we use the word employee. This is a very important change...It will extend the same rights to mothers and fathers to an extended paid leave to provide childcare' (p.13)
I.K.M. CO, ruling coalition	'The proposed solutions aim to *make it easier* to provide care for a child under 12 months. The initiators of the reform want to achieve this by *enabling* the employee [female version in Polish grammar] – the mother, as well as the employee [male version in Polish grammar] – the father to use Maternity Leave, Paternity Leave as well as the new institution of Parental Leave' (p.15)
	'It is worth mentioning that the proposed bill *enables* the employee to use the leave – the mother and employee – the father' (p.16)
B.Sz., PiS, opposition	'The proposed bill aims to *enable* both parents to use paid leave for the one year period following the birth of the child...Furthermore, it aims to *enable* parents to share the parental entitlements to a larger extent' (p.4)
	'The proposed bill aims to *enable* mothers and fathers to provide care for a child during the first year after birth'. (p.4)
	'The proposed solution provides the *opportunity* to divide the additional Maternity Leave into two parts, as well as the availability of this leave for mothers as well as fathers' (p.5)

Note: emphasis added.

Source: Quotations are taken from the transcripts of the 40th sitting of the Polish Parliament, on 14 May 2013 (Sejm, 2013). Page numbers for each quotation refer to the page of the transcript. Translation from Polish were made by the author.

and beings that are valued (Sen, 1999; see also Javornik and Kurowska, 2017; Kurowska, 2018).

As a theoretical perspective, the capability approach was originally proposed for conceptualising and measuring well-being and human development (Sen 1985, 1999). However, recently it has been increasingly applied to the analysis of family policy to determine the extent to which it provides real opportunities for mothers and fathers to achieve valued functionings such as gender equality, employment of mothers, childbearing and fathers' involvement in childcare (see for example, Hobson et al, 2011; 2014; Javornik and Kurowska, 2017; Kurowska, 2018). Following Javornik and Kurowska (2017), the engagement not only of mothers but also of fathers in childcare is interpreted here as one of the crucial valued functionings in a modern European society. A capability approach enables structured insight into the difference between formal rights and the real opportunities that a policy creates for individuals.

The 2013 leave reform in Poland provided fathers with formal rights and statutory entitlements very similar to mothers in taking paid Parental Leave, after the period of Maternity Leave. But, drawing on a capability approach, whether they have the same real opportunity to use those rights and entitlements and achieve the valued functioning of being personally engaged in childcare, is argued to depend on the 'conversion factors' (Sen, 1999) at work. As Javornik and Kurowska (2017) point out, fathers may attain the same legal rights (formal opportunities) to Parental Leave and benefit as mothers, but their *real* opportunities to use this leave may be affected by economic constraints and parental orthodoxies that cast mothers as the proper caregivers, as well as the normative expectations of how a proper male employee behaves (for example, Pfau-Effinger, 2012). That is, the same legal right may be converted into different opportunities for mothers and fathers because of the socio-economic and cultural contexts (conversion factors).

When it comes to the economic conversion factors present in the Polish context at the beginning of the twenty-first century, the relatively low incomes (and thus also living standards) and the gender pay gap both figure prominently. As Javornik and Kurowska (2017) argue, to assess the economic opportunity to use the entitlement to Parental Leave it is necessary to consider financial viability, taking into account the living standards in a particular country. Paid Parental Leave in Poland is available with a 60 per cent replacement rate (the 80 per cent replacement option is available only if the mother declares after childbirth that she wants to use the full leave option). This is much lower than, for example, Sweden's (78 per cent), and likewise lower than the European standard for a generous paid leave (see Gornick and Meyers, 2003; Saxonberg, 2013). Furthermore, the average difference between men's and women's earnings in Poland exceeds 20 per cent (GUS, 2016). This means that the loss in income due to the use of Parental Leave is on average significantly higher for fathers than for mothers. It is, therefore, economically rational for the mother to take the full period of 52 weeks leave. This results in unequal *real* economic opportunity to use the entitlement for mothers and fathers.

Furthermore, fathering is a social phenomenon grounded in cultural patterns of parenting, gender roles and models of masculinity and, moreover, is shaped by family policy (Suwada, 2017). Fatherhood in Poland is mainly perceived as the responsibility to provide the family with economic resources; a 'good father' is one who is able to maintain the family and provide financial security for family members. Suwada's research shows that Polish fathers admit that if they took roles that traditionally are assigned to mothers, such as childcare, they would face negative reactions from the social environment, where it is widely accepted for the mother to go on Parental Leave and still considered out of the ordinary for fathers to be fully engaged in childcare. Therefore, a father choosing to use Parental Leave does not receive the same social support as a mother does.

Finally, despite the fact that the new Parental Leave was aimed at both parents, and the 'additional Maternity Leave' was reformed to be formally available to both parents, the resulting solution was tailored particularly for mothers. Instead of 26 weeks of Maternity Leave paid at 100 per cent of earnings followed by 26 weeks of Parental Leave paid at 60 per cent, mothers had the option of taking all 52 weeks of leave paid at 80 per cent of earnings – but only if they choose that option at the time of the child's birth. This additional right for mothers constituted an additional barrier for fathers, diminishing the real opportunities that they had.

Given the economic and cultural conversion factors, as well as the mother-centred design of the Parental Leave, it is not surprising that in 2015 over 98 per cent of Parental Leave users were mothers (ZUS, 2016), nor that the same percentage was registered in the first quarter of 2017; only 0.86 per cent of leave takers were fathers. One could argue that Parental Leave uptake in Poland (in capability approach terms – the 'observed functioning', that is, what we observe that people do or are; see Robeyns, 2005) could result from a genuine choice of Polish fathers. Yet the majority of fathers (65 per cent) declare that both mothers and fathers should take personal care of children to a very similar extent in the first year after childbirth (Być Tatą, 2014). The fact that it is almost exclusively Polish mothers who in practice use the entitlement to Parental Leave cannot simply be attributed to fathers genuinely choosing not to use it. Again, Polish fathers' individual agency to engage in childcare is constrained by multiple factors: the economic and the cultural context (gender contract), as well as the mother-centred design of the Parental Leave.

One way of diminishing these barriers would be to provide fathers with an individual, non-transferable right to Parental Leave (a 'father's quota') on a par with that of Polish mothers (14 weeks of Maternity Leave is obligatory and non-transferable) and a financially viable leave benefit (preferably replacing 80 to 100 per cent of the father's earnings).

This would provide an economic incentive for fathers to take leave, and help to overcome the cultural/social pressure on women to take the full length of Parental Leave. In Iceland and Sweden, the 'father's quota' has doubled the number of Parental Leave days taken by men (OECD, 2017). In Korea, the father-only entitlement caused the number of men taking leave to rise more than three-fold (OECD, 2017).

The policy narrative during the parliamentary debates around the reform failed to consider the conversion factors that would be involved when the reform was constructed. Politicians ignored not only scientific evidence that provided arguments supporting the introduction of individual and non-transferable entitlements for fathers, but also the experience of other countries that have introduced transferable parental entitlements and the input of social actors during the official public consultations on the bill proposed by the ruling coalition. Paradoxically, one of these actors was the major Polish Confederation of Private Employers (*Lewiatan*), which stated in its response to the consultation that it 'supports the government's proposal to extend Maternity Leave. However, we believe that, due to the difference in wages between men and women (men's are higher), this solution will make the choice of which parent uses the extended leave a fictitious one' (Lewiatan, 2013). It seems, too, that ignoring the economic context of the reform designed to engage fathers in childcare was also driven by the personal views of the majority of political leaders supporting the reform, which corresponded to the conservative ideal of a family, with its belief that 'the mother's bond with the baby cannot be replaced by the father', as well as to a narrowly understood 'freedom of choice' that had to be granted to parents.

Conclusions

In 2013, Poland reformed its Parental Leave system, doubling the period of paid leave available at that time; 26 weeks of a well-paid Parental Leave were introduced on top of 26 weeks of a well-paid Maternity Leave. All the previous reforms that had been undertaken since the introduction of Maternity Leave in 1975 had been very limited and volatile – reflecting heterogenous views on leave policies among the various political parties. The 2013 reform brought about a major change to the system, one that was nearly unanimously supported by parties across the political spectrum. It constituted a rare example of political consensus on family policy in Poland.

In this chapter, drawing on the multiple streams approach, I have argued that the rapid introduction of such an unprecedentedly generous reform in childcare-related leave in Poland was possible due to the skilful integration of three streams – *problems, policies* and *politics* – into a single package during the *policy window of opportunity*. The *window* opened after the coalition won parliamentary elections for a second time, receiving strong proof of public support for its previous policy reforms. Among those reforms had been an incremental increase in the length of paid Maternity Leave.

The new reform was officially promoted to solve Poland's extremely low fertility rate, even though sound scientific research showed that Parental Leave is unlikely to yield a long-term increase in fertility. Nonetheless, the elections gave proponents of familial care policy an overwhelming majority in the parliament, and the idea of a generous leave extension gained strong support among Polish citizens. This generous Parental Leave was also expected to decrease demand for institutional childcare services. As children under one year of age would be covered by parental (in practice maternal) care, the waiting lists in public nurseries were expected to shrink, boosting availability for slightly older children.

Politicians from all of the major political parties in the parliament did not use only conservative (familialistic) arguments in their discussion about the reform, however. As a majority of Polish fathers have declared in studies that both mothers and fathers should be engaged in childcare to a similar extent in the first year after childbirth, the politicians also offered a formal 'gender equal' narrative while discussing the Parental Leave reform. However, statistics show that only a very small share of fathers (under 1 per cent) actually take Parental Leave.

Working from the perspective of the capability approach in the second part of this chapter, I argued that this very low take-up by fathers is due to the fact that the design of the reform does not take account of the economic and cultural context in Poland. Parental Leave is paid at a 60 per cent replacement rate, and taking into consideration living standards in Poland as well as the significant gender pay gap, it is clear that a financially viable solution for Polish fathers has not been put in place. Furthermore, the dominant traditional ideals of masculinity and femininity in Polish culture, which cast mothers as proper caregivers of small children and men as breadwinning employees, erect an additional barrier for fathers in turning their formal entitlement into practice. Finally, the Parental Leave is tailored to mothers, as it grants them an additional entitlement that induces them to claim the full length of Parental Leave at childbirth. This clearly embeds the Polish model of care policy in the (overwhelmingly) supported form of gendered familialism (Kurowska, 2016); the recent introduction of the highest child benefit in Europe (*Rodzina 500 Plus*) by the right-wing PiS government has reinforced this position, making Poland one of the most familialistic and highly supported models of family policy in Europe.

The capability approach-based analysis leads to the conclusion that, in order to provide a truly gender equal entitlement for fathers and mothers, one that provides real opportunities for fathers to take Parental Leave, two basic conditions should be met: a) fathers should be given a non-transferable right to part of Parental Leave, that is, a 'father's quota' (equivalent to the entitlement mothers have within the framework of Maternity Leave); and b) Parental Leave should be paid at a minimum 80 per cent replacement rate in order to be financially viable and avoid creating economic disincentives to taking the leave.

References

Ackrill, R. and Kay, A. (2011) 'Multiple streams in EU policy-making: The case of the 2005 sugar reform', *Journal of European Public Policy*, 18(1): 72–89.

Bill (2012) *Projekt ustawy o zmianie ustawy – Kodeks pracy oraz ustawy o świadczeniach pieniężnych z ubezpieczenia społecznego w razie choroby i macierzyństwa* [*The bill amending the Labor Code and the Law on cash benefits from social insurance in case of illness and motherhood*]. Druk nr [print number] 1175. Warsaw, 23 November 2012.

Bill (2013a) *Projekt ustawy o zmianie ustawy – Kodeks pracy oraz ustawy o świadczeniach pieniężnych z ubezpieczenia społecznego w razie choroby i macierzyństwa* [*The bill amending the Labor Code and the Law on cash benefits from social insurance in case of illness and motherhood*]. Druk nr [print number] 1172. Warsaw, 18 January 2013.

Bill (2013b) *Projekt ustawy o zmianie ustawy – Kodeks pracy oraz niektórych innych ustaw* [*The bill amending the Labor Code and several other laws*]. Druk nr [print number] 1310. Warsaw, 29 April 2013 r.

Bill (2013c) *Projekt ustawy o zmianie ustawy – Kodeks pracy oraz niektórych innych ustaw* [*The bill amending the Labor Code and several other laws*]. Druk nr [print number] 1310. Warsaw, 10 March 2013 r.

Birkland, T.A. (1997) *After Disaster: Agenda Setting, Public Policy and Focusing Events*, Washington, DC: Georgetown University Press.

Być Tatą (2014) *Raport fundacji dajemy dzieciom siłę i Millward Brown* [*Being daddy.report of the foundation empowering children and Millward Brown*]. Available at http://fdds.pl/wp-content/uploads/2016/05/Infografika_Byc_tata_FDN_2014.pdf

CBOS [Centrum Badania Opinii Społecznej] [Public Opinion Research Center] (2013) *Polacy o rocznych urlopach rodzicielskich* [*Poles on parental leaves*]. Available at: www.cbos.pl/SPISKOM. POL/2013/K_081_13.PDF

Czapiński, J. and Panek, T. (eds) (2013) 'Diagnoza Społeczna 2013. Warunki Życia Polaków. Raport' [Social Diagnosis 2013. Living conditions in Poland], *Contemporary Economics*, 7 (special issue): 1–491.

European Values Study (2008) Database. Available at: https://zacat. gesis.org/webview/index.jsp?object=http://zacat.gesis.org/obj/ fCatalog/Catalog5

Gornick, C.J. and Meyers, K.M. (2003) *Families that Work: Policies for Reconciling Parenthood and Employment*, New York, NY: Russell Sage Foundation.

GUS (Główny Urząd Statystyczny) [Central Statistics Office] (2016) *Różnice w wynagrodzeniach kobiet i mężczyzn w Polsce* [*Gender differences in salaries in Poland*]. Available at https://stat.gov.pl/obszary-tematyczne/ rynek-pracy/pracujacy-zatrudnieni-wynagrodzenia-koszty-pracy/ roznice-w-wynagrodzeniach-kobiet-i-mezczyzn-w-polsce-stan-w-2014-roku,12,1.html

Hobson, B. (2014) 'Introduction: Capabilities and agency for work–life balance – a multidimensional framework', in B. Hobson (ed) *Worklife Balance: The Agency and Capabilities Gap*, Oxford: Oxford University Press, pp 1–31.

Hobson, B., Fahlén, S. and Takács, J. (2011) 'Agency and capabilities to achieve a work–life balance: A comparison of Sweden and Hungary', *Social Politics*, 18(2): 168–198.

Javornik, J. and Kurowska, A. (2017) 'Work and care opportunities under different Parental Leave systems: Gender and class inequalities in northern Europe', *Social Policy and Administration*, 51(4): 617–637, DOI: 10.1111/spol.12316

Kingdon, J.W. (1984) *Agendas, Alternatives, and Public Policies*, Boston, MA: Little, Brown.

Kingdon, J.W. (1995) *Agendas, Alternatives, and Public Policies*, 2nd edn, New York: Harper Collins.

Kurowska, A. (2012) 'Wpływ wybranych instrumentów polityki rodzinnej i polityki zatrudnienia na dzietność oraz aktywność zawodową kobiet' [The impact of family and labour market policies on fertility and labour market activity of women], *Polityka Społeczna* [*Social Policy*], 11/12: 14–19.

Kurowska, A. (2013) 'Ocena zasadności założeń reformy urlopów i zasiłków związanych z opieką nad małym dzieckiem' [Assessment of the assumptions of the Parental Leave bill], *Problemy Polityki Społecznej. Studia i Dyskusje* [*Social Policy Problems. Studies and Discussions*], 22: 155–170.

Kurowska, A. (2015) 'Zmiany dostępu do opieki nad dzieckiem w wieku poniżej trzech lat w polskich gminach przed wejściem w życie ustawy „żłobkowej" i po jej wdrożeniu' [The change in access to childcare for children less than 3 years old before and after the "nurseries" law], *Problemy Polityki Społecznej. Studia i Dyskusje* [*Social Policy Problems. Studies and Discussions*], 30: 119–139.

Kurowska, A. (2016) '(De)familializacja i (de)genderyzacja – substytucyjne czy komplementarne perspektywy w porównawczej polityce społecznej?' [(De)familialization and (de)genderization – competing or complementary perspectives in comparative family policy analysis?], in A. Kurowska, B. Pieliński, R. Szarfenberg, and A. Wójtewicz (eds) A. *Perspektywa gender w polityce społecznej* [*Gender perspective in social policy*]. Toruń: Wydawnictwo UMK.

Kurowska, A. (2018) '(De)familialization and (de)genderization: Competing or complementary perspectives in comparative family policy analysis?', *Social Policy and Administration*, 52(1): 29–49.

Kurowska, A. and Słotwińska-Rosłanowska, E. (2013) 'Zatrudnienie a pierwsze i drugie urodzenia kobiet w Polsce' [Employment and the first and the second births in Poland], *Studia Demograficzne* [*Demography Studies*], 1(163): 37–51.

Kurowska, A. and Wolniewicz, K. (2015) 'Opieka nad dzieckiem do lat trzech', in C. Żołędowski, M. Duszczyk and B. Rysz-Kowalczyk (eds) *Dekada członkostwa w Unii. Europejskiej. Perspektywa polityki społecznej* [*Decade of membership in the European Union. Perspective on social policy*], Warszawa: Dom Wydawniczy Elipsa, pp 308–327.

Lewiatan [Polish Confederation Lewiatan] (2013) 'Stanowisko uwzględnione w: Uzasadnieniu do rządowego projektu ustawy o zmianie ustawy - Kodeks pracy oraz niektórych innych ustaw' [Position considered in the justification of governmental project of the changes to the Labor Code]. Available at: http://www.sejm.gov.pl/Sejm7.nsf/druk.xsp?nr=1310

Michoń, P. (2010) 'To the promised land: The work–life balance in Poland 1989–2008', in P. Michoń (ed) *Work–Life Balance Policy in Czech Republic, Hungary, Poland and Slovakia 1989–2009: Twenty Years of Transformation*, Poznań: Dom Wydawniczy Harasimowicz.

OECD (2017) *Key Characteristics of Parental Leave Systems*. Available at www.oecd.org/els/soc/PF2_1_Parental_leave_systems.pdf

Pfau-Effinger, B. (2012) 'Women's employment in the institutional and cultural context', *International Journal of Sociology and Social Policy,* 32(9/10): 530–543.

Robeyns, I. (2005) 'The capability approach: A theoretical survey,' *Journal of Human Development,* 6(1): 93–117.

Saxonberg, S. (2013) 'From defamilialization to degenderization: Toward a new welfare typology,' *Social Policy and Administration,* 47(1): 26–49.

Sejm (2013) *Transcript From the 40th Parliamentary Sitting on 14 May 2013.* Available at www.sejm.gov.pl/Sejm8.nsf/proces.xsp

Sen, A. (1999) *Commodities and capabilities,* Oxford: Oxford University Press.

Suwada, K. (2017) *Men, Fathering and the Gender Trap: Sweden and Poland Compared,* Basingstoke: Palgrave Macmillan.

Zahariadis, N. (2003) *Ambiguity and Choice in Public Policy: Political Manipulation in Democratic Societies,* Washington DC: Georgetown University Press.

Zahariadis, N. (2014) 'Ambiguity and multiple streams', in P.A. Sabatier and Ch. Weible (eds) *Theories of the Policy Process.* Boulder CO: Westview Press.

Zohlnhöfer, R., Herveg, N. and Rüb, F. (2015) 'Theoretically refining the multiple streams framework: An introduction', *European Journal of Political Research,* 54(3): 412–418.

ZUS [The Social Insurance Institution] (2016) Baza wiedzy [Knowledge database]. Available at: www.zus.pl

FOUR

United Kingdom: leave policy and an attempt to take a new path

Peter Moss and Margaret O'Brien

Introduction

The implementation of a statutory right to paid Maternity Leave in the United Kingdom (UK), in 1976 and 1977, following the adoption of the 1975 Employment Protection Act, occurred nearly a century after Maternity Leave rights were first introduced in Germany, and when such leave was already widespread among other industrialised countries. In 1973, when the UK acceded to the (then) European Economic Community (EEC), the original six member states had well-established paid Maternity Leave policies. Indeed, the second wave of leave policies had already begun, with Sweden's introduction of a Parental Leave scheme in 1974, before the UK joined the first wave.

This chapter traces some of the consequences of being a latecomer to leave policy and of the decisions made when the UK did eventually get round to implementing such policy. It also considers how and why a later attempt at reform failed, leaving the UK today still with a maternalist leave policy centred on a long, low-paid Maternity Leave. As such, it is a story of how difficult it can be to turn off a policy pathway once that has become established.

Background: the emergence of a maternalist leave policy

A latecomer to leave policy

Since the end of the Second World War, when women had played a major role in the wartime economy, successive UK governments had opposed mothers going out to work and, more generally, declined to provide support for employed carers. Even after its late adoption of Maternity Leave, in 1975 with implementation in 1976 and 1977, the UK's approach was very different to other European countries.

Whereas Maternity Leave in the six original member states of the EEC ran from 12 to 14 weeks (except for Italy, where it was 20 weeks), the UK's new legislation went for 40 weeks, with up to 29 weeks available after birth;[1] and while the full period of leave in the former countries was paid at a high level of earnings replacement, in the UK only six weeks was highly paid (at 90 per cent of earnings), the remainder being paid at a low flat-rate (12 weeks) or unpaid (22 weeks). The UK also differed from its EEC neighbours by making its Maternity Leave a 'right to reinstatement', that is, to return to a previous job, rather than a 'right to leave', that is, both protecting the job and retaining a woman's employment status while on leave along with all employment-related entitlements. Furthermore, the UK adopted a stringent eligibility condition, that women must have worked for the same employer for at least two years full time or five years part time.

Why did the UK opt for such an exceptional approach to Maternity Leave? It is not clear why the government decided on 40 weeks leave, with 29 weeks available after birth, much longer than leave in most countries. The nearest to an explanation was a government minister stating that 29 weeks post-partum leave would 'give the employee a reasonable time to recover from childbirth and it is also generally accepted that the sixth month after childbirth is the time in which one can wean the baby' (cited in Fonda 1990, p.115). While choosing a starting date 11 weeks before birth may have been related to all women, employed or not, being eligible for a low flat-rate maternity allowance from that date. As to the low level of payment, with only a short period at an earnings-related rate, this may have been because the government originally expected individual employers to pay women taking leave and was reluctant to place high demands on them (the scheme that was finally enacted moved away from individual employer payments to a Maternity Pay Fund, to which all employers contributed 0.05 per cent of their annual wages bill).

Although leave policy was not so well developed internationally as it is today, there was experience from other countries to draw on, as well as the ILO's 1952 Convention on Maternity Rights, which specified 12 weeks of well-paid leave; yet no reference was made to either in the passage of UK Maternity Leave legislation. This is just one example of how ill-considered the original measure was. The 1975 Employment Protection Act, of which Maternity Leave was one part, 'gave many signs of hasty drafting' and was 'rushed

---

[1] Subsequently women could choose when to start Maternity Leave before giving birth, with 11 weeks before birth being the earliest at which leave could begin.

through the legislative process with tremendous speed'; the maternity provisions were 'basically dealt with in two sittings on one day during the Committee stage, and clearly there was little time to reflect on its provisions at any length' (cited in Fonda 1980, pp.114, 117). Not an auspicious start to an important field of social policy, particularly considering, as will become apparent, how this initial long and poorly paid Maternity Leave set the direction of travel for all subsequent developments in UK leave policy.

For two decades after the introduction of Maternity Leave, little further happened to UK leave policy. This was a period dominated by a Conservative government (1979–1997) opposed on principle to regulating the labour market. The government used its veto to block a proposal from the European Commission (EC) (in 1983) for a Directive setting minimum standards for Parental Leave.[2] Similarly, in 1994 the government declined to support a recommendation from the All Party Parliamentary Group on Parenting, for a statutory Paternity and Parental Leave, one of seven recommendations for the International Year of the Family (All Party Parliamentary Group on Parenting, 1994). The only change in UK policy, easing the restrictive eligibility conditions for Maternity Leave in 1994, resulted from another European Directive, which the UK could not veto as it was a 'health and welfare' measure requiring only a majority vote of member states.

Missed opportunities

Movement returned to leave policy with the election in 1997 of a Labour government that explicitly supported gender equality and employed parents. As well as measures to improve the supply of and access to childcare services, steps were taken to develop leave. The government adopted, in 1999, an EU Directive on Parental Leave that other member states had agreed in 1996 (at that time, the UK had an opt-out from such European social policies); introduced paid Paternity Leave in 2003; and enhanced and amended Maternity Leave in 2003, 2007 and 2010.

---

[2] A Parliamentary Committee that considered this EC proposal, reporting in 1985, concluded that 'parental leave can be seen as a bold social innovation bringing important benefits for childcare and equal opportunities at work...[and] is a proper subject for legislation' (House of Lords Select Committee on the European Communities, 1985, para.83). It further concluded that it should be paid, preferably from public funds, but that small businesses should be excluded. This support was to no avail.

The overall effect of these changes was to retain Maternity Leave firmly at the centre of leave policy, despite a rhetoric that fathers should be included in modern family policy. Initiatives on leave policy were taken, but none was used to re-think and re-form an inherited maternalist policy based on a long period of Maternity Leave and premised on women having primary responsibility for the care of young children. The period 1997–2010 can, therefore, be seen as one of missed opportunities for reformulating policy.

The introduction of Parental Leave in 1999 offered the first (missed) opportunity for such reform. This was a new form of leave for the UK, but rather than use this occasion to conduct an overall review of leave policy, Parental Leave was adopted in isolation and as very much the poor relation to Maternity Leave – thin in substance and marginalised in position. The UK opted for the bare minimum required by EU law, three months per parent and unpaid. Furthermore, this leave could only be taken in short blocks (that is, one month per year spread over three years, and not as a single three-month period); some other European countries permitted Parental Leave to be split into short blocks, but all permitted leave also to be taken as one continuous period of time. Not surprisingly, given these circumstances, the UK's Parental Leave has always looked like an afterthought and had minimal impact: unknown of by many, used by few and readily overlooked in future policy changes.

Paternity Leave, introduced in 2003, another new type of leave, provided a second opportunity to review leave policy overall. Again, this never happened, and Paternity Leave, while much publicised, was a modest measure. Its two weeks' duration was not out of keeping with similar leave in other countries; but once again, the low flat-rate payment was.

Finally, any of the proposals to extend and reform Maternity Leave might have led to a wider consideration and reform of overall leave policy, but in practice did not. Instead, policy development focused on further enhancing Maternity Leave, increasing the already long period of leave from nine to 12 months (2003) and extending the low flat-rate payment from 12 weeks to, first, 20 weeks (2003) and then 33 weeks (2007). With the earnings-related payment unchanged at six weeks, this came to nine months of paid leave.

The final reform of the Labour government, in 2010, introduced a new twist to UK leave policy: mothers could transfer unused Maternity Leave and pay to fathers, after the child was 20 weeks. It also brought in another new feature of policy – the distortion of terminology. The new arrangement was called 'Additional Paternity Leave' (APL). A true Paternity Leave is a father-only entitlement, while APL was, in actual fact, a system of transferable Maternity Leave; fathers had no inherent entitlement to this leave, but depended on mothers' eligibility for Maternity Leave and willingness to transfer part of that leave.

When the Labour Party lost power in May 2010 they left a UK leave policy that remained centred on Maternity Leave, indeed even more so than when they came to power. For all its talk of greater gender equality, the administration had retained and indeed reinforced a maternalist approach. True, there had been some concessions to the idea that fathers had caring responsibilities, but these were modest and paled into insignificance beside the central feature of UK policy: women's entitlement to one year's Maternity Leave. Opportunities for fundamental reform, by a government that took parental employment seriously, had been missed.

Politics: trying to take a new path, 2010–2014

The proposal for reform

Prospects for fundamental reform did not seem promising after the May 2010 election returned a coalition government, in which the senior partner was a Conservative party that had previously ignored leave policy, except to veto the adoption of Parental Leave and to improve eligibility for Maternity Leave under duress. Yet within a year, fundamental reform was on the agenda, with the publication of a government document in May 2011: 'Consultation on Modern Workplaces'.[3] As well as changes on flexible working, working time regulations and equal pay, this document proposed a significant re-configuration of leave policy, away from Maternity Leave and towards Parental Leave.

To recap, in May 2011 a two-parent family with a new-born child was entitled to just over 18 months of leave: 12 months Maternity Leave (part transferable to the father); three months per parent of Parental Leave; and two weeks of father-only Paternity Leave. Nine months of Maternity Leave attracted some payment, but mostly at a low flat rate, with only six weeks paid at 90 per cent of earnings, and the two weeks Paternity Leave was similarly paid at a low flat rate. The remaining period, including the whole of Parental Leave, was unpaid.

---

[3] In the legislative process it is normal practice for UK governments to issue a consultation paper in advance and invite views from the public and relevant organisations.

The government proposed changing this system, to further gender equality – referring to 'shared parenting' – and long-term child outcomes:

> The current system therefore gives employed mothers a long period of maternity leave and pay, but employed fathers much less. Moreover, entitlements are quite rigid, with leave having to be taken in large blocks, and only limited opportunity for the sharing of entitlements between parents. We want to change this so that there is greater equity. We want to create a culture where both parents can better balance working and home life, so as to share this crucial early parenting period. There is strong evidence of the benefits of shared parenting and in particular that fathers who are engaged in caring for their children early on are more likely to stay involved. This involvement has been shown to have a range of positive effects, including better peer relationships, fewer behavioural problems, lower criminality, higher educational and occupational mobility, higher self-esteem and higher educational outcomes at age 20. A growing number of fathers say they want to spend more time with their children, but that they are discouraged by the existing system. (HM Government, 2011, p.14)

Another theme ran through all proposals in the consultative document: the need to increase flexibility. Britain, the government stated, 'needs a new system of parental rights fit for the 21st century that provides families with as much support and flexibility as possible so they can choose how best to balance their employment and caring responsibilities' (HM Government, 2011, p.11). At its heart was the idea of what was termed a 'flexible parental leave'.

Under the new proposals, Maternity Leave would be reduced from 52 to 18 weeks, the rationale being that this was the minimum length put forward by the EC in a 2008 proposal to revise the pregnant workers' directive (the proposed new directive has not been agreed, so the 1992 standards remain in place), it was also in line with the recommendations of the ILO. The remaining period of existing Maternity Leave would become 'flexible parental leave', to be divided between parents as they chose, that is, flexibly.

> In addition to allowing parents the possibility of taking leave at the same time (thereby, for example, allowing fathers to

take a longer period when their child is born), we are also seeking views on the desirability of allowing employers and employees to agree greater flexibility in when leave may be taken, such as allowing parents to take leave on a 'part-time' basis or allowing them to break leave into two or more periods. (HM Government, 2011, p.5)

The one exception to flexibility was a proposal for four weeks 'reserved parental leave' for the exclusive use of each parent. To ensure that the four weeks of Parental Leave 'reserved' to the father did not diminish women's existing position, the basic proposal included a further period of (low) paid leave entitlement: '[I]f a family still wishes the mother to take the full 52 weeks of leave currently available, she should be able to do so. An additional four weeks of paid leave will therefore be provided so that the period of paid leave available to the mother is not reduced' (HM Government, 2011).

The rationale for reserving part of the proposed new Parental Leave to fathers was to 'encourage a change in culture towards shared parenting' (HM Government, 2011, p.22), the consultation paper citing '[i]nternational evidence [that] suggests that fathers' usage of parental leave is higher under schemes that offer them targeted or reserved leave as opposed to just making shared leave available to the father' (HM Government, 2011, p.22). What it omitted to say was that international evidence also suggests that fathers are more likely to use Parental Leave not only if a portion is reserved for them but also if that period of leave is well paid. The proposal, however, did not suggest changes to existing rates of payment. Rather, the existing Maternity Leave payments would be re-allocated to the re-configured periods of Maternity and Parental Leave, meaning that six weeks of Maternity Leave would still be paid at 90 per cent of earnings, the remaining 12 weeks at a low flat rate as well as 25 weeks of the new Parental Leave, with the remaining period unpaid.

Also unchanged was the existing two-week Paternity Leave paid at a low flat rate and the existing Parental Leave of three months per parent (rising to four months from April 2013 following a new EU Directive agreed in 2010) – referred to in the consultation document as 'unpaid parental leave'. The Consultation Paper recognised that 'a parent can take no more than four weeks of [unpaid parental] leave in any one year', but made no proposals to change this unusual arrangement, in particular to give parents the right to use leave in one continuous period. Overall, the existing period of 'unpaid' Parental Leave – originating from the Labour government adopting the EU

Directive on Parental Leave – appears in the consultation document as an after-thought, disconnected from the new proposals for converting Maternity to ('flexible') Parental Leave.

Viewed from one perspective, the proposed changes were modest in scope. Yet viewed from another they were significant for attempting to re-configure leave policy. Under the existing dispensation, most leave was Maternity Leave; under the new proposal, most would be Parental Leave, more in keeping with systems in the rest of Europe. From this perspective, it was an attempt to change direction after many years of placing Maternity Leave at the heart of UK leave policy.

Why this proposed change in direction under a Conservative-led coalition? It reflects the transformation that had occurred in UK politics over the previous 20 years. All parties were now signed up to promoting gender equality and supporting parental employment, and all mentioned leave policy in their 2010 election manifestos even though none actually proposed the change, from Maternity to Parental Leave, that eventually emerged in the 2011 Consultation Paper. Moreover, shortly before the election all parties had been influenced by a major report – 'Working better: meeting the changing needs of families, workers and employers in the 21st century' – from the Equality and Human Rights Commission (EHRC) (2009), a statutory but independent body. Published in 2009, this report reviewed options to reform UK leave policy, including a proposal to change Maternity Leave into Parental Leave once a baby had reached six months.

What happened and why

What eventually emerged from the proposed reform of leave policy? In fact, very little. The Consultation Paper's key proposal – re-balancing leave policy from Maternity to Parental Leave – did not appear in the ensuing legislation, the Children and Families Bill introduced in February 2013 and signed into law in March 2014. In this legislation, leave policy remained centred on Maternity Leave, still 52 weeks. The main change was to extend the previous government's transferable Maternity Leave scheme, enabling mothers now to transfer their leave to their partners after two weeks rather than the previous 20 weeks. This scheme acquired a new name – no longer 'Additional Paternity Leave', now 'Shared Parental Leave' (SPL), but an equal distortion of terminology. Parental Leave must be equally available to mothers and fathers, so this revised scheme was no more Parental Leave than its precursor had been Paternity Leave: instead both were Maternity

Leave (an entitlement for women) that could be transferred by the mother to the father – if she so chose.

Why the change from the original proposed re-configuration to a variant on the existing system of transferable Maternity Leave? The government's explanation, in its response to the consultation on the original proposals, is difficult to follow.

> Our initial proposal looked at offering parental leave and pay to fathers whose partners are not currently eligible for maternity leave and pay/allowance. This would have extended the right to leave and pay very widely and it would not have been focused on those working couples who are most likely to benefit from being able to share the care of the baby, enabling them both to maintain an attachment to the labour market while raising their family.
>
> We have therefore decided to create a system whereby *working* families, those where both parents are economically active and who most need to share the leave and pay to combine childcare with working, can share between them up to 50 weeks of the leave and 37 weeks of pay that is currently available to the woman. (HM Government, 2012, p.26, original emphasis)

In sum, the government decided to limit additional leave for fathers to those with a partner both employed and eligible for Maternity Leave – though the rationale for choosing this more 'focused' approach, which makes fathers' access to extra leave dependent on their partners, is not explained, nor is it explained why this option was not included in the original consultation paper. In the absence of a clearer explanation, what might lie behind this retreat by the government of the day? The results of the formal consultation, at least as published, do not provide a clear answer. The original consultation asked for responses to two questions on the proposed change to Maternity and Parental Leave. The first asked: 'Should 18 weeks of maternity leave, accompanied by either statutory maternity pay or maternity allowance, be reserved exclusively for mothers? If not, what proportion should be reserved?' A majority (61 per cent) of the 226 respondents to the consultation answered 'no', but mostly because they preferred a shorter period or no period of reserved leave. However, there was some support for a longer period of Maternity Leave, and 'this view was held particularly strongly by the unions and women's groups' (HM Government, 2012, p.18).

The second question asked 'Should a portion of flexible parental leave be reserved for each parent? If so, is four weeks the right period to be reserved for each parent?', to which only just over half the 206 respondents said 'yes'. In its response the government acknowledged the complexity of its proposed scheme and argued that this merited dropping its move towards more 'father only' leave:

> In the consultation we proposed a system in which there would be several different types of leave available to parents in the first year of their child's life. These would include maternity, paternity, reserved parental, flexible parental and unpaid parental leave. Subsequent discussions with stakeholders suggested that this system was complex and potentially confusing. We concluded that it would be simpler to reduce the amount of different types of leave by retaining paternity leave as the only type of leave reserved exclusively for fathers. (HM Government, 2012, p.20)

The published results of the government's consultation on its proposed reform of leave policy do not explain the backtracking on its original proposal. The responses appear to support a reduction in the length of Maternity Leave. Moreover, the proposals maintained women's right to a year of leave, albeit most would now be Parental Leave and assumed that a woman wanting this full period of leave would be able to negotiate that with her partner.

A clue to the reason for staying with the *status quo* may lie in the passing reference to 'strongly' held support for longer Maternity Leave among trade unions and women's groups. Many of them saw the proposals as threatening employment rights for women that had been in place since the 1970s, as well as some occupational benefits, and were not persuaded by the continued possibility for women to take a year's leave, but mostly as Parental Leave. For example, Maternity Action, a national women's group, supported the government's decision to drop the original model of leave outlined in the Modern Workplaces consultation, which consisted of 18 weeks Maternity Leave and 34 weeks Parental Leave, because 'employers can continue to pay contractual maternity pay during the full 52 weeks of maternity leave without any legal obligation to provide comparable pay to fathers taking [Shared Parental] leave'. While Working Families, an influential NGO, asked the government to maintain Maternity Leave of at least 26 weeks since '18 weeks is insufficient time for most women to recover from birth, arrange childcare and be ready to return to work...

[and would be] likely to create a presumption that this is the amount of leave that women should take'.

Only the Fatherhood Institute, a small NGO and a strong advocate for gender equality in Parental Leave, argued strongly in favour of change:

> These changes are not enough – they won't lead to a lot more sharing right now – but they are an absolutely necessary step towards a system that can do that. If we try hanging on to six months during which only mothers CAN do the caring, we are pushing women backwards. (Fatherhood Institute, 2012)

Overall, therefore, the proposed re-configuration of UK leave policy, to bring it more into line with international understandings of different types of leave and their purposes, did not arouse widespread and ardent backing, certainly not enough to counter opposition voices. Perhaps such backing might have been forthcoming had the proposals been more ambitious, not least offering a substantial increase in payment to leave-takers; but this was never likely at a time when deficit reduction and austerity were the government's priorities and with a welfare system based on low, flat-rate benefit payments. Moreover, while the government's original reforms had been motivated in part by a concern for gender equality, 'shared parenting', when put to the test this took second place to the goal of increasing flexibility.

Some support for this reading – of opposition to change outweighing backing – comes from an attempt to reform leave policy in the previous Labour administration. Patricia Hewitt describes how, as the minister responsible for work–family policy, she sought between 2001 and 2003 to recast leave policy on the basis of equal parental rights, but eventually failed. She puts this down to a 'long-standing ambivalence within the women's movement and childcare profession towards men as fathers or workers with children' and 'no particular demand or support for equal parental leave' – the same mixture as in 2011–2012 of strong opposition and weak backing. Hewitt recalls that, in her time in government,

> most of the people involved in policy-making on family issues, as well as in the care and education of young children, are [sic] women – and women who don't generally see it as a priority to get men playing a more equal role. Most policy debates – and most media coverage – about fathers

focused on absent fathers, generally seen as feckless men refusing to pay child support. (Hewitt, 2014)

Aftermath: the use of 'Shared Parental Leave'

A feature of statutory Parental Leave in the UK – what the government termed 'unpaid parental leave' in its Modern Workplaces consultation – is that because it is unpaid, there are no regularly reported administrative data on usage: how many parents take up leave entitlements, duration of leave taken and variations between groups. No money, no statistics. Some clues on use can be found in the government-funded Fourth Work–life Balance Employee Survey, undertaken in 2012.

When employees with a child under six years were asked whether 'In the last 12 months and with your current employer, [you have] taken any parental leave?', only 11 per cent of these parents said they had (bear in mind that unpaid Parental Leave could, at that time, be taken until a child's fifth birthday). The figure was 12 per cent for men and 10 per cent for women. Lone mothers were more likely to report taking leave (21 per cent) than either 'coupled fathers' (12 per cent) or 'coupled mothers' (8 per cent) (Tipping et al, 2012, Table C5.7). Across all employers surveyed, around one in seven (14 per cent) had at least one employee who had taken unpaid Parental Leave to look after a child in the previous 12 months. No information was provided about how long the period of leave taken had been, though it could not have been more than one month, the maximum period of 'unpaid parental leave' available to take in any given year. However, take-up of paid Paternity Leave has always been high since its inception in 2003: for instance, nationally representative data shows that by 2011, 91 per cent of fathers took time off around the time of birth with 49 per cent taking statutory Paternity Leave and 25 per cent taking additional paid leave provided by employers plus statutory Paternity Leave (Chanfreau et al, 2011).

How has the new 'Shared Parental Leave' fared by contrast? Introduced to cover all births and adoptions on or after 5 April 2015, this was, as already explained, in actual fact transferable Maternity Leave, and an extended version of a similar system introduced three years earlier as 'Additional Paternity Leave', the main difference being that a longer period of Maternity Leave was potentially transferable. The earlier 'Additional Paternity Leave', introduced in 2011, had low take-up: 0.8 per cent of fathers in its first year, 1.4 per cent in its second (2012–2013).[4] A recent study into the reasons for such low

---

[4] www.bbc.co.uk/news/uk-politics-27838255

male take-up identifies four main reasons: financial costs, gendered expectations, perceived workplace resistance and policy restrictions (Kaufman, 2017).

There are no reliable and longer-term statistics on how many fathers are using part of their partner's Maternity Leave under the new SPL arrangement. Some official data show that leave has been shared in only approximately 2 per cent of families in which the mother took Maternity Leave; but this data is from an early stage of implementation and over only a short period, the first three months of 2016. So, it's too soon to tell. However, the prospects of substantial change do not look promising. The UK government itself projected only a modest take-up rate for SPL, of between 2 per cent and 8 per cent of eligible fathers. While a Parliamentary Committee report in 2016 drew attention to some reasons for not expecting too much, including, again, low rates of payment and workplace concerns:

> Research into the first six months of the shared parental leave policy by law firm Hogan Lovells found that cultural perceptions, including concerns that taking leave would be frowned upon or career limiting, were the most commonly cited reason for not taking the time off. However, the research also found that employers not paying men above the statutory benefit was an important factor in low take-up rates.
>
> In its research, the EHRC also found little evidence that SPL would encourage men to become more involved in childcare and so reduce the impact of maternity leave or part-time work on women's careers. Again, it points to levels of paternity pay as a significant barrier to uptake, noting that paternity pay is currently lower than the UK average weekly wage and below the minimum wage. In its view:

> This is likely to be too low to encourage parents to share their childcare roles more evenly, because of the drop in pay most men will incur. In addition, small and medium-sized businesses (SMEs), which make up the majority of employers in the UK are unlikely to supplement the basic additional paternity pay.
>
> (House of Commons Women's and Equalities
> Committee, 2016, p.46)

The same Parliamentary Committee, partly in recognition of failings in SPL, launched an inquiry in early 2017 into how to support fathers in the workplace so that they can 'fulfil their caring responsibilities for children'; while the UK government is committed to evaluating the SPL scheme in 2018. But as things stand, it seems unlikely that either will lead to a major re-forming of UK leave policy, following a new path. The balance of forces, pro and con, has not obviously shifted, while the climate of austerity stretches ever further into the future, ruling out a more generous benefit system for leave-takers that might, just perhaps, smooth a change of course. As things stand, only those families who can afford the financial hit, for instance where maternal salaries are high, can accommodate men's use of the UK's weak work–family reconciliation measures (O'Brien and Twamley, 2017).

Conclusion

Arguably, the UK set out in the wrong direction in 1976, by adopting, late in the day and without sufficient thought, an over-long but poorly paid Maternity Leave, reflecting a basic misunderstanding of the rationale and meaning of this form of leave, that is, that it is intended to protect the health of the mother and newborn child, just before, during and immediately after childbirth. There is a discussion to be had as to how long post-natal Maternity Leave should be to meet this 'health and welfare' criterion; most countries have opted for three or four months, while the case for up to six months' post-partum has been argued. But a maternal health and welfare post-natal leave lasting for up to 12 months is difficult to justify. Yet this was where Maternity Leave had got to in the UK by the time the government attempted to reform leave policy in 2011, by turning away from Maternity Leave towards Parental Leave.

In the event, the existing policy proved too embedded to be easily shifted, a failure to reform that can be seen as a classic case of 'path dependency'. While a few voices favoured fundamental change, more influential voices were against; adapting the existing system, rather than transforming it, became an easier political choice. Perhaps, too, major reform is always harder to implement in a time of austerity, when no financial incentives are available to sugar the pill of change.

But another factor should be included in the equation: the UK's failure, over time, to develop a deep and widespread understanding of the different types of leave and their respective rationales, an understanding that might have led to broader and stronger support for major reform.

Right from the introduction of statutory leave in the late 1970s, the UK made little attempt to learn about leave policies from and with other EEC/EU member states. In particular, the UK paid little attention to leave policy for 20 years after it belatedly adopted Maternity Leave, during which time other European countries and the EEC/EU engaged with the second wave of leave policy – the development of Parental Leave. When the UK re-connected with European social policy, after 1997, adopting the EU Parental Leave Directive in 1999 and the revised Directive in 2013, this opportunity was not used to reflect on existing provision, to gain better understanding of different types of leave, and to think about possible future directions.

Instead, Maternity Leave continued to dominate policy thinking and public discussions, and even increased its hold on leave policy as it was extended in length and payment. This lack of national understanding is seen clearly in the adoption of incorrect and therefore misleading terms for leave policies, such as 'Additional Paternity Leave' or 'Shared Parental Leave', misnomers that disguised the fact that these measures were really forms of transferable Maternity Leave. Even in the attempted reform of 2011–2012, confusion of terminology was rife, with a false distinction drawn between 'flexible' and 'unpaid' Parental Leave. Since Maternity Leave was first introduced in the late 1970s, behaviour and attitudes in the UK have undoubtedly undergone substantive change. Far more women with children are employed, fathers take more responsibility for children, attitudes have become more attuned to gender equality and shared parenting; by 2011 the male full-time breadwinner model only accounted for 22 per cent of British families (Connolly et al, 2016). Yet at the same time, employment itself has become more insecure, more intensive and more stressful, its future increasingly uncertain; and the neoliberal mandate for 'flexible' and less regulated labour markets always trumps the social democratic call for 'gender equality' and attendant greater regulation. The UK, like all Anglophone countries (Baird and O'Brien, 2015) struggles with how to reconcile these two imperatives, and ends up by muddling through with a leave policy that is neither coherent nor effective, unclear in purpose and half-hearted in execution. In the post-Brexit environment, it is even more difficult for the country to think about, let alone adopt, innovative work–

family measures, especially those that will bring about more shared parenting, drawing on the experience of other European countries with the best developed and most effective leave policies. In such a climate, the politics of leave policies continues to favour following the trodden path.

References

All Party Parliamentary Group on Parenting and the International Year of the Family (1994) *Report on UK Proceedings*, London: HMSO.

Baird, M. and O'Brien, M. (2015) 'Dynamics of parental leave in Anglophone countries: The paradox of state expansion in the liberal welfare regime', *Community, Work and Family*, 18(2): 198–217.

Chanfreau, J., Gowland, S., Lancaster, Z., Poole, E., Tipping, S. and Toomse, M. (2011) *Maternity and Paternity Rights and Women Returners Survey* 2009/2010, London: Department of Work and Pensions.

Connolly, S., Aldrich. M., O'Brien, M. and Speight, S. (2016) 'Britain's slow movement to a Gender Egalitarian Equilibrium: Parents and employment in the UK 2001–2013', *Work, Employment and Society*, 30(5): 838–857.

EHRC (Equality and Human Rights Commission) (2009) *Working better: Meeting the Changing Needs of Families, Workers and Employers in the 21st century*. Available at http://webarchive.nationalarchives. gov.uk/20141013170704/http:/www.equalityhumanrights.com/ sites/default/files/documents/working_better_final_pdf_250309.pdf

Fatherhood Institute (2012) *Maternity Leave, Parental Choice and Child Welfare: Setting an Optimum Level for Maternity Leave*. Available at www. fatherhoodinstitute.org/2012/fi-briefing-maternity-leave-parental-choice-and-child-welfare/

Fonda, N. (1980) 'Statutory maternity leave in the UK: A case study', in P. Moss and N. Fonda (eds) *Work and Family*, London: Temple Smith.

Hewitt, P. (2014) 'Gender equality', in C. Clarke (ed) *The Too Difficult Box: The Big Issues Politicians Can't Crack*, London: Biteback.

HM Government (2011) *Consultation on Modern Workplaces*. Available at www.gov.uk/government/uploads/system/uploads/attachment_ data/file/31549/11-699-consultation-modern-workplaces.pdf

HM Government (2012) *Modern Workplaces: Government Response on Flexible Parental Leave*. Available at www.gov.uk/government/ uploads/system/uploads/attachment_data/file/82969/12-1267-modern-workplaces-response-flexible-parental-leave.pdf

House of Commons Women and Equalities Committee (2016) *Gender Pay Gap*. Available at www.publications.parliament.uk/pa/ cm201516/cmselect/cmwomeq/584/584.pdf

House of Lords Select Committee on the European Communities (1985) *Parental Leave and Leave for Family Reasons*, London: HMSO.

Kaufman, G. (2017) 'Barriers to equality: Why British fathers do not use parental leave', *Community, Work and Family*, 1–16, DOI: http://dx.doi.org/10.1080/13668803.2017.1307806

O'Brien, M. and Twamley, K. (2017) 'Fathers taking leave alone in the UK – a gift exchange between mother and father?', in M. O'Brien and K. Wall (eds) *Comparative Perspectives on Work–Life Balance and Gender Equality: Fathers on Leave Alone*, New York: Springer, pp 163–182.

Tipping, S., Chanfreau, J., Perry, J. and Tait, T. (2012) *The Fourth Work–Life Balance Employee Survey (Employment Relations Research Series 122)*, London: Department for Business, Innovation and Skills. Available at www.gov.uk/government/uploads/system/uploads/attachment_data/file/32153/12-p151-fourth-work–life-balance-employee-survey.pdf

FIVE

Israel: leave policy, familialism and the neoliberal welfare state

Nadav Perez-Vaisvidovsky

Introduction

Several researchers in the field of family policy have noted the rapid changes in policy toward families in almost all welfare states in recent decades, adapting it to new family and employment patterns (see for example Kamerman and Moss, 2009; Ferragina and Seeleib-Kaiser, 2015; Naldini and Long, 2017). Israel, however, remains an outlier. Although Israeli family and, most notably, employment patterns have thoroughly changed, no less than elsewhere, family policy in general and leave policy specifically have undergone only minor changes. This chapter will examine the changes (and failed attempts to change) in leave policy in Israel between 2007 (when the provision of leave was the same as in 1954) and 2017, and which culminated in a large-scale public protest, in order to understand why the rapid and massive changes in employment and familial patterns were not matched by changes in leave policy.

The chapter begins by providing, in broad brush strokes, some background on relevant features of Israeli society, before describing family policy in Israel in general and the evolution of leave policy in the years 1954–2007 as an element of this broader policy. Next, the chapter outlines three changes in leave policy that occurred between 2007 and 2016, leading to an analysis of the process of change in 2016–2017, which began with a Facebook protest and ended (for the time being, at least) in a policy change in March 2017.

A final point needs to be made about the scope of this chapter. Its focus is Israeli leave policy, which, in broad terms, covers the area held by Israel prior to 1967, plus inhabitants of eastern Jerusalem and the Golan Heights and Jewish inhabitants in the West Bank. Palestinian inhabitants of the West Bank and the Gaza strip have access to the leave policy of the Palestinian Authority, which is independent of the Israeli programme and is not included in this chapter.

Characteristics of Israeli society

Several characteristics of Israeli society are essential to understanding the development of its leave policy: familialism, increasing participation by women in the labour market, and the society's heterogeneity. Other relevant characteristics of Israeli society, in particular the effects of the Israeli–Palestinian conflict and the neoliberalisation of Israeli economic and social policy, will be touched on in the course of the chapter.

The most prominent characteristic of Israeli society, when discussing family policy, is familialism, the great importance attached to the family over the needs of individual members: the family is central. Israeli families are large. The total fertility rate (TFR) in Israel in 2015 was 3.1 – not only the highest in the OECD, but almost double the OECD average of 1.7, and 40 per cent more than Mexico's, the second-highest.[1] Other indicators confirm the centrality of the Israeli family, albeit less dramatically: the marriage rate is among the highest in the OECD, and marriage age among the lowest; divorce rates are below-average (although rising in recent years), as are rates of single parent families.[2]

From these data, it is easy to imagine that Israeli society promotes traditional caring roles for mothers. However, Israel also has high rates of employment for women, and specifically among mothers. Maternal employment in Israel in 2014 was 72.1 per cent, well above the OECD average of 66.2 per cent, and it varies little by age of youngest child. Women in Israel not only work outside the home – they work long hours; 60.2 per cent of women work more than 40 hours per week, and the average annual working hours for women are 1,700, well above the OECD average of 1,500. However, although Israeli women work more than their average OECD counterparts, they work much less than Israeli men, who average almost 2,000 annual hours worked (OECD, 2017). Thus, the picture that emerges is that parents, and specifically women, face a double burden: on the one hand, large families (which demand large amounts of care work); on the other, long hours of work in the labour market.

The aggregate statistics presented above, however, miss an important part of the story: heterogeneity. Israeli society is deeply divided: Jews and Palestinians; religion and level of religiosity; native-born and immigrants. These divisions are clearly revealed in family characteristics. Ultra-orthodox Jewish families and Muslim Palestinian

---

[1] https://data.oecd.org/pop/fertility-rates.htm
[2] www.oecd.org/els/family/database.htm

families in general have more conservative family structures and higher birth rates (TFR of 6.53 and 3.62, respectively), with lower participation by women in the labour market. Secular Jewish and Christian Palestinian families are at the opposite end of the spectrum, with comparatively small families (although still large by European standards), and high levels of employment (Fogiel-Bijaoui, 2002; Hleihel, 2011; Okun, 2013).

The differences in family size and structure deeply affect the discourse on family policy – and through it, family policy itself. The high rates of low-income families with large numbers of children among certain groups create antagonism toward programmes that target these populations – specifically, means-tested social security programmes aimed at children or families. Such programmes (and specifically child allowance and income maintenance) were at the centre of the debate in the first decade of the twenty-first century, and experienced deep cuts (Doron, 2010). This heterogeneity had little impact on leave policy, aimed as it is at women (and men) participating in the labour market, and the Israeli programme stresses this aspect; it escaped the critique aimed at other programmes.

An overview of family policy in Israel

Family policy in Israel is, naturally, influenced by these characteristics of Israeli families. Another important factor – the most important, some claim – is the Israeli–Palestinian conflict. In the decade following the formation of the Israeli state in 1948, family policy in Israel was formed in the light of this conflict. The governing ethos in Israeli society expressed commitment to gender equality, for example in the Israeli declaration of independence. However, actual policy focused on the role of women as 'mothers of the nation', and their vital part in the 'demographic battle' to maintain a Jewish majority in the state of Israel. Palestinian citizens, having voting rights for the Israeli Parliament, were construed as a threat to the existence of a Zionist–Jewish state. Maintaining the Judaism of the state was dependent, then, on the maintenance of a sizeable Jewish majority, which in turn depended on high birth rates (alongside immigration). Motherhood was seen as a weapon in a demographic battle for the identity of the newly founded nation.

In this context, equal rights legislation was enacted only when it was perceived not to be detrimental to the role of women as mothers. For example, equal military service for women, one of the hallmarks of perceived gender equality, was required only from unmarried young women with no children, and the main legislation for gender equality at the time – the 1951 Women's Equal Rights Law – was limited to areas not affecting the stability of family or marriage. Furthermore, equality was understood as 'the equal right to contribute to nation building' (as the military service example shows). Equality in its contemporary feminist meaning did not appear in the discourse until much later (Berkovitch, 1997).

Israeli society has undergone major changes since then, but this tension between gender equality and the role of women as mothers still shapes family policy. Although Israeli women's participation in waged work has risen dramatically (Hacker et al, 2011), 'women's policy' and 'family policy' is still aimed primarily at protecting mothers participating in the workforce. Women, therefore, are understood mainly as mothers, their roles as workers and citizens taking second place (Ajzenstadt and Gal, 2001; Perez, 2010; Helman, 2011; Herbst and Benjamin, 2012; Herbst, 2013).

One of the major changes, affecting both the Israeli economy and the welfare state, is a sharp move towards neoliberalism. Israel originally had distinct characteristics of a social democratic welfare regime. But since the 1980s, the country has moved toward a neoliberal regime, in a way that appears extreme even compared to a similar shift occurring in western welfare states (Doron, 2001; Hacker et al, 2011).

Renan Barzilay (2012) describes the combined effect of these two processes on family policy as 'fire and forget'. The state supports childbearing – but only until the child is born. Afterwards, parents are left to care for their children with little state support. Thus, public funding for fertility treatments in Israel is the most generous in the world; protections for pregnant workers, including protection from layoff and the provision of leave during pregnancy complications, are comprehensive. However, state assistance and protection for families with children are minimal. It was only during the decade described in more detail below (2007–2017) that free education for three- to five-year-olds was introduced; before then, daycare for parents was subsidised only on a limited scale for low-income families. As discussed, the working week is long (43 hours), and regulation of working hours virtually non-existent. Leave policies, overall, are modest.

Perhaps the most striking example of the 'forget' side of the 'fire and forget policy' are child allowances and income maintenance for families in poverty. These experienced deep cuts in the early 2000s, the explicit logic behind which was that 'some families have too many children' (Doron, 2010, p.21). This brings Israel to the bottom of the league table when measuring government expenditure per child, on early childhood education and care (OECD, 2017) and social security protection for families (OECD, 2017).

Parental Leave before 2007

Prior to the establishment of the state of Israel in 1948, Maternity Leave was eight weeks, based on the British Mandate colonial rule legislation. In 1954, a new Maternity Leave entitlement was introduced, as part of the National Insurance Act, which outlined the new state's social security programme, and the Women Labour Act, which defined protections for working women (and specifically, for working mothers). The new programme included a 12-week Maternity Leave, compensated at 75 per cent of earnings prior to birth. The leave was to be taken in one block of time and could be started from six weeks before birth. Leave payment was based on contributions to social insurance. The programme also included an unpaid leave of up to one year after birth for mothers, dependent on the period of employment with the same employer prior to birth. Both leaves were termed 'Hufshat Leida' (חופשת לידה, literally 'birth leave'), and both included measures of employment protection, though the protection for the paid leave was stronger.

This leave was described at the time by the Minister of Labour, Golda Meirson (later Meir), as a major step towards the protection of women workers and toward gender equality, and as a recognition of the contribution of women to the Zionist struggle. It was also stressed that the leave complied with ILO and WHO recommendations, and was more generous than parallel programmes in '"enlightened" countries such as Sweden and Switzerland' (170th meeting of the 2nd Knesset [Israeli Parliament], 29 December 1952).

Maternity Leave, as introduced in 1954, remained virtually unchanged for four decades, except for fathers being able to share the unpaid leave from 1988. Minor changes included expanding the right to adopting parents and to family members where the child or the mother were hospitalised during leave, and securing social benefits for mothers taking leave. Duration, eligibility criteria and payment, however, remained unchanged for the entire period.

The 1990s were a period of change in Israeli gender policy. A group of feminist legislators transformed gender-related policy in a number of fields, including work–family balance. Although Maternity Leave was not seen as a main target by these legislators, some changes were introduced. The two main ones were, first, in 1994 raising the level of compensation from 75 per cent of earnings prior to birth to 100 per cent; and, in 1998, giving the option for mothers to transfer part of their paid leave to their spouse.[3] However, the length of leave, paid or unpaid, was unchanged, remaining at 12 weeks and one year, respectively.

Subsequently, members of the Knesset (MKs), mainly from opposition parties, continually proposed extensions to the paid Maternity leave. From 1992, in every elected Knesset, a bill to extend the leave to 14 or 16 weeks was laid on the Knesset's table – and in each and every case, it faced government opposition and failed to pass the first stage of the legislative process. Thus, although various changes to the leave were introduced, its length did not change.

2007–2016: small change in leave policy

In 2007, Israeli leave policy consisted of 12 weeks paid Maternity Leave – similar to the situation in 1954, except payment was now 100 per cent of earnings, though still dependent on contribution (that is, participation in the labour force) prior to birth. Out of 12 weeks, six could be transferred to the father (under certain conditions). In addition, an unpaid leave was available for one of the parents until the child reached one year of age. As the first 12 weeks of Maternity Leave are mandatory, take-up is universal by those who are eligible. In 2014 (latest available data), 69 per cent of women giving birth received compensation and 0.39 per cent of fathers shared their spouses' leave.

Other countries, however, had moved on. In the 1950s, 12 weeks of Maternity Leave was considered world-leading, but by 2007, it placed Israel at the bottom of international comparisons (Ray et al, 2008). Moreover, the 1990s and the 2000s witnessed major changes in almost all welfare states, both in the general field of family policy (Ferragina and Seeleib-Kaiser, 2015) and specifically in the field of leave policy (Kamerman and Moss, 2009).

Many Israeli parents, then, faced a problematic situation in 2007. The changes described above in women's employment had already taken place for many groups in Israeli society, if not all. Coupled with Israeli familialism, and specifically high fertility rates, these placed a heavy burden on the shoulders of Israeli women, and the welfare state did little to help them cope with this situation. While the government

---

[3] One may argue that this change constituted a transformation of Maternity Leave to Parental Leave. However, since both legislation and court ruling emphasise that the leave is an entitlement of the mother, who has an option to transfer it, 'Maternity Leave' still describes the programme better.

failed to act to lighten this burden, private legislators did attempt changes, some of which received governmental backing and passed.

2007: Maternity Leave extended from 12 to 14 weeks

The election of the 17th Knesset in 2006 brought about conditions for change. Two MKs – Gideon Saar, from the right-wing Likud Party, and Shelly Yechimovich, from the left-wing Labour Party – introduced a bill to extend Maternity Leave to 14 weeks. As explained both in the Knesset and in interviews, they sought to close the gap between Israel and other industrialised countries and the standards set by international organisations such as the WHO, the ILO and the EU. They were also influenced by rising rates of female employment.

The extension from 12 to 14 weeks was seen as a first step towards a more comprehensive reform of leave policy. This is how MK Saar explained the bill in the Knesset:

> [The extension] will allow Israel to stand in line with at least the minimalist norm, as it exists today even in the European directive of the International Labour Organization [sic]. We know that many studies stress the importance of the connection to the mother in the first months of the baby's life, including breastfeeding, when it exists. Other countries have gone much further. I admit that 14 weeks is not the final destination in my vision, but a realist move that I deemed achievable in this Knesset in the current circumstances.

While previous bills had met with fierce government opposition, this one fared differently. The attitude of the centre-left government was ambivalent. The initial response was support, conditioned by a gradual implementation programme. It then withdrew its support, but did not pressure its MKs to oppose the law, practically ensuring that it would pass the second stage of legislation. In the last stage, the government changed its position again and decided to support the bill, which passed and became law in May 2007, extending Maternity Leave in Israel for the first time in five decades.

Saar and Yechimovich submitted a second bill, a year after the first, to further extend Maternity Leave to 16 weeks, and putting forward the same reasoning. The government reaction was similar, conditioned support on the first stage, opposition on the second stage. Again, the bill passed against government opposition. However, before the third and final stage of legislation, the government collapsed, a new Knesset was elected, and the bill was not passed.

2010: more leave, no extra compensation

Members of the next Knesset attempted to extend Maternity Leave, but using a different strategy. This time, the bill was promoted by MKs Tzipi Hotovely, from the right-wing Likud Party, and Dalia Itzik, from the centrist Kadima Party – again, a cooperation of opposition and coalition MKs. Their bill proposed that paid Maternity Leave be extended to 26 weeks, almost doubling its length, but the compensation for the leave would not change, remaining equal to 14 weeks of the worker's pay prior to birth. The bill passed and became law in March 2010.

As noted before, however, Israeli parents were already eligible for one year's unpaid leave. Thus, the new bill practically created three distinct periods of leave: a paid leave of 14 weeks (hereafter 'paid leave'), an unpaid leave of 12 weeks ('first unpaid leave'), and another period of unpaid leave of 26 weeks ('second unpaid leave'), each under different conditions. To add to the confusion, all three periods were labelled 'Birth Leave'.

The effect of the legislation on the lives of parents was minimal. The main advantage was intended to be the universal availability of the first unpaid leave to all women, whereas the second unpaid leave was only available to those parents working with the same employer for 12 months. However, this was removed during the legislation to maintain government support, and the final bill had the same 12 months requirement.

Thus, the differences between the two types of unpaid leave remained minimal, boiling down to the first unpaid leave being formally part of the paid leave, and therefore covered by its protections; these include an obligation on the employer to continue paying into pension funds, maintenance of seniority-related workers' rights, and somewhat stronger protection from layoff. In addition, because the formal leave was 26 weeks, mothers no longer had to inform their employer if they wanted to extend their leave, but only if they wanted to shorten their leave to 14 weeks. The legislators believed that this would strengthen the position of mothers vis-a-vis their employer when requesting an extension.

Why, then, was the extension needed? The reasoning provided by the legislators did not stress the immediate benefits of the legislation, but rather its value as a step towards a future expansion of leave. As they realised that the government would not allow an extension of paid leave, they worked to extend the leave but not the pay – in the hope that a better political climate in the future would allow an extension not only of leave, but also the compensation period.

2016: Introducing Paternity Leave

The last step in this decade-long period was the introduction of Paternity Leave. Before 2016, mothers in Israel could transfer part of their Maternity Leave to their spouse, but fathers enjoyed no independent entitlement to leave and had no option of taking leave at the same time as their spouse. The only option available was a short period, defined as sick leave, from the beginning of birth contractions until 24 hours after birth, during which fathers could be absent from their work.

Here also, the change came from private legislation. The first to propose a Paternity Leave bill was MK Uri Ariel, of the right-wing Bait Yehudi. His bill in 2011 offered seven days of leave for a newborn daughter and eight days for a newborn son (to allow the father to participate in the Jewish ceremony of circumcision, performed on the eighth day after birth). The leave was to be paid by the employer and deducted from the father's allotted sick leave. The bill's stated rationale was to 'enable parents to spend the first days with their family and to make it easier for the mother'. It enjoyed government support and passed the first and second stages. However, before the third and final stage, the Knesset dispersed for elections.

Following the appointment of MK Ariel as a government minister after the next elections, MK Tamar Zandberg, from the left-wing Meretz party, pushed the bill in the next Knesset. It again enjoyed government support, but due to opposition by the head of the relevant parliamentary committee, MK Haim Katz, who decried the importance of paternal involvement, it did not proceed.

After the next elections, in 2015, Zandberg continued to advance the bill, again with governmental support and this time with a sympathetic committee head. The bill went through a smooth and quick legislative process, and became law in July 2016. However, during the legislation the MKs had to make concessions in order to retain government support. The government, in turn, required the agreement of employer organisations. Thus, the length of the leave was shortened to five days, and the first three days came not from the father's sick allocation, but from his annual leave days. Here, again, the legislators stressed that this was only a partial solution, Zandberg acknowledging that the new leave was insufficient. She expressed the hope that a more comprehensive Paternity Leave measure would soon follow, providing a longer period and public funding of payment for the leave.

Public protests and leave change

The changes described previously originated in the legislature. The MKs proposing them claimed that their bills were based on citizens' demands, and answered societal needs. But they were not the result of actual demands from a social movement or civil society activism. This situation, however, had drastically changed by the second half of 2016.

To understand this change, it is necessary to return to the worldwide waves of social protest of 2011 (for example, the Occupy Movement, the Arab Spring), which did not bypass Israel (Glasius and Pleyers, 2013). In July 2011, an unpreceded wave of protest washed over Israel, including demonstrations, tent cities in city centres, massive social media activity and more. The protests were socio-economic in nature, and their stated goal was 'the people demand social justice', though their exact aims remained unclear and contested. However, the cost of living and the erosion of the welfare state were two main themes of the protesters (Cicurel and Litbeck-Hirsch, 2012; Rosenhek and Shalev, 2014).

Family policy was not at the centre of the protests, but was represented. As part of the general upsurge, a group of parents initiated what they called 'the stroller protest', in which, with their babies and toddlers in strollers, they protested against the cost of childrearing. Although the extension of leave entitlements was presented as part of the demands of this protest, the central demand was free education for children under six years old (Case, 2011, Nachmany, 2011). And indeed, in what is considered by many to be the most prominent tangible achievement of the protests, the Trachtenberg Committee, which was formed by Prime Minister Netanyahu to answer the demands of the protesters, recommended the extension of free public education to 3- to 5-year-olds, a recommendation accepted by the government (Amram, 2013). As can be seen, however, the stroller protest had no effect on leave provision.

This situation changed in June 2016. Osnat Vatury, a mother who had recently given birth to her third child and had no previous political engagement, opened a Facebook page titled 'Parental Leave – It's Not a Right, It's Survival'. She claimed that the current paid leave of 14 weeks was insufficient and called for an extension to six months.

The Facebook protest was an immediate success. Many fathers and (mainly) mothers joined the page, shared its posts and expressed sympathy and support for its causes. It received tens of thousands of 'Likes' within the first month, unpreceded by Israeli standards. Vatury designated 14 June to be a 'Facebook demonstration' day, in which all page followers were expected to change their profile picture in support of the initiative and write or share posts supporting an extension of Maternity Leave.

The success on social media was soon followed by interest from traditional media outlets. The protest received much positive coverage from the main media outlets in Israel, including newspapers and radio and television shows. The two most prominent examples were coverage on the *HaZinor* late night show, focusing on internet trends, which brought many new followers; and later an in-depth coverage of Vatury and the protest on *HaMa'arechet*, a prime-time news magazine on Israel's leading Channel 2.

The high profile of the protest, both on new and traditional media, soon attracted interest from the political arena. The first to bring the issue into the legislative field were opposition MKs. MK Manuel Trajtenberg presented a bill to enable a gradual return from Maternity Leave, permitting mothers to work part-time in the months following leave. MK Merav Michaeli proposed a drastic extension of leave for parents to nine months, following the 'Icelandic model' of three months for the mother, three for the father and three to share. (The author of this chapter took part in designing this bill.)

Unlike previous legislative moves, however, these initiatives were not left only to individual MKs and private bills. Following the massive political pressure, several players in government began to show interest in changes in leave policy, including the Minister of Finance, Moshe Cahlon. Pressured by Vatury, who at this stage was directing her protest towards him, he agreed that the country's leave policy should be changed. The pressure intensified in December 2016. The 2017 state budget was due to be finalised, and it was clear that if an extension of leave was not funded, it would be near impossible to implement any changes in 2017. After massive public pressure and several meetings with Vatury, Cahlon announced that a sum of NIS230 million would be included in the next budget to increase Maternity Leave, a sum estimated to be sufficient for a one-week extension.

Finance Minister Cahlon then appointed MK Rachel Azaria, a feminist from the centrist Kulanu Party (also Cahlon's) with a history of work–family balance legislation, to head a committee to examine the possibility of a change in leave policy, and to bring forward a proposal for such change. Following the work of the committee, a bill was presented to the Knesset, including the extension of paid leave to 15 weeks. For the first time in the history of Israeli leave policy, the additional week was not solely for mothers, but given to the couple to be used either as an extension of the mother's leave or as paid leave for the father, with the possibility to use it while the mother was also on leave. Azaria and Cahlon also agreed a further extension of the leave to 16 weeks within a year. The bill was passed to a special committee, the 'Reform Committee', headed by Azaria, and passed at an accelerated pace, with little opposition. In March 2017, the first part of the bill passed the last stage of legislation and became law, extending paid leave to 15 weeks.

As demonstrated, the initiative received full backing from Cahlon, the Minister of Finance. However, other ministers in relevant offices did not show interest or participate in the legislation. Specifically, the ministers of social equality, labour and welfare took no part in the process.

Judging by posts on the Facebook group wall and from traditional media coverage, responses to the new law were mixed. While the one-week extension was widely seen as positive, many considered it unsatisfactory and some even as insulting. The protest had stressed the importance of half a year of leave; 26 weeks, the length of the 'first unpaid leave', was put forward as a 'magic number' and as the target for the protestors. When the law was amended to provide only one extra week – instead of 12 – many parents expressed dissatisfaction, and some even claimed that the movement had failed.

Vatury, the initiator of the protest, gave a complex message. On the one hand, she stressed the importance of the one-week extension and the other aspects of the legislation; on the other, she claimed that she did not regard this bill, or even the promised future extension to 16 weeks, as the end of the matter, and made public her plans to continue the protest. Even Azaria, who was a main power behind the legislation, did not claim it was satisfactory, or that it should be the end of the reform process. On the contrary, she stressed that this legislation was only the first step of a long journey.

Conclusion: a change failing to happen

From the description above, a distinct tension in the field of leave policy in Israel emerges: on the one hand, according to policymakers and activists interviewed, leave reform enjoys wide support; on the other, such reform fails to come. However, this situation manifests itself differently at the two different stages of legislation.

The most prominent characteristic of the first stage legislation is that it was based on private bills. In every Knesset since 1992, a bill was presented to extend leave; the bills that passed, in 2007 and 2010, passed because of effective political lobbying by the proposing MKs. The bills were not part of a governmental plan, but rather an attempt by individual MKs – both from opposition and coalition parties – to push the length of leave as far as possible.

This leads to the next aspect of the private bills: they were not seen as a comprehensive solution to the social problem of the length of leave available to parents. The MKs behind the legislation did not claim that accepting their offer would provide parents with an ideal leave; rather, they acknowledged that the leave should either be longer (in the 2007 legislation) or fully paid (in 2010 and 2016). Their proposals were always a compromise, presented as the best one could achieve in the current political climate, and as a stepping stone toward future improvements.

Another important aspect of these three legislative attempts was the lack of ideological opposition. In all cases, the government opposed the legislation at certain stages (although in all cases, it finally backed it). However, in most cases, when the government opposed the legislation, it did not give reasons for doing so. Even when a minister did explain government opposition, he did not claim that it stemmed from opposition to the idea of a longer leave period, but rather from economic difficulties. This is how minister Yaacov Deri explained the government's position toward the 2006 legislation, in the first stage: 'The aim is wanted and blessed. The ILO recommends a 14-week parental leave [sic]. However, the cost to the state is enormous. The Ministry of Finance estimated the cost by NIS400 million per year' (105th sitting of the 17th Knesset, 6 May 2007).

One may assume, based on the positions of MKs and of the government, that the claim that paid leave is too short enjoys a wide consensus in Israeli society. The government's inadequate response to this claim probably originates in financial considerations. The Ministry of Finance is one of the strongest players in Israeli politics, and is a staunch supporter of economic austerity (Cohen, 2012). Therefore, the eventual outcome is a process of patching what everyone agrees is a broken programme, with what everyone agrees are inadequate patches.

The 2017 law is different from prior legislation in two important ways: first, it originated in a public protest, and not in MKs' initiatives; and second, it received full and constant backing from government officials, and specifically from Minister of Finance Moshe Cahlon. These two differences might be connected – the public support may have pressured Cahlon to support the legislation. However, in other ways the legislative process seemed very similar to previous attempts at reform; there was no voiced ideological opposition to the legislation, the only argument against an extension being lack of funding. In addition, the legislation was not perceived as the installation of a comprehensive leave policy; rather, it was seen as a small step in the right direction, by all those involved.

To summarise, the decade of 2007–2017 can be seen as the harbinger of change in Israeli leave policy. In the 55 years before this decade, changes to policy were minor, and most notably the length of paid leave remained at 12 weeks for the entire period. But this decade, however, was characterised by real changes, aimed at lengthening the leave and making some of it available to fathers. All these changes were of limited scope and enjoyed limited success, but pointed the way for further extensions.

This pattern of 'insufficient advances', as it might be termed, originates from the tension of two conflicting developments in Israel. The first arises from the combination of familialism, changing women's employment patterns, and the effects of international changes in leave policy. Israeli women are devoting more and more time to wage labour, while maintaining unmatched rates of fertility, which creates growing tensions for the family. At the same time, in an increasingly globalised culture, they are becoming aware of their counterparts in Europe, enjoying more generous leave provisions. Thus, in the debate around leave policy, a prominent argument is international comparison, citing both the example of other countries mainly in Scandinavia but also in other parts of Europe (the Germen *Elterngeld* reform of 2007 receiving much attention) and the recommendations of transnational organisations such the ILO, WHO and EU. Against these raised demands and expectations, the neoliberal character of Israeli social policy, and specifically the 'fire and forget' element guiding family policy, dictate minimal expenditure on social programmes. Thus, while the expansion and extension of leave policies receives strong support among both the public and policymakers, the high costs of such reform lead the powerful Ministry of Finance to oppose such expansion, blocking anything that goes beyond the minimal.

References

Ajzenstadt, M. and Gal, J. (2001) 'Appearances can be deceptive: Gender in the Israeli Welfare State', *Social Politics*, 8(3): 92–324.

Amram, Y. (2013) 'Grass fire: Outbreak of the social protest, its operation style and the results observed in the short term', *American Journal of Social Sciences*, 1(1): 1–12.

Berkovitch, N. (1997) 'Motherhood as a national mission: The construction of womanhood in the legal discourse in Israel', *Women's Studies International Forum*, 20: 605–619.

Case, R. (2011) 'Organisers of the stroller protest: We were surprised, this is just the beginning', *ynet*, 26 July 2011. Available at www.ynet. co.il/articles/0,7340,L-4101597,00.html.

Cicurel, I.E. and Litbeck-Hirsch, T. (2012) 'Personal home, communal tent, and social justice in the Beer Sheva Protest Tents', *Israeli Sociology*, 14(1): 9–28.

Cohen, N. (2012) 'Policy entrepreneurs and the design of public policy: Conceptual framework and the case of the National Health Insurance Law in Israel', *Journal of Social Research and Policy*, 3(1): 1–22

Doron A. (2001) 'Social welfare policy in Israel: Developments in the 1980s and 1990s', *Israel Affairs*, 7(4): 153–180.

Doron, A. (2010) 'Abuse and fraud in the National Insurance System', *Bitachon Soczialy*, 84: 57–78.

Ferragina, E. and Seeleib-Kaiser, M. (2015) 'Determinants of a silent (r)evolution: Understanding the expansion of family policy in rich OECD countries', *Social Politics*, 22(1): 1–37.

Fogiel-Bijaoui, S. (2002) 'Familism, postmodernity and the state: The case of Israel', *Journal of Israeli History*, 21(1–2): 38–62.

Glasius, M. and Pleyers, G. (2013) 'The global moment of 2011: Democracy, social justice and dignity', *Development and Change*, 44(3): 547–567.

Hacker, D., Frenkel, M. and Braudo, Y. (2011) 'Working families in Israeli Law: Between neo-liberalism and human rights', in M. Shilo and G. Katz (eds) *Gender in Israel*, Beer-Sheva: Ben Gurion University, pp 682–727.

Helman, S. (2011) '"Let us help them to raise their children into good citizens": The Lone-Parent Families Act and the wages of care-giving in Israel', *Social Politics*, 18(1): 52–81.

Herbst, A. (2013) 'Welfare mom as warrior mom: Discourse in the 2003 single mothers' protest in Israel', *Journal of Social Policy*, 42(1): 129–145.

Herbst, A. and Benjamin, O. (2012) 'It was a Zionist act: Feminist politics of single-mother policy votes in Israel', *Women's Studies International Forum*, 35(4): 29–37.

Hleihel, A. (2011) 'Fertility among Jewish and Muslim Women in Israel, by level of religiosity, 1979–2009', *ICBS Working Paper Series*, Jerusalem: Israel Central Bureau of Statistics.

Kamerman, S.B. and Moss, P. (2009) 'Introduction', in S.B. Kamerman and P. Moss (eds) *The Politics of Parental Leave Policies*, Bristol: Policy Press, pp 1–13.

Nachmany, N. (2011) 'מחאת העגלות בת"א: "חינוך הוא מוצר יסוד"' [The Stroller Protest in Tel-Aviv: "Education is a Basic Commodity"], *nrg.*, 30 August 2011. Available at www.nrg.co.il/online/1/ART2/277/658.html

Naldini, M. and Long, J. (2017) 'Geographies of families in the European Union: A legal and social policy analysis', *International Journal of Law, Policy and the Family*, 31(1): 94–113.

OECD (2017) *Starting Strong 2017*, Paris: OECD.

Okun, B.S. (2013) 'Fertility and marriage behavior in Israel: Diversity, change, and stability', *Demographic Research*, 28: 457–504.

Perez, N. (2010) 'The abandoning of fathers as surveillance of families: Fathers in the Israeli legislative discourse', in C. Katz and E. Izfadia, E. (eds) *Abandoning State: Surveillancing State*, Tel Aviv: Resling, pp 271–290.

Perez-Vaisvidovsky, N. (2013) 'Fathers at a crossroads: The combined effect of organizational and cultural factors on the making of gender-related policy', *Social Politics: International Studies in Gender, State and Society*, 20(3): 407–429.

Perez-Vaisvidovsky, N. (2017) 'Fathers as frauds: On the criminalization of fathers in the parental leave for fathers program in Israel', *Men and Masculinities*, DOI: 10.1177/1097184X17696175

Ray, R., Gornick, J.C. and Schmitt, J. (2008) *Parental Leave Policies in 21 Countries: Assessing Generosity and Gender Equality*, Washington DC: Center for Economic and Policy Research.

Renan Barzilay, A. (2012) 'Working Parents: Multidimentionalism and working-class social feminism – lessons for reconciling family and work in Israel', *Tel Aviv University Law Review*, 35: 327–328.

Rosenhek, Z. and Shalev, M. (2014) 'The political economy of Israel's "social justice" protests: A class and generational analysis', *Contemporary Social Science*, 9(1): 31–48.

SIX

Japan: leave policy and attempts to increase fathers' take-up

Hideki Nakazato

Introduction

Japan has developed a Parental Leave scheme that allows fathers one year of paid leave regardless of the employment status of their partner, and which has been described as 'by far the most generous paid father-specific entitlement in the OECD' (OECD, 2017, p.6). This is a result of frequent amendments to the leave scheme since its first implementation in 1992. Yet despite its generosity, take-up of Parental Leave by men in Japan remains low, at just over 3 per cent of all eligible fathers.

This chapter will describe the characteristics of Japan's leave policy and explore how it has developed since its inception in 1976, when leave was only for mothers in certain public sector occupations including teachers, nurses and childcare workers; it pays particular attention to the increasing emphasis on use by fathers, including an important change in 2014. The chapter will also examine political processes at different stages of policy development and the involvement of various actors within and outside the country; in particular, positions taken by these actors in policy debates, common and conflicting goals and interests, and how these have shaped policy changes. In addition to attempting to explain how and why the leave scheme was established, it will also consider why, despite the current policy's design, leave-taking by fathers in Japan is still so rare. It will conclude by considering what potential the current scheme has to promote more equal use of Parental Leave by mothers and fathers, and what conditions are needed to realise that potential.

In a comparative study of Japan and three other countries, Boling (2015) has examined the politics of work–family policies in areas such as childcare, leaves, child allowances and workplace-oriented policies, based on wide-ranging interviews. This chapter will focus specifically on Parental Leave, and draws mainly on records of discussions and negotiations, including proceedings of the National Diet (the Japanese Parliament), the Labour Policy Council (a body composed of representatives of public interests, workers and employers, offering advice on labour policies to the Minister of Health, Labour and Welfare), and the related research committee of the Ministry of Health, Labour and Welfare (before 2000, the Ministry of Health and Welfare and the Ministry of Labour). In addition, the chapter refers to newspaper articles and to two publications from the early 1990s by key government officials: a book by Yaeko Itohisa from the Japan Socialist Party (Itohisa, 1990), and an article by Fujii Ryuko, the head of the Women Welfare Division of the Ministry of Labour (Fujii, 1991). These sources were analysed using NVivo 11, a qualitative data analysis programme, and coded based on the topics, roles, political parties of speakers and the time periods when the statements were made.

Background to the introduction of Parental Leave

In Japan, the first phase of the post-war history of women's participation in the labour force has been described as 'popularisation of the housewife' (Ochiai, 1994). Labour force participation rates of 25- to 35-year-old women fell from 1955 to 1975 (Figure 6.1), as

Figure 6.1: Labour force participation of women by age (1955–1975)

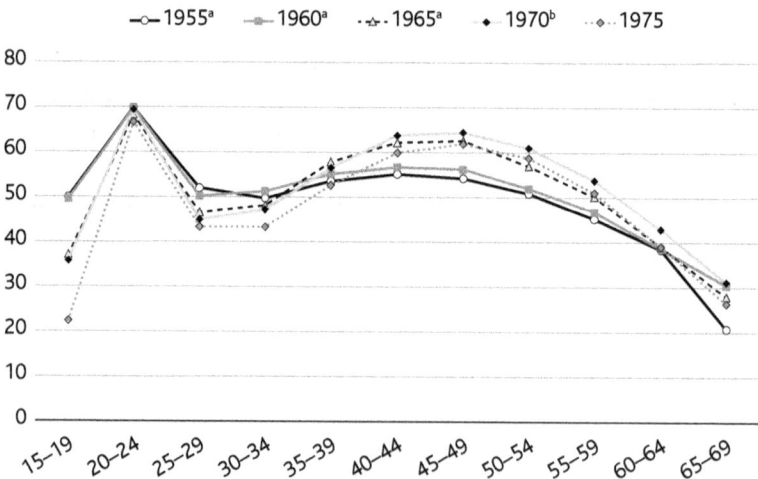

Note: [a] based on 1% sample; [b] based on 20% sample.
Source: Population Census (Table 19-1, Longitudinal Statistics, Statistics Bureau, www.stat.go.jp/data/chouki/zuhyou/19-01.xls)

more women stopped employment after they got married or when they got pregnant. After this phase, labour force participation among women in their late 20s rapidly increased, but that of women in their early 30s remained low with only a small increase (Figure 6.2). Thus, the male breadwinner model became more prevalent among married couples between 1955 and 1975, which overlapped with the period of the Japanese Economic Miracle, when Japan grew to become the world's second largest economy, and it was dominant when the introduction of Parental Leave was being discussed.

When the fall in women's employment reached its lowest point in the mid-1970s, another change set in, which was to raise widespread public concerns in the 1990s: the birth rate. After a rapid decrease from the immediate post-war baby boom, the total fertility rate stabilised around replacement level for 15 years (Figure 6.3). The rate then began to decrease again after 1973 and kept decreasing with several short-term recoveries. This fertility decline was often mentioned in the Diet and in the Labour Policy and other Councils from the late 1980s in their discussions about pensions, leave and other topics related to social welfare and social security.

Figure 6.2: Labour force participation of women by age (1970–1990)

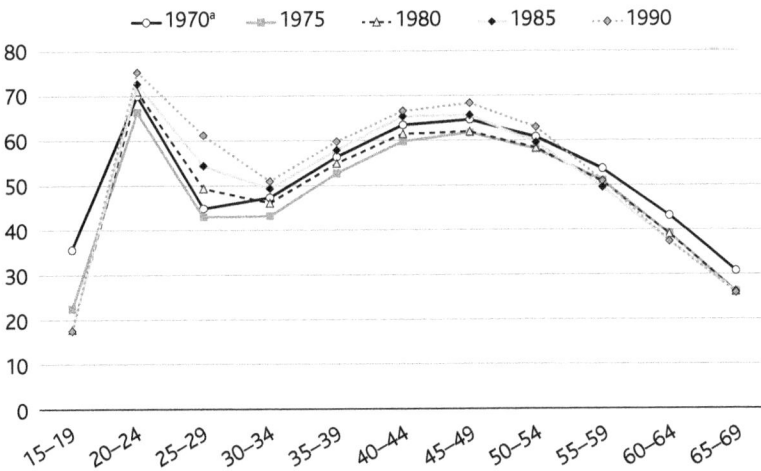

Note: a based on 20% sample.

Source: Population Census (Table 19-1, Longitudinal Statistics, Statistics Bureau, www.stat.go.jp/data/chouki/zuhyou/19-02.xls)

Figure 6.3: Total fertility rates in Japan (1947–1995)

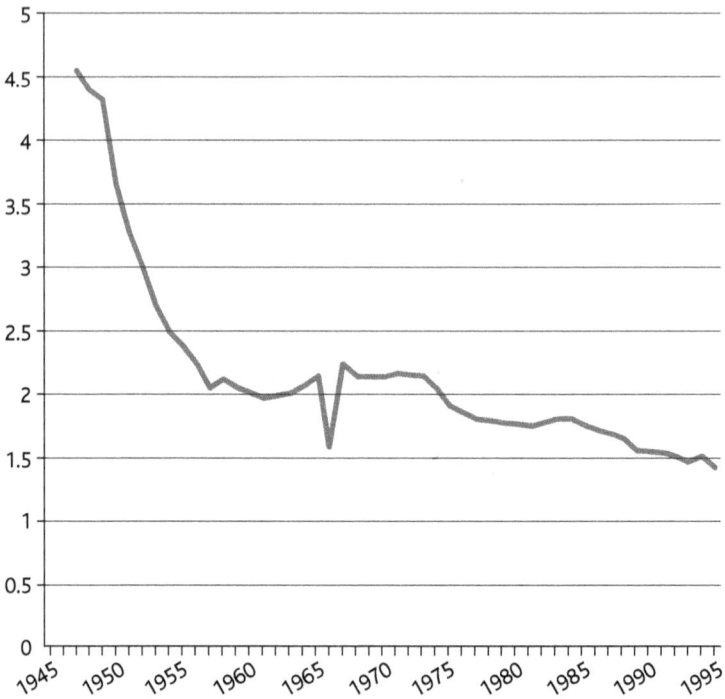

Source: 'Vital Statistics', Statistics and Information Department, Minister's Secretariat, MHLW (www.mhlw.go.jp/english/wp/wp-hw9/dl/01e.pdf)

Japan's Parental Leave policy and its amendments

Statutory Maternity Leave (termed 'prenatal and postnatal leave') was first introduced in 1947. It was extended in 1985, from six to eight weeks after birth, with compulsory leave increasing from five to six weeks, and from six to ten weeks before birth for a multiple pregnancy; and then again in 1998, from ten to 14 weeks before birth for a multiple pregnancy. A maternity benefit, financed by the Employees' Health Insurance system, was paid from 1922, well before Statutory Maternity Leave, with 60 per cent of the mother's average earnings for six weeks after birth and four weeks before birth; the period was extended in 1947 to match the newly introduced leave entitlement (Noshiro, 2017), and increased to two-thirds of average earnings in 2007. A statutory leave scheme to follow Maternity Leave (termed 'childcare leave') was first established in July 1975, but only for mothers in limited public sector occupations, such as teachers, nurses and childcare workers.

Under Japan's current Parental Leave scheme, each parent is entitled to take leave until the day before their child becomes one year old. When it was first introduced in 1992, workers were entitled to take this leave only when their partner was not on leave or not at home as a primary carer of the child. Payments were introduced in 1995 at 25 per cent of an employee's average earnings, with part of this payment (5 per cent) only made after employees returned to work. Payment increased from 25 per cent to 40 per cent (30 per cent during the leave, 10 per cent after return) in 2001, then to 50 per cent (30 per cent, 20 per cent) in 2007. From 2005, leave and payment could be extended until a child reached 18 months under certain conditions, such as there being no childcare places available.

Further amendments were introduced in 2010. Both parents could now take leave and receive payment at the same time, including employed parents whose spouse was not employed. Furthermore, leave could be extended until the child reached 14 months *if both* parents took some of the leave – even though each parent is only entitled to 12 months after birth including the Maternity Leave period. Under this arrangement, a typical situation might be that a mother takes leave until a child is 12 months old and the father either starts leave on the same day that the mother finishes or starts his leave some time before and then returns to work when the baby becomes 14 months old. Finally, the timing of the payment of leave benefit was simplified so that all the benefit could be received during the leave period.

After April 2014, the benefit payment rose again, to 67 per cent of earnings for the first six months for each parent, after which it drops to 50 per cent for the remaining leave period. This could be an incentive for fathers to take leave after the mother has taken leave for six months. The benefit payment is tax-free, and the recipients are exempted from social insurance contributions. The leave benefit is funded from the Employment Insurance system, financed by contributions from employees, employers and the state.

Introduction of Parental Leave

Japanese politics after the Second World War has been described as the '1955 system', which 'functioned as a one-party system under the control of the Liberal Democratic Party (LDP) for 38 years, from 1955 through 1993' (Boling, 2015, p.107). In this situation, where the conservative LDP had a majority in both the Upper House (the House of Councillors) and Lower House (the House of Representatives), it was not surprising that several bills put forward by the Japan Socialist

Party (JSP) between 1982 and 1984 to introduce Parental Leave for male and female workers in both public and private sectors, failed to pass into law.

In 1987, several opposition parties – the JSP, *Komeito*, the Democratic Socialist Party, and the United Social Democrats – jointly proposed a Parental Leave bill to the Upper House in response to a request by the federations of trade unions. This bill provided that either the mother or the father should be entitled to take leave until the day before their child became a year old. Most notably, the bill proposed a leave benefit, set at 60 per cent of earnings, funded by employers, employees and the state (Itohisa, 1990). The bill was finally considered in the House Committee on Society and Labour in May 1988. However, because of the political battles on other important bills and a bribery scandal, the Parental Leave bill was dropped in the last Diet session before Upper House elections in 1989, without further substantial discussion (Itohisa, 1990).

The LDP lost many seats in these elections, emerging with only 109 seats out of 252, the end of their long-term majority. The JSP won 46 seats, which gave them a total of 66 seats in the Upper House. What is also notable about this election is what was described as the 'Madonna Sensation', the largest number of women ever to be elected. The JSP, headed by Takako Doi, the first female leader of any political party in Japan, contributed half of the newly elected seats won by women.

In November 1989, the Parental Leave bill by the four parties was proposed again in the Upper House. After a Working Committee on the Parental Leave issue was established, the bill was referred to the House Committee on Society and Labour and Yaeko Itohisa of the JSP set out the rationale for the proposal. She explained that, while increasing numbers of married women were employed and more and more mothers with small children were expected to work, many of them had to leave their workplace and experienced difficulties in returning to work; it was necessary to establish a Parental Leave system as well as flexible childcare services to cope with this problem. She also insisted that this was internationally recognised, promoted by the United Nations and ILO, and that leave entitlements should be given to both female and male workers. On the same day, the two largest trade unions presented the Diet with a petition supporting the bill, signed by nearly five million people. This time the LDP, still the ruling party, also established their own working committee for Parental Leave and related issues (Itohisa, 1990). Although the bill was dropped because of the dissolution of the Lower House in January 1990, the LDP showed a supportive attitude to the idea of Parental

Leave in the report of its working committee and also in its election manifesto.

Even after the LDP secured another comfortable majority in the Lower House, Prime Minister Kaifu supported Parental Leave in a policy speech, insisting 'We will make an active effort to establish a Parental Leave system' (Itohisa, 1990, p.158). In this political climate, the Parental Leave bill from the four opposition parties was proposed for the third time, along with a further bill proposing a supplementary resolution requiring continuing consideration of a Parental Leave benefit payment. A Working Committee on Parental Leave was established within the House Committee on Society and Labour in May, in which LDP members expressed their positive attitude toward Parental Leave legislation, despite negative opinions coming from business associations (Itohisa, 1990). Adding to the supportive political climate, the Japanese Communist Party (JCP) put up its own bill proposing compensation for parents taking leave of 30 per cent of earnings, and referring to the examples of Italy and Australia (Itohisa, 1990).

Faced by this situation, the Japan Federation of Employers' Associations presented 'Opinions on Parental Leave Issues' in June 1990. They opposed both legislation on economic compensation and the extension of leave entitlements to fathers.

> The necessity of dual expenditures on salaries both for the employees on leave and their replacements should be decided by individual companies, and it is not appropriate to uniformly force [companies] to make the decision. Even if it is covered by means of social insurance, the balance with the existing social security contributions such as child allowance should be considered first. The mothers' role in children's development cannot be doubted. However, extending the entitlement to fathers should be considered carefully by taking into account the practical aspects including social conventions. (Itohisa, 1990, pp.398–399)

In December 1990, the Working Committee agreed that the government should prepare a bill and the Ministry of Labour requested the Council on Women and Youth Affairs, consisting of representatives from business associations, trade unions and public interests, to discuss legislation for establishing a Parental Leave system. The Council submitted a report to the Minister of Labour in March 1991 (Fujii, 1991), which recommended the introduction of statutory Parental

Leave and referred to the position taken by some that payment should be 60 per cent of previous earnings. The Council, however, concluded that legislation on economic compensation needed more discussion given the diversity of views on the subject.

Drawing on these recommendations, the Ministry prepared an outline bill and consulted the Council. The Council approved, with workers' representatives proposing that economic compensation during leave should be discussed and provided as soon as possible, while employers' representatives argued against employers having to make payments or establishing an insurance system for Parental Leave (Council on Women and Youth Affairs, 1991). Following Council approval, the Ministry submitted the bill to the Diet on 29 March 1991, and it was discussed in both Houses. All the opposition parties criticised the bill for making no provisions for economic compensation for parents taking leave; as one member put it, 'We think that as long as you [Minister of Labour] say that the Parental Leave is a right, 60 per cent of the wage should be paid as leave benefit for economic compensation during the leave period' (Yaeko Itohisa, JSP). The Minister replied and explained the difficulty posed by differing opinions among stakeholders.

> Honestly speaking, the point you have raised is among those that we are also interested in and have examined. I have considered this sincerely and with political sympathy as one of the issues we should address as a political issue. I would like to emphasise and would like you to understand this. However, unfortunately, there have been opposing opinions in the Diet and among the stakeholders such as the members of the Council on Women and Youth Affairs, and so this has been a very difficult administrative decision. (Labour Minister Sadatoshi Ozato, LDP)

After discussion, the opposition parties except the JCP, which continued its support for payment at 30 per cent of earnings, agreed to a revised bill, supported by the LDP, which added an article that required the government to examine the payment issue and take necessary action after the implementation of the Act. Once this revised bill was approved in the Upper House Committee on Society and Labour, the legislation was quickly approved by both Houses of the Diet, and the Childcare Leave Act was promulgated on 15 May 1991.

In this newly introduced Parental Leave scheme, which was termed 'Ikuji Kyugyo' (Childcare Leave), both parents had the right to ask for a year's leave that included the eight weeks of post-natal Maternity Leave; but employers were allowed, based on collective agreements with their employees, to reject a request for leave by an employee whose partner was on leave or not working, unless it was during the eight weeks immediately after the birth (that is, the Maternity Leave period). Leave could be taken for a continuous period only, which meant that fathers could not take leave when their partner returned to work after her Parental Leave if they (the fathers) had already been on leave during the first eight weeks. Although the Act became effective in April 1992, employers with 30 employees or fewer were exempted for three years. In 1995, the Act was amended to introduce statutory family care leave, a limited period of leave to care for a sick or injured child, and renamed the Act on Childcare Leave, Caregiver Leave, and Other Measures for the Welfare of Workers Caring for Children or Other Family Members; this new provision was implemented in 1997.

The introduction of leave benefit

The first amendment of the Parental Leave scheme was the introduction of leave benefit. As noted previously, opposition parties had all along insisted on the need for payment during Parental Leave, but it was missing from the initial legislation. This issue, however, started to be discussed in the Central Employment Security Council, which advises government on the Employment Insurance System, and the Women and Youth Affairs Council, even as the Childcare Act was coming into force. The Women and Youth Affairs Council proposed that economic compensation during Parental Leave should be made through the Employment Insurance scheme, which provided unemployment benefits, with Council members representing trade unions insisting on a benefit set at 60 per cent of earnings to be paid by establishing a new fund (Asahishinbun Newspaper, 1993).

Following the recommendation, the Central Employment Security Council proposed a leave benefit set at 25 per cent of earnings, and paid via the Employment Insurance scheme. Based on this proposal, an amendment of the Employment Insurance Act was discussed and passed in the Diet in 1994. The Minister of Labour explained that the purpose of the amendment was to cope with the difficulties faced by parents wanting to take leave and the consequent avoidance of having children (Labour Committee, House of Councillors).

Increasing fathers' take-up becomes a goal

Among the discussions about introducing leave benefits, it is hard to find any statements before 2001 referring to increased use of Parental Leave by fathers as a goal of leave policy. This was also the case when the Employment Insurance Act was amended in 2000, increasing leave benefit from 25 per cent to 40 per cent. However, one witness at the Upper House Committee on Labour and Social Policies in April 2000, Professor Mari Osawa, who had taken a major role in preparing the Basic Act for a Gender Equal Society passed in 1999, did raise the low take-up of leave by fathers and suggested the need for positive action, such as a higher benefit rate when fathers take Parental Leave.

The situation changed soon after the 2000 amendment. In 2001, most statements about further amendments of the Parental Leave scheme referred to the low take-up rate among fathers and the necessity to increase it. For example, Ikuo Yamahana from DPJ asked the Ministry of Health, Labour and Welfare about how they were analysing this issue, mentioning the low take-up rate for leave by fathers reported in the Basic Survey on Women's Employment Management in 1999 and three documents submitted from 2000 to 2001: 'Basic Policy on Measures for Equal Employment Opportunities for Men and Women' (14 July 2000), the 'Recommendation to the Minister of Labour by the Women and Youth Affairs Council' (22 December 2000), and the 'Report by the Expert Committee on Measures to Reconcile Work and Childcare' from the Council for Gender Equality established in the Cabinet Office (19 June 2001). All mentioned the necessity to promote take-up of Parental Leave by fathers.

Following discussion in the Lower House, Yukiko Kawahashi from DPJ asked questions about the research into increasing fathers' leave take-up.

> The proportion of fathers who take Parental Leave is 0.42 per cent, which means that only 4 out of 1000 men take Parental Leave when their partners give birth to a child. Promoting fathers' take-up of Parental Leave or any other leave is said to be necessary to balance work and life and to strengthen the bond between fathers and children. This was intensively discussed in the Lower House and the amended Act has the supplementary resolution providing that 'The government should conduct research on the increase of fathers' leave take-up and take necessary actions.' What kind of research will the government conduct and when

will it take the necessary action? (Yukiko Kawahashi, DPJ, Upper House Committee on Health, Labour and Welfare, 8 November 2001)

As you [Kawahashi] have pointed out, the proportion of men among all employees who take Parental Leave is tiny. It was only 2.4 per cent in 1999, it is an important issue how to increase the proportion...The supplementary resolution was recently made and the content and the schedule of the research and necessary actions are yet to be decided. It will not be too long before we start, and we would like to explore examples in other countries or in companies with good practices in Japan, and promote the research on what will be effective actions to increase fathers' leave take-up. (Kimie Iwata, The Director-General of Equal Employment, Children and Families Bureau, Ministry of Health, Welfare and Labour)

Although both speakers used different ways of calculating take-up by fathers, both emphasised low take-up. The proportion of *eligible* fathers who took Parental Leave would become the main indicator for fathers' take-up when discussing further revision of the Parental Leave scheme.

This focus on leave take-up by fathers in the policy-making process from around 2000 can be understood as in part a response to the Basic Act for a Gender Equal Society passed in 1999, and its enforcement in 2001, as it reflected a shift from women's policy to gender equality policy. This new law emphasised the necessity of men's involvement in activities both in the home and in communities if low fertility rates were to be addressed.

Special extension of leave period

An important change to Parental Leave was agreed on in 2004. From January 2005, leave and payment could be extended until a child was eighteen months when 1) admission to a childcare centre had been requested but was not forthcoming; or 2) the spouse of the employee who was expected to take care of the child was not able to do so for reasons such as death, injury, and illness. This was intended to help parents stay at home when they could not find a childcare place, and was introduced to cope with a shortage of services. Although this extension of leave was likely to keep working mothers away from the workplace longer without incentivising fathers to take any part of Parental Leave, some voices called for an even longer extension, such as until the end of March when many childcare services admitted children, or even until the third year in primary school (when a child is 8 years old). 'I would like you to extend the Parental Leave until the child enters Year 3 of the primary school, rather than [just to] 18 months. This is what working women hope' (Masako Owaki, DPJ, Upper House Committee on Health, Labour and Welfare, 14 June 2004).

Papa Mama Parental Leave Plus: a Japanese version of Fathers' Quota?

A number of significant initiatives occurred in 2007. In April, benefit payments were increased to two-thirds of previous earnings for Maternity Leave and to 50 per cent for Parental Leave. While the increase in the Maternity Leave benefit was in line with an increase in Invalidity Benefit, the enhanced Parental Leave benefit was intended to increase take-up by fathers. The same year also saw the publication, by government and other stakeholders, of a Charter for Work–Life Balance and an Action Policy for Promoting Work–Life Balance. The Charter followed discussions at the Council of Public and Private Sector Executives (a body consisting of government ministers and representatives of employers' associations, trade unions and local government) about the need to collaborate in supporting the development of a Japanese society with a more harmonious work–life balance. In the Action Policy, various targets were set, including a 10 per cent Parental Leave take-up rate for men by 2017.

In September 2007, the Research Committee on Future Support of Work and Family was established by the Ministry of Health, Labour and Welfare to conduct research and discuss improving support for working families who cared for children, elderly people and family members with disabilities. It consisted of five academics from law, economics, sociology and management, a newspaper reporter, a trade union official and a HR manager, and met 12 times, collecting research findings and opinions from its members and from invited witnesses. In July 2008, the Research Committee published a report 'Realising a society where working while raising children is not so special'. It mentioned in its preface various actions, including the setting of a target for fathers' take-up of leave, and presented recommendations for amending the statutory Parental Leave scheme. These included making Parental Leave an individual entitlement, so that fathers could take Parental Leave regardless of the mother's situation; and changing how leave could be taken, to permit it to be split into several short periods, enabling fathers to take a second period of Parental Leave even when they had already taken some leave during the first eight weeks after birth (although business associations had mentioned management difficulties if leave was to be divided into separate periods).

A sharing bonus called 'Papa Mama Ikukyu Plus' [Father Mother Childcare Leave Plus] was also suggested. Under this scheme, leave could be extended until the child was 14 months old *if both* parents took leave, even though each parent was initially entitled to only 12 months after birth, including the Maternity Leave period. The Committee noted that there had been other opinions about the length of bonus months for couples who shared leave, such as six months instead of two. The report further proposed calling leave for the first eight weeks after birth 'Papa kyuka' [Paternity Leave], to emphasise that this was an entitlement for fathers and might be taken separately from later periods of leave.

Most of the suggestions, except for the 'Papa kyuka', were also supported in discussions at 11 meetings of the Labour Policy Council from 27 August to 25 December 2008 and included in recommendations sent to the Ministry, for inclusion in an amendment bill it was preparing for debate in the Diet. These proposed amendments to the Parental Leave scheme were discussed in June 2009 in both Houses of the Diet. The amendments were mostly welcomed, even by the opposition parties, although some changes were suggested in the Lower House Labour Committee, such as six bonus months instead of two by the DPJ and the Social Democratic Party, and benefit payment at 60 per cent of previous earnings rather than 50 per cent by the JCP. But the main recommendations by the Labour Policy Council, such as two bonus months for leave-sharing parents and an entitlement to take leave even if the other parent was not working, were supported and approved in the Diet. The amended Act came into force in 30 June 2010.

Increasing incentives for fathers

Even after the introduction of the sharing bonus, 'Papa Mama Ikukyu Plus', fathers' take-up of Parental Leave remained very low, at around 2 per cent of eligible fathers. To increase the incentive for fathers, another amendment was made in 2014, to provide a leave benefit of 67 per cent of earnings for the first 180 calendar days of Parental Leave, and 50 per cent for the remaining leave period. This proposal was not discussed beforehand in any research committees or Councils, such as the Labour Policy Council, but first proposed by the Minister of Health, Labour and Welfare in the Diet on 7 March 2014. Replying to a question in the Committee on Health, Labour and Welfare of the Lower House about the reason why the increase of leave benefit would be limited to six months, the Minister explained the intention of the revised scheme.

> A family where a man shares the care of the first child is likely to have another child, while, in Japan, men's time in childcare is said to be very small based on various statistics. So we would like men to cooperate in the care of children. In this sense, the idea to limit the increased benefit of 67 per cent of earnings to the first six months means that parents can receive 67 per cent of earnings for a whole year if both a father and a mother take six months of leave. It is said that one of the reasons why men do not take Parental Leave is economic. The fact that fathers can receive 67 per cent of earnings will facilitate fathers to take Parental Leave. This is the reason we propose the increase of benefit for the first 6 months. (Norihiro Tamura, Minister of Health, Labour and Welfare, Committee on Health, Labour and Welfare of the Lower House, 12 March 2014)

Although the stated objective was to increase fathers' take-up of Parental Leave, it is apparent from the Minister's explanation that the goal of increasing fertility also lay behind this proposed policy change.

It should also be noted that 67 per cent is higher than the compensation rate of 60 per cent that opposition parties had been calling for back in 1987 when they proposed a joint bill, and had never been suggested before by the government. In reaction to a question about whether the proposed increased compensation rate would be enough, compared to 80 per cent in some other countries such as Sweden, the Director-General of the Employment Security Bureau emphasised that the new rate would in fact match the benefit payments made in Sweden and other countries.

> Although leave benefit in Sweden is 80 per cent, that in Japan is tax-free and the employees are exempted from paying social insurance premium during the leave, and thus about 80 per cent of income will be compensated. So, we understand that our benefit system will be as good as those of Sweden and other countries. (Junichi Okazaki,

the Director-General of the Employment Security Bureau, Committee on Health, Labour and Welfare of the Lower House 12 March 2014)

Some consequences of changes to Parental Leave

Have these amendments to the Parental Leave scheme worked? Have they increased take-up by fathers and more sharing of childcare in the early months of parenthood? This section addresses these questions, drawing on the latest statistics about leave-taking of fathers and mothers and women's career continuity after childbirth to examine the relation between changes in policies and practices.

Unlike some other countries where changes in leave policy have led to a rapid increase in fathers' take-up of leave (Erler, 2011; Wall, 2014), take-up rates of Japanese fathers remain very low (Figure 6.4). Despite relatively generous statutory provision, the proportion of eligible fathers taking Parental Leave was still less than 3 per cent in 2015. However, there has been a steady increase, with small spurts around the time of important amendments, such as an increase of leave benefit and permitting fathers to take leave on full benefit at the same time as their partner is at home.

The low take-up rates of fathers until 2010 are understandable given the high proportion of mothers who were not in the labour force after

Figure 6.4: Proportion of eligible fathers taking Parental Leave (1996–2016)

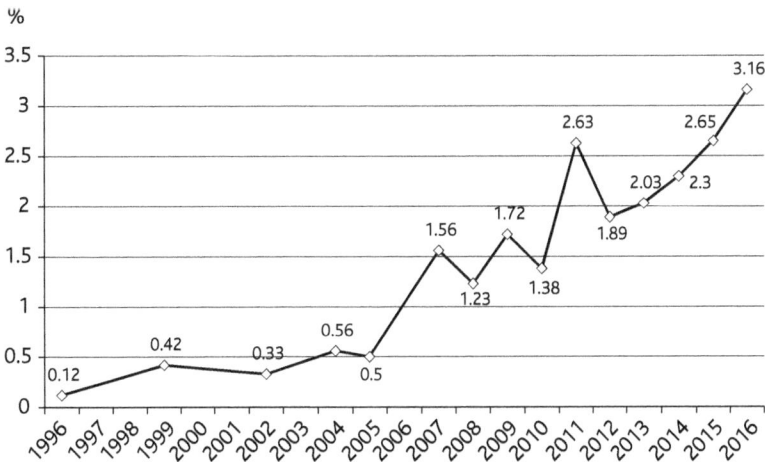

Source: Ministry of Health, Labour and Welfare, Basic Survey of Gender Equality in Employment Management (based on a national sample of 10,000 private sector workplaces that employ five or more permanent employees)

the birth of a child (Figure 6.5), and the legal requirement that workers were only entitled to take leave when their partners were not at home as a primary caregiver. The lower rate of income compensation until the recent change could also have been an important obstacle to fathers' leave-taking. Recent changes in the proportion of mothers who take Parental Leave and stay in the labour force are notable (Figure 6.5); this could encourage or force more fathers to take Parental Leave. However, it is important to note a huge, continuing gender difference in the periods of leave that are taken (Figure 6.6).

One important figure to note is the proportion of mothers who take more than 12 months of leave. The basic Parental Leave entitlement is until the child turns one year old; yet nearly 40 per cent of mothers use some extra leave period. In some cases, this might be the result of giving birth to more than one child and taking leave consecutively for each of these children. However, it is also likely that women take extra months of leave while waiting for their child to be admitted to a childcare service.

Figure 6.5: Work status of mothers around the birth of a first child by the year of birth of the child (1985/1989–2010/2014)

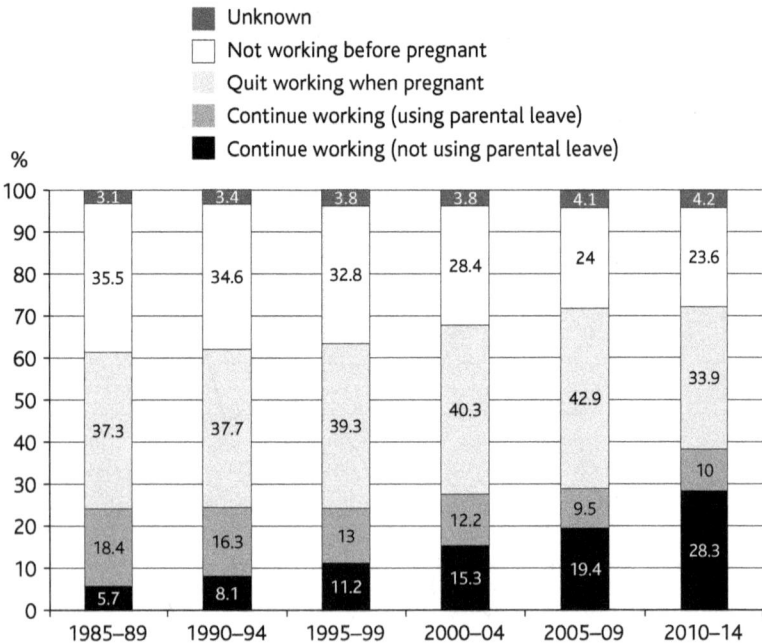

Legend:
- Unknown
- Not working before pregnant
- Quit working when pregnant
- Continue working (using parental leave)
- Continue working (not using parental leave)

	1985–89	1990–94	1995–99	2000–04	2005–09	2010–14
Unknown	3.1	3.4	3.8	3.8	4.1	4.2
Not working before pregnant	35.5	34.6	32.8	28.4	24	23.6
Quit working when pregnant	37.3	37.7	39.3	40.3	42.9	33.9
Continue working (using parental leave)	18.4	16.3	13	12.2	9.5	10
Continue working (not using parental leave)	5.7	8.1	11.2	15.3	19.4	28.3

Source: National Institute of Population and Social Security Research, Japanese National Fertility Survey

Figure 6.6: Leave period taken by fathers and mothers (2015)

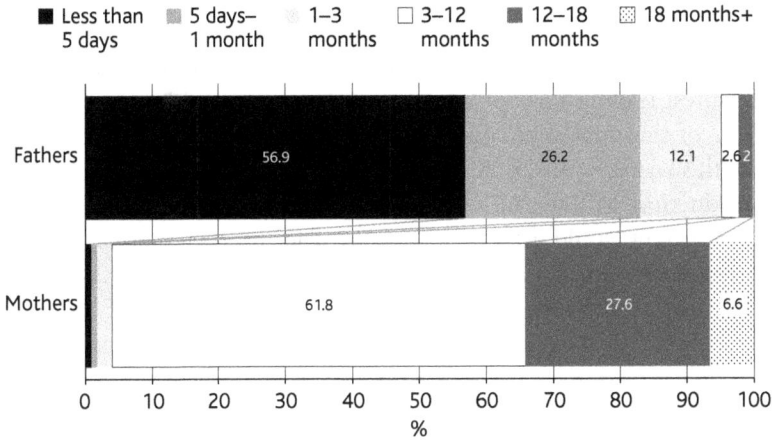

Source: Ministry of Health, Labour and Welfare, 2015 Basic Survey of Gender Equality in Employment Management

Conclusion

This chapter has examined how statutory Parental Leave was introduced and developed in Japan. Until it was first approved in 1991 under the LDP conservative government, there were repeated efforts to introduce legislation, with advocates referring to research on European countries and recommendations by international organisations, and with the trade unions playing an important role. Later on, most of the amendments were based on recommendations by the Women and Youth Affairs Council, the Central Employment Security Council, and the Labour Policy Council, then agreed by government and designed by civil servants. The proposal for a leave benefit of 60 per cent, put forward by opposition parties in the 1980s, was finally realised in 2014, the latest of a number of gradual amendments motivated by increasing concern about low levels of involvement by fathers in the care of children and the likely link to fertility, which started around the turn of the century.

Regardless of this development, however, fathers leave take-up rate is still very low. Looking ahead, limiting the maximum benefit payment to the first six months for each parent, which was introduced in 2014, might work as an incentive for fathers to take more leave, and the accelerated increase of take-up after 2014, albeit from a very low level, might be related to this new measure. But given the workplace climate that discourages fathers in Japan from taking Parental Leave, further strong incentives and other measures will be necessary to increase take-up rates significantly.

This short history also reveals another big issue. Developments in leave policy have not been part of a wider and coordinated set of measures, leading to contradictory forces at work. For example, the effect of the implementation of the 'Papa Mama Ikukyu Plus' two-month sharing bonus in 2010 may have been weakened by the earlier introduction of a special extension of leave for six months in cases where parents could not find a childcare place for their child. A further amendment, agreed and implemented in 2017, allows an extension of leave until a child turns two years old, for the same reason of childcare not being available. Though some members of the Labour Policy Council argued that this further extension should be restricted to the parent who has not taken leave before, this idea was not included in the Council's final recommendation nor in the government's bill, the justification being that this is an emergency measure to address the problem of the shortage of childcare places.

If Japan is to achieve its two stated goals, eliminating barriers for mothers to stay in the labour force and increasing fathers' involvement in childcare and family life, it will require a broad and large-scale policy package, combining childcare policy, working hours legislation, changes to workplace culture and Parental Leave policy. This study of leave policy development reveals frequent amendments to tackle immediate problems, such as shortage of childcare places, but no wide-ranging and coherent approach to policy design which might address more long-term challenges such as gender equality and low fertility.

References

Asahishinbun Newspaper (1993) '"Koyo hoken wo tsukai ikujikyugyo enjo wo" Fujinshonenshin ga kengi' ['Use Employment Insurance to help take parental leave' proposes The Women and Youth Affairs Council]. Asahishinbun Newspaper Morning Edition, 28 September.

Boling, P. (2015) The Politics of Work–Family Policies: Comparing Japan, France, Germany and the United States, Cambridge: Cambridge University Press.

Council on Women and Youth Affairs (1991) 'Ikujikyugyo To ni kansuru Horitsuan (Kasho) nitsuite [About the Outline of the Childcare Leave Bill' (20 May 1991). Available at www.ipss.go.jp/publication/j/shiryou/no.13/data/shiryou/roudou/538.pdf

Erler, D. (2011) 'Germany: Taking a Nordic turn?', in S.B. Kamerman and P. Moss (eds) *The Politics of Parental Leave Policies: Children, Parenting, Gender and the Labour Market*, Bristol: Policy Press, pp 119–134.

Fujii, R. (1991) 'Ikuji to Shigoto no Ryoritsu heno Atarashii Ippo' [A new step for balancing childcare and work], *Fujin Rodo* [*Women's Labour*], 16: 24–32.

Itohisa, Y. (1990) *Ikuji Kyugyo Ho: Yonto kyodo hoan to oshu shokoku no hosei* [*Childcare Leave Law: Joint bill by four parties and legislation in European countries*], Tokyo: Rodokyoiku Centre.

Nakazato, H. (2017) 'Fathers on leave alone in Japan: Lived experiences of the pioneers', in M. O'Brien and K. Wall (eds) *Comparative Perspectives on Work–Life Balance and Gender Equality: Fathers on Leave Alone*, Springer Nature, pp 231–255.

Noshiro, H. (2017) 'Shakai Hoken Seido ni Miru 'Kosodate Shien' Kinou' [The function of child-care support in social insurance system], *The Bulletin of the Institute of Human Sciences, Toyo University* (19), pp 199–211.

Ochiai, E. (1994) *Toward the Twenty-First Century Family*, Tokyo: Yuhikaku.

OECD (2017) *Family Database. PF2.1: Key Characteristics of Parental Leave Systems*. Available at www.oecd.org/els/soc/PF2_1_Parental_leave_systems.pdf

Wall, K. (2014) 'Fathers on leave alone: Does it make a difference to their lives?', *Fathering: A Journal of Theory, Research, and Practice about Men as Fathers*, 12(2): 196–210.

SEVEN

China: leave and population policies

Shirley Gatenio Gabel, Wen-Jui Han
and Xiaoran Wang

Introduction

Rising life expectancy, fertility concerns, increasing parental employment particularly among mothers with young children, and rising inequality have brought work and family issues into the spotlight globally, including China. The recent ending of China's one-child policy has provided a major impetus for China to formally restructure its Maternity Leave policy. China first adopted such a policy in the 1950s, but it is only since 2001 that the country has significantly expanded Maternity Leave and many provinces have recently introduced Paternity Leave. Even though China now offers generous Maternity Leave policies, great disparities in entitlement and coverage continue, such as between rural and urban areas, and between employees in public and private sectors.

This chapter reviews the evolution of modern Maternity Leave policy in China since the first measures in 1951 and traces the origins of present-day policies that are part of social insurance schemes and rapidly expanding. In its earliest period, China's leave policy was driven mainly by socialist ideals, then by economic goals and women's rights from the 1980s into the new century. We suggest that the most recent shift in family policies was primarily led by social science research, that has raised concerns regarding demographic structure and economic growth. This chapter ends with a discussion of how current changes may affect future directions. The policies described overleaf generally apply to all citizens in theory, urban and rural alike; however, in reality, most, if not all, of the policies and practices are limited to residents who hold urban household registration status, unless indicated otherwise.

Background

Economically, China has transformed from a state-planned to a market economy since the early 1980s, and is now the second largest economy in the world after the United States.[1] Just three decades ago, China was one of the poorest countries in the world with a GDP per capita of only US$156 in 1978; by 2015, it stood at US$8,069 (World Bank, 2016). With an average annual GDP per capita growth rate of more than 8 per cent over the last three decades, China has progressed from a deprived, low-income country to a middle-income developing country. During this same period, individual and family well-being substantially improved, with rapid economic growth lifting more than 800 million people out of poverty. Yet China remains a country in development where per capita income is low compared to countries with advanced economies (World Bank, 2017).

While economic reforms ushered substantial improvements in health and poverty reduction, the accompanying demographic and economic changes also brought unforeseen social consequences associated with a market-oriented economy, such as income inequality. China's Gini coefficient is estimated to be about 0.55, placing China among the most income unequal nations in the world (Xie and Zhou, 2014). A substantial part of this high level of income inequality is due to regional and rural–urban disparities. The widening income gap in China is likely to have repercussions for both childrearing and child well-being.

In large part, the highly stratified social welfare system in China, favouring urban and highly skilled labour over rural and low skilled labour, can be traced back to the birth of the People's Republic of China (PRC), in September 1949. During the subsequent Maoist period, economic production was transferred from private to public entities and all industry was nationalised by 1955 (MacFarquhar, 1987). Full employment was the goal and social benefits were attached to employment. Comprehensive welfare packages and moderate living wages for able-bodied, urban Chinese citizens were provided through *danweis* (work units). *Danweis* encompassed state-owned enterprises, state agencies, government departments, and other organisations in the public sector (Saunders and Shang, 2001). Each *danwei* established its own welfare system, which was composed of three basic elements: job tenure (iron rice bowl), an egalitarian wage (big rice pot) and a welfare package (for example, housing, healthcare and Maternity Leave

---

[1] www.weforum.org/agenda/2017/03/worlds-biggest-economies-in-2017

benefits) (Lu, 1989). Wages were typically moderate and supplemented by social benefits. Prior to the economic reform of 1978, more than 80 per cent of the urban labour force was covered by the *danwei* system (Ringen and Ngok, 2017). The more skilled and capital intensive, the higher the *danwei's* position in the hierarchy, which meant that the *danwei* had more influence with central planners and could offer its workers more generous benefits (Bian, 1994).

In rural areas, farmers were organised into communes based on collective ownership of land. Communes provided farmers and their families with basic needs in return for their labour. The 'five guarantees' system (food, clothing, housing, medical care and burial expenses) was funded by rural collectives and subsidised by the government (Chan et al, 2008).

The urban–rural division was reinforced by the household registration system, *hukou*, which documented household information for every individual and distinguished between those with urban or rural origins. Under the *hukou* system, established in 1958, Chinese local governments had to approve any internal migration within China and social supports were only available from the area in which an individual was registered (Chan, 2010).

The evolution of leave policies

Leave policies in China have been closely related to socio-economic planning and family planning policies, and reflect political goals. To best understand how these policies evolved in China, three time periods are identified – Maoist China, the Post-Maoist period, and current reforms.

Maoist China: the birth of maternity insurance and a one-child policy

Built on socialist ideals, the newly founded PRC sought to end centuries of male hegemony and foster female labour participation and equality (Liu et al, 2015). During the Maoist period (Mao Zedong, first chairman of the Chinese Communist Party (CCP) died in 1976), gender equality was prioritised by the state, and women were equally appointed to leadership positions and agricultural collectives along with men (Edwards, 2000). At the time China emulated the economic models and labour policies of the Soviet Union, and this is thought to have motivated the enactment by China's State Council in 1951 of the Labour Insurance Regulation, which included maternity insurance for the first time in modern Chinese history. This regulation provided

56 days (eight weeks) of paid Maternity Leave to employees of state-owned enterprises, state organs and public institutions[2] (Liu and Sun, 2015). Maternity benefits for female employees of enterprises were paid by the enterprises themselves, whereas those for employees of state organs and public institutions were paid from state finances (Liu, 2010). The Labour Insurance Regulation was, therefore, an enterprise-based insurance system, not a collective pooling of risk in a social insurance fund (Liu and Sun, 2015). No information documenting compliance by enterprises was found by the authors of this chapter.

During the Maoist period, urban and rural communities initially experienced significant growth; but by the 1960s the combination of poor government planning, unusual weather patterns and natural disasters led to widespread famine and millions of deaths. Officials searched for solutions to avoid a repeat of these events and in the late 1970s, China launched a birth control campaign to curb population growth. Many countries, especially developing nations, were concerned about population growth in the 1960s and 1970s, but China's response was perhaps the most draconian. The CCP had also been challenged by efforts to modernise following Mao's death and persistent food shortages. It decided, therefore, to take immediate action by publicly decreeing a policy restricting child bearing to one child per couple (Bongaarts and Greenhalgh, 1985).

This one-child policy took the form of a directive issued by the CCP's political leadership, and was not actually passed into law until 2001 (Wang, 2012).[3] The policy was announced in an open letter in 1978 to members of the CCP and the Communist Youth league. The task of implementing and enforcing was left to party leaders in lower

---

[2] A state-owned enterprise (SOE) is a legal entity that is created by the government to take part in commercial activities on the government's behalf; it can be wholly or partially owned by government. SOEs should be differentiated from other forms of government agencies or state entities established to pursue purely non-commercial objectives. During this early period in modern Chinese history, all commercial activities were owned and controlled by the government, www.investopedia.com/terms/s/soe.asp#ixzz4YaatvPca.

[3] Generally speaking, laws in China are not the same as in a rule-of-law system. The tendency in China that continues today is for social policy to be regulated by directives, decisions and circulars rather than set in law (Chan et al, 2008). This allows for considerable variance in implementation across local governments, and the monitoring and enforcement of the policies can easily be inadequate (Blaxland et al, 2014).

levels of government,[4] including specifying policy requirements and exemptions. Accompanying the population control directive was the 'late, long and few' slogan adopted in the late 1970s that promoted 'late' marriage, 'long' intervals between children, and 'few' children, meaning one child (or two in special circumstances) per couple. The directive and slogan would later justify widespread sterilisation and abortion campaigns, as well as involuntary abortions, infanticides and sterilisations (Whyte et al, 2015).

The implementation of the directive led to an accepted practice of offering longer Maternity Leave and Marriage Leaves (7–30 days paid time off from work after marriage) to couples who married late (age 23 years for women and 25 years for men) and waited until they were older to become first-time parents; the additional leaves varied from several days to months and were determined by local governments. Couples with only one child were also rewarded with other government assistance and better employment opportunities, while those who had more than one child (without permission) typically faced hefty fines and might be denied public education for their children (Wang, 2012).

Because China's social policies were interpreted and implemented by governments and local party leaders in the provinces and autonomous regions, Maternity Leave varied across the country. But since monitoring of implementation was not done systematically during this period, it is not possible to document how the policies and their implementation varied across China (Blaxland et al, 2014).

China became a member of the United Nations in 1971 and its isolationism decreased thereafter as China ratified and integrated international treaties and conventions into its reformed constitution in 1982 (Kent, 2002). Its open-door policy starting in 1979 sought to find opportunities for China to join world organisations and global markets (Kent, 2002). Toward this end, China adopted the ILO's standards and other international documents on Maternity Leave (Liu and Sun, 2015).

---

[4] China is divided into 34 different administrative regions, 23 provinces, five autonomous regions, four centrally administered municipalities (Beijing, Chonqing, Shanghai and Tianjin) and two special administrative regions (Hong Kong and Macao). The highest administrative level of government is the State Council, followed by government of provinces, autonomous regions, the large municipalities and special regions. Below these are the county, city and district levels, followed by town and township governments.

Post-Maoist period: Reforms of the 1980s into the 1990s

Following the death of Mao in 1976, China embarked on a transformation that prioritised the economy and market-based strategies, and by 1986 had officially replaced its full-employment policy as the key to social welfare benefits with a system of individual contracts. The opening of employment to enterprises that were not state-owned and migration to urban areas in search of employment left millions of Chinese without social benefits, including Maternity Leave insurance, because newly formed non-state-owned enterprises did not have obligations to provide social benefits as was the case for state-owned enterprises (Guan, 2000). Migrant workers were generally without social protection because their rural *hukou* status cut them off from benefits and services in their new urban homes. Among urban employers, state-owned enterprises now competed with non-state-owned enterprises who were not required to offer benefit packages (Giles et al, 2006). Large-scale layoffs became common and state employers often did not honour wage and social protection obligations (Cai, 2006).

State-owned enterprises employing a large proportion of female workers complained that Maternity Leave obligations diminished their competitiveness. In response, some state-owned enterprises adopted measures to reduce the number of female employees and/or benefits for women with young children, such as forcing nursing women to stay at home (without paid benefits), closing childcare facilities or not allowing time off to breastfeed during the day (Liu, 2010). Women organised in response and as early as 1980, a joint report by the All-China Federation of Trade Unions and the All-China's Women's Federation was submitted to the Secretariat of the Central Committee of the CCP arguing that women were disadvantaged and discriminated against in employment by these practices, and urging policymakers to establish a social insurance scheme for Maternity Leave and dismantle the existing enterprise-based system (Liu, 2010). Once again it was left to regional and local government authorities to adjust social benefits to the rapidly changing economy and to respond to women's grassroot campaigns. As a result, the types of Maternity Leave insurance and benefits offered grew increasingly diverse by region and types of employer.

Women organising to assert their rights was part of a backlash to China's retreat from its earlier priority of gender equality (Edwards, 2000). This retreat came at the same time that China sought to increase its international relations, for example by ratifying the United Nations

Convention to Eliminate Discrimination Against Women in 1980 (UN CEDAW, 1997). Paradoxically, as the state lessened its role in the economy, social protection and employment, women in China became more aware of women's issues and of their rights.

To level the competitive playing field across different types of employers and uphold women's right to employment, several localities, such as Zhuzhong in Hunan province in south-central China, developed Maternity Leave schemes based on social insurance principles, funded by employers and administered by local labour departments (Liu, 2010). In such schemes, child-bearing female employees drew their maternity allowance from local labour departments on a monthly basis by producing a certificate issued by their employers. These were among the first efforts toward introducing risk-pooling, social insurance schemes. Other localities experimented with different ways to reconcile parenting responsibilities with work and this further increased the diversity of administrative systems and benefits across China (Liu, 2010). The diversity, coupled with weak enforcement of local regulations governing payment of maternity insurance contributions, resulted in low claimant levels for these payments and low coverage rates as well as other administrative challenges, all of which pointed to the need to establish a national Maternity Leave system (Liu, 2010).

In 1988, the State Council promulgated the Women Workers' and Employees' Labour Protection Regulations aimed at establishing a unified maternity insurance system for state organs, public institutions and enterprises, expanding the coverage of maternity insurance from the original state-owned organisations to all enterprises both state- and non-state-owned, the latter including also collectively-owned, foreign-invested and rural enterprises. The new Regulations also increased the length of Maternity Leave from the original 56 days to 90 days (including 15 days before childbirth), but they continued to impose the cost of Maternity Leave payments on the employers of female employees; the situation for women who were not eligible was unclear (UN CEDAW, 1997).

By the late 1980s, the whole national social protection system, not just maternity benefits, was no longer in synch with economic policies, and the *hukuo* system heightened the vulnerability of the rural-to-urban migrants who were excluded from social protection despite the expansion of mandated coverage. The continued variation in social benefits by type of employer and region meant a confusing provision of maternal insurance benefits and left many women with little or no coverage (World Bank, 1997; Sin, 2005).

Organised women's efforts continued and women petitioned the CCP and government officials to reinforce the state's responsibility towards women (Edwards, 2000). In 1992, China enacted the Women's Act, which was a comprehensive and systematic approach to women's rights and interests covering all aspects of women's social and economic roles (UN CEDAW, 1997). The Act required the state to develop social insurance (for example, public pensions and employment benefits), social assistance, and health services to protect women. It explicitly mandated local government at all levels to develop maternity insurance and gave local authorities responsibility to provide maternity assistance for impoverished women (UN CEDAW, 1997). Such locally piloted social insurance programmes led to a new framework for a new social protection system in the early 1990s, in which benefits were funded by pooling contributions from individuals, enterprises and local and central governments, and was paid to individual employee accounts. However, implementation and enforcement of this new system were, once again, not regularly monitored (Zhang, 2002).

In 1994, the Ministry of Labour, in conjunction with the AllChina Women's Federation, the AllChina Federation of Trade Unions and other organisations, drafted the Proposed Methods for Maternity Insurance of Enterprise Workers, also known as Trial Measures on Maternity Insurance, which went into effect in 1995. In addition to formally requiring all urban enterprises (state- and non-state owned) to provide at least 90 days of Maternity Leave, the Trial Measures sought to resolve the employment bias affecting women by encouraging experimental pilot programmes to publicly pool insurance contributions; for example, enterprises might deposit contributions for maternity benefits, calculated according to a fixed percentage of employees' wages, with designated insurers to establish maternity insurance funds. Maternity benefits consisted of a maternity allowance, Maternity Leave with pay and healthcare. Maternity Leave was paid at the level of average monthly earnings in the previous year and disbursed by a maternity insurance fund. Two-thirds of China's provinces experimented with similar reforms (UN CEDAW, 1997). Unmarried mothers were excluded, not by the Trial Measures but under the Law on Population Planning that required forfeiture of any social and maternity benefits when the Law was broken, such as bearing a child outside of marriage.

The Women's Act and Trial Measures paved the way for better protection of employed women's equal rights with employed men. Together, they forced labour departments at various levels of government to pay close attention to the implementation of labour-related laws and regulations protecting female workers.

Current reforms: 2000 to the present day

The 2001 Population and Family Planning Act officially recognised China's one-child policy in law and also formally linked the one-child policy with Maternity Leave policy, though unofficially the two had worked in conjunction for some time. Provinces, autonomous regions and certain municipal governments were instructed to formalise the enhanced benefits, such as longer leave periods, that had long been granted in practice.

By 2008, out of over 302 million urban employees, 93 million or 30 per cent had employers directly making contributions toward maternity insurance coverage (MOHRSS, 2009). Statistics are difficult to locate, but it is estimated that in 2008 there were 1.4 million recipients of maternity benefits for 16 million births (MOHRSS, 2009), so many mothers did not receive any benefit. While all urban enterprises were directed to pay for maternity insurance by making contributions for both male and female employees, only women were entitled to benefits. Despite China moving toward a public system of employers pooling costs into social insurance funds for social benefits, many millions of rural residents and migrants continued to be disadvantaged.

The 1994 Trial Measures did not apply to rural employees and were difficult to enforce. But by the mid-2000s, Beijing had enacted policies to allow rural migrants to participate in all major social insurance schemes, including maternity benefits (Cheng et al, 2014), and similar policies were put in place in other urban areas that absorbed large numbers of migrant workers, such as Guangdong and Shanghai (Cheng et al, 2014). Yet, enterprises did not always pay statutory contributions to maternity insurance and the lack of funds meant that millions of women did not receive benefits or received less in benefits than stipulated by law (Liu, 2010). There was also considerable ambiguity as to whether birth-related medical expenses were to be covered by maternity insurance funds or health insurance funds (Liu, 2010).

The 2010 Social Insurance Law was an attempt to enhance the social protection system by establishing a legal foundation for all five branches of social insurance in China: maternity, old-age, health, unemployment and work-injury insurance (Liu and Sun, 2015). This national law entitled employed women to cash benefits and healthcare coverage for maternity, childbearing, family planning and related needs; and it regulated the employer's obligation to pay contributions for maternity insurance. This was followed by the Special Rules on the Labour Protection of Female Employees, implemented in 2012 ('2012 Rules' hereafter), detailing employer obligations and employee rights (Wei, 2016). Employers were prohibited from reducing earnings or dismissing employees due to pregnancy, childbirth or breastfeeding, and were required to reduce working hours or allow time off due to pregnancy. The 2012 Rules established mandatory Maternity Leave of 98 days, including 15 days before birth, and while on leave, female employees were entitled to benefits based on average earnings over the previous year; on returning to work, they were entitled to one hour each day for breastfeeding.[5]

The 2012 Rules reinforced the 2001 Population and Family Planning Law, which entitled women who married late and delayed childbearing to longer periods of Maternity Leave, and there were additional benefits (determined by local government) for one-child families, including enhanced monthly childcare allowances. Couples who had more than one child risked losing employment, eligibility to children's healthcare and education (Zhu, 2003; Hesketh et al, 2005). In practice there were many exceptions to the one-child policy; it is estimated that by 2007 only 36 per cent of the population were subject to a strict one-child limit and 53 per cent of couples who had a daughter were given permission to have a second child and another 11 per cent were allowed two children for other reasons that included disability of the first child, death of the first child, and other special circumstances (Callick, 2007). China's fertility rate hovered around 1.6 (NBSC, 2012; CIA, 2015).

Using Maternity Leave benefits as an incentive for limiting childbearing came to an abrupt end in 2015. Beginning in 2001, scholars from leading institutions of population research in China formed research teams to study how the one-child policy would affect China's economic growth potential (Feng et al, 2016). Concerns were expressed about meeting future labour force needs, but also about sustaining filial piety, a cultural expectation rooted in Confucian ideals that adult children should care for their ageing parents (Thompson, 2010). This is referred to as the '4:2:1' problem, meaning there were now four grandparents and two parents for every one working Chinese

---

[5] Breastfeeding was almost universal in China 40 years ago and has since declined markedly to about 28 per cent due to mothers returning to work, access to milk substitutes and mothers' perceived lack of milk. With the goal of improving child health and development, a campaign by UNICEF and the National Center for Women and Children's Health was launched in 2013 to increase breastfeeding rates in China (Yang et al, 2016).

man and woman. Studying such issues emerging from the one-child policy led scholars, elected officials and policymakers to advocate abolishing the policy (Zhou, 2016).

In all, demographers organised three collective appeals to policymakers, in April 2004, January 2009 and January 2015, each time urging policymakers to relax restrictions and finally to revoke the policy (New Citizen Movement, 2015; Feng et al, 2016). The imbalance of the male–female ratio, the slowdown in China's economic growth, and the burden that the one-child policy placed on young couples were all believed to contribute to growing support among policymakers for relaxing the one-child policy (New Citizen Movement, 2015; Feng et al, 2016).

By the end of 2015, the Central Committee of the Communist Party of China issued a directive amending the Population and Family Planning Law to allow married couples to have two children, with effect from 2016. This amendment eliminated incentives for late marriage and late parenthood and authorised provincial-level governments to implement this directive and to determine which couples may be allowed to have more than one child. Many provinces announced changes to local regulations to comply with the national decision, including the ending of additional Maternity Leave for late marriage and other leave extensions. Instead, most provinces have provided 30 extra days for first-time mothers, thus increasing the 98-day Maternity Leave to between 128 and 158 days (Covington, 2016). In addition, employer-financed paid Paternity Leave is now being introduced in many places on a provincial level ranging between seven days to one month, though typically 15 days. It has been suggested that Paternity Leave has replaced previous rewards for late childbearing (Zhang, 2016).

Newly revised Maternity Leave policies encourage women to have two children and maintain labour force attachment (Li, 2017). Details of local implementation are still evolving, but Table 1 summarises the Maternity and Paternity Leave policies across China to date. Generally speaking the leaves include pre- and post-natal leave, are paid at the average rate for an industry and guarantee job security. As Table 7.1 demonstrates, the variation across China is significant.

Coverage and benefit levels for maternity insurance are the lowest of the five types of social insurance in China. And despite laws mandating contributions across employment sectors and regions, evidence from household survey data suggests that they are still difficult to enforce and that coverage rates remain low (MOHRSS, 2016). At the time of writing, it remains unresolved if maternity insurance funds will cover

Table 7.1: Current duration of Marriage, Maternity and Paternity Leave across provinces and regions in China, 2016

Provincial region	Marriage Leave (days)	Maternity Leave (days)	Paternity Leave (days)
Anhui	3	158	10 days or 20 days if a couple does not reside in the same locality
Beijing	10	128 days and an additional 1–3 months with employer approval	15
Chongqing	15	128 days or up to 1 year with employer approval	15
Fujian	15	158–180	15
Gansu	30	180	30
Guangdong	3	178	15
Guangxi	3	148	25
Guizhou	13	158	15
Hainan	13	158	15
Hebei	18	158	15
Helongjiang	15–25	180	15
Henan	21–28	158	1 month
Hubei	3	128	15
Hunan	3	158	20
Inner Mongolia	18	158	25
Jiangsu	13	128	15
Jiangxi	3	158	15
Jilin	15	158 days up to 1 year with employer approval	15
Liaoning	10	158	15
Ningxia	3	158	25
Qinghai	15	158	15
Shaanxi	3–13	158 days or 168 days with a pre-pregnancy physical exam	15 days or 20 days if a couple does not reside in the same locality
Shandong	3	158	7
Shanghai	10	128	10
Shanxi	30	158	15
Sichuan	3	158	20
Tianjin	3	128	7
Tibet*	10	1 year	30
Xinjiang	23	158	15
Yunnan	18	158	30
Zhejiang	3	128	15

Source: Information extracted from provincial amendments of family planning regulations and Tibet's notice on adjusting the welfare of cadres and workers in universal two-child policy. Full details available from the authors on request.

the costs of leave for second children and if additional revenues will be derived from taxes or elsewhere.

Going forward

It is commonly believed that the one-child policy prevented over 400 million births in China, although this figure has been challenged as overstating the number of births averted and for attributing reduced births to the one-child policy alone (Feng et al, 2013). There is, however, little dispute that as a result of interconnected policies, fertility rates were reduced below replacement levels. The consequences of this have included an ageing population – one-third of the population is aged 60 years or over and retirement age in China is 50 or 55 years for women and 60 years for men – without a sufficient working population to support them in retirement,[6] labour force shortages particularly in certain regions, and abnormal sex ratios as a result of female infanticide and sex selective abortions (Peng, 2011; Feng et al, 2016). Economic stagnation has also been a concern as the growth rate in jobs has decreased since 2010.

Since the 1980s, the overall fiscal capacity of China's government has grown, yet social spending as a share of overall government expenditures has remained relatively low (NBSC, 2016a). At the same time, many social issues are facing China, including disparities between rural and urban areas and among geographic regions, and the slow progress in creating a social security safety net (NBSC, 2016a).

It is estimated that 72 per cent of women between 25 and 34 years of age with children under the age of six years are employed in China (ACWF, 2011) and that labour force participation among this group would be higher but for the limited and unaffordable childcare options available (Cook and Dong, 2001). The United Nations Human Rights Council continues to report maternity-related discrimination practices in China; employers hire women who already have children, deny pregnant women statutory leave, or dismiss women during pregnancy (UNHRC, 2014). A recent report documented that more than 72 per cent of women said that they were not hired or promoted due to gender discrimination and over 75 per cent believed that they were dismissed due to marriage or childbirth (Yang, 2012).

---

[6] China's current retirement age was established after the founding of new China, when the population's life expectancy was less than 50 years old. China is expected to introduce reforms gradually delaying the retirement age (Beijing Times, 2015).

Despite improved coverage and funding, the majority of new mothers remained uncovered and did not receive maternity benefits in 2015, only 6.4 million recipients for 16.6 million births (NBSC, 2016b). While out of more than 404 million urban employees, only 44 per cent had employers paying contributions toward maternity insurance coverage on their behalf, though this was up from 30 per cent in 2008 (MOHRSS, 2016). The Chinese government estimates that only 6.6 per cent of 166 million rural migrant workers were covered in 2013 by maternity insurance (Chan and Seldon, 2014).

So though China may offer generous Maternity Leave to some, limited eligibility and poor enforcement has not yet allowed mothers and fathers in China to truly benefit from the protection mandated by law. The most recently enacted two-child policy is a response to the undesirable consequences resulting from the one-child policy, which may have stagnated economic growth as well as contributed to the familial burdens and responsibilities that only children shoulder. The two-child policy may stimulate a surge in fertility for the next decade, but we do not expect the increase in the fertility rate will continue in the long run without further incentives. China's one-child policy may have substantially curtailed fertility since its inception in late 1970s, but the recent decrease in the fertility rate since the 2000s may have more to do with the rising costs of childrearing, the strong motivation and desire to work continuously as educational levels, particularly among women, have risen, as well as the trend among young generations to marry late or to not marry at all.

We do expect, however, that a family-friendly policy such as the one currently mandated in China, if coupled with strong enforcement, may help stimulate a more productive labour force and thus economic growth for years to come. Families usually need financial assistance when facing the newly incurred costs of having newborn children. Paid leave policies, such as the one currently implemented in China, would likely yield long-term economic benefits for both families and employers, if enforced effectively.

With China having the second largest child population in the world and the largest labour force, providing the optimal environment to promote family well-being as well as children's optimal healthy development, is ever more important. With its currently implemented family-friendly policy, coupled with strong enforcement, China holds a promising key to enhance the welfare of families and future generations of productive citizens, to the benefit not only of the country but also of the world's economy and well-being.

References

ACWF (All-China Women's Federation) (2011) *Report on Major Results of the Third Wave Survey on the Social Status of Women in China*. Available at http://landwise.resourceequity.org

Beijing Times (2015) 'Renshebu: woguo pingjun tuixiu nianling buzu 55 sui, quanqiu zuizao' [Ministry of Human Resources and Social Security: China's average retirement age of less than 55 years old the world's earliest], *China Economic Net*, 15 Oct 2015. Available at www.ce.cn

Bian, Y. (1994) *Work and Inequality in Urban China*, Albany, NY: SUNY Press.

Blaxland, M., Shang, X. and Fisher, K.R. (2014) 'Introduction. People oriented: A new stage of social welfare development in China', *Journal of Social Service Research*, 40(4): 508–519.

Bongaarts, J. and Greenhalgh, S. (1985) 'An alternative to the one-child policy in China', *Population and Development Review*, 11(4): 585–617.

Cai, Y. (2006) *State and Laid-Off Workers in Reform China: The Silence and COLLECTIVE Action of the Retrenched*, London: Routledge.

Callick, R. (2007) 'China relaxes its one-child policy', *The Australian*, 24 January 2007. Available at www.theaustralian.com.au

Chan, C.K., Ngok, K.L. and Phillips, D. (2008) *Social Policy in China: Development and Well-being*, Bristol: Policy Press.

Chan, J. and Selden, M. (2014) 'China's rural migrant workers, the state, and labor politics', *Critical Asian Studies*, 46(4): 599–620.

Chan, K.W. (2010) 'The household registration system and migrant labor in China: Notes on a debate', *Population and Development Review*, 36(2): 357–364.

Cheng, Z., Nielsen, I. and Smyth, R. (2014) 'Access to social insurance in urban China: A comparative study of rural–urban and urban–urban migrants in Beijing', *Habitat International*, 41: 243–252.

CIA (Central Intelligence Agency) (2015) *China, People and Society: The World Factbook*. Available at www.cia.gov/library

Cook, S. and Dong, X. (2011) 'Harsh choices: Chinese women's paid work and unpaid care responsibilities under economic reform', *Development and Change*, 42(4): 947–965.

Covington (2016) *Changes to Chinese Parental Leave Benefits*. Available at www.cov.com/-/media/files/corporate/publications/2016/06/changes_to_chinese_parental_leave_benefits.pdf

Edwards, L. (2000) 'Women in the People's Republic of China: New challenges to the grand gender narrative', in L. Edwards and M. Roces (eds) *Women in Asia: Tradition, modernity and globalization*, Ann Arbor, MI: The University of Michigan Press, pp 59–84.

Feng, W., Cai, Y. and Gu, B. (2013) 'Population, policy, and politics: How will history judge China's one child policy?', *Population and Development Review*, 38(s1): 115–129.

Feng, W., Gu, B. and Cai, Y. (2016) 'The end of China's one child policy', *Studies in Family Planning*, 47(1): 83–86.

Giles, J., Park, A. and Cai, F. (2006) 'How has economic restructuring affected China's urban workers?', *The China Quarterly*, 185: 61–95.

Guan, X. (2000) 'China's social policy: Reform and development in the context of marketization and globalization', *Social Policy and Administration*, 34(1): 115–130.

Hesketh, T., Lu, L. and Xing, Z.W. (2005) 'The effect of China's one-child family policy after 25 years', *New England Journal of Medicine*, 353: 1171–1176.

Kent, A. (2002) 'China's international socialization: The role of international organizations', *Global Governance*, 8(3): 343–364.

Li, H. (2017) 'Lianghai lai le, chanjia chang le' [Two-child policy comes, maternity leave extends], *People's Daily Online*, 4 May 2017. Available at www.people.com.cn

Liu, B., Li, L. and Yang, C. (2015) *Gender Equality in China's Economic transformation*, Beijing: United Nations System in China.

Liu, C. (2010) (X. Bi, Trans.) *Current Situation of Maternity Insurance Legislation and its Implementation in China*. Available at www.iolaw.org.cn

Liu, T. and Sun, L. (2015) 'Maternity insurance in China: Global standards and local responses', *Asian Women*, 31(4): 23–51.

Lu, F. (1989) 'Danwei: A special form of social organization', *Social Sciences in China*, 10(3): 100–122.

MacFarquhar, R. (1987) 'The succession to Mao and the end of Maoism', in R. MacFarquhar (ed) *The Politics of China: The Eras of Mao and Deng*, Cambridge: Cambridge University Press, pp 248–339.

MOHRSS (Ministry of Human Resources and Social Security of the PRC) (2009) *2008 nian renli ziyuan he shehui baozhang shiye fazhan tongji gongbao* [*2008 Statistical Bulletin on the Development of Human Resources and Social Security*]. Available at www.mohrss.gov.cn

MOHRSS (Ministry of Human Resources and Social Security of the PRC) (2016) *2015 nian renli ziyuan he shehui baozhang shiye fazhan tongji gongbao* [*2015 Statistical Bulletin on the Development of Human Resources and Social Security*]. Available at www.mohrss.gov.cn

NBSC (National Bureau of Statistics in China) (2012) *Women and Men in China – Facts and Figures 2012*. Available at www.unicef.cn/cn.

NBSC (National Bureau of Statistics of China) (2016a) *China Statistics Yearbook 2015*, Beijing, China: China Statistics Press. Available at www.stats.gov.cn/tjsj/ndsj/2015/indexeh.htm

NBSC (National Bureau of Statistics of China) (2016b) *2015 nian guomin jingji he shehui fazhan tongji gongbao* [*2015 Annual Statistical Communiqué on the National Economic and Social Development*]. Available at http://www.stats.gov.cn/

New Citizen Movement (2015) *39 ming xuezhe lianming cu quanmian kaifang erhai, quxiao shengyu xianzhi (jianyi quan wen shu)* [*39 scholars collectively advocate for allowing universal second child birth and abolish restriction on fertility control*]. Available at https://xgmyd.com

Peng, X. (2011) 'China's demographic history and future challenges', *Science*, 333: 581–587.

Ringen, S. and Ngok, K. (2017) 'What kind of welfare state is emerging in China?', in I. Yi (ed) *Towards Universal Health Care in Emerging Economies*, Basingstoke: Palgrave Macmillan, pp 213–237.

Saunders, P. and Shang, X. (2001) 'Social security reform in China's transition to a market economy', *Social Policy and Administration*, 35(3): 274–289.

Sin, Y. (2005) 'Pension Liabilities and Reform Options for Old Age Insurance', *Working Paper* 2005-1, Washington DC: World Bank. Available at www.worldbank.org

Thompson, W. (2010) 'China's rapidly aging population', *Today's Research on Aging*, 20: 1–5. Available at www.prb.org

UN CEDAW (United Nations Committee on the Elimination of Discrimination Against Women) (1997) *China Report*, report number: CEDAW/C/CHN/34. Available at http://womenwatch.unwomen.org

UNHRC (United Nations Human Rights Council) (2014) *Report of the Working Group on the Issue of Discrimination Against Women in Law and Practice: Mission to China*, report number: A/HRC/29/40/Add.3. Available at www.ohchr.org

Wang, C. (2012) 'History of the Chinese family planning program: 1970–2010', *Contraception*, 85(6): 563–569.

Wei, N. (2016) *A Study of Employment Discrimination Against Women in China from a Comparative Perspective*, Unpublished Master's thesis, University of Oslo. Available at www.duo.uio.no/handle/10852/51396

Whyte, M.K., Feng, W. and Cai, Y. (2015) 'Challenging myths about China's one-child policy', *The China Journal*, 74: 144–159.

World Bank (1997) *Old Age Security: Pension Reform in China (China 2020)*, Washington, DC: The World Bank.

World Bank (2016) *China Overview*. Available at www.worldbank.org/en/country/china

World Bank (2017) *World Bank Indicators, GDP Per Capita (Current US$) and China*. Available at http://data.worldbank.org

Xie, Y. and Zhou, X. (2014) 'Income inequality in today's China', *Proceedings of the National Academy of Sciences*, 111(19): 6928–6933.

Yang, H. (2012) 'Urban women's gender discrimination issues in employment', *Specialist Viewpoints, Women of China*. Available at www.womenofchina.cn

Yang, Z., Lai, J., Yu, D., Duan, Y. et al (2016) 'Breastfeeding rates in China: A cross-sectional survey and estimate of benefits for improvement', *Poster Abstract*, Beijing: Department of Maternal and Child Nutrition, National Institute for Nutrition and Health, Chinese Center for Disease Control and Prevention

Zhang, C. (2002) *The Interaction of the State and the Market in a Developing Transition Economy: The Experience of China*. Available at www.semanticscholar.org

Zhang, L. (2016) 'China: Maternity leave further extended by provinces', *Global Legal Monitor*, 3 May 2016, US Library of Congress. Available at www.loc.gov/law

Zhou, W. (2016) 'Qunguo renda daibiao Youlin He: Jianyi erhai chanjia yanchang yige yu'e' [NPC representative Youlin He: Recommend to extend maternity leave for 1 month], *Yangcheng News*, 3 March 2016. Available at http://news.sohu.com/20160303/n439204842.shtml

Zhu, W.X. (2003) 'The one-child family policy', *Archives of Disease in Childhood*, 88(6): 463–464.

EIGHT

Mexico: leave policy, co-responsibility in childcare and informal employment[1]

Cándido Pérez-Hernández and Anna Escobedo

Introduction

This chapter analyses leave policy developments in Mexico, up to 2018, looking at the transition from a system based on Maternity Leave to a broader approach related to childhood and labour policies. Maternity Leave was anchored in the Mexican Constitution as early as 1917, in the context of the Mexican Revolution that transformed the country's culture and government. A century later fathers came to the fore with the introduction of Paternity Leave in 2012. The recent changes illustrate how the dual-earner/dual-carer model along with social policies supporting a caring fatherhood are spreading to Mexico as well as to the rest of Latin America.

We aim to identify structural conditioning factors, obstacles and challenges to improving leave policies in Mexico. We also review the proposals that have been generated during the last five years. Given the emerging research on leave policies in Latin America, an additional purpose is to integrate the specific features and challenges from this region into the international academic debate.

The chapter starts with a section introducing the context of leave policies in the Latin American region. We then present some basic information on Mexico and an overview of the development of leave policies, including a description of the legislative initiatives presented in the Congress of the Union (*Congreso de la Unión*, the Federal Chamber of Deputies and Senate) between 2012 and mid-2017, which were designed to extend leave and increase co-responsibility between men and women for the care of children. We discuss structural

[1] The authors are grateful to Olga Molina-Herrera for helping with the translation and revision of the chapter.

impediments and challenges to improving leave policies in Mexico, some of which have been pointed out by international organisations, such as the informal economy, funding and the growth, complexity and fragmentation of ECEC services. We conclude by identifying the need to link leave and ECEC policies, in order to focus efforts not just on parents' co-responsibility and equality but also on children's well-being. These policies can also act as pull factors for the formalisation of informal employment, so that the associated costs could then be reformulated as social investments.

The spread of the social politics of parenthood to Latin America

Research on the cultural and institutional construction of motherhood, fatherhood and the relationship between working parents, the labour market and social policies has spread all over the world. The promotion of a family model based on citizenship combining breadwinning and caregiving has become central to contemporary family policy, with the search for measures to achieve equal opportunities for mothers and fathers; interest has been growing since the 1990s, particularly in the social politics of fatherhood (Flaquer and Escobedo, 2014). Besides the role of fathers as economic providers, their contribution to families as potential carers has become a significant research theme (O'Brien, 2009). Fatherhood has shifted from relative obscurity to a central position, primarily, but not exclusively, for its potential to improve child and family well-being (Cabrera et al, 2007). In the field of public policy, Parental Leave has shown potential for promoting men's involvement in children's care and upbringing (Brandth and Kvande, 2009; O'Brien, 2009; Meil, 2013).

Research in Latin America on the work/family dynamic has also started to focus on the role of Paternity and Parental Leaves. They are visible, efficient and symbolically powerful instruments that both reflect and potentially promote social and institutional change towards more gender and social equality. Leave policies in the region remain overwhelmingly targeted towards mothers, but in the last decade Paternity Leave and Parental Leave measures have been expanding and bringing fathers to the fore. According to the ILO, Latin America as a global region has witnessed one of the largest increases in the provision of statutory Paternity Leave over the last two decades, even though it is paid for by the employer in two-thirds of countries (ILO, 2014). Across the region in 2013, six countries had no Paternity Leave, nine had leave of between one and five days and four had leave of between

10 and 14 days. But only three countries had shared Parental Leave: Cuba (2003), Chile (2011) and Uruguay (2013).

Maternity Leave exists throughout Latin America with an average length of 12 to 13 weeks (ILO, 2014). In most countries it is funded by the state, not employers, in order to avoid labour market discrimination against women (Lupica, 2016). All countries have measures and sanctions to prevent employees' dismissal for maternity-related reasons; but though job protection is mostly guaranteed, discrimination is still reported. For example, when a woman is applying for a job, requiring her to complete a pregnancy test is still common practice even though illegal.

When comparing Maternity and Paternity Leaves, some authors consider that the region is experiencing inequitable policies for women and men (Pautassi and Rico, 2011). The duration is on a totally uneven scale: from eight to 26 *weeks* for female employees, but only two to 14 *days* for men. It is also observed that in labour regulations the provision of care entitlements is focussed on, and in many cases limited to, mothers, under the assumption that they are the main carers for children; other policies that might encourage the universal caregiver model, such as Parental Leave, are practically non-existent (Lupica, 2016).

Leave policies in Mexico

There is a growing body of literature on leave policies in Latin America, particularly on Paternity Leave (Lupica, 2016). Research in this field is spreading to Mexico (Frías, 2014; Moguel, 2014; García and Mendizábal, 2015; INMUJERES DF, 2016; Pérez, 2017); fatherhood and low paternal involvement in childcare, upbringing and housework, as well as policies around these issues, are receiving increasing attention (Figueroa, 2014). However, information about Maternity and Paternity Leave in Mexico is sparse. Working with data provided by the Mexican Social Security Institute, the Institute for Social Security and Services for State Workers and the National Institute of Statistics and Geography, we estimate that about 26 per cent of the 2,353,596 births in 2015 were covered by Maternity Leave benefits paid by the social security system; but no information is available for Paternity Leave, which is paid by employers (the different funding of these two types of leave is discussed further overleaf). We have found no further information on the use of leave in Mexico. Three national surveys include at least one item related to leave policies: the National Time Use Survey, the National Occupation and Employment Survey, and the National Household Income and Expenditure Survey, but none permit detailed analysis, mainly because Maternity and Paternity Leave are conflated with sick leave in the same question.

The Mexican context

Mexico is a federal republic, composed of 31 states plus Mexico City and 122 million inhabitants (INEGI, 2015a; 2016a). Since 1970, the total fertility rate has been continuously decreasing, from 6.7 children per woman to 2.2 by 2016 (CONAPO, 2014). Births outside marriage have increased from 37 per cent in 1995 to 65 per cent in 2014.[2] The number of divorces per 100 marriages has tripled from 7.4 in 2000 to 22.2 in 2015 (INEGI, 2016b). As a consequence, the number of households headed by women is increasing, for example, growing from 24.6 per cent in 2010 to 29 per cent in 2015, an increase of 2.3 million households now headed by women (INEGI, 2010; 2015b).

Female employment is relatively low in Mexico, 47 per cent among those of working age, compared to 67 per cent on average across the OECD, or, if we focus on the Latin American region, around 60 per cent in countries such as Chile, Colombia, Peru or Brazil (OECD, 2017). Female employment is strongly impacted by early motherhood, with an employment rate of only 33.4 per cent for women with children under three-years-old, then increasing to 43.2 per cent when children are three to five-years-old, and to 50.8 per cent when children are between six to 14 years old.[3] While the employment rate for partnered mothers is 41 per cent (indicating a prevalence of male breadwinners in two parent families with children under 15 years), it is 72 per cent for single mothers.[4]

The profound family changes that Mexico has been experiencing in recent decades call for the development of new work/family policies, for both mothers and fathers, to promote gender equality and paternal engagement to strengthen child-father bonds.

Historical development of leave policies in Mexico

The Mexican Constitution introduced Maternity Leave in 1917 in the following terms (Article 123):

---

[2] www.oecd.org/els/family/SF_2_4_Share_births_outside_marriage.pdf
[3] www.oecd.org/els/family/LMF_1_2_Maternal_Employment.pdf
[4] www.oecd.org/els/soc/LMF_1_3_Maternal_employment_by_partnership_status.pdf

> During the three months prior to childbirth, women shall not perform physical labour that requires excessive material [sic] effort. In the month following childbirth they shall necessarily enjoy the benefit of rest and shall receive their full wages and retain their employment and the rights acquired under their labour contract. During the nursing period, they shall have two special rest periods each day, of a half hour each, for nursing their infants.

Maternity Leave remained unchanged until 1960, when it was extended to one paid month prior to birth and two paid months after. In 1974, Article 123 was amended by stating that the leave period should be six weeks prior to birth and six weeks following, involving a redistribution of pre- and post-natal periods (Bermúdez, 2006). Although there have been no further changes to the Constitution, other lower-level laws have been reformed, such as the Federal Labour Law, the Social Security Law and the Law on State Workers Social Security Institute.

In 2012, a six-week period of leave for adoptive mothers was introduced, as well as an extension of post-natal Maternity Leave to eight weeks for a child born with any kind of disability or requiring hospital care. During 2016, a flexible system was initiated, allowing the transfer of up to four of the six pre-natal leave weeks to the post-natal period, meaning mothers could take up to ten weeks following childbirth. Also in that year, both the management and payment for Maternity Leave for private sector employees were facilitated. Currently, Maternity Leave lasts for six weeks before birth and six weeks after, is paid at 100 per cent of earnings and is funded through social security contributions as it is considered a labour benefit.

Paternity Leave was approved in 2012. Prior to the labour reform that included Paternity Leave, there were several legislative initiatives, of which one of the most important was in April 1997. This initiative was presented in the Chamber of Deputies and aimed at reforming Constitutional Article 123 to include Paternity Leave as a labour right, granting ten paid leave days to all fathers who worked within the formal economy. The initiative, however, failed to secure support (Frías, 2014).

During 2012, the President presented a labour reform initiative that attempted to respond to insufficient employment generation (an economic dimension), poor protection of vulnerable groups (a social dimension), and lack of transparency and accountability by trade unions (a political dimension). This proposal was limited to changing the Federal Labour Law without attempting to amend the Constitution. Many of the proposed reforms regarding the economic dimension were strongly supported by employers' organisations such as the Employers' Confederation of the Mexican Republic and the Business Coordinating Council, which considered the reforms to benefit their interests. This made it possible to include, as part of the social dimension of the reform, some changes favourable to employees, such as the prohibition of the requirement that women applying for jobs present a 'certificate of not being pregnant' (*certificado médico de no embarazo*) and the introduction of ten days of Paternity Leave (Bensusán, 2013).

Due to the importance of the proposed reform, intense debates were organised by universities, social organisations and political parties across the country. The issues under discussion included several individual labour rights, such as Paternity Leave (SEGOB, 2013). The end result was Article 132 of the Federal Labour Law, which established that men should have five working days of leave, for childbirth or adoption, paid at 100 per cent of earnings; but unlike Maternity Leave, which is paid for through social security, Paternity Leave was to be paid by employers. Public funding of Paternity Leave through social security was never considered, probably to avoid increasing federal government expenditure; and so to limit the cost to employers, the proposed Paternity Leave length was shortened from the original proposal of ten days to five days.

Alongside these legislative proposals, a few public agencies and academic institutions since the mid-2000s have introduced their own Paternity Leave measures, usually offering between ten and 15 fully paid days. Among them are the Ministry of Social Development, the Ministry of the Interior, the Ministry of Foreign Affairs, the Electoral Tribunal of the Federal Judiciary, the Federal Police, the National Workers' Housing Fund, the National Women's Institute, the *Colegio de la Frontera Sur*, the National Polytechnic Institute, the Human Rights Commission of Mexico City and the Government of Mexico City.

Legislative proposals for leave policies: 2012 to mid-2017

Since the Federal Labour Law Reform in 2012, with its introduction of Paternity Leave, 85 leave-related legislative initiatives have been proposed in the Congress of the Union. Although these initiatives have been presented by different political parties, none has succeeded. A systematic review of these initiatives, presented from 2012 to mid-2017 has been conducted for this chapter. For the purpose of analysis, this information was classified into the following fields: name of the initiative, promoter, political affiliation, status, objectives and motivation of the proposal, type and characteristics of the leave proposal, scope and limits.

Most of the proposals have aimed at increasing leave periods granted to women and men since the current ones are considered insufficient, especially for Paternity Leave. The main motives of the proposals were: a) non-discrimination against women, b) women's employment stability, c) encouraging work and family harmonisation, d) parental balance and equality in family co-responsibility, and e) employment equality between men and women. It is worth mentioning that there are no references to children's well-being and the potential positive impact of having both parents as caregivers.

There is also no mention of the relationship between leave policies and other early childhood policies. Therefore, the initiatives are exclusively focused on employment and its regulation. Moreover, there is no analysis of the initiatives' likely economic impact for employers, or for public expenditure in the case of those proposing that leave should be funded by social security. Nor is there any prospective analysis of the potential impacts, including costs and benefits, on the labour market or on the relationship between formal and informal employment, which (as we shall discuss further below) is a fundamental challenge for Mexican society. Overall, therefore, these are isolated proposals focussed on the extension of leave periods. None consider, for example, the implementation of a comprehensive system of Parental Leave nor any specific measures addressed towards integrating working parents who currently cannot access leave arrangements, either because they are self-employed or in informal employment.

Finally, the fact that the initiatives have been presented by different political parties, including the three main ones, points not only to leave policy being on the political agenda but to the potential for future political agreements. However, the fact that none of these initiatives includes any data about current use of leave policies, the cost of existing policies or the possible economic impact of increasing, for example, Paternity Leave, suggests that the emerging political interest is not yet matched by a capacity to design effective policies.

Leave policy challenges in Mexico

International organisations have described some challenges for leave policies in Latin American countries, and particularly in Mexico. The Inter-American Development Bank (Banco Interamericano de

Desarrollo) (BID), which in 2015 presented a relevant study on early childhood, discusses the difficulties of extending statutory leave policies in Latin America because of the large proportion of informal workers, which hinders effective monitoring of compliance. It also mentions funding as a key issue, and one of the main difficulties the region faces in developing social security. The BID states that leave policies can influence the decision to take formal or informal employment, depending on how they are financed (BID, 2015).

The OECD has recently issued a series of recommendations based on a study of gender equality policies in Mexico. These include measures to improve access to childcare services for children under four years old, and extending Maternity Leave to at least 14 weeks and Paternity Leave from the current five days to at least eight weeks. The OECD anticipates that such measures should be accompanied by efforts to encourage parents to take advantage of the policies). Like the BID, it recognises that reducing informal employment is a great challenge, which, although it affects men, is much more serious for women (OECD, 2017).

In the next section we will probe deeper into three challenges for the development of leave policies: the informal economy; the funding of leave policies; and the growth, complexity and fragmentation of ECEC.

The informal economy

The informal economy in Mexico produces about Mex\$3,559 billion per year (about US\$178 billion), which, in 2013, represented 24.8 per cent of GDP (INEGI, 2015c). There are two components to an understanding of 'informality' or, the informal economy, in Mexico: 1) the informal sector and 2) informal work (Galindo and Ríos, 2015).

According to the National Institute of Statistics and Geography (INEGI, 2014), the *informal sector* is comprised of private companies that are not considered separate financial entities from their owners, that is, there is no financial separation between the enterprise's productive activities and the owner's individual activities. Typically uncompetitive, they function at a low organisational level, on a small scale, and with little division or separation between labour and capital. Labour relations within them – if they exist – are based on casual employment, kinship or personal and social relationships, rather than contractual agreements with formal guarantees. The informal sector is also typically outside the social security system.

Informal work includes people who have employment but do not have labour rights such as social security, or labour benefits, such as when they lose their job. In Mexico, informal work is widespread, even within public institutions, among both front-line workers and suppliers. Thus, informal employees have a strong presence within private enterprises and public institutions, and even more so within domestic work (INEGI, 2014). In 2015, around 30 million people (57.6 per cent of the total employed population) were so employed (INEGI, 2015c). However, levels vary across Mexico; in 2013, for example, the State of Oaxaca registered 81.2 per cent informal employment while the State of Nuevo Leon registered 39.5 per cent (Galindo and Ríos, 2015).

Due to informality, social security is highly segmented and unequal. On the one hand, formal workers must be registered with and contribute to social security, which includes a complex system of insurance and benefits covering sickness, maternity, pensions, survivors, housing, childcare services and disability. Employers and formal employees pay about 84 per cent of social security costs through a payroll tax, and the government contributes the remaining 16 per cent from the federal budget (Levy, 2012). On the other hand, informal workers make no such contributions and are, therefore, excluded from contributory social security benefits such as Maternity Leave, but also from Paternity Leave which, although not derived from social security contributions, requires a formal labour relationship with an employer. However, informal workers do receive so-called non-contributory social protection, benefiting from health programmes, non-contributory childcare services and housing subsidies, since the costs of such benefits are assumed, almost entirely, by the government.

This situation raises a dilemma: how to avoid promoting informality while trying to improve living conditions and social protection coverage for informal workers, including extending policies such as Maternity or Parental Leave that are currently inaccessible to informal employees. Levy (2012) argues that the root of the problem lies in the asymmetric financing of social security, depending as it does on the employee's labour status. This asymmetry leads to some employees having the right to social security and others not, a situation that is exacerbated by the great mobility between formal and informal jobs in some sectors. For this reason, Levy's central proposal is to eliminate asymmetric financing and replace it with universal social security, as exists for public education where funding comes from general taxation and, consequently, children of formal and informal employees go to the same public schools – unlike the situation in ECEC, where the children of parents with informal and formal employment usually go to different nurseries.

So, the informal economy contributes to inequality of care for young children. For while some parents have access to leave policies, the majority do not. As a consequence, considerable differences in children's development might be due to their parents' employment status.

As a final consideration on this challenge, international experience has shown the potential of social security benefits, particularly at this early stage of parenthood, to act as pull factors to promote the formalisation of female employment. In order to access more generous Parental Leave schemes, women have a strong incentive to be previously attached to formal employment. On the other hand, benefits after taking leave may retain mothers in formal employment; for example, a measure that the Spanish government introduced in 2003 to incentivise mothers' attachment to formal employment after the end of Maternity Leave, by implementing a generous monthly payment until the child's third birthday as a return of social security contributions, has proved very successful (Flaquer and Escobedo, 2009; Pfau-Effinger et al, 2009).

Funding

As previously stated, Maternity Leave is funded by social security contributions while Paternity Leave is generally funded by employers. Unlike EU member states, in two out of three Latin American countries, employers pay for Paternity Leave. In the Mexican context, among the reform bills analysed, only two proposed that Paternity Leave should no longer be funded by the employer, but by social security. The first was discarded, while the second is still pending at the end of 2018.

In the short term, it seems unlikely that any agreement will be reached for social security funding of Paternity Leave. Thus, the extension of Paternity Leave faces significant difficulties, since it would require approval from and negotiation with the business community. Any such proposal could be particularly sensitive for micro-, small- and medium-sized enterprises, which together employ 75.4 per cent of all employees (INEGI, 2015d). Moreover, in these kinds of enterprise, employees could face major obstacles if they claim the use of an extended Paternity Leave that is paid for by the employer.

Furthermore, the development of publicly-funded leave would face funding obstacles in the Mexican social security system, whose financial deficits have been widely criticised (Martínez and Cabestany, 2016). Regardless of the social security funding model, the resources for sustaining social security funds always appear to be insufficient. A number of factors contribute to inadequate social security finances: high levels of expenditure, mainly related to liabilities accrued by the pensions system; the equipment and expansion needs of operating units; the high costs of care caused by the growing numbers of beneficiaries; and an increase in disease outbreaks (Sánchez-Castañeda, 2012).

In recent years, while the amount of social protection for people who do not contribute to social security has increased, some critics suggest that there has been insufficient effort directed towards developing a healthier revenue stream, which is currently dependent on the contributions of the formally employed population (Martínez and Cabestany, 2016). Looking to the future, any significant development of leave for fathers or a parental leave scheme beyond Maternity Leave seems unfeasible in current funding conditions, and thus will require a reorganisation of the funding of social security.

Growth, complexity and fragmentation of ECEC

In Latin America, governments' efforts in the provision of ECEC are recent and their focus is mainly on coverage (Rodríguez, 2010; Marco, 2014). The regional rate of enrolment of children aged three- to five-years-old increased from 56 per cent in 1999 to 65 per cent in 2007 (UNESCO, 2010), Information on access to ECEC for children under three years old is incomplete and scattered, but it has been observed that enrolment rates are lower among younger age groups (Marco, 2014). In addition to social inequalities, there are cultural factors that affect children's access, even in families with economic resources, such as the perceived lack of legitimacy of early education (Itzcovich, 2013).

In Mexico, education is compulsory for children from three years old, but at the beginning of the school year 2014–2015 only 42.8 per cent of three-year-olds were enrolled in school, compared to 89.9 per cent of four-year-olds and almost 100 per cent of five-year-olds (INEE, 2016). Further, it is estimated that coverage by public childcare services for younger children is low, although some of these services have grown exponentially in recent years with an overall fourfold increase in children attending between 2000 and 2015 (see Figure 8.1).

Currently, ECEC is diverse and fragmented in Mexico, especially for children under three years old. The reasons for such fragmentation are many but one of the most important is the number of public bodies that provide services, including the (federal) Ministry

Figure 8.1: Number of children attending childcare services of the three main public providers (thousands) (2000–2015)

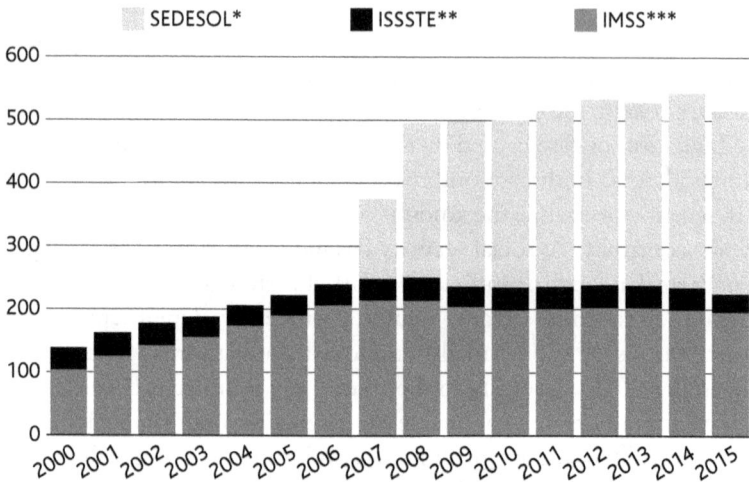

Notes:
* SEDESOL – Ministry for Social Development (*Secretaría de Desarrollo Social*);
** ISSSTE – State Workers Social Security Institute (*Instituto de Seguridad y Servicios Sociales de los Trabajadores del Estado*);
*** IMSS – Mexican Social Security Institute (*Instituto Mexicano del Seguro Social*).

Source: Author's own calculation using information from Social Studies and Public Opinion Centre (CESOP, 2016)

of Public Education, the Education Ministry of each State, the Ministry of Health, the Ministry of Labour and Social Welfare, the Ministry of Social Development and the Integral System for Family Development. There is no horizontal coordination between the different programmes, nor vertical coordination for children of different ages and developmental stages attending these services, apart from some programmes coordinated within the same institution. A central concern, therefore, is the need for greater coordination between different sectors, such as education, health and labour, as well as an urgent need to link ECEC programmes for children under three-years-old to those for children over three.

Currently, there is no governing system that coordinates ECEC programmes, authorities and institutions. Children who have access to education and care services do so because their parents are eligible for a particular programme or employment benefit; given the diversity of public ECEC schemes, access to these services depends not only on labour law but on parents' particular employment. The result is significant differences in access to such services among children of, for example, workers in the public and private sectors (see Table 8.1).

Table 8.1: Some eligibility conditions for access to ECEC services offered by main public providers

Mexican Social Security Institute (IMSS)	State Workers Social Security Institute (ISSSTE)	Ministry for Social Development (SEDESOL)
Mothers with social security (formal work)	Mothers (government employees)	Working/studying (or looking for a job) mothers; low socio-economic status; no access to other ECEC services
Widowed or divorced fathers with social security and with custody of children	Fathers (government employees)	Single fathers with custody of children; low socio-economic status; no social security
Children from 45 days to four years old	Children from two months to six years old	Children from one to four years old

Source: IMSS, ISSSTE and SEDESOL official websites

When looking at the relationship between leave and services, Maternity Leave, at best, ends ten weeks after birth, but a child's right to receive ECEC may start only from one or four years of age, producing a wide gap between these policies. This happens because Maternity and Paternity Leaves are labour entitlements and not linked to a right to ECEC during a child's first three years of life.

Conclusions

Leave policies for mothers and fathers in Mexico, as in other Latin American countries, are starting to be seen as a necessary mechanism for moving from the male breadwinner to a dual-earner family model, in which the role of both parents as providers and as carers is recognised and promoted. These policies are gaining increasing attention in response to the growing interest throughout Latin America in measures that encourage both parents' involvement in child-raising and care, while at the same time protecting maternal employment and positively nurturing well-being in early childhood. These policies will have to respond to new family patterns such as an unprecedented growth in the number of divorces, a high proportion of children born outside marriage, and the proliferation of households that are headed by women. Yet despite increasing awareness of the importance of this field, there are still very few studies that analyse leave policies in Mexico; this is due, on the one hand, to a lack of data from national surveys and, on the other, to the late awakening of academic interest in the subject.

While Maternity Leave in Mexico is more than 100 years old, Paternity Leave is much younger, with only five years of history. There are important differences between the two leaves, including length, funding and flexibility. Parental Leave, understood as extended leave after Maternity Leave and available to both mothers and fathers, is not yet on the political agenda.

In the five years since Paternity Leave was introduced, in 2012, dozens of further initiatives have been proposed, and these legislative initiatives have been reviewed in this chapter. From this, it is clear that they have focused, above all, on extending the duration of leave; there has been no analysis of the current state or use of leave policies, nor of potential economic, labour or family impacts. Despite these limitations, the approval of any one of these proposals might have represented some advance; but none has been approved. On the contrary, most have been discarded.

The chapter has also deepened awareness of three of the main challenges to progress with regard to the development of leave policies in Mexico, which have been raised by international organisations such as the Inter-American Development Bank and the OECD: the informal economy, the funding of leave policies and the growth, complexity and fragmentation of ECEC policies. At present, informal labour means very unequal access to (and conditions of) care for young children, because leave policies and childcare services depend on the labour affiliation of parents, mainly mothers. Furthermore, as we have shown, ECEC services today are excessively complex and disjointed, and children have not been the centre of attention in the development of policies. A further problem is that leave policies and ECEC programmes are unrelated, with one consequence being a substantial gap for most parents between the end of Maternity Leave and when a child becomes entitled to an ECEC service.

The transformation of informal employment into formal employment is a major national concern and policy driver. To further this goal, we recommend linkage of leave policy and ECEC policy and enhancement of both policy areas as incentives for the formalisation of informal work. Regarding leave funding, we can see no reasons that might justify the current funding of Paternity Leave by employers; on the contrary, it seems unsustainable in the long term, especially if there is a future introduction of Parental Leave, shared by mothers and fathers. The long-term aim should be reform of early childhood policies (including leave and ECEC) to overcome current excessive complexity and social and gender inequalities. Comparative learning and benchmarking methodologies promoted by international organisations, together with knowledge production in this field by academic networks, provide a context for well-informed reform. The alternative, continuing along the same path, offers a bleaker scenario, continuing the current institutional complexity, where private initiatives favour the better off while making little impact on inequality.

References

Bensusán, G. (2013) *Reforma laboral, desarrollo incluyente e igualdad en México* [*Labour Law, Inclusive Development and Equality in Mexico*], Mexico: CEPAL.

Bermúdez, G. (2006) 'Análisis comparativo de las prestaciones de seguridad social por maternidad' [Comparative analysis of maternity social security benefits], *Boletín Mexicano de Derecho Comparado*, XXXIX(116): 453–479.

BID (2015) *Los primeros pasos: el bienestar infantil y el papel de las políticas públicas* [*The Early Years: Child Well-being and the Role of Public Policy*]. Available at https://publications.iadb.org/bitstream/handle/11319/7259/Los_primeros_a%C3%B1os_El_bienestar_infantil_y_el_papel_de_las_pol%C3%ADticas_p%C3%BAblicas.pdf

Brandth, B. and Kvande, E. (2009) 'Gendered or gender-neutral care politics for fathers?', *The Annals of the American Academy of Political and Social Science*, 624(1): 177–189.

Cabrera, N.J., Shannon, J.D. and Tamis-LeMonda, C. (2007) 'Fathers' influence on their children's cognitive and emotional development: From toddlers to pre-k', *Applied Development Science*, 11(4), 208–213.

CESOP (2016) *Guarderías/estancias infantiles en México* [*Nurseries in Mexico*], Mexico: Cámara de Diputados.

CONAPO (2014) *Proyecciones de la población 2010–2050* [*Population Projections 2010–2050*], Mexico: CONAPO.

Figueroa, J.G. (coord.) (2014) *Políticas Públicas y la Experiencia de Ser Hombre. Paternidad, Espacios Laborales, Salud y Educación* [*Public policies and the experience of being a man: fatherhood, work spaces, health and education*], Mexico: El Colegio de México.

Flaquer, L. and Escobedo, A. (2009) 'The metamorphosis of informal work in Spain: Family solidarity, female immigration and development of social rights', in B. Pfau-Effinger, L. Flaquer and P. Jensen (eds) *Formal and Informal Work: The Hidden Work Regime in Europe*, New York, NY: Routledge, pp 143–168.

Flaquer, L. and Escobedo, A. (2014) 'Licencias parentales y política social de la paternidad en España', [Parental leave and social policy of fatherhood in Spain], *Cuadernos de Relaciones Laborales*, 32(1): 69–99.

Frías, H.M. (2014) 'El camino hacia la igualdad de género, la licencia por paternidad en México' [The road to gender equality, Paternity Leave in Mexico], in J.G. Figueroa (ed) *Políticas públicas y la experiencia de ser hombre: Paternidad, espacios laborales, salud y educación* [*Public policies and the experience of being a man: fatherhood, work spaces, health and education*], Mexico: El Colegio de México, pp 79–109.

Galindo, M. and Ríos, V. (2015) 'Informalidad' [Informality], *Serie de Estudios Económicos*, 1 (August 2015). Available at http://scholar.harvard.edu/files/vrios/files/201508_mexicoinformality.pdf?m=1453513195

García, J.N. and Mendizábal, G. (2015) 'Análisis jurídico de la paternidad con perspectiva de género: Una visión desde la masculinidad' [Legal paternity analysis gender: a view from masculinity], *Revista Latinoamericana de Derecho Social*, 20: 31–59.

ILO (International Labour Office) (2014) *Maternity and Paternity at Work: Law and Practice Across the World*, Geneva: ILO.

INEE (2016) 'La educación obligatoria en Mexico' [Compulsory education in Mexico], *Informe 2016*, Mexico: INEE.

INEGI (2010) *Censo de población y vivienda* [*Census of population and housing units*], Mexico: INEGI.

INEGI (2014) *La informalidad laboral: Encuesta nacional de ocupación y empleo* [*Labour informality: National occupation and employment survey*], Mexico: INEGI.

INEGI (2015a) *Estadísticas de natalidad* [*Birth Statistics*], Mexico: INEGI.

INEGI (2015b) *Encuesta intercensal* [*Intercensal survey*], Mexico: INEGI.

INEGI (2015c) *Medición de la economía informal* [*Measuring the informal economy*]', Mexico: INEGI.

INEGI (2015d) *Encuesta nacional sobre productividad y competitividad de las micro, pequeñas y medianas empresas* [*National survey on productivity and competitiveness of micro, small and medium businesses*], Mexico: INEGI.

INEGI (2016a) *Encuesta nacional de ocupación y empleo: Indicadores estratégicos* [*National occupation and employment survey: Strategic indicators*], Mexico: INEGI.

INEGI (2016b) *Estadísticas de nupcialidad* [*Marriage statistics*], Mexico: INEGI.

INMUJERES DF (2016) *Informe de resultados de la investigación cualitativa sobre 'Paternidad en condiciones equitativas en el ámbito laboral 2015'* [*Report on the results of the qualitative research on 'Paternity under fair conditions in the workplace 2015*], Mexico: Instituto Nacional de las Mujeres del Distrito Federal.

Itzcovich, G. (2013) *La expansión educativa en el nivel inicial durante la última década*, Cuaderno N° 16 [*Educational expansion in the initial level during the last decade*], Buenos Aires: Sistema de Información las Tendencias Educativas de América Latina-SITEAL, IIPEUNESCO. Available at www.siteal.iipe.unesco.org/sites/default/files/siteal_cuaderno_16_nivel_inicial.pdf

Levy, S. (2012) 'Seguridad social universal: Un camino para Mexico' [Universal social security: A road for Mexico], *Nexos*. Available at www.nexos.com.mx/?p=15047

Lupica, C. (2016) 'Licencias de paternidad y permisos parentales en América Latina y el Caribe: herramientas indispensables para propiciar la mayor participación de los padres en el cuidado de los hijos e hijas' [Paternity and parental leave in Latin America and the Caribbean: essential tools to promote greater participation of fathers in the care of children], *Masculinities and Social Change*, 5(3): 295–320.

Marco, F. (2014) *Calidad del cuidado y la educación para la primera infancia en América Latina*. [Quality of care and education for early childhood in Latin America], Mexico: CEPAL.

Martínez, J. and Cabestany, G. (2016) 'La reforma de la seguridad social en México frente a los desequilibrios del mercado de trabajo' [The reform of social security in Mexico against market imbalances of work], *Economía Informal*, 397: 89–104.

Meil, G. (2013) 'European men's use of parental leave and their involvement in child care and housework', *Journal of Comparative Family Studies*, XLIV(5): 557–570.

Moguel, M.J. (2014) *Políticas institucionales y cambios en los significados sobre la masculinidad: un análisis de caso de la licencia de paternidad en la Comisión de Derechos Humanos del Distrito Federal* [Institutional policies and changes in the meanings of masculinity: A case analysis of Paternity Leave in the Human Rights Commission of the Federal District], Mexico: FLACSO.

O'Brien, M. (2009) 'Fathers, parental leave policies and infant quality of life: International perspectives and policy impact', *The Annals of the American Academy of Political and Social Science*, 624(1): 190–213.

OECD (2017) *Building an inclusive Mexico: Policies and Good Governance for Gender Equality*, OECD: Paris.

Pautassi, L. and Rico, M.N. (2011) 'Licencias para el cuidado infantil: derecho de hijos, padres y madres' [Leaves for childcare: children, fathers and mothers' entitlement], *Boletín de la infancia y adolescencia sobre el avance de los Objetivos de Desarrollo del Milenio*, 1(July 2011): 4–9.

Pérez, C. (2017) 'Mexico country note', in S. Blum, A. Koslowski and P. Moss (eds) *International Review of Leave Policies and Research 2017.* Available at www.leavenetwork.org/lp_and_r_reports/

Pfau-Effinger, L., Flaquer, L. and Jensen, P. (eds) (2009) *Formal and Informal Work: The Hidden Work Regime in Europe*, New York, NY: Routledge.

Rodríguez, C. (2010) 'La organización del cuidado de niños y niñas en la Argentina y el Uruguay' [The organization of children's care in Argentina and Uruguay) in *El cuidado en acción: Entre el derecho y el trabajo* (Cuadernos de la CEPAL Nº 94 (LC/G.2454-P) [Care in action: Between right and work], Santiago de Chile: Comisión Económica para América Latina y el Caribe (CEPAL).

Sánchez-Castañeda, A. (2012) *La seguridad y la protección social en México: su necesaria reorganización* [Security and social protection in Mexico: its necessary reorganization], Mexico: UNAM, Instituto de Investigaciones Jurídicas.

SEGOB (Secretaría de Gobernación) (2013) *Reforma laboral, derecho del trabajo y justicia social en Mexico* [Labor reform, right to work and social justice in Mexico], Mexico: SEGOB.

UNESCO (2010) *Atención y educación de la primera infancia en América Latina* [Early childhood care and education in Latin America], Santiago de Chile: UNESCO-Oficina para América Latina y el Caribe.

NINE

United States: leave policy, failure and potential

Gayle Kaufman

Introduction

The United States (US) stands out as the only country highlighted in this book, and one among very few countries in the world, that does not offer a statutory entitlement to paid Maternity Leave (ILO, 2014). Such leave as exists to care for newborn or recently adopted children is most commonly labelled 'Family Leave', and covers caring for family members (for example, child, spouse, parent) who are ill, as well as newborns; the US may be exceptional in combining these two types of leave into one measure. Furthermore, this leave at the national and state level refers to individual employees rather than mothers or fathers; hence, there is little or no reference to 'Maternity' or 'Paternity' Leave.

According to the Bureau of Labor Statistics (2013), 85 per cent of all American workers had access to unpaid Family Leave, mainly through the Family and Medical Leave Act (FMLA). However, the same report shows that only 12 per cent of workers had access to *paid* Family Leave, mainly through employer policies; this has increased slightly in the last few years, but as of 2016, only 14 per cent of civilian workers in the US had access to paid Family Leave (Desilver, 2017). The same is true when it comes to paid Maternity Leave. According to a recent survey of a national sample of working mothers, only 41 per cent received paid leave, and the average amount of paid leave was just 3.3 weeks at 31 per cent of wages (Shepherd-Banigan and Bell, 2014). How can this be? Why is there no paid leave at the national level? What has happened at the state and local level? Have employers stepped in to fill the need for paid leave? Will we ever see the US adopt paid Parental Leave?

This chapter attempts to address these questions. It focuses on leave policy in the US, namely the absence of paid statutory leave for parents at the national level and efforts to fill the gap at the state and local levels. While there is no federal paid Maternity, Paternity or Parental

Leave, six states (of 50) have passed legislation for paid Parental Leave, and others have used short-term disability leave to offer paid Maternity Leave. This is a distinct feature of the US as many policies that are not supported at the federal level are left to be determined by individual states. Increasingly, too, private employers are creating and expanding paid leave policies, though these tend to benefit more professional workers (National Partnership for Women & Families, 2017). It seems progress is being made at lower levels of government, but the current climate suggests limited hope for a national policy in the near future.

Before reviewing the development of leave policies for parents in the US, it may be useful to provide an overview of relevant terminology. The first distinction is between paid and unpaid leave. There is no paid leave at the federal level, but some states and employers provide a percentage of employees' wages or salary. Those who are eligible for unpaid leave may be able to use vacation or sick days, if available from their employer, to cover their pay. The second distinction is between Maternity, Paternity and Parental Leave. Maternity refers to leave for mothers, Paternity to leave for fathers, and Parental to leave for parents. Some states and employers make distinctions between Maternity and Paternity Leave, but most policies refer to Parental or Family Leave, the latter including leave to care for a newly born or adopted child and to provide care for sick family members. The following sections focus on leave policies at the national level, state level and city and employer level. The final section discusses possibilities for policy moving forward.

The absence of statutory paid Parental Leave at the national level

The only federal policy that addresses Parental Leave is the Family and Medical Leave Act (FMLA), which was passed in 1993 under President Bill Clinton. There was much resistance, with FMLA being introduced in Congress each year between 1984 and 1993, finally passing in 1991 and 1992 only to be vetoed by President (H.W.) Bush. Much of the opposition to FMLA focused on the potential damage to businesses and employers. On the other hand, much of the motivation for introducing Family Leave centred on women's increasing participation in the labour force. In particular, legislators noted the need to respond to the dramatic rise in employment among mothers of young children and the growing need for dual earner households, as well as the surge in single parent families. Arguments in favour of FMLA raised the potential benefits to businesses, including lower turnover rates and increased productivity. Interestingly, some representatives also noted that the US was out of touch with the rest of the world on this issue. Notably, however, there was very limited discussion of fathers at this time (Karr, 2017).

The final version signed by President Clinton in January 1993 and in effect since August 1993 allows up to 12 weeks of unpaid leave for eligible employees. FMLA, as its name suggests, covers family and medical reasons for leave. Medical leave includes time off to care for oneself or for a family member (spouse, child, parent) who is experiencing a serious medical condition; it may be useful to note upfront that a majority of those who use FMLA do so for their own illness (Klerman et al, 2014). Family Leave also includes time off for pregnancy, adoption or foster placement and care of newborn or newly adopted children.

FMLA leave is an individual right of each eligible employee. To be eligible, an employee has to work for an eligible worksite, which includes only firms that have at least 50 employees. Even if an employee works for an eligible employer, they must have worked for the same employer for at least one year and must have worked at least 1,250 hours during the previous year. Leave is job-protected, which means that the employer must allow the employee to return to their original job or an equivalent job (as determined by pay, benefits and other conditions) and must continue health insurance coverage for the employee while on leave. Those working for small businesses, particularly businesses with fewer than ten employees, and those working in service and retail comprise many of those not covered by FMLA (US Department of Labor, 2000).

Some states have extended the number of weeks covered by FMLA, lowered the requirement that employers have at least 50 employees, or broadened temporary disability insurance (TDI), which attracts benefit payments, to include pregnancy and childbirth. Most states do not provide these benefits, and therefore there is no paid leave for many new parents, including mothers who are recovering from childbirth. Under the Pregnancy Discrimination Act of 1978, employers with 15 or more employees cannot discriminate against an employee based on current pregnancy, past pregnancy, potential pregnancy, or medical conditions related to pregnancy or childbirth. It also requires employers to treat pregnant employees the same as they would treat other temporarily disabled employees. This may involve paid leave but that is not required.

In order to assess the effectiveness of FMLA, the Department of Labor commissioned surveys in 1995, 2000 and 2012. In the most recent survey, only 17 per cent of worksites report that the policy applies to them and another 30 per cent are unsure if FMLA applies. Meanwhile, Klerman, Daly and Pozniak (2014) have estimated that only 10 per cent of worksites meet eligibility requirements. In considering employee eligibility, only 59 per cent of employees meet all requirements, that is, worked full-time or for at least 1,250 hours over the preceding 12 months at a worksite with 50 or more employees continuously for the past year. Awareness of FMLA increased from 56 per cent in 1995 to 66 per cent in 2012, with the most common way of learning about the legislation coming from a poster or Human Resources. Based on analysis of the Current Population Survey in 2011–2014, only 38 per cent of working adults who are eligible for FMLA can afford unpaid leave. This varies from 28.6 per cent in Idaho to 44.7 per cent in Virginia (Institute for Child, Youth and Family Policy, 2015). The bottom line is that few workplaces are covered under FMLA, 41 per cent of employees are not eligible for FMLA, and even fewer workers feel they can afford to take unpaid leave.

Taking some form of Family and Medical Leave is fairly common among American workers; each year, 13 per cent of *all employees in the country* take leave for a new child, their own illness, or to care for a sick family member. Extended over several years, the proportion of all workers taking some form of leave is likely to be sizeable. However, there is a notable difference in leave-taking by eligibility, with 16 per cent of those who are eligible for FMLA taking leave compared to 10 per cent of those not eligible for FMLA. It is also important to note that only a minority of leave taken is to care for a new child – only 21 per cent of leave takers fall into this category. On the other hand, a slight majority of leave takers (55 per cent) take leave for their own illness and 18 per cent take leave to care for a parent, spouse or child. Close to half of employees (48 per cent) receive pay while on leave, mainly through paid sick leave, vacation leave and personal leave, while 17 per cent receive partial pay and 34 per cent receive no pay; these statistics are not broken down by reason for leave, so paid leave taken to care for a new child cannot be isolated. Not surprisingly, low-income workers and those taking longer leave are less likely to receive pay, and the second most common reason for returning to work, after no longer needing leave, is the inability to afford leave (reported by 40 per cent of employees who take leave). On the other hand, most employers seem to have a positive or neutral view toward FMLA; a large majority (85 per cent) report that it is easy to comply with FMLA, and only a very small number (2–3 per cent) report confirmed or suspected misuse of FMLA.

Studies of FMLA show benefits for women's employment and children's health. For example, Hofferth and Curtin (2006) find that following FMLA, women's post-birth employment and job retention increased. Examining the impact of FMLA on birth outcomes, Rossin (2011) finds a connection between Maternity Leave and higher birth weight and reduced risk of premature birth as well as lower infant mortality, particularly among college-educated, married mothers. Nevertheless, returning to work within 12 weeks (the maximum period of FMLA) may reduce important health behaviours such as breastfeeding and immunisations (Berger et al, 2005).

There have been recent attempts to pass paid Parental Leave at the national level, most notably in the form of the proposed FAMILY (Family and Medical Insurance Leave) Act, but they have failed thus far. In 2013, Democrat Senator Kirsten Gillibrand and Democrat Representative Rosa DeLauro first introduced the FAMILY Act. When they reintroduced the bill in 2015, it was referred to the Committee on Finance in the Senate and moved to the Subcommittee on Social Security in the House. Most recently, on 7 February 2017 Senator Gillibrand reintroduced the FAMILY Act to the 115th Congress (Zillman, 2017). The FAMILY Act would provide up to 12 weeks of paid leave for the birth or adoption of a new child, to care for a sick child, partner or parent, or to care for oneself. Workers on leave would receive 66 per cent of their wages, up to a maximum of US$4,000 per month. Funding for the programme would come from a small tax of 0.2 per cent of earnings collected from employers and employees (Farrell and Glynn, 2013). The main difference between the existing FMLA and the proposed FAMILY Act is that the latter would provide *paid* leave; eligibility and amount of time (12 weeks) are the same. At the time of writing (January 2018), the FAMILY Act has been referred to the House Committee on Finance.

State level policies

Six states have passed laws establishing paid leave programmes, and four are currently in effect. The US seems to be exceptional in having such stark differences in policy between states. As Lipset (1997) argued, the historical absence of a monarchy and the prominence of individualism in its creation means that Americans are less deferential to government. Many believe that politicians, especially those at the national level, cannot know what is best for them. These are the same arguments that have been made around issues as diverse as education, abortion and same-sex marriage. Passing paid leave at the state level has not been easy, but there have been stronger local actors involved. The policies passed in California, New Jersey, Rhode Island and New York are highlighted below and overleaf (see also Table 9.1 for a summary of the main features of paid leave in these states).

California

California was the first state to introduce paid Family Leave, with the passage of Paid Family Leave (PFL) in 2002. As with FMLA, this policy covers care for newborn and newly adopted/fostered children, called bonding claims. Like FMLA, it also covers care for a spouse, child or parent with a serious medical condition, called caring claims. Unlike FMLA, it included registered domestic partners from the start and added siblings, parents-in-law, grandparents and grandchildren in 2014 as eligible family members for care. This programme offers up to six weeks of leave paid at approximately 55 per cent of earnings up to US$1,216 per week (as of 1 January 2018) and is based on State Disability Insurance (SDI). Individual employees have rights to paid Family Leave so that both mothers and fathers can take six weeks of paid leave.

Efforts to legislate for paid Family Leave began in the late 1990s, when Democrat State Senator Hilda Solis introduced a bill that required the Employment Development Department (EDD) to conduct a study on the costs of expanding SDI benefits to individuals on Family Leave. When the study was released in 2000, it showed that Family Leave could be covered under SDI for as little as 0.1 per cent increase in the state payroll tax. Democrat State Senator Sheila Kuehl introduced Senate Bill 1661 in February 2002. It originally included 12 weeks of paid leave (parallel to the amount of unpaid time offered by FMLA) and cost-sharing between employees and employers.

While the bill garnered large support among Democrats and work–family organisations, business groups lobbied against it. After negotiations, the bill reduced paid leave to six weeks, deleted the employer contribution, and allowed a requirement that employees use up their vacation time (up to two weeks) before obtaining state benefits. Once these changes were made, the bill was approved quickly in September 2002 and went into effect on 1 January 2004. In 2016, the law was amended to increase benefits and eliminate the seven-day waiting period. Workers whose earnings are close to the minimum wage are eligible for 70 per cent of their earnings, while those with higher wages are eligible for 60 per cent.

The evidence so far suggests that California's Paid Family Leave programme has been successful in increasing parents' use of leave while having minimal impact on employers. Between 2004 and 2009, the number of claims per 100 live births increased from 24 to 30 (Zigler et al, 2012). The percent of 'bonding claims' filed (that is, including new children via birth, adoption or fostering) has remained high at 88 per cent, with the remaining 12 per cent being 'caring claims' (Employment Development Department, 2016). Another hopeful sign is that the percent of male bonding claims has risen from 23 per cent in 2007 and 2008 to 35.5 per cent in 2015 and 2016 (Employment Development Department). In a quasi-experimental study of the programme, Bartel et al (2015) find that Paid Family Leave increases fathers' leave-taking by 50 per cent for leave alone (while the mother is at work) and by 28 per cent for concurrent leave (at the same time as the mother).

Nevertheless, there remains a gap in how much leave men and women take; while men take a median of three weeks bonding leave, women take a median of 12 weeks (Appelbaum and Milkman, 2011). While there are limited studies thus far, Bartel et al (2014) conclude that PFL has had a positive impact on children and families through increased breastfeeding and time with children. In terms of employer effects, Appelbaum and Milkman's (2011; 2013) research suggests that employers are quite satisfied, with approximately 90 per cent of the 250 California firms in their study saying that the law has had a positive effect or no effect on outcomes such as productivity and morale.

California's Paid Family Leave programme still lacks job protection. Those who are covered by FMLA and PFL can take paid leave under PFL and have their job protected under FMLA; but though workers who are not eligible for FMLA may be able to take paid leave under PFL, they have no guarantee that their job will be available upon their return. Employers are also not obligated to tell employees that there is no job protection.

New Jersey

New Jersey Family Temporary Disability Leave law (commonly known as Paid Family Leave) went into effect in 2009, five years after California's PFL. Similar to California, the jobs of employees who take leave but are not covered by FMLA are not protected.

The number of Paid Family Leave claims increased from 14,127 in 2009 to 29,456 in 2012. Bonding claims make up 82 per cent of claims with the other 18 per cent being family care claims. Unlike in California, there has been no notable increase in men's bonding claims with men representing 12 per cent of bonding claims in 2009 and 2012 (Lerner and Appelbaum, 2014). There is limited research on this state policy, but an early study showed positive views of the programme but limited awareness (White et al, 2013). Lerner and Appelbaum (2014) interviewed 18 employers across the state to look at the impact of Paid Family Leave. Most employers in their study reported no or minimal effects. Some reported an improvement in morale, but almost all reported no change in productivity, profitability or turnover.

Rhode Island

Rhode Island passed legislation called Temporary Caregiver Insurance (TCI) in July 2013, and the policy went into effect on 1 January 2014, five years after New Jersey and ten years after California. As with these states, Rhode Island's law builds on its Temporary Disability Insurance programme. With a payroll tax just above 1 per cent, workers are able to take up to four weeks of leave at 60 per cent wage replacement, with benefits set at a minimum of US$89 and a maximum of US$831 per week. Unlike the policies in California and New Jersey, Rhode Island's policy provides job protection similar to FMLA.

An early study shows that many workers have benefited from TCI, but awareness remains an issue; only about half of workers are aware of the benefit, with lower awareness among Hispanics and low-income workers. Women make up the majority of TCI leave takers (84 per cent compared to 16 per cent of men), and are more likely to use the full allocation of time, four weeks (92 per cent compared to 68 per cent). TCI users seem to benefit in a number of ways; they are more likely to report an increase in income and fewer work absences as well as longer breastfeeding and more 'well-baby visits' (that is, regular medical check-ups) (Silver et al, 2016).

New York

The official website of the state of New York states that it has 'the nation's strongest and most comprehensive Paid Family Leave policy'.[1] The policy was passed in 2016 and began on 1 January 2018. It will be phased in over three years so that workers are provided eight weeks of leave at 50 per cent pay in 2018, ten weeks of leave at 55 per cent pay in 2019, ten weeks of leave at 60 per cent pay in 2020, and 12 weeks of leave at 67 per cent pay from 2021. Maximum pay is based on a percentage of the state average weekly wage, which is currently US$1,306. While employers cannot require employees to

---

[1] www.ny.gov/programs/new-york-state-paid-family-leave

use vacation or sick leave (as in California), they may allow employees to use this leave in combination with Family Leave to achieve their full earnings. Like the other states, New York funds this programme with an employee payroll deduction. Like Rhode Island, New York's policy provides job-protected leave. It is more generous than existing policies in a couple of ways: first, it will provide the longest leave when fully implemented in 2021; second, it covers part-time workers and workers regardless of citizenship or immigration status.

Other states

In 2007, Washington State passed the Family Leave Act, which parallels the FMLA in providing 12 weeks of job-protected leave. It would have provided paid leave, but it never went into effect. However, the state recently passed Paid Family Leave, which will go into effect in 2020. In 2018, Massachusetts passed Family and Medical Leave, which will go into effect in 2021.

Several states are considering Family Leave legislation. Arizona introduced a measure in May 2016 that mandates a report with a cost analysis for a Family Leave programme by July 2020. Other states, including Arkansas, Colorado, Connecticut, Florida, Nebraska, New Mexico, Virginia and Wisconsin, have introduced bills that have failed, died, been tabled or been indefinitely postponed. The policies have mainly been introduced by Democrats.

To summarise, of the 50 US states, four currently have a paid Family Leave policy in effect (California, New Jersey, New York, Rhode Island) (see Table 9.1), and two have passed legislation on paid leave that will go into effect in 2020 and 2021 (Washington and Massachusetts). All of these states are considered politically liberal with higher proportions of Democrats than Republicans. As of January 2018, 21.4 per cent of the US population live in a state with paid leave.

Beyond the national and state levels

City level policies

Cities such as Pittsburgh and Austin provide paid Parental Leave to city employees (Lemire, 2015). In January 2016, New York City Mayor Bill de Blasio signed a personnel order that provides paid leave for maternity, paternity, adoption or foster care to those who work for the city, numbering around 20,000 employees. The order provides six weeks of leave at 100 per cent salary, and this can be extended

Table 9.1: Summary of state-level policies in the United States

	Year passed/ in effect	Length of leave	Level of pay	Maximum pay per week	Job protection
California	2002/2004	6 weeks	60–70%	$1,216	No
New Jersey	2008/2009	6 weeks	66%	$637	No
Rhode Island	2013/2014	4 weeks	60%	$831	Yes
New York	2016/2018	8 weeks	50%	$653	Yes

Note: When fully implemented in 2021, New York state will provide 12 weeks at 67% pay

to 12 weeks if combined with existing leave. The policy was funded by cancelling a planned managerial pay rise and capping vacation at 25 days (NYC Government, 2016).

The city of San Francisco recently introduced paid leave for all new parents, which went into effect on 1 January 2017. This policy goes beyond California's PFL by offering 100 per cent of earnings for six weeks; while the state policy provides 55 per cent of earnings, the city policy requires employers to pay the remaining 45 per cent. This policy gradually applies to more and more workplaces, starting with companies that employ 50 or more workers; but from 1 July 2017 it has applied to companies with 35 or more employees, and from 1 January 2018 to companies with 20 or more employees. A report from the city controller showed that the policy would increase parents' income while on leave from an average of US$743 per week to US$1,351 per week; moreover, as the upper limit for total benefits from the state and employer is US$2,133, this means that those who earn under approximately $111,000 per year would receive full pay for the six weeks of leave (Green, 2017). Under San Francisco's law, a national company with a branch in San Francisco must provide the remaining amount to cover full pay, regardless of its policy at headquarters or other branches.

The District of Columbia (Washington, DC) is the most recent to pass legislation with the Universal Paid Leave Amendment Act in April 2017, to be effective in July 2020. The policy will provide eight weeks of paid leave for the birth, adoption or fostering of a new child, as well as six weeks to care for a sick family member. All full-time and part-time private sector workers who are employed in Washington, DC are eligible, regardless of residence, as long as they spend at least 50 per cent of their work time in the District of Columbia. Benefits will be determined differently depending on earnings (O'Connor, 2016). Unlike previous policies, a business tax will fund this leave policy.

Like the states that have passed paid Family Leave laws, the cities that have followed suit are left-leaning, with Democratic mayors.

Company policies

In the last few years, several companies have introduced or expanded their Family Leave policies. Video streaming company Netflix received considerable attention in August 2015 when it introduced 'unlimited' paid leave for salaried employees during the first year after their child's birth or adoption; they later revised the policy to include more employees for shorter periods of time. Other companies that offer paid Parental Leave include Spotify (six months), Etsy (26 weeks), Twitter (20 weeks), Facebook (4 months), Bank of America (16 weeks) and Ernst & Young (16 weeks), all of which offer 100 per cent pay during leave.

Many others make a distinction between Maternity and Paternity Leave or Maternity and Parental Leave. Companies such as Accenture, Amazon, Coca-Cola, eBay, Fidelity Investments, The Honest Company, Johnson & Johnson, Microsoft, PayPal, and Zillow offer about twice as much Maternity Leave as Parental Leave. Hilton Worldwide and Land O'Lakes offer ten weeks of Maternity Leave for birth mothers and two weeks of Parental and adoption Leave for other parents. Campbell Soup Company, JPMorgan Chase, M & T Bank and Wells Fargo distinguish between primary caregiver leave and secondary caregiver leave, offering between ten and 16 weeks of paid leave to the primary caregiver and two to four weeks to the secondary caregiver. Some only offer Maternity Leave, such as Blackstone Group, Nestle, Vodafone and Western Union (National Partnership for Women & Families, 2017).

Access to paid leave varies considerably by industry, with 37 per cent of finance and insurance workers and 33 per cent of information workers having access to paid leave compared to only 5 per cent of construction workers and 6 per cent of leisure and hospitality workers. Those working for larger companies are also more likely to have access to paid leave, 23 per cent of those working for companies with 500 or more employees versus 9 per cent of those working for companies with fewer than 100 employees (Desilver, 2017). Overall, access to paid leave reflects the great inequality in the American labour force and society more generally, with more educated workers and those with higher incomes also having better leave benefits.

The politics of stalemate

The National Partnership for Women & Families (2016) finds that 78 per cent of voters support having a national law to establish paid Family and Medical Leave. While support is greatest among Democrats (93 per cent), a majority (66 per cent) of Republicans and Independents (77 per cent) also favour a paid leave policy. Much of this support may be due to the possibility of financial strain if there is a need for leave; the same study finds that 71 per cent of voters indicate that time off to care for a new child or an ill family member would likely create financial hardship. The Pew Research Center conducted a more extensive survey following the last Presidential election, from mid-November to early December 2016. They also find majority support for paid Family and Medical Leave. However, support varies based on the reason for leave, with 85 per cent supporting paid leave for workers who have a serious health condition and 67 per cent supporting paid leave for workers to care for an ill family member. There is more support for new mothers than fathers (82 per cent versus 69 per cent) to take such leave (Horowitz et al, 2017).

Since it is clear that most people on both sides of the political spectrum support paid leave, why has the US not been able to pass this measure at the national level? One reason may be the low relative importance placed on paid leave. A Pew survey conducted in early January 2017 finds that paid leave is a top priority for only 35 per cent of adults, lower than 20 other issues, including terrorism, economy, education, jobs and healthcare costs (Horowitz et al, 2017). It may be that Americans do not see how paid Maternity or Parental Leave fits into larger issues of employment protection, maternal and child health, and long-term stability for families.

Another reason may be disagreement about how paid leave should be implemented. For example, among those who support paid leave for new mothers and fathers, about three-quarters say that pay should come from employers rather than federal or state government. However, only half of adults surveyed think the federal government should require employers to provide paid leave, while the other half think employers should be able to decide for themselves (Horowitz et al, 2017).

A third reason may be perceptions about the impact of a paid leave policy on businesses. While an overwhelming majority of Americans (94 per cent) thinks that access to paid leave would have a very positive or somewhat positive impact on families, 57 per cent think that it would have a somewhat negative or very negative impact on small businesses and attitudes are split on the impact on employers more generally (Horowitz et al, 2017). We might ask why Americans care so much about small businesses. The historical absence of a feudal system or monarchy has meant that class divisions are less visible.

Furthermore, Americans tend to believe in the idea of meritocracy and the possibility that they will improve their own class position. In other words, a lower-class American might see themselves as a future small business owner (Lipset, 1997).

This is related to a fourth reason, which is the particularly strong emphasis on individualism in the US. As Brad Harrington, executive director of the Boston College Center for Work & Family, states: 'People would prefer to try to keep taxes low, let individuals be responsible for their own care, and that's sort of become the accepted value system in the US' (Peltz, 2016). While many parents struggle to balance work and family, most do not necessarily see it as a government issue but rather an individual or couple problem that they themselves need to solve (Kaufman, 2013).

Finally, Republican legislators do not favour programmes that help working mothers or families, and do not seem to care that the US is an outlier on this and other issues. With Republicans in control for the moment in both the House and Senate, it seems unlikely that paid Parental Leave will be passed any time soon. While most Americans are in favour of such a policy, Republicans tend to respond more to the desires of business owners.

Where do we go from here?

During the 2016 Presidential campaign, paid leave finally became an issue. Democratic candidate Hillary Clinton proposed a paid Family and Medical Leave policy that would provide 12 weeks of leave to new parents and to those caring for ill family members. Paid at two-thirds of wages, this proposal was basically the same as the FAMILY Act. Meanwhile, Republican candidate Donald Trump's proposal, prompted by his daughter Ivanka, included only married mothers. Since the election, and possibly based on a backlash for his exclusion of fathers, single mothers and adoptive parents, Trump revised his proposal. In his proposed budget, Trump includes six weeks of paid Parental Leave, which would be open to birth and adoptive mothers and fathers. However, a major weakness of this proposal is that it leaves the details of Parental Leave up to the states. Because it would be based on state-level unemployment insurance programmes, benefit levels would vary tremendously. Unemployment insurance benefits tend to be lower than average earnings and are currently less than one-third of average wages in 22 states (Frothingham and West, 2017). At these rates, many, if not most, new parents would be unable to afford to take Parental Leave.

The good news is that changes in federal social policies related to education, health and families often occur at the state level first. If we consider marriage equality, this is an example of a very quickly changing policy. In 2005, same-sex marriage was only legal in Massachusetts. By 2009, Connecticut, Iowa, New Hampshire and Vermont legalised same-sex marriage. New York, Maine, Maryland and Washington joined this group by 2012. By the time the Supreme Court ruled in favour of same-sex couples in *Obergefell v. Hodges* in June 2015, only 13 states still had same-sex marriage bans. Paid Parental Leave is unlikely to move so swiftly, but the increasing attention to this topic and the developments occurring at company and state levels indicate some progress and hope for a national policy in the future. The abundance of evidence suggests that paid leave is good for workers, families and businesses. Let's make it happen!

References

Appelbaum, E. and Milkman, R. (2011) *Leaves that Pay: Employer and worker experiences with Paid Family Leave in California,* Washington, DC: Center for Economic and Policy Research.

Appelbaum, E. and Milkman, R. (2013) *Unfinished Business: Paid Family Leave in California and the Future of US work–family Policy*, Ithaca, NY: ILR Press.

Bartel, A., Baum, C., Rossin-Slater, M., Ruhm, C. and Waldfogel, J. (2014) *California's Paid Family Leave law: Lessons from the First Decade. Report Prepared for the US Department of Labor.* Available at www.dol.gov/wb/resources/california_paid_family_leave_law.pdf

Bartel, A., Rossin-Slater, M., Ruhm, C., Stearns, J. and Waldfogel, J. (2015) *Paid Family Leave, Fathers' Leave-Taking, and Leave-Sharing in Dual-Earner Households. Report Prepared for the US Department of Labor.* Available at www.dol.gov/asp/evaluation/completed-studies/Paid_Family_Leave_Fathers_Leave_Taking_and_Leave_Sharing_in_Dual_Earner_Households.pdf

Berger, L.M., Hill, J. and Waldfogel, J. (2005) 'Maternity leave, early maternal employment and child health and development in the US', *The Economic Journal*, 115(501): 29–47.

Bureau of Labor Statistics (2013) *Employee Benefits Survey.* Available at www.bls.gov/ncs/ebs/benefits/2013/ownership/private/table21a.htm

Desilver, D. (2017) *Access to Paid Family Leave Varies Widely Across Employers, Industries*, Washington, DC: Pew Research Center, 23 March. Available at www.pewresearch.org/fact-tank/2017/03/23/access-to-paid-family-leave-varies-widely-across-employers-industries/

Employment Development Department, State of California (2016) *Disability Insurance (DI) and Paid Family Leave (PFL) Weekly Benefit Amounts*. Available at www.edd.ca.gov/Disability/pdf/qspfl_PFL_Program_Statistics.pdf

Farrell, J. and Glynn, S.J. (2013) *The FAMILY Act: Facts and Frequently Asked Questions*, Washington, DC: Center for American Progress. Available at www.americanprogress.org/issues/economy/reports/2013/12/12/81037/the-family-act-facts-and-frequently-asked-questions/

Frothingham, S. and West, R. (2017) *Trump's Paid Parental Leave Plan Won't Work for Women and Families*, Washington, DC: Center for American Progress. Available at www.americanprogress.org/issues/women/reports/2017/06/08/433895/trumps-paid-parental-leave-plan-wont-work-women-families/

Green, E. (2017) 'Historic SF parental leave law kicks in', *SF Gate*, 3 January. Available at www.sfgate.com/politics/article/Historic-SF-parental-leave-law-kicks-in-10831209.php

Hofferth, S.L. and Curtin, S.C. (2006) 'Parental leave statutes and maternal return to work after childbirth in the United States', *Work and Occupations*, 33(1): 73–105.

Horowitz, J.M., Parker, K., Graf, N. and Livingston, G. (2017) *Americans Widely Support Paid Family and Medical Leave, But Differ over Specific Policies*, Washington, DC: Pew Research Center, 23 March. Available at www.pewsocialtrends.org/2017/03/23/americans-widely-support-paid-family-and-medical-leave-but-differ-over-specific-policies/

ILO (International Labour Organization) (2014) *Maternity and Paternity at Work: Law and Practice Across the World*. Available at www.ilo.org/wcmsp5/groups/public/---dgreports/---dcomm/documents/publication/wcms_242617.pdf

Institute for Child, Youth and Family Policy (2015) *Working Adults Who are Eligible For and Can Afford FMLA Unpaid Leave*. Available at www.diversitydatakids.org/data/ranking/529/working-adults-who-are-eligible-for-and-can-afford-fmla-unpaid-leave-share/#loct=2&tf=17

Karr, J.E. (2017) 'Where's my dad? A feminist approach to incentivized paternity leave', *Hastings Women's Law Journal*, 28(2): 225–263.

Kaufman, G. (2013) *Superdads: How Fathers Balance Work and Family in the 21st Century*, New York, NY: New York University Press.

Klerman, J.A., Daly, K. and Pozniak, A. (2014) *Family and Medical Leave in 2012: Technical Report. Prepared for the US Department of Labor*, Cambridge, MA: Abt Associates Inc. Available at www.dol.gov/asp/evaluation/fmla/FMLA-2012-Technical-Report.pdf

Lemire, J. (2015) 'Paid parental leave programs starting to expand in US cities', *CNS news*, 25 December. Available at www.cnsnews.com/news/article/paid-parental-leave-programs-starting-expand-us-cities

Lerner, S. and Appelbaum, E. (2014) *Business as Usual: New Jersey Employers' Experiences with Family Leave Insurance*, Washington, DC: Center for Economic and Policy Research. Available at http://cepr.net/documents/nj-fli-2014-06.pdf

Lipset, S.M. (1997) *American Exceptionalism: A Double-Edged Sword.* New York, NY: W. W. Norton and Company.

National Partnership for Women and Families (2016) *Key Findings: 2016 Election Eve/Election Night Survey*. Available at www.nationalpartnership.org/research-library/work-family/key-findings-2016-election-eve-election-night-survey.pdf

National Partnership for Women & Families (2017) *New and Expanded Employer Paid Family Leave Policies (2015–2017)*. Available at www.nationalpartnership.org/research-library/work-family/paid-leave/new-and-expanded-employer-paid-family-leave-policies.pdf

NYC Government (2016) 'Mayor de Blasio signs paid parental leave personnel order for NYC workers. January 7'. Available at www1.nyc.gov/office-of-the-mayor/news/025-16/mayor-de-blasio-signs-paid-parental-leave-personnel-order-nyc-workers#/0

O'Connell, M. (2015) 'Obama authorizes up to six weeks of paid parental leave', *Federal News Radio*, 15 January 2015. Available at https://federalnewsradio.com/pay-benefits/2015/01/obama-authorizes-up-to-six-weeks-of-paid-parental-leave-for-feds/

O'Connor, C. (2016) 'Washington, D.C. passes 8 week paid parental leave bill', *Forbes*, 20 December 2016. Available at www.forbes.com/sites/clareoconnor/2016/12/20/washington-d-c-passes-8-week-paid-parental-leave-bill/#fa7c1966bfa4

Peltz, J.P. (2016) 'Why paid parental leave won't go national', *Los Angeles Times*, 28 April 2016. Available at www.latimes.com/business/la-fi-qa-parental-leave-20160428-story.html

Rossin, M. (2011) 'The effects of maternity leave on children's birth and infant health outcomes in the United States', *Journal of Health Economics*, 30(2): 221–239.

Shepherd-Banigan, M. and Bell, J.F. (2014) 'Paid leave benefits among a national sample of working mothers with infants in the United States', *Maternal and Child Health Journal*, 18(1): 286–295.

Silver, B.E., Mederer, H. and Djurdjevic, E. (2016) *Launching the Rhode Island Temporary Caregiver Insurance Program (TCI): Employee Experiences One Year Later. Submitted to the US Department of Labor, Women's Bureau. RI Department of Training and Labor*. Available at www.dlt.ri.gov/tdi/pdf/RIPaidLeaveFinalRpt0416URI.pdf

US Department of Labor (2000) *FMLA Survey*. Available at www.dol.gov/whd/fmla/foreword.htm

White, K., Houser, L. and Nisbet, E. (2013) *Policy in Action: New Jersey's Family Leave Insurance Program at Age Three*, New Brunswick, NJ: Center for Women and Work.

Zigler, E., Muenchow, S. and Ruhm, C.J. (2012) *Time Off with Baby: The Case for Paid Care Leave*, Washington, DC: Zero To Three.

Zillman, C. (2017) 'Kirsten Gillibrand is giving her paid family leave proposal its first Trump-era test', *Fortune*, 7 February. Available at http://fortune.com/2017/02/07/trump-paid-family-leave-gillibrand/

PART II

Some current issues in leave policy

TEN

What do people want?
Leave policy preferences
in different countries[1]

Isabel Valarino

Introduction

Leave policies related to parenting are often studied from a policy development perspective or in relation to their outcomes, such as uptake, fertility, child development, maternal employment or father involvement. This chapter addresses another important, yet under-explored dimension: individual preferences regarding leave policies. This is an important issue since it contributes to the legitimacy of existing social arrangements and can point to possible grounds for reform (Svallfors, 2012).

Leave policies in industrialised countries have developed at different rates, within specific social and economic contexts and political ideologies and following distinct policy objectives (Kamerman and Moss, 2009). Today there is considerable heterogeneity across leave schemes, notably the total duration of paid leave available for parents, including Maternity, Paternity and Parental Leaves, and the extent to which mothers and fathers have individual entitlements and/or are encouraged to share them. Leave schemes vary on further dimensions such as the amount of payment, flexibility or eligibility criteria, as discussed throughout this book, but this chapter focuses on these two aspects specifically. For instance, while in the Nordic countries, such as Sweden and Norway, well-paid leave of about one year for both parents was already implemented in the 1970s, in liberal welfare states, statutory paid leave is available for a relatively shorter duration – or does not yet exist in the extreme case of the US (see Chapter Nine) – and tends to target mothers more than fathers.

[1] Funding for the project on which this chapter draws was provided by the Swiss National Science Foundation (P300P1_171457).

Do these different institutional contexts influence what individuals consider as 'good' leave policies? When it comes to the care of a new-born child, do attitudes vary across countries? How satisfied or dissatisfied are individuals with leave arrangements? This chapter addresses these largely unexplored questions by analysing leave policy preferences in 27 industrialised countries, mostly in Europe (for a full list, see Table 10.1). The first objective is to describe preferences across countries and welfare regimes regarding leave duration and the gender division of leave. The second is to identify, across welfare regimes, the factors associated with individuals' dissatisfaction with the duration of leave currently available in their own country, which includes the development of an indicator for dissatisfaction.

Framework of the study

Welfare attitudes, welfare regimes and leave policies

'Welfare attitudes' refer to individuals' values and preferences regarding the degree and type of state intervention for citizens' social and economic security (Svallfors, 2012). In this chapter, individuals' preferences regarding leave policies are referred to as 'leave policy preferences'. Two specific aspects of the design of leave policies are considered (there are more, as discussed throughout the book): the total duration of paid leave to which parents should be entitled and how it might be shared between mothers and fathers.

In comparative studies, three sets of factors are usually considered as influencing individuals' attitudes to welfare policies (see Blekesaune and Quadagno, 2003; Jaeger, 2006; Svallfors, 2012). First, according to *self-interest theory*, those benefiting from or likely to become recipients of social protection are expected to have more positive attitudes toward the welfare state. Second, *ideational theory* suggests that subjective characteristics such as individuals' values will also influence welfare attitudes. Third, *institutional theory* suggests that individuals' views about justice principles and solidarity are shaped by the welfare state context and reflect the existing degree of state support.

In order to analyse in a comparative framework how welfare states may influence leave policy preferences, the study reported in this chapter draws upon welfare state literature (Esping-Andersen, 1990) and its gender critique (for example, Lewis, 1992; Orloff, 1993). The latter sees public policies as distributing responsibilities for the social care of dependants in distinct ways, as based on different ideologies, and as shaping gender relationships differently. Family policies, among them leave policies, are part of the institutional context that influences the gender division of work and defines norms about good parenting (see also Rostgaard, 2002; Pfau-Effinger, 2005).

Esping-Andersen's (1990) three-fold welfare regime typology is used together with Aidukaite's (2009) conceptualisation of Central and Eastern European countries as forming a 'post-communist' regime. Countries which have not been classified consistently in the literature are considered as 'hybrid' (see Ferragina and Seeleib-Kaiser, 2011). Regimes are used as descriptive and organising tools to make sense of the main patterns of leave policy preferences and to provide an encompassing view of the 27 selected countries. Such a macro-level approach undoubtedly implies reducing complexity and to some extent the variety within each regime.

In *social democratic* regimes, typically found in the Nordic countries, state benefits and services are universal and reliance on the family and the market for the care of dependent family members is limited. These countries were among the first to introduce paid Parental Leave as well as incentives for fathers' uptake through reserved quotas. Parents have access to between nine and 16 months of paid post-natal leave (including Maternity, Paternity and Parental Leaves) (see Table 10.1 for the exact duration in each country). Finland is an exception in this regard as parents may receive a home care allowance up to the child's third year. However well-paid leave – about 70 per cent of earnings – lasted around ten months in 2012.

In *conservative* regimes, found in continental Europe, the family and in particular women have been regarded as the main care providers for dependent family members. The traditional male breadwinner family model has been supported by the state, even if in the last decades some welfare states have departed from this model. As a result, countries grouped in this regime show considerable heterogeneity in their leave schemes. In northern countries paid leave ranges from 12 to 36 months, while southern European welfare states grant shorter paid entitlements. Different types of leave are available for fathers: Paternity Leave as well as individual Parental Leave entitlements in Belgium, France and Portugal; while extra Parental Leave is offered when fathers use leave in Austria, Germany and Portugal.

Liberal welfare regimes are found in Anglophone countries where individual responsibility prevails. Individuals rely mainly on the market, especially for childcare services. Paid leave policies are generally limited (they range from zero to 12 months) and provide above all maternity protection to women. Paternity and Parental Leaves are less widespread and generally there are no father-targeted incentives. The

US is the only industrialised country without any statutory paid leave and Canada stands out with a one-year leave, paid at 55 per cent of earnings.

Finally, Central and Eastern European (CEE) countries represent *post-communist regimes* (Aidukaite, 2009). They have had a comprehensive social insurance system but low benefits due to the economic hardship that followed the end of Communist regimes. While mothers had access to relatively generous family benefits, Parental Leave and childcare services allowing their continued full-time employment, the transition greatly undermined public resources and commitment to these services, pushing care work back onto women (Pascall and Manning, 2000). The (re)emergence of cultural and religious identities after the Communist era also supported the return of the male breadwinner family model. Leave policies range from 12 to 36 months but often entail low or flat-rate benefits, with negative effects for gender equality. Slovenia and Croatia do not quite fit this regime, as they followed a somewhat different post-transition path and have more gender equal policies than other CEE countries (for example, Blum et al, 2014).

Review of the literature on attitudes toward leave

Several comparative studies have analysed attitudes toward family policies such as childcare services, family allowances and leave. In line with the institutional theory previously mentioned, some have found a relationship between the level of state contribution to such policies and individuals' support for them. For instance, individuals were found most supportive of childcare services in regimes with the most developed service systems (Mischke, 2014; Dobrotić and Vučković Juroš, 2016; Chung and Meuleman, 2017). Analysing attitudes toward duration, gender division and funding source in four countries, another study found that preferences largely reflected existing leave schemes (Valarino et al, 2018).

Further results point to some inconsistencies, however. For instance, Valarino et al (2018) found that in liberal Switzerland and the USA – countries with limited or no statutory paid leave respectively – many respondents nevertheless expected longer entitlements. A study on attitudes towards childcare services in 14 European countries showed that preferences for state responsibility in this field were among the highest in southern European countries, where state services are typically limited (Mischke, 2014). Finally, one of the rare comparative studies that has analysed attitudes towards leave policies found no clear regime influence in the ten countries studied, and 'a weak correlation between the actual duration of Parental Leave in different countries and people's evaluation of its sufficiency'; the authors concluded that 'Europeans on the whole want to have an option of Parental Leave lasting 2–3 years' (Stropnik et al, 2008, p.410). To sum up, the question of whether there is an influence from existing leave schemes and welfare regimes on leave policy preferences remains open.

According to welfare attitudinal theories, not only institutional but also individual factors will influence individuals' preferences on family and leave policies. Indeed, several studies have found that self-interest variables exert a significant influence on attitudes (for example, Stropnik et al, 2008; Mischke, 2014; Valarino et al, 2018; Chung and Meuleman, 2017; Dobrotić and Vučković Juroš, 2016). Women, younger cohorts and parents are generally found to be more supportive of family policy measures. The influence of education is not consistent and results suggest the significance and direction of relationships are context specific (see Stropnik et al, 2008; Mischke, 2014; Chung and Meuleman, 2017; Dobrotić and Vučković Juroš, 2016).

Finally, studies also confirm that ideational variables should be taken into account when analysing attitudes toward family policies. Thus, individuals who are non-religious and who support solidarity and gender equality have overall more positive attitudes toward childcare services and leave policies (for example, Stropnik et al, 2008; Mischke, 2014; Valarino et al, 2018; Chung and Meuleman, 2017; Dobrotić and Vučković Juroš, 2016).

Analytic approach and hypotheses

In order to address some of the gaps in the literature as identified in the previous section, leave duration preferences have been explored through central tendency measures; that is, country aggregate means and medians for 27 countries. Contrary to Stropnik et al (2008), but in line with Valarino et al (2018), it was hypothesised that following 'institutional theory' as previously discussed, preferences will be correlated with existing country leave durations and that distinct leave duration preferences will be identifiable across regimes. To further explore whether there is consensus within countries, the proportion of individuals who agree on an ideal leave duration has been analysed; consensus was hypothesised to be highest in welfare regimes where state support for balancing work–family, including leave, have been implemented for the longest period of time, that is social democratic and post-communist regimes.

In order to explore the legitimacy of leave policy across countries, the study develops two indicators of dissatisfaction. The first is the percentage of respondents who consider that there should be no paid leave at all; according to institutional theory, leave should be most rejected in liberal regimes where it is least institutionalised. The second indicator is whether individuals' preferred leave duration exceeds the existing leave policy in their country or not. Given the scarcity and inconclusiveness of previous research (Stropnik et al, 2008; Valarino et al, 2018), there is no strong hypothesis regarding whether there will be more dissatisfied individuals in 'short-leave' (for example, liberal regimes) or in 'long-leave' (that is, social democratic and post-communist regimes) countries.

Apart from cross-national and welfare regime differences, the study sought to identify correlates of leave duration dissatisfaction at the individual level. The expectation was that those more likely to face work–family challenges (that is, women, the young, parents) would be dissatisfied with current leave and want a longer entitlement. However, since there are stark regime differences in the leave schemes, it is possible that such relationships will vary by welfare regime.

Finally, the study addresses gender differences in leave preferences. Following up on previous research (Valarino et al, 2018), it was expected that welfare state contexts would influence what individuals consider an appropriate use of leave by mothers and fathers. Consequently, gender egalitarian social democratic regimes were expected to have the highest proportion of individuals wanting a gender equal division of leave, while preferences might favour a more gendered use of leave in conservative and post-communist regimes.

Data and methods

The data come from the 2012 module *Family and changing gender roles IV* in the International Social Survey Programme (ISSP Research Group, 2016). The 27 countries included are the ones for which data were available in the ISSP and that were also represented in the data source used for legislative details on leave policies (Moss, 2012/2013/2014); these details refer to 2012, 2013 or 2014, depending on which year the data collection for the ISSP survey was conducted in each country. The ISSP data are representative for the population aged 18 years and over, except in Finland, Iceland and Japan where respondents were aged 15+. Country sample sizes range from 814 respondents in the UK to 2,528 in Spain, with a total sample of 35,501 respondents, excluding 1,726 individuals who did not answer the main survey item on leave duration preference. When provided, country weights were used in all analyses.

The main survey item used to measure leave duration preferences is: 'Consider a couple who both work full-time and now have a new born child. One of them stops working for some time to care for their child. Do you think there should be a paid leave available and, if so, for how long?' This continuous variable (ranging from 0 to 95) represents the number of months of paid (Maternity, Paternity and Parental) leave individuals consider legitimate for parents to receive.

The dissatisfaction indicator, which captures an individual's preference for longer leave, is computed by comparing this preferred leave duration with the statutory paid leave duration available in their country in the year the survey was conducted. This duration was retrieved from Section 2 of each country note in the international network's annual review (Moss, 2012/2013/2014), except for Poland, Portugal and the UK where information could not be retrieved and was interpreted from other parts of the country notes. Additional leaves conditional on earnings, father uptake or multiple births were excluded. Since the ISSP question does not mention any specific level of financial compensation, it is not clear what individuals understood exactly by 'paid leave'; namely at which rate; therefore, the total amount of paid leave available, whatever the payment rate, is used as reference.

The dissatisfaction indicator is a binary variable that distinguishes between those whose leave duration preference is equal or inferior to the available leave (*satisfied*) and those whose leave duration preference is superior (*dissatisfied*). It is important to bear in mind that individuals might not have answered that they were dissatisfied had they been asked this specific question in a survey. This measure of dissatisfaction is a computed one, and is highly sensitive to the reference statutory duration used for each country.

The gender division of leave preferences indicator is based on this item: 'Still thinking about the same couple, if both are in similar work situations and are eligible for paid leave, how should this paid leave period be divided between the mother and the father?' The question taps into individuals' ideal representations of gender leave division, offering three alternatives: a) the mother should take the entire period of leave (*fully gendered*), b) the mother should take most and the father should take some of it (*partly gendered*), c) mother and father should take half each (*gender equal*). Respondents who answered that the father should take more leave than the mother or all the leave (0.4 per cent of the sample) are included in the latter category. This survey item

Table 10.1: Statutory leave entitlements and leave preferences by country and welfare regimes (2012–2014)

| | | Statutory leave entitlements[a] | | Leave duration preferences[b] | |
| | | | | Central tendency | |
Welfare regime	Country	Paid leave in months	Entitlement for fathers	Mean (months)	Median (months)
Social democratic Nordic countries	Denmark	14	3	7.9	6
	Finland	36	✓	15.1	12
	Iceland	9	✓	12	12
	Norway	13	✓	12.6	12
	Sweden	16	✓	16.7	15
	Pooled			**12.5**	**12**
Conservative Continental European countries	Austria (North)	24	✓	28.9	30
	Belgium (North)	34	✓	8.1	6
	France (North)	36	✓	13.2	12
	Germany (North)	12	✓	16.1	12
	Israel (South)	3		7.8	6
	Portugal (South)	11	✓	10.4	6
	Spain (South)	5	✓	15.9	12
	Pooled			**14.1**	**12**
Liberal Anglophone countries	Australia	4		6.5	6
	Canada	12		9.3	12
	Ireland	6		8.2	6
	UK	9		8	6
	USA	0		5	3
	Pooled			**7.2**	**6**
Post-communist Central and East-European countries (CEE)	Croatia	12	✓	17	12
	Czech Rep.	36		36.2	36
	Lithuania	24	✓	24.9	24
	Poland	12	✓	16.3	12
	Russia	36		28.9	36
	Slovak Rep.	36		36.6	36
	Slovenia	14	✓	10.1	12
	Pooled			**25.7**	**24**
Hybrid	Japan	12	✓	9.7	6
	Netherlands	14	✓	5.7	4
	Switzerland	3		6.3	6
	Pooled			**7.3**	**6**
Total sample				**14.8**	**12**

Notes: Paid leave duration refers to the total post-natal paid leave (different compensation levels) including Maternity, Paternity, Parental and Childcare Leaves. Additional conditional leaves (depending on earnings, father uptake or multiple births) are excluded. The 'entitlement

Leave duration preferences (continued)[b]			Gender division of leave preferences[b]		
Consensus	Dissatisfaction				
Largest group with same answer (duration in months)	Want no leave	Want a longer leave	Mother takes all	Mother takes most	Half each
33% (12)	17%	4.8%	5.3%	47.5%	47.1%
30.5% (12)	9%	3%	3.2%	52.4%	44.4%
47.8% (12)	1.8%	67.1%	2.7%	48.7%	48.6%
47.4% (12)	10.2%	23.2%	4.5%	52.5%	43%
33.6% (12)	5.1%	49%	1.4%	28.2%	70.4%
38.7% (12)	**9.1%**	**27.9%**	**3.5%**	**46.5%**	**50%**
32.6% (36)	8.3%	52.3%	38.5%	39.9%	21.6%
22.2% (6)	19.3%	3.7%	14.2%	41%	44.8%
24% (12)	15.4%	0.9%	14.6%	37.8%	47.5%
37.9% (12)	7.1%	37.4%	15.9%	34.1%	50%
42.4% (6)	2.2%	83.9%	56.6%	21.9%	21.5%
30% (6 and 12)	1.9%	43.8%	27.2%	47%	25.8%
31.8 (12)	5.4%	79.7%	32.9%	33.6%	33.5%
25.7% (12)	**9.9%**	**39.9%**	**26.8%**	**36.3%**	**36.9%**
30.1% (0)	30.1%	58.1%	19.6%	50%	30.5%
42.1% (12)	14.4%	11.2%	24.3%	48%	27.8%
25.2% (12)	20.9%	42.5%	16.5%	47.8%	35.6%
32.5% (12)	11.4%	38.1%	19.9%	53.1%	27%
22% (6)	16.5%	83.5%	32.3%	31.4%	36.4%
26.3% (12)	**20%**	**49.9%**	**22.6%**	**45.5%**	**31.9%**
54.6% (12)	0.8%	37.8%	48.5%	27%	24.5%
39% (36)	2.4%	33.2%	69.3%	21%	9.6%
39.5 (24)	1.5%	34.5%	54%	35.2%	10.7%
46% (12)	1%	31.6%	32.5%	33.5%	34%
43.7% (36)	2.4%	7.7%	81.1%	10.7%	8.2%
50.4% (36)	1.2%	24.1%	68.5%	21.5%	9.9%
65.6% (12)	14.4%	5.3%	41.4%	43.3%	15.3%
28.7% (36)	**3.2%**	**24.6%**	**59.2%**	**25.7%**	**15.1%**
28.3% (12)	11.7%	17.2%	19.8%	61.8%	18.4%
24.8% (6)	24.2%	4.3%	12.3%	39.4%	48.3%
27.3% (6)	11.7%	63.2%	19.6%	41.3%	39.1%
23.3% (6)	**15.7%**	**28.8%**	**17.6%**	**48%**	**34.4%**
27.2% (12)	**10.4%**	**34.8%**	**29.9%**	**37.6%**	**32.5%**

for fathers' indicator consists of any period of paid Parental Leave reserved for fathers and/or paid Paternity Leave. [b] Percentages calculated on samples excluding missing responses.

Source: [a] Moss, 2012; 2013; 2014, to match the year of survey does not allow assessing attitudes toward the division of leave between same-sex parents.

The data on entitlements aimed at fathers taking leave in each country are also taken from the international network's annual review (Moss, 2012/2013/2014). As a rough indication of whether schemes intend fathers to also take leave, the existence of paid Paternity Leave and/or of a reserved period of paid Parental Leave for the father is used (for details of leave provision and preferences in the 27 countries, see Table 10.1).

Methods include descriptive statistics for leave duration and gender division of leave preferences by country and welfare regimes, scatterplots and chi-square tests. Logistic regression is used to analyse the individual factors related to leave dissatisfaction. They are performed on pooled samples by welfare regimes and control for country effects. Individual level variables entered in the models were selected following self-interest and ideational theories and previous research results, as well as based on available data in the survey.

Variables include *sex*, where men are the reference group. *Parenthood* distinguishes between parents with at least one child under 18 years living in the household, parents without a child under 18 years living in the household, and childless respondents (reference group). *Age* is a categorical variable distinguishing between a younger cohort (18–40 years), a middle one used as a reference (41–65 years), and an older cohort (65+ years). Individuals' *level of education* separates three groups: those with none or a primary level (reference group), with a secondary level, and with a tertiary level. *Employment status* is a dummy variable distinguishing between those outside the labour market (in education, housework, military, disabled, retired, other) coded as the reference group, and those in paid work or searching for a job.

Gender ideology captures individual values about gender roles and parenthood. It is computed as the mean of answers (on a 1–5 scale) to four survey items touching upon attitudes towards what is considered best for the child, maternal employment and men's and women's role in the family; to avoid sample size reduction, the mean was computed allowing one missing value out of four. The lowest values indicate the most egalitarian gender ideology and the highest value indicates most traditional gender ideology. Further ideational variables such as individuals' political stance, which might shape leave policy preferences, could not be included in the analysis because of too many missing data.

Several robustness checks were performed in order to verify the sensitivity of the logistic regression results to the composition of welfare regimes. Alternative groupings were used, for instance separating Northern and Southern European countries or excluding Slovenia and Croatia from post-communist regimes since these two countries differ in terms of gender equality. Results showed overall very similar relationships, although a few lost significance. The model was also run on the full sample, again replicating results.

Leave policy preferences: descriptive results

What leave duration do people prefer?

As hypothesised, descriptive statistics show large country differences regarding individuals' views about the legitimate duration of paid leave. Preferred leave durations range from a mean of five months in the USA, to 36 months in the Slovak Republic and the Czech Republic. There are marked differences across welfare regimes, but not all regimes are equally homogeneous.

In social democratic regimes preferences tend towards a paid leave of about one year, though preferences in Denmark are slightly shorter. Consensus is high; about one third or more of respondents in these countries agree that 12 months is the right amount of leave. A roughly similar preferred duration of one year is observed in continental European countries, with the exception of Austria where the mean exceeds two years. However, there is a weaker consensus in these countries, since a smaller proportion of respondents agree on a specific leave duration and the most frequent duration cited varies significantly from one country to another. Germany and Israel stand out with a high consensus for one year and six months paid leave respectively.

The longest average preferred leave durations are among post-communist countries; reaching two and three years in Czech Republic, Slovak Republic, Russia and Lithuania. Croatia, Poland and Slovenia stand out with shorter average preferences. Overall, it is in post-communist regimes that consensus about paid leave is strongest. In Croatia, 66 per cent of respondents agree on one year of leave.

Shorter average preferred leaves prevail in liberal and hybrid regimes. Aggregate mean preferences are about six months or slightly more (for example, Japan and Canada). Except for Canada, consensus is as low as in conservative countries, indicating no clear norm about the leave duration in these societies.

Do average preferences correlate with existing statutory leave durations?

As expected, there is a positive correlation between the country-specific statutory duration of paid leave and country average preferred leave durations (see Figure 10.1). Belgium, France and Finland are outliers, with average preferences substantially shorter than the statutory leave; these countries share a long leave available with low flat-rate benefits (Parental Leave in France, childcare leave in Finland and the time credit system in Belgium). Several liberal, south European and hybrid regimes show the opposite pattern, suggesting statutory entitlements do not meet average preferences. The largest gap is found in Spain, where parents are entitled to a total of five months of paid Maternity and Paternity Leave, while average preferences reach 16 months; a longer Parental Leave does exist but is unpaid. Another noteworthy case is the US, where on average respondents consider there should be five months paid leave, while there is currently none at all.

Figure 10.1: Scatterplot of statutory leave durations and average preferred leave durations by country

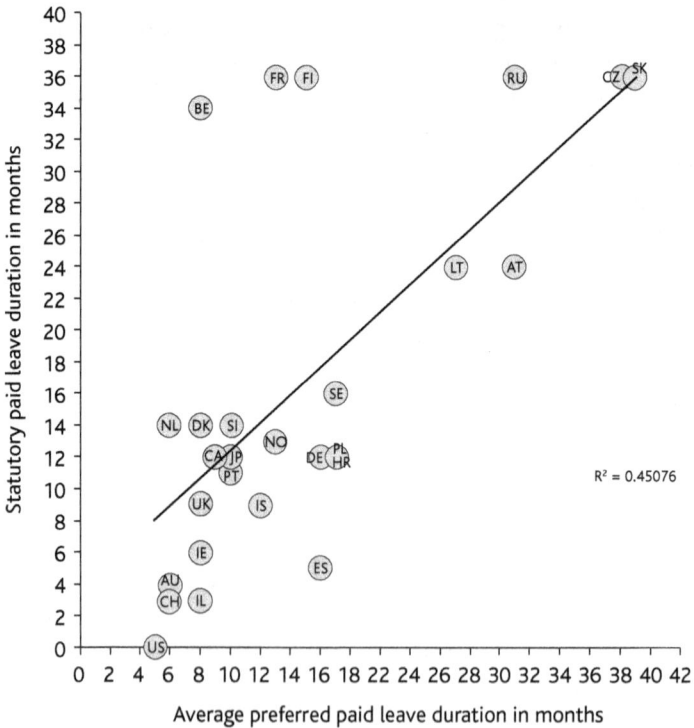

How dissatisfied are individuals with leave?

The proportion of 'dissatisfied' individuals who would prefer a longer period of paid leave is about 35 per cent of the total sample, but varies greatly by welfare regime. Table 10.1 shows that the largest proportion are in liberal regimes (50 per cent of pooled samples), followed by conservative (40 per cent), hybrid (29 per cent), social democratic (28 per cent) and post-communist (25 per cent) regimes. This macro-picture suggests that there is a larger share of individuals who would prefer a longer leave in 'short-leave countries'. Figure 10.2 confirms this trend, and provides a more complex view into cross-country differences. Dissatisfaction is especially high in the US, Israel, Spain, Switzerland and Australia. Iceland is also noteworthy, with about two-thirds of respondents preferring a longer leave, one year instead of nine months.

It is important to note that substantially more individuals would have been coded as 'dissatisfied' if the duration of statutory *well-paid*

Figure 10.2: Scatterplot of statutory leave durations and percentage of dissatisfied by country

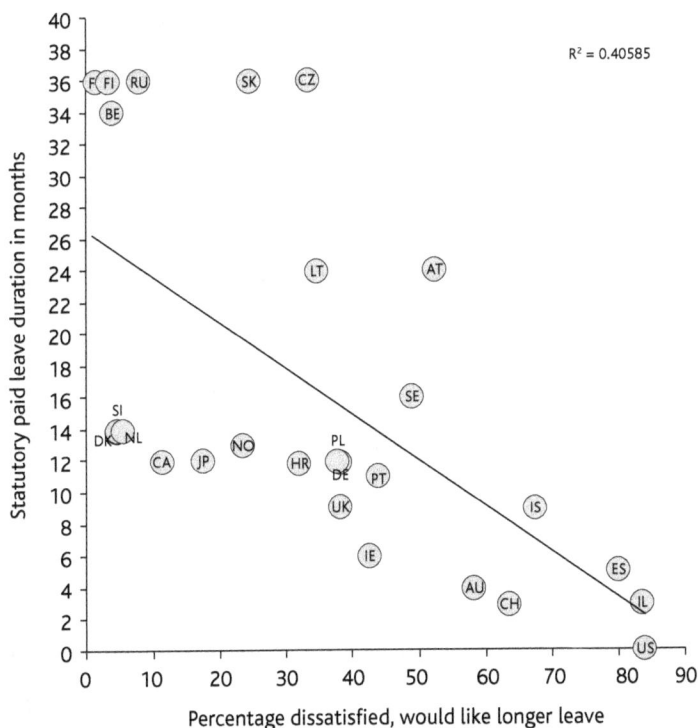

leave (that is, at least two-thirds of previous earnings) had been taken as reference instead of the leave duration paid at any rate. Therefore, the estimate that a little over one third of individuals in the total sample would prefer a longer leave than their current statutory entitlement is likely to be a conservative one.

Turning to the second indicator of 'dissatisfaction', there is a relatively small (10 per cent) proportion of respondents who consider that there should be no paid leave at all. The largest proportion is in liberal regimes (20 per cent), which confirms the hypothesis that leave is most contested in countries where it is most recently introduced and least institutionalised; the fact that Australia stands out with 30 per cent of the sample rejecting paid leave possibly reflects social divisions on this issue at the time of the survey, with paid Parental Leave only introduced shortly before the survey took place, in 2010. As expected, paid leave is clearly most accepted in post-communist regimes, followed by social democratic countries, only 3 per cent and 9 per cent of respondents respectively rejecting paid leave. Other results are more unexpected, such as the rather large proportion of respondents rejecting paid leave in Denmark (17 per cent). While among conservative regimes, paid leave seems slightly more legitimate in southern than northern Europe.

How should the mother and the father share the leave?

Fairly clear patterns of preferences for the gender division of leave are observed in social democratic and post-communist regimes. Fully gendered leave uptake is clearly rejected in the former, though there is a divide about the extent to which fathers should be involved in childcare – both gender equal and a partly gendered division are supported. Sweden is an exception, with a large majority (70 per cent) preferring a gender equal division, perhaps reflecting the long-standing priority given to gender equality and fatherhood (Rostgaard, 2002). In post-communist countries, a gendered pattern dominates; leave is mainly considered the mothers' prerogative. This result can be explained by leave schemes in CEE countries historically designed as a work–family measure aimed particularly at mothers (Pascall and Manning, 2000). Exceptions include Poland, where the three patterns are equally favoured, and Slovenia, where the fully and the partly gendered leave uptake options receive similar support.

There is considerably more heterogeneity in the other regimes. In liberal welfare states, the partly gendered division of leave is predominant, followed by the gender equal division, the US being an exception with no predominant pattern. Overall, this suggests that in countries with limited leave schemes and few incentives to promote fathers' leave use, there is weaker consensus regarding the ideal gender division of leave. It was expected that conservative regimes would favour a fully gendered pattern, but it is not the case. The fact that no clear norms can be identified may be attributed to the fact that these countries have followed different paths since the 1990s in reforming family and leave policies. It is noteworthy that Germany's 2007 leave policy reform, which increased incentives for fathers' leave use, is mirrored in the high level of support for a gender equal leave division (50 per cent).

A chi-square test shows that there is a significant relationship between the existence of father incentives in the national leave schemes and wanting a gender equal division, $\chi^2(1) = 704.15$, $p < 0.001$. The odds of wanting a gender equal division of leave are twice as high if individuals live in a country with such an incentive. These complementary analyses suggest that leave scheme design is indeed associated with individuals' views of how parents should share the leave.

Correlates of dissatisfaction: logistic regression results

Descriptive results contribute to evidence that institutions shape individuals' leave policy preferences. Logistic regression analyses enable the exploration of further factors of influence at the micro-level and whether these vary by welfare regime or not. The focus hereafter is on the correlates of individuals' dissatisfaction with leave schemes and their preference for a longer duration of leave in their country. Results suggest that in addition to country effects, self-interest and ideational mechanisms are at play (see Table 10.2). Women have higher odds of being dissatisfied and wanting a longer leave in all regimes except in CEE countries, where leaves are already long. This probably reflects women's primary role in childcare. Parents, in particular those with at least one child still living in the household, are also more likely to be dissatisfied.

There is also a clear age effect. In all regimes except post-communist, the younger cohort is more likely to be dissatisfied. This reflects 18- to 40-year-olds being in the family formation life stage, when individuals are most likely to be concerned about leave policies. Across all regimes, the oldest cohort is significantly less likely to be dissatisfied.

Interestingly, gender ideology has opposite effects in different welfare regimes. In countries with better developed leave policies,

Table 10.2: Logistic regression results for being dissatisfied with current leave duration (being satisfied is the reference group). Separate models by welfare regimes. Odds ratios.

	Social-democratic	Post-communist	Conservative	Liberal	Hybrid
Sex					
Man	Ref.	Ref.	Ref.	Ref.	Ref.
Woman	1.75***	1.10	1.25***	1.33***	1.46***
Parenthood					
Childless	Ref.	Ref.	Ref.	Ref.	Ref.
Parent of child <18 yrs	2.68***	1.38***	1.60***	1.49***	1.32*
Parent of child 18+ yrs	1.99***	1.25*	1.20*	1.00	0.91
Age category					
15–40 years	1.23*	1.07	1.16*	1.92***	1.33*
41–65 years	Ref.	Ref.	Ref.	Ref.	Ref.
65+ years	0.53***	0.83*	0.72***	0.64***	0.74
Education degree					
Primary	Ref.	Ref.	Ref.	Ref.	Ref.
Secondary	0.98	1.05	1.17*	1.10	1.13
Tertiary	1.10	1.01	1.14	1.20	1.90***
Employment status					
Not in paid work	Ref.	Ref.	Ref.	Ref.	Ref.
In paid work	1.01	0.97	1.06	1.00	0.94
Gender ideology score	1.17***	1.27***	1.26***	0.92*	0.89
N	5,679	7,865	10,970	4,977	3,175
Model	χ^2 (df 13) = 2,078.64***	χ^2 (df 15) = 786.10***	χ^2 (df 15) = 5,772.49***	χ^2 (df 13) = 1,526.90***	χ^2 (df 11) = 1,173.01***
Nagelkerke	0.443	0.141	0.550	0.352	0.437
Cox and Snell R square	0.307	0.095	0.409	0.264	0.309

Notes: Models control for the country effects in each welfare regime. Significance levels: $p<0.001$***, $p<0.01$**, $p<0.05$*

that is, social democratic, post-communist and conservative, the more traditional gender values individuals hold, the more likely they are to want a longer leave. This may mean that longer leaves are seen by respondents as an instrument to prolong maternal childcare. By contrast, in liberal welfare regimes, more traditional individuals are less likely to want a longer leave; this is also the case for hybrid countries, where the estimate is very close to significance level. This suggests that in contexts where welfare state benefits are more limited, a traditional family model is seen as best achieved through private solutions, for example women's withdrawal from employment, while those with gender equal attitudes would prefer a longer leave to improve mothers' (and possibly fathers') work–family balance.

Results show only limited or no effect of employment status and education. This finding confirms that the influence of such variables may be very context-dependent, as previous results have suggested, and that gender, cohort and family life course variables matter most.

Conclusions

This is the first study to provide a large-scale analysis of preferences about the duration and gender division of leave policies. Overall, it shows high acceptance of the principle of paid leave across welfare states; only one in ten respondents in the total sample rejects paid leave altogether. But ideas of what is a 'good' leave policy vary substantially across welfare regimes, with leave duration preferences ranging from about six months in liberal regimes to roughly one year in social democratic and conservative ones, and up to two and three years in some post-communist regimes. This study found more variation than in a previous smaller-scale study (Stropnik et al, 2008).

As hypothesised, leave policy preferences are significantly associated with welfare regimes and current statutory leave schemes. This means that for duration, the longer the existing statutory leave, the longer the preferred leave at the aggregate level; while when leave schemes are designed to encourage fathers' uptake, there is also a larger proportion of individuals wanting a gender equal division of entitlements. In line with institutional theory, this suggests that when leave policies are well institutionalised and have been implemented for a long time – as in social democratic and post-communist regimes – policies and preferences match best. The weaker consensus about leave duration and leave gender division observed in conservative, liberal and hybrid regimes reflects the different stages and more recent institutionalisation of leave policies.

It is important to note, however, that there are outlier countries within welfare regimes, which points to the limits of the typologies used and the challenge of grouping complex and evolving welfare states. Another limit concerns the cross-sectional data used, which does not prove any causal mechanism. Thus, it is likely that there are feedback mechanisms through which individuals' attitudes also shape policies (see Brooks and Manza, 2006).

Another contribution of this study is to show that beyond this overall picture, there are sometimes high levels of dissatisfaction across countries and regimes. Results show a significant negative correlation between leave durations and dissatisfaction levels: the shorter the statutory paid leave in a country, the larger the percentage of individuals who would prefer a longer paid leave. This has potential policy implications, suggesting that in several contexts there may be social demand and political grounds for leave extension. Gender division of leave preferences also point to possible reforms, such as implementing or increasing father incentives through individual leave entitlements and quotas; this is, for example, the case in some conservative and liberal welfare states where unexpectedly high proportions of respondents favour a gender equal division of leave. Such results call for small-scale comparative case studies.

Finally, the study provides insights into the micro-level factors related to leave dissatisfaction and the correlates of preferring a longer leave. Regression results confirm self-interest mechanisms and the influence of values. In line with previous studies (Stropnik et al, 2008; Valarino et al, 2018), parents, younger cohorts and women are more likely to be dissatisfied. Correlates of dissatisfaction generally behave in the same way across welfare regimes, except for gender ideology where opposite effects are observed in 'long leave' and 'short leave' regimes. This result suggests that leave policies can contribute to reproducing the male breadwinner family model and a specialisation of gender roles or can promote a more gender equal division of work within the family. This depends on the design of leave policies and whether or not they target fathers individually and encourage their involvement in childcare (for example, Kamerman and Moss, 2009; Haas and Rostgaard, 2011).

To sum up, this study shows that paid leave for parents is considered a legitimate family policy across all welfare regimes, but that stark differences exist regarding what is considered as a 'good' leave for parents. It sheds light on the institutional shaping of leave policy preferences and also highlights the varying levels of dissatisfaction across countries and what this may mean for further policy development. At the individual level, in addition to country effects, gender values and family life course circumstances are the main factors driving individuals' preference for longer leave. While the macro-level approach reported in this chapter entails an inevitable loss of complexity, it nevertheless contributes to our understanding of leave policy preferences as profoundly socially, politically and historically shaped.

References

Aidukaite, J. (2009) 'Old welfare state theories and new welfare regimes in Eastern Europe: Challenges and implications', *Communist and Post-Communist Studies*, 42(1): 23–39.

Blekesaune, M. and Quadagno, J. (2003) 'Public attitudes toward welfare state policies: A comparative analysis of 24 nations', *European Sociological Review*, 19(5): 415–427.

Blum, S., Formánková, L. and Dobrotić, I. (2014) 'Family policies in "hybrid" welfare states after the crisis: Pathways between policy expansion and retrenchmen', *Social Policy and Administration*, 48(4): 468–491.

Brooks, C. and Manza, J. (2006) 'Social policy responsiveness in developed democracies', *American Sociological Review*, 71(3): 474–494.

Chung, H. and Meuleman, B. (2017) 'European parents' attitudes towards public childcare provision: The role of current provisions, interests and ideologies', *European Societies*, 19(1): 49–68.

Dobrotić, I. and Vučković Juroš, T. (2016) 'Who should finance childcare? Multilevel analysis of 24 countries', *Croatian Journal of Social Policy*, 23(3): 323–357.

Esping-Andersen, G. (1990) *The Three Worlds of Welfare Capitalism*, Cambridge: Polity Press.

Ferragina, E. and Seeleib-Kaiser, M. (2011) 'Welfare regime debate: Past, present, futures?', *Policy and Politics,* 39(4): 583–611.

Haas, L. and Rostgaard, T. (2011) 'Fathers' rights to paid parental leave in the Nordic countries: consequences for the gendered division of leave', *Community, Work and Family*, 14(2): 177–195.

ISSP Research Group (2016) *International Social Survey Programme: Family and Changing Gender Roles IV – ISSP 2012 GESIS Data Archive*, Cologne: GESIS.

Jaeger, M.M. (2006) 'Welfare regimes and attitudes towards redistribution: The regime hypothesis revisited', *European Sociological Review*, 22(2): 157–170.

Kamerman, S.B. and Moss, P. (2009) *The Politics of Parental Leave Policies: Children, Parenting, Gender and the Labour Market*, Bristol: Policy Press.

Lewis, J. (1992) 'Gender and the development of welfare regimes', *Journal of European Social Policy*, 2(3): 159–173.

Mischke, M. (2014) *Public Attitudes Towards Family Policies in Europe: Linking Institutional Context and Public Opinion*, Wiesbaden: Springer VS.

Moss, P. (ed) (2012/2013/2014) *International Review on Leave Policies and Related Research*. Available at www.leavenetwork.org

Orloff, A.S. (1993) 'Gender and the social rights in citizenship: The comparative analysis of gender relations and welfare states', *American Sociological Review*, 58(3): 303–328.

Pascall, G. and Manning, N. (2000) 'Gender and social policy: Comparing welfare states in Central and Eastern Europe and the former Soviet Union', *Journal of European Social Policy*, 10(3): 240–266.

Pfau-Effinger, B. (2005) 'Welfare state policies and the development of care arrangements', *European Societies*, 7(2): 321–347.

Rostgaard, T. (2002) 'Setting time aside for the father: Father's leave in Scandinavia', *Community, Work and Family*, 5(3): 343–364.

Stropnik, N., Sambt, J. and Kocourková, J. (2008) 'Preferences versus actual family policy measures', in C. Höhn, D. Avramov and I.E. Kotowska (eds) *People, Population Change and Policies*, The Hague: Springer, pp 391–410.

Svallfors, S. (ed) (2012) *Contested Welfare States: Welfare Attitudes in Europe and Beyond*, Stanford, CA: Stanford University Press.

Valarino, I., Duvander, A.-Z., Haas, L. and Neyer, G. (2018) 'Exploring Leave Policy Preferences: A Comparison of Austria, Sweden, Switzerland, and the United States', *Social Politics: International Studies in Gender, State & Society*, 25(1): 118–147.

ELEVEN

Gender equality: Parental Leave design and evaluating its effects on fathers' participation

Ann-Zofie Duvander, Guðný Björk Eydal,
Berit Brandth, Ingólfur V. Gíslason,
Johanna Lammi-Taskula and Tine Rostgaard

Introduction

The promotion of gender equality is a major aim behind many Parental Leave systems and an important part of the family policy discourse in all the Nordic countries, namely: Denmark, Finland, Iceland, Norway and Sweden. The extensive and well-paid leave rights for both men and women contribute to consistently placing these countries high on gender equality rankings, such as, for example, the Global Gender Gap (World Economic Forum, 2016). Entitlement to leave rights alone is not sufficient to create gender equality, but Nordic fathers increasingly make use of the legislation, which should move these countries towards that goal. Leave legislation is the cornerstone for the take-up of leave by fathers and any subsequent impact this may have, but take-up is also related to other labour market legislation, ECEC services and other arrangements, as well as cultural norms that restrict or enable Parental Leave use.

Often-mentioned outcomes of fathers taking Parental Leave are that they become more involved in childcare, and that it enhances the earlier return of mothers to paid employment; job-protected Parental Leave has historically proved important primarily for mothers' labour market participation and work hours. Other outcomes referred to in the Nordic countries include relatively low child poverty rates and relatively high fertility rates. Mothers' and fathers' Parental Leave use, as well as their division of leave, may have an immediate effect on sharing childcare and household work. It may also in the long run consolidate a certain gendered division of responsibility for these tasks. However, generous leave entitlements may weaken parents' positions in the labour market and reduce career opportunities if employers expect them to take long spells out of working life.

Even if the Parental Leave system in the Nordic countries is part of a policy context that generally seeks to encourage gender equality, for example through the support of shared parenthood and protection of parents in the labour market, there is still a long way to go. The Nordic countries have highly gender-segregated labour markets, a persistent gender wage gap, and women do most unpaid housework and childcare. This is partly related to the fact that women still use much more of the entitlement to Parental Leave than men (Nordic Council of Ministers, 2016).

This chapter highlights the various and varied policy approaches within the Nordic countries to support equal sharing of Parental Leave by both parents. While the Nordic countries share the goal of gender equality and all have well paid Parental Leave available to both parents, the details of their policies differ, revealing divergences in essential dimensions of policy design. None of the Nordic countries have successfully reached the goal of gender equality, but may in some aspects have come further than many other countries, and have more often made gender equality an explicit policy goal.

Sharing of Parental Leave is often seen as an indicator of gender equality, but it is important to acknowledge the many dimensions of gender equality and also the somewhat elusive nature of the concept. Gender equality is hard to define and, regarding Parental Leave, to apply; it is not always clear that a 50/50 division is the goal; sometimes the goal may be any sharing between parents. Still, in all the Nordic countries the goal is set higher than the current situation. In the chapter, we present different dimensions of policy design, and then ask how these facilitate sharing of leave, namely: quotas, flexibility in use and compensation levels. We use earlier research and data from the country reports to be found in the annual review of the international network (see Chapter One). The chapter concludes with a discussion of the most successful paths towards a more gender equal sharing of Parental Leave.

Nordic Parental Leave: developments over time

As in most countries, Parental Leave systems in the Nordic countries build upon Maternity Leave legislation for working women, introduced in the first half of the twentieth century. From the 1970s, Maternity Leave was generally extended and renamed Parental Leave as it now covered both parents; but in Denmark and Finland, a period of Maternity Leave only for mothers has remained. The transformation of Maternity Leave into a Parental Leave indicates a break with the earlier model where childcare responsibility rested solely with the mother. However, even if the political goals were now discussed in more gender-neutral terms, Parental Leave was still mainly used by mothers. Today, Parental Leave legislation generally aims to depart from the image of the mother as primary carer, but parental behaviour still does not reflect equal sharing of care.

Parental Leave rights in all Nordic countries gradually increased in length during the 1980s and 1990s, although there is great variation in how this was done and at what speed. Iceland remained the laggard with a short period of paid Parental Leave, mainly directed at mothers, until 2000; then it introduced what can be considered to be the most radical leave reform in gender equality terms among the Nordic countries, with the introduction of a non-transferable quota of three months to each parent. A one-month quota for fathers (and mothers) had already been introduced in Norway and Sweden in the early 1990s, and today all the Nordic countries have such quotas (that is, periods of paid leave that can only be taken by fathers or mothers), except Denmark, whose father's quota only lasted from 1998 to 2001 (Duvander and Lammi-Taskula, 2011; Rostgaard and Lausten, 2015). Today, the length of Parental Leave and its division between mother, father and sharing between both parents, vary across countries (Figure 11.1).

Similarities in leave legislation across the Nordic countries include a fairly high compensation level, paid by national social insurance (and not by employers) (Table 11.1). Benefits for those in work are earnings-related, at 70 to 100 per cent of earnings, often with a ceiling, with minimum flat-rate benefits for those without work. The compensation levels have varied over time but have remained relatively high by international standards. Another dimension to have varied over time is the period over which leave can be used, varying from the Finnish case where leave can only be used by mothers immediately following birth to the Swedish case, where one fifth of the leave can be saved for use up until the child is 12 years old (Eydal et al, 2015).

Eligibility for Parental Leave is mainly based on residence in the country and on the parents' prior employment record and individual earnings. However, in Norway eligibility for the father's quota requires that both parents have been employed for six out of the ten months prior to birth. In Finland, fathers have historically had to share residence with the mother in order to use the leave; but since 2017, fathers responsible for childcare but not living with the mother can

Figure 11.1: Length of paid Parental Leave per parent (weeks) in Nordic countries (2016)

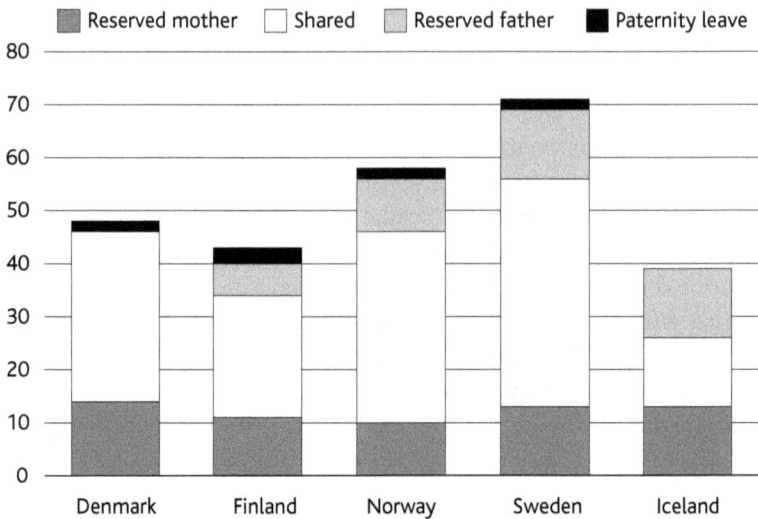

Source: Compiled by authors based on data from country reports in Koslowski et al, 2016

Table 11.1: Comparison of the main elements of Parental Leave legislation in Nordic countries

	Denmark	Finland	Iceland	Norway	Sweden
Year Parental Leave introduced	1984	1985	1981	1978	1974
Length at introduction (months)	5.6	6	3	4.2	6
Length in 2016 (months)	11	9.5	9	11.7/14	16
Year quotas introduced	1997	2003	2000	1993	1995
Length of fathers' quota in 2016 (months)	0	2.2	3	2.5	3
Length of mothers' quota in 2016 (months)	3.3	2.6	3	2.5	3
Wage replacement level (%)	100 to ceiling	70–90 different periods	80 to ceiling	100/80 to ceiling	77.6 to ceiling

Note: In Denmark, the first 18 weeks are a Maternity Leave, with four weeks prior and 14 weeks following birth.

Source: Compiled by authors based on data from country reports in Koslowski et al, 2016

also use the leave. In Iceland and Sweden, fathers' rights are more protected; in Sweden the only requirement for leave take-up is custody over the child, while in Iceland only agreement with the custodial parent is needed. In Denmark, the father should be in a recognised partnership with the other parent. In all countries, same-sex parents are treated in the same way as other parents, rights being based on legal (biological or adoptive) parenthood status (Hakovirta et al, 2015).

Gender equality from a Parental Leave perspective

Despite the general emphasis on gender equality in the Parental Leave legislation, Nordic countries are still far from achieving equal sharing of Parental Leave. Often fathers' share of Parental Leave use is taken as an indicator of the degree of gender equality, particularly in international comparisons, as other measures are hard to come by, but also when measuring gender equality over time within one country. Fathers' share of Parental Leave obviously depends on eligibility, the length of leave available and other conditions of use, thus caution is needed in any comparison.

It should also be acknowledged that gender equality may be conceptualised in various ways. On the one hand, it may imply that both mothers and fathers have equal opportunities to take leave and care for the child and that decisions on how to share the Parental Leave are preference-based and not determined by norms, legislation, economic constraints or other external pressure. In this way, we may see gender equality as a precondition for sharing leave. On the other hand, gender equality may refer to the actual division of leave or the outcomes of equal leave-sharing, such as position in the labour market, or equal division of housework. With regard to Parental Leave, it is often assumed that the participation of fathers is the first step to gender equality and in particular gender equal sharing of childcare.

Considering women's and men's work historically, research has shown that men's participation in unpaid work in the private sphere has been increasing over time, in particular in the Nordic countries, just as women's participation in paid employment increased somewhat earlier (Goldsheider et al, 2015; Stanfors and Goldscheider, 2017). As mothers are now participating in the labour market to almost the same degree as fathers in the Nordic countries, focus on gender equality is mainly centred on changing fathers' behaviour. Generally, it is assumed that both women and men will benefit from such change, both on individual and societal levels. Also, for children, positive outcomes are associated with fathers' participation in childcare, sometimes measured by Parental Leave use (Sarkadi et al, 2007; Brandth and Gíslason, 2011).

A situation with no gendered economic or normative constraints on the distribution of work would perhaps lead to a normal distribution (in a statistical sense) of Parental Leave use: fathers taking the major part in some families, and mothers in some families, but most families sharing more or less equally. Often, however, individual preferences hide or incorporate prevalent gendered structures that shape choices on how to share leave. Instead, it is common to understand gender equality as a 50/50 sharing of Parental Leave, as well as other childcare, unpaid housework and income; the Swedish measure of sharing leave – somewhere between 40 and 60 per cent to indicate gender equal couples – is an example of this (Swedish Social Insurance Agency, 2013).

Another dimension of sharing leave is the duration of leave necessary to reach the desired outcome of gender equality, which may be a question of how long fathers have to take leave for it to potentially lead to longer-term changes in gendered care responsibility norms. Perhaps a threshold of a certain length has to be reached before we can expect the leave sharing to tip any balance in favour of gender equality (Almqvist and Duvander, 2014). So, a single day of fathers' Parental Leave may not contribute to a shift in behaviour (Hosking et al, 2010), but a month with sole care of the child may be of importance (see examples in O'Brien and Wall, 2017). There may also be different thresholds leading to various 'degrees' of gender equality (Brighouse and Wright, 2008). Thus, the relationship between sharing of Parental Leave and gender equality is far more complicated than a linear association. However, just as mothers' entering the labour market was part of a trend in a particular direction, fathers' leave use may indicate a similar trend.

Parental Leave uptake and long-term consequences

When Parental Leave sharing is compared across the Nordic countries, it is mainly taken for granted that all mothers use some leave, and the main interest is the proportion of fathers using any leave, as well as their share of all leave used. The Nordic Council of Ministers has attempted to collect annual statistics of how leave is shared for many years (Nordic Council of Ministers, 2016). Even though such numbers are useful to indicate time trends across countries, one has to take careful note of the differences in national legislation. For example, Iceland's relatively short leave may statistically show a higher *share* of leave to the father, while the *number* of days is lower than in Sweden, which has a longer leave. Also, when simultaneous use of leave is possible, fathers and mothers are likely to use some of the leave together, which may have different consequences for gender equality than fathers at home alone. The more flexible and longer period possible for use by Swedish fathers will facilitate their use compared to the stricter timeframe in, for example, Finland, but not necessarily lead to more gender equal care practices. In addition, eligibility criteria exclude a considerable share of Norwegian fathers (and mothers) but include, for example, almost all Icelandic fathers (and mothers). Despite these differences, it is obvious that the trend is towards more sharing of Parental Leave in all the Nordic countries (Figure 11.2). Nevertheless, not all fathers use leave, in particular fathers who are not living with mothers, and fathers on the extreme ends of the income scale; economically marginalised and very high earning men.

The most obvious long-term effect of fathers' leave use is continued engagement in childcare. Studies have shown that fathers who share the care of young children with their partner continue to be active in childcare as well as in household chores after the end of leave. Furthermore, fathers who take leave are more likely to stay in contact with the child after divorce (Ottesen, 2015). Across the Nordic countries, fathers' use of leave is also found to have

Figure 11.2: Fathers' share of total Parental Leave use in Nordic countries (1990–2015)

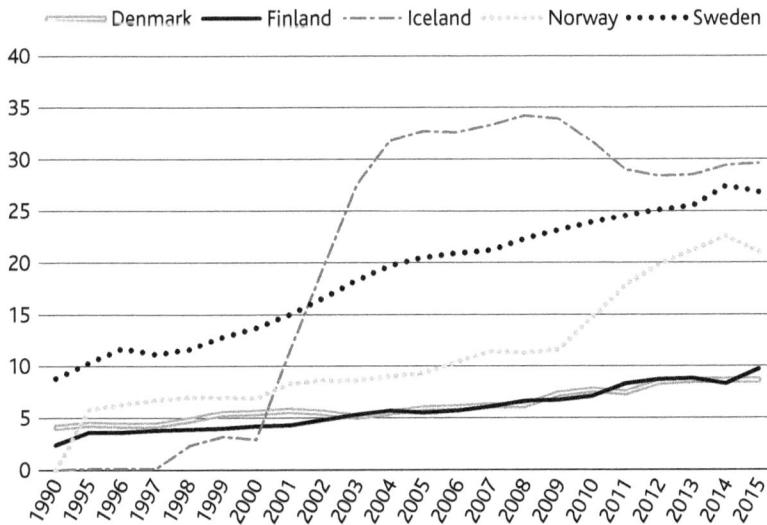

Source: Nordic Council of Ministers, 2016

consequences for the father–child relationship (Hwang and Lamb, 1997; Sarkadi et al, 2008; Duvander and Jans, 2009; Arnalds et al, 2013; Brandth and Kvande, 2018). The division of Parental Leave is also related to how unpaid domestic work is shared, with fathers' take-up of longer Parental Leave positively associated with sharing domestic work, but to a different degree for different (gendered) activities (Kitterød, 2013; Duvander et al, 2015). It has to be noted, however, that these studies generally do not take into account whether fathers who took leave were initially more child-oriented, that is, whether fathers with certain characteristics are more likely to take Parental Leave, rather than leave-taking itself leading to these differences in later outcomes.

Parental Leave sharing may also be associated with the labour market careers of both parents. Due to employment breaks such as Parental Leave, women may accumulate fewer years of work experience and seniority than men, imposing a 'motherhood penalty' on their careers and earnings. For example, research shows that a long Parental Leave (over a year) inhibits mothers' promotion prospects (Evertsson and Duvander, 2010), but taking Parental Leave is also found to have a slight negative effect on fathers' earnings. Thus, both mothers and fathers may suffer financially for taking leave (Rege and Solli, 2013; Evertsson, 2014).

Key dimensions for gender equal use of Parental Leave

In this section, we consider the possible gender equality effects of three dimensions in the design of Parental Leave policies.

Quotas

Quotas in Parental Leave mean that part of paid leave is reserved for each parent and forfeited if not used by him/her. This is a strong incentive particularly for fathers to take at least some leave and the introduction of quotas in Nordic countries has been aimed at a gender equal use of Parental Leave; recently, quotas have also been introduced elsewhere, such as Germany (Reimer et al, 2017), Québec (Doucet et al, 2017) and Portugal (Wall and Leitão, 2017). Some have also reversed the development. Denmark abolished their quota and Norway reduced their quota from 14 to ten weeks due to ideological differences between political parties in government. Indeed, there has been considerable political controversy around quotas, except in the case of Iceland, due to differences of view about policy goals or the methods used for reaching gender equality (Eydal and Rostgaard, 2011; Eydal et al, 2015; Salmi and Lammi-Taskula 2015).

Even if there has been political and popular resistance to a father's quota for various reasons, there is clear evidence that quotas have increased fathers' take-up of leave. This is an indication that this policy design does change behaviour, even in an area such as early years childcare, where traditional gender roles have persisted. In Iceland, the great majority of fathers started to use the full length of their quota right away (Eydal and Gíslason, 2015). In Norway, fathers' leave use was very low before the quota was introduced and the immediate increase was remarkable, from 4 to 39 per cent of all fathers (Cools et al, 2015). In Sweden, about half of all fathers used leave already before the quota was introduced, but this increased to about nine out of ten fathers after the reform (Duvander and Johansson, 2015). Also in Denmark, the quota influenced fathers' leave use, and the use decreased immediately after the quota was abolished (Rostgaard and Lausten, 2015). Recent figures from Finland also indicate a large increase in leave use after the quota was made more flexible and easy to use in 2013 (Salmi and Närvi, 2017).

Quotas, however, do not seem to be as effective in persuading fathers to use more than their personal entitlement; statistics show that only a small minority of fathers take more than their quota of leave (see for example Arnalds et al, 2013). The quota seems to create a norm of how much leave fathers should use, the sharable part of Parental Leave being often seen as primarily for the mother to take. However, more variation in use seems to occur over time between subgroups of fathers (Duvander and Johansson, 2015).

Overall, we can conclude that quota reforms have been essential and efficient in leading to an increasing number of fathers using at least some leave; but that generally, mothers still take most leave days, and in some cases are still the only parent to take any leave.

Flexibility

Another important policy dimension is the flexibility in how leave can be used, accommodating a particular family's needs and preferences, as well as the needs of work organisations and employers. Flexibility is mainly motivated by the different situations of parents, and from a gender equality perspective flexibility should facilitate both the labour market participation of mothers and Parental Leave use by fathers. During the last decades, the need for flexibility has also been related to family change and diversity, as well as a more flexible working life. All the Nordic countries have some flexibility incorporated into their policy design, specifying when Parental Leave can be used and how much at a time. Flexibility and free choice have consequently become a policy rationale for framing contemporary work–family policies (see Chapter Twelve; also Ferrarini and Duvander, 2010; Eydal and Rostgaard, 2015). Also for work organisations this may be seen as important, as employers can negotiate times spent on leave and potentially request that certain work tasks be performed during the leave period.

There are many types of flexibility in the design of leave policies (see Koslowski et al, 2016). The most prevalent are: stretching the leave over several years; combining leave with part-time work; splitting leave up into several blocks of time; and taking leave with or without the other parent present at the same time. An extensive right to unpaid job-protected leave may make the use of the paid leave flexible in, for example, extending leave periods by a combination of paid and unpaid leave. In the Nordic countries, all of these options are available to a varying degree (Table 11.2).

The flexibility of the system may influence Parental Leave use and facilitate gender equal parenting. For example, a comparison between Sweden and Finland concluded that the less flexible scheme in Finland is the reason for lower take-up rates by fathers, both among natives and immigrants (Tervola et al, 2017). Nevertheless, flexibility in how leave can be used may also have contrary consequences. Flexibility in leave use is found to make it difficult to set boundaries to the demands of work; according to Brandth and Kvande in Chapter Twelve, fathers who combine part-time leave with work seem to experience a double stress as both work and care require their full focus, and this makes them feel that they are not living up to the expectations of either (see also Chapter Thirteen about Québec). Besides, it is the mothers who have to manage caregiving when the fathers attend to their work, called 'work-oriented leave practice' (Smeby, 2013).

Another aspect of flexibility relevant for gender equality is whether fathers take leave with or without the mother being at home at the same time (O'Brien and Wall, 2017). The possibility to be home together may facilitate fathers' leave. In Sweden a transition period from one carer to another where both are home is acknowledged by giving the right to use 30 days simultaneously during the child's first year; this is a recently introduced and popular policy, used for about a third of all children (Swedish Social Insurance Agency, 2016). In Iceland, many fathers use part of their quota to be with the mother in the first weeks after births, but also take leave on their own later

Table 11.2: Overview of flexibility options in Parental Leave schemes in Nordic countries

Country	Use until a certain age	Split up the leave into blocks	Part-time leave combined with part-time work and/or unpaid leave	Both parents have option to be home at the same time
Denmark	9 years	Yes	Yes	Yes
Finland	2 years for fathers' quota, rest no flexibility	Yes	Yes, in combination with work	Partly (3 weeks)
Iceland	2 years	Yes	Yes, in combination with work or unpaid leave	Yes
Norway	3 years	Yes	Yes, in combination with work	Partly (only during the father's quota)
Sweden	4 years to use 384 days, 96 days can be used until the child is 12 years old	Yes	Yes, in combination with work or unpaid leave	Partly (1 month during the first year, not during quota)

Source: Compiled by authors based on data from country reports in Koslowski et al, 2016

(Arnalds et al, 2013). When the quota was four weeks in Norway, about half of fathers took leave when the mother was home (Brandth and Kvande, 2003), but as the quota has lengthened, parents more often take only part of it together. Taking leave together shortens the total leave period and may create care gaps; while fathers taking leave without the mother present has different effects on fathers' caregiving than if they are at home together (Bungum, 2013; Kvande and Brandth, 2017).

The effects of flexible leave for gender equality are thus highly debatable. On the one hand, flexibility increases use by fathers, and is likely to be important for the career possibilities of mothers who are employed in white-collar or superior positions. On the other hand, it seems obvious from studies that when parents are at home together, the father becomes more of a mother's helper than an independent carer, something that shapes his continued involvement in caring.

Compensation

The level of payment is a decisive factor for take-up of Parental Leave, and the fact that the father's income is often higher than the mother's is a commonly used explanation for the unequal division of leave. In the Nordic countries, Parental Leave is part of national social insurance, which covers income loss associated with caring for a young child with an earnings-related benefit. Women and men without employment are in most cases covered by a basic minimum benefit, which has varied over time and may be paid as a lump sum at birth or as a flat rate for every day on leave (Koslowski et al, 2016). The criteria of employment to qualify for the earnings-related benefit is part of the dual-earner model, rewarding work before having children; this incentive is particularly important for women's continued labour force participation and thus a basis for a more gender equal economic situation.

The level of compensation paid when on leave varies across the Nordic countries, and ceilings on payments also differ. The ceiling was decreased dramatically in Iceland during the financial crisis of 2008, leading to fewer fathers using leave and also using fewer days (Eydal and Gíslason, 2015). The level of compensation needs to be considered alongside the level of the ceiling. A high ceiling can be combined with low compensation, or the other way around, and various combinations are likely to attract different subgroups of parents to take different amounts of leave; thus, raising the ceiling makes taking leave more attractive to higher earning fathers. Overall, compensation levels and ceilings are related to gender equality as they make it more or less possible for fathers (and mothers) to take longer leave, thus increasing a more equal use of Parental Leave.

In addition to the social insurance benefit for Parental Leave, it is quite common for employers to pay a supplement based on collective agreements. In Sweden today, almost all employees are covered by such agreements, but they have developed in male dominated sectors only recently. There is no overview of Nordic collective agreements, but they exist to various degrees in all the countries; for example, in Norway and Denmark employers often provide such supplements.

Conclusions

Parental Leave sharing is clearly associated with gender equality, and the Nordic countries are often considered as case examples of the successful use of this policy instrument. Specific dimensions in policy design are particularly successful in increasing fathers' take-up of leave. First and foremost, the quota has reserved rights for fathers, and also signalled public support for active fatherhood and a gender equal division of care in the early years of the child. Increasingly, fathers take leave and use their quotas. However, the sharable part of Parental Leave is still used mainly by mothers. There is thus still considerable gender inequality in Parental Leave use, as well as in later childcare, household work and labour market participation in all the Nordic countries.

Regarding flexibility in how Parental Leave can be used, the Nordic countries have more ambivalent experiences. On the one hand, flexibility in how and when to use leave enhances fathers' leave use; but on the other hand, it may adversely affect the quality of care and may have negative consequences for the father–child relationship and continued sharing of unpaid work. Furthermore, different types of flexibility may have different consequences for gender equality. In particular, it seems imperative that fathers are at home without the mother for an extended period of time, in order to gain independent experience, confidence and abilities as carers.

Nordic experience also indicates that the level of compensation is important. Fathers' take-up seems more sensitive to economic incentives than mothers', as fathers mainly use the leave when it is highly compensated and the economic costs are less severe.

In addition, the basic dimension of how long the leave is, and whether care gaps are present, will be important for how parents share the leave and the length varies considerably between the Nordic countries. Another dimension of Parental Leave design is who is eligible to use it; eligibility criteria may exclude some groups of fathers within the Nordic countries, in particular those not living with the mother, or in families where the mother does not have a sustained and recent employment record (see also Chapter Fifteen). This questions the universal ideal behind Nordic family policy and may inhibit fathers' potential to take care responsibility.

Caution is needed about how to conceptualise and measure gender equality in the take-up of Parental Leave, and thus the evaluation of success against this goal; for example, gender equality may mean 50/50 sharing, but often much lower levels are accepted. Parental Leave, too, is only one of many policies in a social policy context where gender equality is emphasised. Yet it may work as a very important driver. It kicks in at a crucial point in women's and men's lives when inequality often accelerates. Fathers' take-up of Parental Leave is associated with participation in childcare and housework at later stages in life, and it may influence women's labour market situation in a positive way.

In conclusion, the Nordic experience of Parental Leave makes a few results clear. One is that given generous incentives fathers will make use of Parental Leave; they are not, in the Nordic case, particularly constrained by traditional ideas of masculinity. Social reactions to such usage may be ambivalent, but there is no strong resistance. Nevertheless, not all fathers use the leave and non-users are important groups to consider as they add up to at least one fifth of all fathers, even in countries with a non-transferable quota.

We can also conclude that the various dimensions of leave policy design and the way in which they interact with each other are important. For example, quotas have to be considered in the context of benefit levels and flexibility; a low flat-rate benefit or no flexibility in timing of taking leave may discourage leave-taking by fathers, while a mother's use of flexibility may be restricted if she is not eligible for earnings-related benefit and has to use the low flat rate.

Moreover, as discussed in Chapter Fourteen, it is important to see Parental Leave in the broader context of other family policies; such as the availability of public ECEC services with suitable hours and affordable fees, childcare allowances, as well as the right to leave from work to care for sick children and to work reduced hours. Care gaps between leave and public ECEC entitlements will inhibit gender equality, with mothers mainly covering any gaps in care by reducing labour market work or extending their labour market interruptions.

There is a fairly broad social and political consensus in all the Nordic countries that Parental Leave is an important social right for a number of reasons, one of which is gender equality. The political goal is that the leave should be shared as equally as possible. How to accomplish that has been widely debated, but it seems indisputable that non-transferable periods have produced the fastest and most comprehensive results for gender equality.

References

Almqvist, A.-L. and Duvander, A. (2014) 'Changes in gender equality? Swedish fathers' Parental Leave, division of childcare and housework', *Journal of Family Studies*, 20(1): 19–27.

Arnalds, A., Eydal, G. and Gíslason, I. (2013) 'Equal rights to paid Parental Leave and caring fathers – the case of Iceland', *Icelandic Review of Politics and Administration*, 9(2): 323–343, DOI: http://dx.doi.org/10.13177/irpa.a.2013.9.2.4

Brandth, B. and Gíslason, I.V. (2011) 'Family policies and the best interest of children', in I.V. Gíslason and G.B. Eydal (eds) *Parental Leave, Childcare and Gender Equality in the Nordic Countries*, TemaNord 2011: 562, Copenhagen: Nordic Council of Ministers, pp 109–145.

Brandth, B. and Kvande, E. (2003) 'Father presence in childcare', in A.M. Jensen and L. McKee (eds) *Children and the Changing Family: Between Transformation and Negotiation*, London: Routledge Falmer, pp 61–76.

Brandth, B. and Kvande, E. (2018) 'Masculinity and fathering alone during Parental Leave', *Men and Masculinities*, 21(1): 72–90. DOI: 10.1177/1097184X16652659

Brighouse, H. and Wright, E.O.S. (2008) 'Strong gender egalitarianism', *Politics and Society*, 36(3): 360–372.

Bungum, B. (2013) 'Barnas fedrekvote – tid sammen med far' [Children's father's quota – time with their father], in B. Brandth and E. Kvande (eds) *Fedrekvoten og den farsvennlige velferdsstaten* [*The father's quota and the father friendly welfare state*], Oslo: Universitetsforlaget, pp 60–73.

Cools, S., Fiva, J.H., Kirkeboen, J.L. (2015) 'Causal effects of paternity leave on children and parents', *The Scandinavian Journal of Economics*, 117(3): 801–828.

Doucet, A., Lero, D.S., McKay, L. and Tremblay, D.-G. (2017) 'Canada country note', in S. Blum, A. Koslowski and P. Moss (eds) *International Review of Leave Policies and Research 2017*. Available at www.leavenetwork.org/lp_and_r_reports/

Duvander, A. and Jans, A. (2009) 'Consequences of fathers' Parental Leave use: Evidence from Sweden', *Finnish Yearbook of Population Research 2009*, pp 49–62.

Duvander, A. and Johansson, M. (2015) 'Parental Leave use for different fathers: A study of the impact of three Swedish Parental Leave reforms', in T. Rostgaard and G. Eydal (eds) *Fatherhood in the Nordic Welfare States: Comparing Care Policies and Practice*, Bristol: Policy Press, pp 349–369.

Duvander, A. and Lammi-Taskula, J. (2011) 'Parental Leave', in I. Gislason and G.B. Eydal (eds) *Parental Leave, Childcare and Gender Equality in the Nordic Countries*, Tema Nord 2011: 562, Copenhagen: Nordic Council of Ministers, pp 29–62.

Duvander, A., Ferrarini, T. and Johansson, M. (2015) *Familjepolitik för alla? En ESO-rapport om föräldrapenning och jämställdhet* [*Family policy for all? A report on parental benefits and gender equality*] Report to the expert group in public economics (ESO) 2015: 5, Stockholm: Finance Ministry.

Evertsson, M. (2014) 'Föräldraledighet och karriär: Kvinnors och mäns lön efter en föräldraledighet' [Parental Leave and career: Women's and men's wages after Parental Leave], in K. Boye and M. Nermo (eds) *Lönsamt arbete – familjeansvarets fördelning och konsekvenser. SOU 2014: 28 [Work for profit – division and consequences of family responsibility]*, Stockholm: Fritzes, pp 187–226.

Evertsson, M. and Duvander, A. (2010) 'Parental Leave: Possibility or trap? Does Family Leave length effect Swedish women's labour market opportunities?', *European Sociological Review*, 27: 1–16.

Eydal, G.B. and Rostgaard, T. (2011). 'Gender equality re-visited: Changes in Nordic child-care policies in the 2000s', Regional issue, *Social Policy & Administration*, 45(2): 161–179.

Eydal, G.B. and Gíslason, I.V. (2015) 'Caring fathers and Parental Leave in prosperous times and times of crisis: the case of Iceland', in G.B. Eydal and T. Rostgaard (eds) *Fatherhood in the Nordic Welfare States: Comparing Care Policies and Practice*, Bristol: Policy Press, pp 327–348.

Eydal, G.B. and Rostgaard, T. (2015) 'Introduction', in G.B. Eydal and T. Rostgaard (eds) *Fatherhood in the Nordic Welfare States: Comparing Care Policies and Practice*, Bristol: Policy Press, pp 1–22.

Eydal, G.B., Gíslason, I.V., Rostgaard, T., Brandth, B., Duvander, A.-Z., Lammi-Taskula, J. (2015) 'Trends in Parental Leave in the Nordic countries: Has the forward march of gender equality halted?', *Community, Work and Family*, 18(2): 167–181.

Ferrarini, T. and Duvander, A.-Z. (2010) 'Earner–carer model at the cross-roads: Reforms and outcomes of Sweden's family policy in comparative perspective', *International Journal of Health Services*, 40(3): 373–398.

Goldscheider, F., Bernhardt, E. and Lappegard, T. (2015) 'The gender revolution: A framework for understanding changing family and demographic behaviour', *Population and Development Review*, 41(2): 207–239.

Hakovirta, M., Haataja, A., Eydal, G.B. and Rostgaard, T. (2015) 'Fathers' rights to family cash benefits in Nordic countries', in G.B. Eydal and T. Rostgaard (eds) *Fatherhood in the Nordic Welfare States: Comparing Care Policies and Practice*, Bristol: Policy Press, pp 79–102.

Hosking, A., Whitehouse, G. and Baxter, J. (2010) 'Duration of leave and resident fathers' involvement in infant care in Australia', *Journal of Marriage and the Family*, 72(5): 1301–1316.

Hwang, P. and Lamb, M. (1997) 'Father involvement in Sweden: A longitudinal study of its stability and correlates', *International Journal of Behavioral Development*, 21(3): 621–632.

Kitterød, R. (2013) 'Mer familiearbeid og mindre jobb blant småbarnsfedre' [More family work and less job for parents to small children], in B. Brandth and E. Kvande (eds) *Fedrekvoten og den farsvennlige verferdsstaten* [*The father's quota and the father friendly welfare state*], Oslo: Universitetsforlaget, pp 42–58.

Koslowski, A., Blum, S. and Moss, P. (eds) (2016) *International Review of Leave Policies and Research 2016.* Available at www.leavenetwork. org/lp_and_r_reports/

Kvande, E. and Brandth, B. (2017) 'Fathers on leave alone in Norway: Changes and continuities', in M. O'Brien and K. Wall (eds) *Comparative Perspectives on Work–Life Balance and Gender Equality: Fathers on Leave Alone*, London: Springer Open, pp 29–44.

Nordic Council of Ministers (2016) 'Nordic statistical yearbook'. Available at http://norden.diva-portal.org/smash/record.jsf?pid=di va2%3A763002&dswid=-519

O'Brien, M. and Wall, K. (2017) *Comparative Perspectives on Work–Life Balance and Gender Equality: Fathers on Leave Alone*, London: Springer.

Ottesen, M.H. (2015) 'The long-term impact of early paternal involvement in childcare in Denmark', in G.B. Eydal and T. Rostgaard (eds) *Fatherhood in the Nordic Welfare States: Comparing Care Policies and Practice*, Bristol: Policy Press, pp 251–276.

Rege, M. and Solli, I. (2013) 'The impact of paternity leave on future earnings', *Demography*, 50(6): 2255–2277.

Reimer, T., Erler, D. and Blum, S. (2017) 'Germany country note', in S. Blum, A. Koslowski and P. Moss (eds) *International Review of Leave Policies and Research 2017.* Available at www.leavenetwork.org/ lp_and_r_reports/

Rostgaard, T. and Lausten, M. (2015) 'Gender equality incentive policies and their consequences for men's and women's take-up of Parental Leave in Denmark', in G. Eydal and T. Rostgaard (eds) *Caring Fathers in the Nordic Welfare States: Policies and Practices of Contemporary Fatherhoods*, Bristol: Policy Press, pp 277–302.

Salmi, M. and Lammi-Taskula, J. (2015) 'Policy goals and obstacles for fathers' Parental Leave in Finland', in G.B. Eydal and T. Rostgaard (eds) *Fatherhood in the Nordic Welfare States: Comparing Care Policies and Practice*, Bristol: Policy Press, pp 303–324.

Salmi, M. and Närvi, J. (eds) (2017) 'Perhevapaat, talouskriisi ja sukupuolten tasa-arvo' [Parental Leave, economic crisis and gender equality]. *Raportti* 4/2017, Helsinki: THL.

Sarkadi, A., Kristiansson, R., Oberklaid, F. and Bremberg, S. (2008) 'Fathers' involvement and children's developmental outcomes: A systemic review of longitudinal studies', *Acta Paediatrica*, 97(2): 153–159.

Smeby, K.W. (2013) 'Fedrekvoten – stykkevis og delt eller fullt og helt?' [The father's quota – divided and piecemeal or complete and whole], in B. Brandth and E. Kvande (eds) *Fedrekvoten og den farsvennlige velferdsstaten [The Father's Quota and the Father Friendly Welfare State]*, Oslo: Universitetsforlaget, pp 150–164.

Stanfors, M. and Goldscheider, F. (2017) 'The forest and the trees: Industrialization, demographic change, and the ongoing gender revolution in Sweden and the United States,1870–2010', *Demographic Research* 36(3): 173–226.

Swedish Social Insurance Agency (2013) De jämställda föräldrarna [Equal parents], *Socialförsäkringsrapport 2013: 8*, Stockholm: Swedish Social Insurance Agency.

Swedish Social Insurance Agency (2016) *Social Insurance in Figures*, Stockholm: Swedish Social Insurance Agency.

Tervola, J., Duvander, A.-Z. and Mussino, E. (2017) 'Promoting Parental Leave for immigrant fathers: What role does policy play?', *Social Politics* 24(3): 269–297.

Wall, K. and Leitão, M. (2017) 'Portugal country note', in S. Blum, A. Koslowski and P. Moss (eds) *International Review of Leave Policies and Research 2017*. Available at www.leavenetwork.org/lp_and_r_reports/

World Economic Forum (2016) *Global Gender Gap Report*. Available at www.weforum.org/reports/the-global-gender-gap-report-2016

TWELVE

Flexibility: some consequences for fathers' caregiving[1]

Berit Brandth and Elin Kvande

Introduction

This chapter deals with fathers' experiences of using Parental Leave in a flexible way. Flexibility is often lauded in policy documents and research reports as an opportunity for mothers and fathers to control the timing of their leave-taking and as having the potential to increase the use of leave, particularly by fathers. Leave policies differ greatly between countries, reflecting many different political values, goals and designs, and many countries offer flexible use of Parental Leave to a greater or lesser extent (see Koslowski et al, 2016). This chapter focuses on Norwegian leave policy where the Parental Leave system is a mix between a family entitlement and an individual entitlement.

When fathers in Norway were given the opportunity to use 12 weeks of shared Parental Leave in 1978, this leave was a family entitlement aiming to increase gender equality in work and family. As the measure turned out to have little effect in terms of fathers' and mothers' sharing of leave days, fathers were given an individual right of four weeks in 1993 – the so-called 'father's quota'. The quota was not only an earmarked entitlement for employed fathers; it was also made non-transferable to the mother, and the weeks had to be taken during the child's first year. This rigid design proved to be effective as fathers soon adapted to it as part of their work–family practice (Brandth and Kvande, 2001).

At the time of writing, Norway has 25 years of experience with an earmarked, non-transferable leave for fathers. Over the years, the quota has been lengthened and measures have been introduced to make more fathers eligible and to encourage them to take leave. One aspect

---

[1] Part of the empirical analysis in this chapter has been published earlier in: Brandth and Kvande (2016), copyright © 2016 by the Authors (2015). Reprinted by permission of SAGE Publications, Ltd.

of the regulation meant to encourage fathers is increased flexibility in how leave may be taken. As the neoliberal ideology of choice made an increasingly strong impact on politics, authorities introduced flexibility into the leave design to compensate for the original rigidity of the quota. Flexibility seemed particularly important as the quota was lengthened. According to a government proposal (Ot.prp. no. 104, 2004–2005, p 28), the most important rationale for a flexible father's quota was 'to make it simpler to combine work and childcare'. Flexible leave was intended to help achieve the broad goal of the father's quota: dual earning/dual caring. Even though the Nordic countries put priority on home-based care for the first year of the child's life, they permit the leave to be spread out over a longer period (see Chapter Eleven). Norway offers the possibility to use all or part of the leave until the child reaches three years of age.

In the recently proposed EU Directive on Work–Life Balance for Parents and Carers, one of the proposed measures is an individual, non-transferable Parental Leave of four months for each parent, compensated at the level of sick pay. Parents should be able to request to take this leave on a part-time basis or split it into shorter blocks until the child reaches 12 years (European Commission, 2017), up from eight years in the current Directive on Parental leave. Like flexible work, flexibility in leave design seems to be taken for granted as a positive solution for combining work with childcare. However, flexible leave may have different effects to those of flexible work.

As noted, flexible leave design takes a number of forms. In this chapter, focus is on *time flexibility*, taking the father's quota as part-time leave in combination with part-time work or split into shorter blocs – piecemeal leave. There is reason to expect that the different forms of flexibility may affect fathers' caregiving differently. The chapter will explore part-time leave and piecemeal leave, asking how they influence fathers' caregiving practices. Although the study relates to the Norwegian situation, the knowledge produced may be useful to other countries in the process of redesigning leave rights for fathers.

The Norwegian Parental Leave system for fathers

How to increase fathers' use of Parental Leave is a relevant question for all countries that want to promote men's involvement in childrearing and gender equality more broadly. The explicit intention of the Norwegian father's quota is to improve the fathers' role, strengthen the father–child relationship and contribute to gender equality in both family and working life.

Table 12.1: Norwegian Parental Leave: distribution of weeks with 100% earnings compensation between mothers and fathers (selected years)

Year	Total leave	Mother's quota	Shared Parental Leave	Father's quota
1993–2005	42	3* + 6	29	4
2013	49	3* + 14	18	14
2014–2017	49	3* + 10	26	10

Note: * These three weeks must be taken before birth

As Table 12.1 shows, the length of the father's quota has varied and is today ten weeks of a total Parental Leave period of 49 weeks, with 100 per cent earnings compensation up to a fairly high ceiling of about NOK550,000 (€55,734) a year. It reached an all-time high of 14 weeks in 2013 before it was reduced to ten weeks when a conservative government took office. Almost all eligible fathers (over 90 per cent) take all or part of the father's quota. The period of shared Parental Leave is mostly taken by mothers (Kitterød et al, 2017).

Since the 1990s, choice and flexibility have increasingly been promoted in Norwegian political debates, and in 2007 the father's quota was made flexible. Fathers' part-time leave may be concurrent with mothers' part-time leave and flexible working hours, and a block of the father's quota may be taken together with the mother's holidays from work. The alternative to flexible leave is continuous leave on a full-time basis.

Flexible use of the father's quota has been increasing since it was first introduced. Official statistics from the Norwegain Labour and welfare Administration (nav.no) show that in 2016, 23 per cent of eligible fathers chose part-time leave, compared with 5 per cent of mothers. There is no record of how many fathers split the quota into blocks. When the father's quota was extended in 2013, it was expected that fathers would divide their father's quota more often than when the quota was shorter (Fougner, 2012). It is this new pattern of use we will examine in more detail in this chapter. As a longer father's quota combined with an opportunity to use it flexibly has influenced fathers' take-up patterns, it may in turn also have consequences for their caregiving.

Research on Parental Leave design

In social policy scholarship concerned with gender equality, there has been increased focus on Parental Leave policies and their potential to strengthen women's ties to employment and men's to caregiving. Parental Leave designs are often multidimensional and complex (Ray et al, 2010). The designs vary between countries in terms of eligibility, financing, duration and flexibility. Research has documented that individualised and non-transferable Parental Leave rights, rather than gender-neutral family rights, are more effective when it comes to fathers taking leave (Brighouse and Wright, 2008; O'Brien, 2009; Brandth and Kvande, 2009; 2012; Ray et al, 2010; Duvander and Lammi Taskula, 2011; Haas and Rostgaard, 2011, Eydal and Gíslason, 2013). Daly (2011) applies the term 'individualization processes' for the change in family policy designs towards a dual earner/dual carer model.

The presence of the father's quota in the Norwegian and other Nordic Parental Leave systems has had a positive effect on fathers' involvement in caring (see also Chapter Eleven). In order to understand why this is so, Kvande and Brandth (2017) have explored how the design elements have worked in fathers' everyday practices. Their findings show that the quota being a statutory, earmarked and non-transferable leave with generous income replacement is experienced as important because then employers accept it. To use their quota has become a norm for fathers in Norway (Halrynjo and Kitterød, 2016).

While much research has been concerned with the effects of Parental Leave use, research on the effects of flexibility in the Parental Leave design for mothers and fathers is rather scarce. Some exceptions are Brandth and Kvande, 2013; 2016; Smeby, 2013; Duvander, 2013; Boyer, 2017.

Shared Parental Leave has been flexible since 1994 in Norway. The so-called 'time account scheme' allowed for part-time and piecemeal use, but within the child's first year only. It was meant to enable leave to be tailored to each family's special situation and make it easier for employed parents to manage the time squeeze of combining work and family. Since it reduced the period of total absence from work, it was argued that it would make it particularly attractive for men to use the leave (NOU, 1993, p.52).

A study found that flexible use was low for mothers as well as fathers (Holter and Brandth, 2005). Only 2.2 per cent of mothers, who are the main users of shared Parental Leave, used the leave flexibly. These mothers had university education and careers, and they wanted to return to work as soon as possible, albeit part time. The authors pointed out that this practice represented a break with the moral obligations of parenting in Norway, which is for parents to care for the child at home during its first year. It also showed that use of flexible leave for parents in career jobs demanded competent planning as the borderline between work and home became diffuse. Parents tended to work more than they had agreed upon, and the study concluded that working life more than the parents profited from flexible leave. Smeby (2013) has called this take-up pattern a 'work-oriented' leave practice, in contrast to an 'equality oriented' practice where fathers take their leave all in one piece.

Another take-up pattern can be described as 'family oriented' (Smeby, 2013). When the father times his leave so that the mother is home at the same time, the mother's main responsibility for the child is not interrupted, and the father becomes her support person. These fathers are more likely to need the mothers to translate the child's needs for them, and fathers' care practices based on knowing the child are not as well developed. As a result, they feel more comfortable with older children, often giving priority to older siblings (Brandth and Kvande, 2003).

Flexible leave may be a useful work–family balancing tool in some contexts. A French study describes the effects of flexible Parental Leave taken one day a week in the child's first three years (Boyer, 2017). Since it is rare for French fathers to take Parental Leave, part-time leave is positively assessed by fathers as giving 'a good mix' of work and time with the children. However, the study concludes that part-time leave does not change the cultural norm of mother–child primacy, with fathers not fully accepted as nurturers, and thus it is not effective as a gender equality tool.

Data and method

This chapter is based on interviews with 20 fathers who have taken the father's quota on a part-time or piecemeal basis. Thirteen fathers had used part-time leave in combination with work, while seven had split the quota into blocs of time of various lengths. The sample was selected from a larger sample of cohabiting or married heterosexual fathers who had used the father's quota. The fathers were recruited by contacting a university and private firms, as well as snowballing, and most interviews were conducted in 2012 and 2013. The interviews were semi-structured, lasted from one to two hours, and for the most part the fathers were interviewed in their homes. At the time of the interview, their leave experiences were quite recent, the oldest children being two-and-a-half years old. In the interests of confidentiality, real names are not used.

Considering the Norwegian eligibility rules, where the right to Parental Leave is earned through employment, all the fathers and mothers had been permanently employed full-time before the birth of the child. An extra effort was put into finding interviewees with lower educational backgrounds. This was only partially successful, as 14 of the 20 fathers had high- to medium-level education. However, the occupational composition of the sample is varied.

Most commonly, fathers in Norway take their leave after the mother has taken hers, usually starting when the child is about nine months old. Flexible use, as in this sample, means that leave tends to be more spread out over the child's first three years than would be the case if not taken flexibly. Some of the fathers on part-time leave had a well-organised system alternating between work and leave every other day, or taking leave for one day a week while working the other four days. The part-time leave could also be more fluidly organised, for instance some fathers agreeing with their employers on a certain division between work and care but leaving open how this would be applied in practice. Other fathers in the sample used the part-time leave option to shorten the working day. Concerning piecemeal leave, its most common usage was to take one block of leave relatively early during the first year as a family holiday, and a second and third block later. Splitting leave into just two or three blocks results in relatively long leave periods, which may have different consequences for fathers' caregiving than if leave is split into shorter blocks of time.

Some consequences of flexible leave-taking

The main reasons fathers gave for choosing flexible leave were their pursuit of the optimal arrangement, their feeling irreplaceable at work, and their tendency to define the leave as a holiday (Brandth and Kvande, 2013). This section focuses on what fathers say about the *consequences* of part-time leave for their caregiving.

Part-time leave and fathers' interrupted caregiving

Fathers who chose part-time leave in combination with work did so because they believed it would work well in their situation. It would enable them to attend to work at the same time as taking leave. In retrospect, however, many of these fathers were dissatisfied with their choice, for several reasons. It often created stressful situations, not enabling childcare and work to be combined satisfactorily. Gustav, a graduate engineer, who took his whole quota on a part-time basis, stated:

I did not envision that there would be so much stress because I was actually also at work at the same time. So this is a thing I...I don't think I would do this again. It wasn't really leave because I never got into it as a routine. Then it wasn't really work either, because I couldn't go to work every day. So it became very...it was really two things that both were sort of half-way. And that was really not a good solution.

Gustav took his part-time leave on the days when his wife, a nurse, worked her daytime shift. Although it had seemed like a good solution in the planning, neither work nor care benefited, as his job disturbed his focus on childcare and vice versa. Since this was his first child, he felt it was particularly important to be able to establish good routines, but this was hindered by part-time leave-taking.

That you establish a routine every day, if you get up and do this and that, then I think it would be easier. Then I think there's less work too. For example, clothing and that stuff, and that she has, like...that you make it flow.

It was this flow in the caregiving that he missed. He did not experience 'the slow time', in which the child's needs direct how time is spent, and where not too many other things have to take place at the same time. He believed that being able to totally disregard the job during the period of leave would have been much better 'because it's a little bit like this, there are phone calls and mails'.

Ben, who worked as a financial advisor in a bank, had planned to stay home on leave for two or three days a week. He related how it worked in his case:

Monday I went to work, Tuesday I was home, Wednesday I went to work again, and like this...You felt that when you were at work, you were always lagging behind. You would bring some of this grind home with you, and then you're home and the baby is crying and then you need to feed it. It was more of a hassle for me than not, so if I were to do it again...but let's be clear, we're not having any more babies! But if I were to do it again, I would have chosen to take out the full leave in one go, could have made some plans, perhaps travelled to see grandparents, done more trivial things together. You don't have that option in an off–on situation.

He described how making himself available to work caused many interruptions, when passing the following judgement on his experience with part-time leave:

> It simply didn't work; it was a horrible lesson to learn. Really, having such a part-time set-up...In my job, customers call early and late, mail pops in, inquiries come in. They don't know when I'm on father's leave or not. If I had been able to tell them that I'll be back on this or that date [full-time leave], they could have related to that. But the point is that they also called when I was home with the baby. I muted the phone eventually, and then I saw 13 unanswered calls and there were texts. So this was far too poorly organised by me. I must admit that my boss at work told me to do what was best for me, so I had free rein to do this as I wanted. But as it turned out this was not a success.

It was only in retrospect that he saw that he had made a poor choice when he opted for part-time leave, and he had to accept the consequences of this choice. From Gustav's and Ben's experiences, it is clear that part-time leave demands strict organisation. What Ben recommended to others was:

> to put the job entirely on the sidelines! Even if you're in sales, you just have to say that this is how it is during this period of time! Just put everything else aside and say to yourself: Now you're taking your father's quota for so and so many weeks and nothing else. That's my hot tip.

Many fathers on a part-time father's quota talked about how it felt as if they were working full-time, while additionally having a one-year-old to care for. Nicolai, a research scientist, who was on leave one day a week, described this feeling:

> I needed to switch off and on all the time. You can't work normally, so it was stress...It might be my job, because I'm doing research, and then you're working more than the hours you spend sitting in your office. So you must be strong and not check your e-mail when you're home. It wasn't easy.

Julio, an engineer working in telecommuting, who also took his father's quota as part-time leave, reported how 'the plan, or idea, was that I shouldn't lose so much contact with the job, but it didn't work out in practice'.

Part-time use of the father's quota meant that leave was not used to get mentally involved in day-to-day childcare and other domestic chores. The chaotic lives that fathers described, attempting to handle both work and care, weakened their chances to establish autonomous care routines. 'Multitasking' by combining part-time care with part-time work did not supply the continuous slow time that childcare requires. As a result, part-time use of the father's quota confirmed the mother's position as the primary caregiver in the family, as she needed to be available as the ground crew.

Piecemeal leave: various caregiving consequences

Some of the fathers involved in the study were quite pleased with their choice of flexible leave after it was over, particularly those who had divided the father's quota into two or three blocks of some length. One of them was Arne, a cultural worker. As the father of three children he had used the father's quota three times. His last time, when the father's quota had been expanded to ten weeks, he split into two parts. He reflected that 'my experience is that it is nice to have father's leave and stay home, so that's what I will remember…I would really have liked to have had longer leave, but this is about finding a good solution with my wife'. With all their experience, this couple had found that leave in two parts worked well for them since it gave Arne two continuous periods of five weeks, each of which was not interrupted by work.

> As a man I have been used to prioritize myself, career, studies and such, so this is a completely different role… When she [youngest daughter] is awake you can't do anything else than mind her, and that is the purpose, of course. So I felt privileged. You get a different form of contact with the child when you don't compete with the mother. Feeding and nursing the baby are clearly the mother's advantage. So in that way, it is lovely that she is not there as you get a better contact then.

Although he took piecemeal leave, the length of the two blocks of leave resulted in the type of father–child relation that is described as happening during continuous, fairly long leaves (Brandth and Kvande, 2003). Another father, Steinar, a consultant engineer, who first had a period of full-time leave and then part-time leave for a second period, was also fairly pleased with his choice, but he described full-time leave the most positively:

> I would say that the first period, when I had this nice daddy-on-leave feeling where I was at home alone and had the ongoing run of the household with Emilia. And this was…it was just like I had envisioned. Bliss, really! It was very nice and time to spare and calm and lots of nice things.

It seems relatively common among fathers who took leave in several blocks to define one part of the father's quota as a holiday spent together with mother and child. After the quota was extended to ten weeks, additional leave was left over after this perceived holiday period. Some fathers in the sample took the rest of their leave part time, but others, like Ivar, took it in one full-time block. He and his wife organised Parental Leave so that she first took six months, then a three-week 'holiday break' together with Ivar who used his father's quota. After this, Ivar's wife went back to work and Ivar took the rest of his father's quota plus the remaining three months of shared Parental Leave. His choice is an example of how the father's quota is split up and partly defined as holidays, but it is also an example of a father who took longer leave than the father's quota and was home alone with the child for a relatively long period.

It is not customary to see the whole father's quota as a holiday, but one father did so. After the mother had taken leave for five months, David took five weeks father's quota plus four weeks of his saved summer holiday. In this period the mother was also home. David planned to repeat this arrangement next summer: 'so I will do it like this next year as well. Nine weeks holiday, two years in a row! I haven't had that since I left school, ha, ha'. David worked in a private consultancy firm, and nine weeks absence during the summer seemed possible for the firm to manage.

> Before I left I said that I am going to have nine weeks holiday, and I was laughed at a bit at work. Holiday, like! Ha, ha. Honestly, I did have nine weeks' holiday. We were together as a family for nine weeks and shared the caring. So, it would have been more of a drudgery to mind the

child if I had been alone than it is when we are two and can share it and take it a bit as it comes.

We see from the quote how David describes his daily caring during this period as being shared with the mother. Sharing as they see fit is quite different – and less a moral obligation for fathers – from what would have been the case if he had had sole responsibility for caring. Timing the leave to coincide with the mother's holiday does not serve to strengthen fathers' own caring competence and responsibility. The common leave period parents spend together without work obligations was experienced by the fathers in Smeby's (2013) study as 'a golden period'. To be two parents together sharing the daily caregiving tasks was experienced as a relaxed time, a longed-for break and absence of stress. But, according to Smeby, even if a 'family oriented' leave is experienced as positive for the family, it does not challenge the father to take actual responsibility, and thus the full gender-equality potential of the father's quota is not realised.

Flexible leave for avoidant fathering

The literature has shown that an earmarked, non-flexible father's quota has the power to get fathers who would never have thought of taking leave by themselves to use Parental Leave (Brandth and Kvande, 2002; 2012). This section will explore how flexible leave rather opens up the possibility for fathers to *avoid* taking the main responsibility for childcare.

Nicolai, a father of two, stated: 'Really, when I was thinking about leave, I couldn't envision staying at home for ten weeks with the kids. It's simply too much'. He described his reluctance the following way:

It's very difficult, not really that much fun, to be frank. I don't want to shock anybody; really, I'm just saying how it felt like. Caring for a baby is demanding; it's really difficult, you know. You can't turn your back, or go to the loo without the child coming with you, more or less. Or if your turn your back, the child is holding a knife, it's like…it's so hard! I thought ten weeks at home, that will be hard physically and mentally, and it'll be boring too! When the child is so young, there's not that much you can do, I feel. But I thought that it was a very good idea to do it… working 80 per cent over one year.

Nicolai decided that one day of leave per week was what he would be able to manage. He also fetched the other children earlier from kindergarten and argued that this way of taking leave benefited the entire family because there was less stress on a day-to-day basis. For first-time parents, the hard and externally unvalued work of nurturing and caring for a very young child often comes as a shock (Miller, 2011), and this might be the underlying reason behind Nicolai's choice.

This may also have influenced some fathers who expressed a wish to postpone taking leave if they were to have another child. 'I might want to have my leave when the child is a little bit older, really', Gustav said, his reason being that 'for my part at least, when the child is a little bit older, there is slightly more, how to say it, response with the child, like, so I feel this is more rewarding for my part, really'. This idea that it could be more rewarding to take Parental Leave when children are rather older was a main reason why some fathers in the sample had postponed taking leave. This was the case with Dag who decided to take the leave when his son had become older. He had negotiations with his wife, who would have preferred him to have longer periods of leave during the child's first year, but Dag steadfastly insisted that he 'take it in periods until he [their son] turns three', the longest period of leave he ever took being four days in a row. He believed that the relationship between father and son would benefit from having some common experiences that they would both appreciate:

> It means more for the future development between me and my son that I do something that he is able to understand, remember and enjoy. And then I thought that enjoying things together must be something he thinks is exciting and fun, thus he must learn what an excavator is first! Otherwise, we cannot go together and look at construction sites. Because I knew for certain that we would be stopping to look at construction sites. He must be old enough first, then I'll take out father's leave. Now he thinks this is great fun!

Dag and his son often took a drive to look at construction sites, and he felt it had given him richer experiences with his son than if he had stayed home minding him. For Dag, infant care did not qualify as a meaningful father–son experience:

> I did it, I took some Fridays and walked him in his baby carriage while he was sleeping and burping and drinking

milk from a bottle. But I felt that this didn't give me the same, because I could have done this on Saturday and Sunday as well. But now I feel that it is much more rewarding to be with him because now he is much more interested in being with his father, now it's not just about feeding him.

It is interesting to note that Dag treats the father's quota as something that should be rewarding for himself; so for him, the father's quota became days off with his son and not ongoing daily caregiving. He constructed a different type of fathering as he attached more importance to fun and games with his three-year-old child. These findings confirm research about men participating in the more enjoyable aspects of child-rearing, leaving ongoing, primary responsibility for children to mothers (Klinth and Johansson, 2010). Fathers' ability to choose the character of their involvement shapes their fathering, and in such cases leave-taking does not seem to represent any real shift towards fathers taking greater responsibility for childcare. Flexible leave, therefore, increases the risk that leave policies will only partially dismantle the gendered division of care responsibility.

Conclusions

In this chapter we have focused on the individual, non-transferable right to Parental Leave for fathers in Norway – a right that has now become mature. Over the years, flexibility options have been introduced, and this has made Norway a country with many choices in its Parental Leave system. Addressing the increasing body of research, which focuses on the design of Parental Leave, we have studied part-time and piecemeal leave as alternatives to taking all of the leave at the same time, which was the main option in the first 14 years after the introduction of the father's quota. Full-time leave is thus the alternative and fathers' standard reference situation. In other countries where flexible leave is introduced from the start and men's family involvement is less well established, this may be different; flexible use of leave is preferable to no use of leave.

Our results show that taking leave on a part-time basis in combination with part-time work has negative effects on fathers' caregiving. Choosing this as an alternative implies fathers making themselves available for work, something that often creates stressful situations and interrupted caregiving. The boundaries between work and childcare become blurred and prevent men from getting fully immersed with their babies. Part-time use of the quota assumes that the mother is available, and thus it tends to confirm her as the primary caregiver. Consequently, there is no clear change in the main responsibility for caring. Institutionalising the opportunity to work during the leave is, therefore, not a guaranteed way of increasing fathers' involvement in caregiving.

Piecemeal leave seems to have two different types of effect on fathering. When a block is taken by fathers as a holiday together with the mother, the opportunity to take responsibility and increase their caregiving competence is hampered. This resonates with studies comparing what effects staying at home alone with the baby or staying at home together with the mother has for fathering. However, when the blocks of leave are fairly long and the mother is at work, the situation for caregiving is different. In such situations, the effect of staying home on leave alone corresponds to what previous studies have found about the effects of continuous, solo fathering (Brandth and Kvande, 2003; 2017; O'Brien and Wall, 2017).

We have also seen that flexible leave is an option for fathers who are reluctant to take on childcare. It supports the idea of the choice-making father who has the privilege of making his own choices when it comes to work and care. Part-time leave over several years thus weakens the effects of non-transferability. Interestingly, one motive for taking leave when the child is older is that fathers might see it as more rewarding for themselves.

The aim of this chapter has been to get insight into an important issue in leave policy: how flexibility as a design element in Parental Leave may affect fathers' caregiving. The experience of Norwegian fathers suggests that offering a part-time leave option and the possibility of taking leave over a long period may stall progress towards dual caring and gender equal practices. This lesson may be important for the EU, whose proposed directive envisages spreading leave-taking over 12 years, as well as individual countries developing their Parental Leave system. The results also indicate the need to consider the effects of flexibility when assessing the much-commended Nordic leave systems. It is, however, important to note that the period over which leave-taking may be spread is relatively short in the Nordic countries, and that there may even be a trend to reduce the period; Sweden just did so, and a recent white paper on family policies in Norway suggests the leave-taking period be reduced to two years (NOU, 2017, p6).

References

Boyer, D. (2017) 'Fathers on leave alone in France: Does part-time parental leave for men move towards an egalitarian model?', in K. Wall and M. O'Brien (eds) *Comparative Perspectives on Work–Life Balance and Gender Equality*. London: Springer, pp 183–204.

Brandth, B. and Kvande, E. (2001) 'Flexible work and flexible fathers', *Work, Employment and Society*, 15(2): 251–267.

Brandth, B. and Kvande, E. (2002) 'Reflexive fathers: Negotiating parental leave and working life', *Gender, Work and Organization* 9(2): 186–203.

Brandth, B. and Kvande, E. (2003) 'Father presence in childcare', in A.M. Jensen and L. McKee (eds) *Children and the Changing Family: Between Transformation and Negotiation*, London: Routledge Falmer, pp 61–75.

Brandth, B. and Kvande, E. (2009) 'Gendered or gender-neutral care policies for fathers?', *Annals of the American Academy of Political and Social Science*, 624(1): 177–189.

Brandth, B. and Kvande, E. (2012) 'Free choice or gentle force? How can parental leave change gender practices?', in A.T. Kjørholt and J. Qvortrup (eds) *The Modern Child and the Flexible Labour Market*, Houndsmills, Basingstoke: Palgrave Macmillan, pp 56–70.

Brandth, B. and Kvande, E. (2013) 'Fedrekvotens valgfrihet og fleksibilitet' [Father's quota's freedom of choice and flexibility], in B. Brandth and E. Kvande (eds) *Fedrekvoten og den farsvennlige velferdsstaten [Father's quota and the father-friendly welfare state]*, Oslo: Universitetsforlaget, pp 134–149.

Brandth, B. and Kvande, E. (2016) 'Fathers and flexible parental leave', *Work, Employment and Society*, 30(2): 275–290.

Brandth, B. and Kvande, E. (2017) 'Masculinity and fathering alone during parental leave', *Men and Masculinities*, DOI: 10.1177/1097184X16652659

Brighouse, H. and Wright, E.O. (2008) 'Strong gender egalitarianism', *Politics and Society*, 36(3): 360–372.

Daly, M. (2011) 'What adult worker model? A critical look at recent social policy reform in Europe from a gender and family perspective', *Social Politics*, 18(19): 1–24.

Duvander, A.-Z. (2013) 'Er den svenske permisjonsordningen for fleksibel?' [Is the Swedish parental leave too flexible?], in B. Brandth and E. Kvande (eds) *Fedrekvoten og den farsvennlige velferdsstaten [Father's Quota and the Father-Friendly Welfare State]*, Oslo: Universitetsforlaget, pp 165–179.

Duvander, A.-Z. and Lammi-Taskula, J. (2011) 'Parental leave', in I.V. Gíslason and G.B. Eydal (eds) *Parental Leave, Childcare and Gender Equality in the Nordic Countries*, TemaNord 2011: 562, Copenhagen: Nordic Council of Ministers, pp 31–64.

European Commission (2017) Proposal for a Directive of the European Parliament and of the Council on Work–Life Balance for Parents and Carers and Repealing Council Directive 2010/18/eu (COM(2017) 253 final). Available at https://eur-lex.europa.eu/legal-content/EN/TXT/HTML/?uri=CELEX:52017PC0253&from=EN

Eydal, G.B. and Gíslason, I.V. (2013) 'Tredelt permisjon og lang fedrekvote. Erfaringer fra Island' [Parental leave in three parts and long father leave. Experiences from Iceland], in B. Brandth and E. Kvande (eds) *Fedrekvoten og den farsvennlige velferdsstaten* [*Father's quota and the father-friendly welfare state*], Oslo: Universitetsforlaget, pp 222–237.

Fougner, E. (2012) 'Fedre tar ut hele fedrekvoten – også etter at den ble utvidet til ti uker', [Fathers use the whole father's quota – also after extension], *Arbeid og velferd*, 2: 71–77.

Gornick, J. and Meyers, M.K. (2003) *Families that Work: Policies for Reconciling Parenthood and Employment*, New York: Russel Sage Foundation.

Haas, L. and Rostgaard, T. (2011) 'Fathers' rights to paid parental leave in the Nordic countries: Consequences for the gendered division of leave', *Community, Work and Family*, 14(2): 177–195.

Halrynjo, S. and Kitterød, R.H. (2016) *Fedrekvoten – norm for fedres permisjonsbruk* [*Father's quota – a norm for how much father use leave*] I *Norge og Norden. Report 2016: 06*, Oslo: Institute for Social Research.

Holter, T. and Brandth, B. (2005) 'Tidskonto: Valgfrihet for elitemødre?' [Time account: freedom of choice for elite mothers?], in B. Brandth, B. Bungum and E. Kvande (eds) *Valgfrihetens tid* [*Time for choice*], Oslo: Gyldendal Akademisk, pp 79–94.

Kitterød, R.H., Halrynjo, S. and Østbakken, K.M. (2017) *Pappaperm? Fedre som ikke tar fedrekvote – hvor mange, hvem og hvorfor? Report 2017: 2*. Oslo: Institute for Social Research.

Klinth, R. and Johansson, T. (2010) *Nya svenska fäder*, Umeå: Borea Bokförlag.

Koslowski, A., Blum, S. and Moss, P. (2016) *International Review of Leave Policies and Research 2016*. Available at www.leavenetwork.org/lp_and_r_reports/

Kvande, E. and Brandth, B. (2017) 'Individualized, non-transferable parental leave for European fathers: Migrant perspectives', *Community, Work and Family*, 20(1): 19–34.

Miller, T. (2011) *Making Sense of Fatherhood*, Cambridge: Cambridge University Press.

Nav.no (2016) *Foreldrepenger, engangsstønad og svangerskapspenger.* Available at www.nav.no/no/NAV+og+samfunn/Statistikk/Familie+-+statistikk/Foreldrepenger%2C+engangsstonad+og+svangerskapspenger

NOU (Norges offentlige utredninger) (Official Norwegian Reports) (1993) *Tid for barna*, NOU 1993: 12, Government.no. Available at www.regjeringen.no/globalassets/upload/kilde/odn/tmp/2002/0034/ddd/pdfv/154809-nou1993-12.pdf

NOU (Norges offentlige utredninger) (Official Norwegian Reports) (2017) *Offentlig støtte til barnefamiliene*, NOU 2017: 6, Government.no. Available at www.regjeringen.no/no/dokumenter/nou-2017-6/id2540981/sec1

O'Brien, M. (2009) 'Fathers, Parental Leave policies and infant quality of life: International perspectives and policy impact', *The Annals of the American Academy of Political and Social Science*, 624: 190–213.

O'Brien, M. and Wall, K. (eds) (2017) *Comparative Perspectives on Work–Life Balance and Gender Equality: Fathers on Leave Alone*, London: Springer Open.

Ot.prp. no. 104 (2004–2005) *Om lov om endringer i folketrygdloven og enkelte andre lover* [*Concerning the Act on Amendments to the National Insurance Act and certain other laws*], Oslo: Ministry of Children and Family Affairs.

Ray, R., Gornick, J. and Schmitt, J. (2010) 'Who cares? Assessing generosity and gender equality in parental leave policy designs in 21 countries', *Journal of European Social Policy*, 20(3): 196–216.

Smeby, K. (2013) 'Stykkevis og delt eller fullt og helt?', in B. Brandth and E. Kvande (eds) *Fedrekvoten og den farsvennlige velferdsstaten*, Oslo: Universitetsforlaget, pp 150–164.

THIRTEEN

The workplace: challenges for fathers and their use of leave

Valérie Harvey and Diane-Gabrielle Tremblay

Introduction

Up to the present day, public gender equality policies have aimed to improve women's situation by giving them rights equal to those of men or supporting positive discrimination. But this has not been sufficient to ensure effective equality between men and women. Indeed, Esping-Andersen (2009) does not hesitate to qualify the movement that began in the twentieth century as an 'incomplete revolution'. Women are still earning less than men per hour for full-time jobs and they often perform several 'jobs': career woman, domestic worker and carer. This creates tensions that weigh on the shoulders of these 'superwomen', trying to combine their careers with family life and household chores (Conway, 2003). An enduring unequal division of housework not only makes work–life integration extremely difficult, but may even have a negative impact on the birth rate (Holloway, 2010, p.178).

Should future public policies designed to achieve genuine gender equality be aimed not at women, but at men? In an arena such as work–family balance, it may well be a prerequisite for gender equality. According to the OECD, the involvement of fathers is not only essential to the welfare of the family, but it has an impact on the perception of workplaces regarding female employees and wage inequality:

> As long as mothers rather than fathers reduce labour force participation in the presence of children, and make use of parental leave provisions, [there] are of course employers who perceive women as less committed to their career than men, and are therefore less likely to invest in female career opportunities. (OECD, 2007, p.59)

Yet it is not always easy for fathers to take leave from work for family reasons, since this responsibility traditionally belongs to the mother and firms are not always open to fathers' desires to be more active in sharing family responsibilities. Thus, public policies play a very important role in bringing about change: Paternity Leave and father-only Parental Leave become ways to bypass 'mother gatekeeping' based on the traditional parental roles (Tremblay and Lazzari Dodeler, 2015). By encouraging fathers to take a break from work, because if they do not take their leave entitlement they will lose it, the state sends a clear message about the importance of the father's role in the family.

This chapter examines the opportunities that Paternity and Parental Leaves create for fathers, based on the findings of two qualitative studies of leave-taking fathers in Québec. It reveals some difficulties encountered in the workplace by fathers who do take leave, such as being asked to take a shorter leave, to postpone the taking of leave, or to compromise part of their leave by working from home (telework). We also investigate the problems that arise when fathers, upon their return to work, try to reconcile new family responsibilities with their previous routine working schedule.

We consider the literature before presenting our findings from extensive interviews with fathers. To support our conclusions, we use extracts from these interviews relating to discussions which the fathers had with their employers. Altogether, just over 60 interviews were conducted: around 30 interviews with fathers who took Paternity Leave and, in some cases, Parental Leave, being at home alone with their child, and drawn from a variety of sectors and occupations (Tremblay and Lazzari Dodeler, 2015); and a similar number with fathers in the IT multimedia sector, many of whom encountered challenges in the use of the Parental Leave, in particular with regard to timing and length.

Family public policies: a brief history and ideal type classifications

As the fertility rate has declined in many industrialised countries, the introduction of Parental Leave is part of the broader set of family policies that have been developed to help parents reconcile work and family. The labour market has also undergone profound changes during the twentieth century. Atypical work, self-employment, competition for quality jobs and pressure for greater job performance have all steadily increased (Tremblay, 2012). Because it is difficult to manage the combination of demanding work and time required by the family, parents in the twenty-first century often experience a lot of tension: 'Parents who are in the workplace and who have young children are twice as stressed as the population on average' (Pronovost, 2015, p.47).

In order to counteract the decline in birth rates and promote work–life balance (among other rationales as discussed elsewhere in this volume), many governments have therefore put in place a series of family policies. According to Esping-Andersen's typology (1990), the Nordic countries belong to the group of social democratic welfare states, in which the state is heavily involved in redistribution among citizens and provides innovative family support (Haavind and Magnusson, 2005). There are two other categories: the conservative states that allow the intervention of the government, but in a less direct way, such as France and Germany, for example. Finally, unlike the social democratic regimes, the liberal states minimise government interventions in favour of market intervention (Tremblay, 2017; 2019). The Anglophone countries, including the United States, the United Kingdom, Australia and Canada (except for Québec province), largely constitute this liberal group.

When discussing Parental Leave, the institutional models described by Hantrais and Letablier (1996) arguably offer more helpful explanations and categorisations for understanding the types of relations between family and work in different countries than are to be found in Esping-Andersen's work. The ideal types of Esping-Andersen and of Hantrais and Letablier cover different categories and as such are difficult to combine analytically. It could be said that Esping-Anderson's liberal ideal type, placing a greater emphasis on individual freedom, overlaps to a certain extent with Hantrais and Letablier's non-interventionist model; the ideal type country in this case largely delegates responsibility to employers to negotiate agreements with their employees about leave when there is a birth (Tremblay, 2019).

Countries typically classified as 'liberal', which have introduced Maternity, Paternity and Parental Leave, and several 'conservative' countries, which have also done so, would arguably fit better in Hantrais and Letablier's ideal type model based on alternation between work and family, however. This model allows parents (mostly mothers) to leave the labour market or reduce their hours to care for children (Netherlands for example, see Tremblay, 2019). They will then be supported by public policies before returning to work, often part-time, when children enter school.

Iceland also stands out because even if classified as 'liberal', it should clearly be included, like the 'social democratic' countries, in the work–family balance ideal type proposed by Hantrais and Letablier that has put in place measures to allow work to be pursued while also allowing for family life. This latter set of countries gives priority to equal treatment between men, women and children (Tremblay, 2019, p.263) and they develop family policies that are consistent with these values. Faced with these hybrid states, the classification developed by Esping-Andersen is then less useful than that of Hantrais and Letablier from the point of view understanding the dynamics of family policies, even if both typologies may be considered complementary to some extent.

A feature of those countries in the work–family balance ideal type has been the treatment of fathers in leave policies, in particular the provision of a 'father's quota' of non-transferable and well-paid leave. Norway (1993), Sweden (1995) and Denmark (1997) were the first countries to introduce such a quota, followed by Iceland (2003). The Canadian province of Québec followed in 2006 with its own non-transferable Paternity Leave of three to five weeks, of which more in the next section.

The consequences of these non-transferable Paternity and Parental Leaves have been positive for the division of tasks at home. Icelandic parents in 2003 reported a better sharing than parents in 1997 and fathers' participation in tasks increased from 30 per cent in 2005 to 40.4 per cent in 2010 (Gíslason, 2011). Over the years, Parental Leave 'increases the likelihood of fathers being involved in childcare' (Ásdís et al, 2013, p.335) and fathers continue to be present even after the end of the leave period. A study conducted in 1997, 2003 and 2009 with fathers in Iceland showed that care is more equally divided if the father uses at least three months (Ásdís et al, 2013, p.340), a conclusion which is consistent with research in Québec that concludes that Paternity Leave allows men to develop more confidence in their abilities to take care of a newborn (Tremblay and Lazzari Dodeler, 2015). With this new-found confidence, the longer the time a father spends on leave, the greater his subsequent involvement is likely to be at home. Also, as mothers have done for a long time, according to a Swedish study, these fathers tend to decrease their working hours thereafter, taking more days off work for children's illness. They also make more use of the various working time arrangements intended to support carers (Haas and Hwang, 2008). Thus, generous family policies specifically aimed at fathers could help gradually reduce the inequalities between men and women at home as well as in the labour market.

The case of Québec

In Canada, the province of Québec has sufficiently different family policies to be considered distinct from the rest of Canada. Many consider it closer to the 'social democratic' welfare states, with its family policy clearly closer to the 'work–family balance' model of the Nordic states than to the 'liberal' model of the US and the rest of Canada (Tremblay, 2019). Around 2000, both the Canadian federal and Québec provincial governments aimed at improving leave policies. If the federal Maternity Leave did not change, remaining at 15 weeks, Parental Leave was extended from 10 to 35 weeks (with an income replacement of 55 per cent); and as of 1 December 2017, an option of 61 weeks 'extended Parental Leave' at 33 per cent of earnings is available (for a fuller discussion of leave policy in Canada, see Chapter Nineteen).

In Québec, in 2006, the provincial government introduced the Québec Parental Insurance Plan (QPIP), which replaced the federal programme in the province. The QPIP is more generous than provision in the rest of Canada, not only for the mother but also for the father: it allows him to take three or five weeks Paternity Leave, with income replacement of either 75 per cent for three weeks leave or 55 per cent for five weeks (details of all leave policies in Québec are given in Table 13.1, showing how options that trade off duration against payment level are also available for Maternity and Parental Leaves). As a result, Québec is the only province in Canada to provide fathers with a non-transferable paid leave, and it leads to impressive statistics: while fewer than 20 per cent of Québec fathers used (federal) Parental Leave between 2001 and 2014, today 80 per cent take the QPIP, for an average length of seven weeks, which combines the full length of the Paternity Leave (five weeks) plus an average of two weeks of Parental Leave (Tremblay, 2018; Harvey and Tremblay, 2019); fathers who take both Paternity and Parental Leave average 13 weeks. The Québec provincial government has also created an affordable childcare programme, which has provided further support for employed parents.

The leaves described in Table 13.1 can be taken so that both parents are at home at the same time. QPIP data indicate that mothers are on leave at the same time as fathers in 89 per cent of cases when fathers only take Paternity Leave, but in only 51 per cent of cases when fathers use both Paternity and Parental Leave, as mothers are more likely to have resumed employment when fathers take Parental Leave.

In Québec, fathers who have used Paternity Leave are afterwards 'more likely to be absent [from the workplace] for family reasons,

Table 13.1: Québec Parental Insurance Plan (QPIP): summary table

Type of leave	Basic Plan		Special Plan		Benefit Payment	
	Number of weeks	Income replacement	Number of weeks	Income replacement	Begins no earlier than:	Ends no later than:
Maternity Leave (exclusively for the birth mother)	18	70%	15	75%	the 16th week before the expected week of delivery.	18 weeks after the birth week.
					*the week the pregnancy was interrupted (after the 19th week of pregnancy)	*18 weeks after the pregnancy is interrupted.
Paternity Leave (exclusively for the father)	5	70%	3	75%	the week the child is born.	52 weeks after the birth week.
Parental Leave (may be shared by the parents)	7	70%+	25	75%	the week the child is born.	52 weeks after the birth week.
	25	55%				

Source: Régime Québécois d'assurance parentale, 2017

which in turn would contribute to changing attitudes in workplaces that were once very resistant to men's absenteeism for family reasons' (Baillargeon, 2013, pp.232–233). In terms of gender equality, a study that focused specifically on the effects of the QPIP shows that while the new regime has not succeeded in eliminating the large gap between the number of weeks of leave taken by mothers (46 weeks on average) and fathers (nearly seven weeks now), QPIP contributed to reducing this gap, as fathers' participation jumped from two to five weeks almost immediately after the plan was introduced (Patnaik, 2016).

The same study also looked at the labour market and the division of labour within couples between two censuses, just before QPIP (2005) and after (2010). In 2010, on average mothers were more active in the labour market, working more hours per week and more often in full-time work. Since the introduction of the new public childcare and leave policies at the start of the twenty-first century, Québec has moved from being one of the Canadian provinces with the lowest employment rates among women with young children (under six years old) to being one of the highest – 70.3 per cent in 2014 compared with 65.1 per cent for the rest of Canada (Demers, 2015). Moreover, between 2005 and 2010, fathers' average working hours had declined. There is therefore a more equal distribution of working time between parents than previously.

Judged by family policies, fathers' leave-taking, the number of childcare centres and the labour market participation of women, Québec now compares with Iceland and other Nordic countries, and sits beside them, using Hantrais and Letablier's typology, as a model of work–family balance.

Difficulties experienced by Québec fathers in the workplace

While it is clear that the QPIP is well appreciated by parents, including fathers, the perception of leave has not changed in all sectors and occupations, especially when it comes to fathers wanting to take Paternity *and* Parental Leaves. One problem seems to be that fathers on Paternity Leave (unlike mothers on Maternity Leave) are not often replaced, even if they go on to take more than five weeks by using some Parental Leave, as they usually do not take so many continuous weeks; where fathers take both kinds of leave, they mostly take Paternity Leave earlier on and Parental Leave later, after the mother has gone back to work. This means that their work is split between the remaining employees or that projects are postponed. This poses particular challenges in industries where there is no slack and where employees are already on a tight schedule with a high-level of work intensity.

To explore such workplace issues further, two studies were conducted in 2013 and 2014 by the authors of this chapter, with fathers who were using Paternity and Parental Leaves. The first was conducted with some 30 fathers who had taken at least four weeks of Paternity Leave, spending time alone with their child. Many took much longer, up to a few months, including some Parental Leave, but they usually had to take Paternity Leave and Parental Leave separately. Fathers in the study were from various sectors and occupational categories (employees, professionals, blue collar workers). They were contacted by phone from a list provided by the agency responsible for administering the QPIP of fathers who had taken leave.

The second study included 31 fathers working in IT multimedia in urban areas; an invitation to participate was sent by participating companies and the fathers answered directly to the researcher to set a date for meeting. Fathers had taken leave for 49 children (some participants had more than one child), and in two-thirds of cases (32 children) this had involved non-consecutive weeks, meaning that fathers had returned to work after a few weeks at home, and then taken some weeks of leave later. Only 17 cases were consecutive and these fathers (13) mostly took less than seven weeks. For the analysis presented in this chapter, the data from both studies have been integrated.

Several fathers across both studies mentioned the difficulty of taking more than five weeks off as they were not replaced during their leave; while in order to avoid being overloaded on their return, fathers often did not completely cut off from work. Technology allowed them to be connected at all times to continue with tasks already in progress, and several fathers even checked their professional emails every day. Consulting emails or responding to calls from colleagues, if necessary, seems to be the norm in the IT multimedia sector in particular, and this can have an impact on family life even before the baby comes along, as the quote below illustrates:[1]

> Yes, we kept in touch…Even for my first, when we were in the hospital for the birth, I got a call, in front of the doctor! When my girlfriend told me she was pregnant with the second, I had a call that night and I made a mistake, I made a mistake of 30,000 dollars! But we corrected it, we

---

[1] All quotations from fathers have been translated from French.

corrected it! But I was so nervous that I made a mistake and I was too fast. (Ryu, two children, ten and 11 weeks off for Parental/Paternity Leave)

Moreover, births do not always take place at a favourable moment for the company, which may force a father to compromise on the dates for taking his leave. A position of responsibility can also prevent a father from using all the weeks to which he is entitled, also setting a negative example for other fathers. Occupying a leadership position in the firm may mean refusing to be absent, even for the birth of a child, or making greater compromises so as not to disturb the workflow in the company.

I wanted to take five weeks, as the plan allows. But I was at that point in a crunch, so I could not. I was in a leadership position. I had the pressure on my own, I did not feel it from the boss, but I certainly anticipated it. So I took three weeks and took two weeks around Christmas break. I had to adapt the leave a little, considering the situation at work, it was not easy. Now I can say that after three weeks, my spouse would have liked to have me stay at home because at the third week, it was still a little difficult at home. (Prolog, one child, five weeks leave)

I said: 'Can I take three–four weeks?' And they said, 'It would be best not to do that.' No pressure, you can take them anyway, there are people who do it... But no, I did not take them. (Luigi, two children, five weeks for the last child)

While some have encountered difficulties in simply asking for and using the weeks of Paternity Leave, those who wanted to use a few weeks of Parental Leave in addition to Paternity Leave were faced with more stress when they put forward this request.

To announce that I was going to take a leave, I found it really hard. Because I was the first, nobody had ever done that. I was willing not to take it! If it was a problem for them...I did not want that, but I was trying to be flexible, to take less than six months. I said: 'I understand that, we can manage...' You see, this kind of thing, I really left all the doors open. That's what I found most difficult about my job. (Pascal, one child, 22 weeks leave)

There's a stress…You're really scared, because all your career you've been working in the same place for ten years. Every week, you're there 40 hours a week, that's what gives you cash to live, that's what pays your house, that's what makes your children live, you do not want your children to miss anything…But in the company, about the leave, I never had to blame anyone. No pressure, nothing. No encouragement, no discouragement. You have the leave, you are not encouraged to take the weeks, but nobody will say anything. (Marcus, two children, 24 and 28 weeks)

The feeling of being a troublemaker, of betraying or threatening the stability of the company, of perceived resistance from senior colleagues possibly leads many fathers to take a shorter period of leave than they would ideally want. This can also explain why fathers can go beyond merely an email and telephone presence, usually without remuneration, agreeing to continue working part-time even while taking leave, in which case remuneration is common; Paternity and Parental leave regulations permit receiving up to 25 per cent of gross weekly earnings. Such arrangements can make the management of their personal schedules very complex.

I had asked for a full-time leave, because I thought I needed it, I was tired. At work, I was a little tired, there were things that did not suit my taste and it would have done me good, but it was a little more difficult to negotiate. Finally, they preferred that I do some telework. I could take care of my daughter the way I wanted, but they trusted me that my work would go forward anyway. I found it very difficult. Super difficult. (Vincent, three children, 24 weeks each)

When fathers returned to work, some had seen promotions escape them because of having taken leave, whether it was clearly mentioned to them or just implicit.

During my leave, I received the results of an exam I had done at the beginning of the year. While I was away, there were promotions in the firm and I was not called. My employer did not consider my resumé, he did not ask me for it. As I was not there, I went unnoticed in the process. (Mario, one child, five weeks leave)

> Before I had children, I was a representative of my company in an organisation with international travel and all that. And since then, this has been taken away from me and they have given it to someone else who is not very interested in doing it. It may just be a coincidence, I don't know, I'll never know, but it is weird. (Vincent, three children, 24 weeks each)

> At the annual evaluation, having a baby has held me back. I was criticised for not necessarily being up-to-date about the products on the market and all that. (Java, two children, six and five weeks)

The most difficult aspect of working life to manage after leave for many fathers seemed to be overtime, especially in jobs with specific delivery dates and where it was common to work overtime to get projects completed. When they become fathers, employees are faced with the impossibility of being as available at the workplace as they used to be. Yet because the new parent does not have the benefit of special treatment, he is reintegrated at the same level as other workers, with the same expectations.

> Since the birth, I have accumulated 190 overtime hours in two years. (Dante, one child, six weeks)

This takes us onto a new issue, that of fathers' continued commitment to involved parenting following leave-taking. Many can no longer work as much as before, which becomes a source of daily friction; peak moments of high intensity at work raise the problem of work–life balance and the stress it causes.

> It was not something new, in the sense that I had lived that before. I've already had the impression that I've been rushing for two or three months. But I found it even more difficult to face this now that I had other responsibilities at home. My boss did not expect us to take a day off, he expected us to work more. (Abel, two children, 37 and 38 weeks)

> Before, I worked up to 50 hours a week and it was not a big deal! Then, when you do things like that, you get noticed... While now, it is 4 o'clock, I have no choice but to stop working and get the child from daycare. With one

of my bosses, it causes friction. He absolutely wants me to do overtime, overtime, and overtime: 'I cannot stay, I have to go get the child at the daycare.' He said: 'Yeah, but we all make sacrifices here!' Yes, but the little one, she cannot come back alone from the daycare. I gotta go, I just have no choice! (Faris, two children, nine weeks each)

Some fathers find other ways to continue working overtime as before, by teleworking, for example, when the company is open to this possibility.

The employer is very, very, very nice, I have an online access key that allows me to work from home. So when my daughters sleep, I go back to work. I prefer to arrive early in the morning and leave early at night, and I have to work again after the girls are sleeping, if possible. (Mac, two children, four weeks each)

I was always doing at least five more hours per week. I have a laptop, I can do telework. So I arrive home, I take care of the children, I make supper, then I…Bathing, sleeping, then at 8 o'clock, I open the laptop and I go on until about 11 pm. (Link, two children, six weeks each)

The issue of availability to work overtime in the evening or at weekends generates workplace tension, and it also causes a lot of stress and guilt for fathers. Their refusal to participate and be present as much as others, to be less present than before and not to be there outside standard office hours, is not always easy for them to manage (as has long been an issue for mothers).

I have conditioned myself to say that it is totally acceptable that I do my 40 hours. I consider myself a productive person when I am at work. But it is certain that sometimes we make small scenarios in our head: sometimes we say that the world will say that I am a 'coward', that I work less or whatever, that I left the job for others to do. (Rockman, two children, six and five weeks)

Some fathers cannot find a solution and end up leaving their jobs. They clearly refer to work–family conflict as the main reason for moving to a new job with more conducive working conditions. This is often also explained by other frustrations, amplified by conflicts and tensions that have grown since the arrival of a child.

> I finally left my job to go to the public sector. I found that it did not make sense for my child: I left at 7:00 am, I arrived home at 7:00, or 7:15 pm and my child is sleeping, I did not see him! He spends more time at the daycare than at home…Where I am now, overtime is extremely rare. So it was a matter of work–life balance, that was really my reason for leaving. (Joel, three children, ten, eight and eight weeks)

> I was tired of always having to struggle when it was time to leave work, feeling guilty because I was leaving and there were people who stayed. I did not quite agree with this way of operating. Because even if I knew that sometimes we had rushes, I found the rushes that we had lasted relatively long. (Abel, two children, 37 and 38 weeks)

Our interviews confirm that if Québec fathers are very positive about leave-taking and wish their employer to be supportive, this is not always the case. In sectors where work is very intense, such as IT multimedia in particular, some fathers have had their employer ask them to change the timing of leave and to take only the Paternity Leave part (of three to five weeks) and not share the later Parental Leave with the mother. This has led to some tensions and to some fathers leaving their job for another where there is more flexibility.

Conclusions

With its Paternity Leave, Québec stands out from the rest of North America. But despite this innovative measure, we can see that there are still challenges for fathers. As our research shows, Paternity and Parental Leave are not straightforwardly happy events for fathers, not breaks from the office that will make it possible for them to return relaxed to a conducive office routine. Many fathers in our research had difficulty in negotiating the length and the timing of leave-taking. So, even if mothers still take most of the Parental Leave weeks, it is not always easy for fathers to apply or take leave, especially if they wish to exceed the standard now established in Québec for the first five weeks of Paternity Leave, and go on to take some weeks of Parental Leave as well.

Employers accept the weeks of Paternity Leave as something which is not really negotiable, even if they sometimes try to change the timing planned by fathers; but it is more difficult for some fathers to take weeks of Parental Leave, especially in sectors with strong work intensity such as IT. Furthermore, firms often ask fathers to do some work during the five weeks of Paternity Leave. Because of this, not only are fathers in these intensive sectors somewhat apprehensive at asking for leave and having to negotiate their departure, but they cannot always detach themselves completely from their work, using technologies to stay in touch (email, telework) and undertake part-time work, which adds to stress (see also Chapter Twelve on possible impacts of flexible leave in Norway).

Becoming a father is a big change in life, especially when it is the first child. Yet the term 'leave' leads some employers to consider that, once this temporary absence from work is completed, the arrival of the child has been taken care of by the workplace, that the situation is resolved as soon as the father goes back to work, and that he no longer requires more time at home (Brinton and Mun, 2016). It is then up to the employee to manage the new reality of his personal life by trying to minimise as much as possible the impacts of these changes on his professional life. One solution is to change job, to a position more compatible with parenting; in a recent poll of 1000 fathers, 54 per cent stated that they will certainly or probably consider a job change in order to obtain a better reconciliation between work and family (Regroupement pour la valorisation de la paternité, 2017, p.10). Our results are in tune with other research on employees' and employers' opinions: the former say that their priorities are the family and the couple, while the latter seem to think that existing measures are sufficient and nothing more needs to be done (Mercure, 2008, p.170).

The childcare network developed since 2000 and the Québec Parental Insurance Plan undoubtedly make things somewhat easier for employed parents in Québec than in other Canadian provinces. Fathers in Québec seem to be very attached to the Paternity Leave offered by the QPIP. They use it, and some even go beyond the number of weeks reserved for fathers and not transferable to the mother. Québec is thus moving closer to what is offered in the Nordic countries, namely the work–family balance model of Hantrais and Letablier (1996). But this may not be enough. In a context where the Québec population is ageing and some sectors of the economy already have job shortages, losing workers because of insufficient work–family balance can be a real issue. Childcare and leave entitlements offered by the state are very important, but workplaces also need to be supportive of parents, not only accommodating both mothers and fathers taking Parental Leave but also offering working time flexibility and telework in order to facilitate the longer-term integration of work and family.

References

Ásdís, A.A., Eydal, G.B. and Gíslason, I.V. (2013) 'Equal rights to paid Parental Leave and caring fathers: The case of Iceland', *Icelandic Review of Politics and Administration*, 9(2): 323–344.

Baillargeon, D. (2013) *Brève histoire des femmes au Québec* [*Short History of Québec Women*], Montréal: Boréal.

Bernard, P. and Saint-Arnaud, S. (2003) 'Convergence or resilience? A hierarchical cluster analysis of the welfare regimes in advanced countries', *Current Sociology*, 51(5): 499–527.

Bernard, P. and Saint-Arnaud, S. (2004) 'Du pareil au même? La position des quatre principales provinces canadiennes dans l'univers des régimes providentiels' [The Same or Not? The place of four Canadian provinces in the providential regimes system], *Cahiers canadiens de sociologie*, 29(2): 209–239.

Brinton, M.C. and Mun, E. (2016) 'Between state and family: Managers' implementation and evaluation of Parental Leave policies in Japan', *Socio-Economic Review*, 14(2): 257–281.

Caldwell, J.C. (2004) 'Demographic theory: A long view', *Population and Development Review*, 30(2): 297–316.

Conway, J.F. (2003) *The Canadian Family in crisis*, Toronto: James Lorimer.

Demers, M.-A. (2015) *Les Québécoises en couple, principalement les mères, sont plus susceptibles d'occuper un emploi que les autres Canadiennes* [*Québec women in couples, especially mothers, more frequently have a job than other Canadian Women*], Québec: Institut de la statistique du Québec.

Esping-Andersen, G. (1990) *The Three Worlds of Welfare Capitalism*, Princeton, NJ: Princeton University Press.

Esping-Andersen, G. (2009) *The Incomplete Revolution: Adapting to Women's New Roles*, Cambridge: Polity Press.

Gíslason, I.V. (2011) *Changing Fathers: Reluctant Mothers?* Available at: www.leavenetwork.org/fileadmin/user_upload/k_leavenetwork/seminars/2011/2011_Gislason.pdf

Gíslason, I.V. (2012) 'Introduction', in Nordic Council of Ministers (ed) *Parental Leave, Childcare and Gender Equality in the Nordic Countries*, Copenhagen: Norden, pp 13–30.

Haas, L. and Hwang, C.P. (2008) 'The impact of taking Parental Leave on fathers' participation in childcare and relationships with children: Lessons from Sweden', *Community, Work and Family*, 11(1): 85–104.

Haavind, H. and Magnusson, E. (2005) 'The Nordic Countries: Welfare paradises for women and children?', *Feminism and Psychology*, 15(2): 227–235.

Hantrais, L. and Letablier, M.-T. (1996) *Familles, travail et politiques familiales* [Families, work and family policies], Paris: Presses Universitaires de France.

Harvey, V. and Tremblay, D.-G. (2018) 'Paternity leave in Québec: between social objectives and workplace challenges', *Community, Work and Family*. Available at: https://doi.org/10.1080/13668803 .2018.1527756

Holloway, S.D. (2010) *Women and Family in Contemporary Japan*, New York: Cambridge University Press.

Koslowski, A., Blum, S. and Moss, P. (2016*) International Review of Leave Policies and Research 2016*. Available at www.leavenetwork.org/ lp_and_r_reports/

Mercure, D. (2008) 'Travail et familles. Des tensions croissantes au cours de la prochaine décennie' [Work and families. Growing tensions for the next decade], in G. Pronovost, C. Dumont and I. Bitaudeau (eds) *La famille à l'horizon 2020*, Québec: Presses de l'Université du Québec.

Moyser, M. (2017) 'Women and paid work', *Statistics Canada*. Available at www.statcan.gc.ca/pub/89-503-x/2015001/article/14694-eng. htm

OECD (2007) *Babies and Bosses: Reconciling Work and Family Life*, Paris: OECD.

Patnaik, A. (2016) *Reserving Time for Daddy: The Short and Long-Run Consequences of Fathers' Quotas*. Available at https://ssrn.com/ abstract=2475970 or http://dx.doi.org/10.2139/ssrn.2475970

Pronovost, G. (2015) *Que faisons-nous de notre temps? Vingt-quatre heures dans la vie des Québécois. Comparaisons internationales* [*What are we doing with our time? Twenty-four hours in Québecers Life. International comparisons*], Québec: Les Presses de l'Université du Québec.

Régime québécois d'assurance parentale (2017) 'QPIP Benefits – Summary Table'. Available at www.rqap.gouv.qc.ca/includes/ tableaux/tab_synthese_prestations_en.html

Regroupement pour la valorisation de la paternité (2017) '*Perceptions des pères québécois à l'égard de l'engagement paternel et de la conciliation famille et travail*' [*Perceptions of Québec fathers about paternal involment and work–family balance*]. Available at www.semainedelapaternite.org/files/ sondage_cft_rvp_rapport_final.pdf

Scaillerez, A. and Tremblay, D.-G. (2016) 'Le télétravail, comme nouveau mode de régulation de la flexibilisation et de l'organisation du travail: analyse et impact du cadre légal européen et nord-américain' [Teleworking, a new mode of flexibility and work organization: Analysis and impacts of European and North-American legal systems], *Revue de l'organisation responsable*, 11(1): 21–31.

Tremblay, D.-G. (2017) *L'éclatement de l'emploi* [*Explosion of employment*], Québec: Téluq University and Presses de l'Université du Québec.

Tremblay, D.-G. (2019) *Conciliation emploi–famille et temps sociaux* [*Work–family balance and social times*] (4th edn), Québec: Presses de l'Université du Québec.

Tremblay, D.-G. and Lazzari Dodeler, N. (2015) *Les pères et la prise du congé parental ou de paternité: Une nouvelle réalité* [*Fathers and Parental and Paternity Leave' use : A new reality*], Québec: Presses de l'Université du Québec.

Weber, M. (1965) *Essai sur la théorie de la science* [*Methodology of social sciences*]. Paris: Plon.

FOURTEEN

Care-work policies: conceptualising leave within a broader framework[1]

*Sara Mazzucchelli, Luca Pesenti
and M. Letizia Bosoni*

Introduction

Since the early 1990s, the demand for Parental Leave and formal ECEC services has been increasing in all European countries as more women have entered the labour market (Annesley, 2007). Although the EU Directive on Parental Leave has obliged member states to introduce appropriate legislation, significant differences in this leave can still be found among countries in relation to eligibility, duration, levels of payment and flexibility (Koslowski et al, 2016). The aim of this chapter is to explore whether the often-used approach (*à la* Esping-Andersen) to identify welfare regimes according to their unique and mutually exclusive characteristics helps us to adequately understand this variation in the way Parental Leave is implemented across countries. The chapter is part of a wave of new analyses offering a theoretical link between the arena of welfare policies and the wider configuration of socio-economic, cultural and institutional frameworks within which the different welfare regimes are placed (Hall and Soskice, 2001; Den Dulk et al, 2013). In particular, the central argument is that reflection on Parental Leave must be conceptualised within a broader framework of structural dimensions (such as care-work resources provided either publicly or privately, as well as family structures) and cultural resources (such as ideas about care tasks).

[1] This chapter is the joint work of all three authors; however, the Introduction, Theoretical approach, The structural dimension and The cultural dimension are attributed to Pesenti; the Comparison of Leave Systems between countries: case selection to Bosoni; Leave, structure and culture: interactions and effects and Conclusions to Mazzucchelli.

Theoretical approach

As noted by Hinrichs (2000), the choice to focus on a specific policy area permits more precise observations of the existence of stability or change within the broader field of work–life balance policies. This choice seems methodologically appropriate where the aim is to capture any elements of convergence or, conversely, differentiation of leave policies, avoiding the risk of analysing these policies 'from above', which might favour the impression of 'regime stability' (Natali and Rago, 2010, p.63). However, this restriction of the object of analysis leaves the comparative researcher with a problem, as a given policy area rarely, if ever, exists in isolation. Parental Leave policies are, on the one hand, related to a wider range of policies (in particular, work–life balance, education, health, fertility and social mobility policies); while on the other hand, they interface with the actors (and their cultures) related to other political and institutional arenas.

Therefore, this analytical approach requires a change of perspective with respect to theoretical models of the welfare regime, such as that proposed by Esping-Andersen (1990). The pattern of 'welfare regimes', built on the basis of a range of data collected at the end of the 1980s, was centred on the analysis of welfare systems in which the state exercised a hegemonic role both as regulator and provider. The subsequent changes introduced since the mid-1990s, however, have led to a progressive pluralisation of the relevant welfare actors, in particular political and institutional subsystems. This has arguably generated, in all European national contexts, the structuring of specific 'welfare systems' characterised by complex configurations between these actors and a state that no longer appears hegemonic. Alongside this systemic transformation (as well as with reference to a wider range of theoretical and methodological critical observations), an extensive critical literature on the theory of 'welfare regimes' has developed (Bertin and Campostrini, 2015).

In line with this literature, we propose a model based on two main analytical dimensions, proposing that social policy scholarship on Parental Leave should become integrated with a number of elements that, in a distinct manner, have been proposed by various authors in recent years in an attempt to improve the theoretical perspective on the subject. We specifically consider a 'structural dimension', determined by the contribution of the relevant actors in relation to care-work arrangements, that is, the state, employers and families; and a 'cultural dimension', defined by values and social models.

The structural dimension

Some reflections in recent years indicate how welfare policies should be analysed within a broader framework that connects them to the structural and systemic dimensions of each country. The work of Hall and Soskice (2001) was among the first to connect theoretically the two approaches of 'welfare models' and 'varieties of capitalism' (VoC). In this way, the classic concept of 'occupational welfare', originally proposed by Richard Titmuss (1958), has been rediscovered today as a potential tool for analysing the set of market-driven social benefits provided by private employers (or the state in its role as employer). Following these theoretical lines, we think it might be possible to improve the analysis of leave policies and work–life balance measures, accepting the premise that employers could be seen 'under specific conditions as important actors contributing to…the stability [of welfare state and social policy arrangements]' (Seeleib-Kaiser and Fleckenstein, 2009, p.741).

Some analyses show that the adoption of work–life balance measures by employers is only partially related to welfare regimes, so that there are important differences between countries in the same cluster. The lowest level of such care benefits is recorded in the social democratic and post-communist countries, but in the former there is the highest level of flexible working time policies. On the other hand, the highest level of work–life measures is present in workplaces in conservative regime countries. In general, the presence of workplace benefits, including forms of flexible working hours designed to facilitate the reconciliation of work and family life, is associated with institutional pressures in the country for such reconciliation, much more than the presence of economic pressures (Den Dulk et al, 2013). The presence of explicit public support for reconciliation is positively associated with the adoption of both leave and other policies to make the care of children easier for workers. But apart from these differences, the authors point out that corporate organisational features show the highest correlation rates with this type of welfare policy at firm level (Den Dulk et al, 2012).

If, therefore, we widen our gaze from statutory provisions to include occupational welfare that includes programmes introduced either by social partners, bilaterally or through unilateral employers' actions (OSE, 2014), we typically get a more complex picture. In addition to workplace arrangements, leave policies (Maternity, Paternity, Parental) need to be conceptualised in relation to other structural elements, such as ECEC services and the relationship/gap between leave and ECEC entitlements, as well as trends in family stability (such as the presence of both parents in the household).

The cultural dimension

The role of culture is also helpful in illuminating welfare regime differences in cross-national comparisons, but has frequently been marginalised (Pfau-Effinger, 2005; Jo, 2011). In Pfau-Effinger's highly cited work, culture is defined as collective constructions of meaning by which human beings define reality (Neidhard et al, 1986; Pfau-Effinger, 2005), including stocks of knowledge, values and ideals. In the debates on the interrelations of welfare state policies and culture, it is common today to talk about 'welfare culture' (Ullrich, 2000; Dallinger, 2001), referring to relevant ideas in a given society about the welfare state and the way it is embedded in society, in particular ideas about paid work and the labour market; about social inclusion, social exclusion and the nature of citizenship; and about social services, the welfare mix, the family and care. Of particular interest for our discussion are ideas about who is responsible for the care of elderly or young people, in particular the role of the state and family, and how work and family interrelate; for example, formal and informal care in a country may depend on the provision of formal services, but also on ideas about the role of family as primary care provider (Pfau-Effinger and Geissler, 2002; Rostgaard, 2002).

Different cultural models often coexist within the same country, and these may sometimes conflict or change over time. Moreover, welfare policies depend on both the material interests of individuals and cultural values and ideals, which influence the degree to which policies are accepted by people and their impact on an individual's social practices. Social policies are the outcome of negotiation and compromises between ideas and interests of different social actors (individuals, policy-makers, market, state, third sector, and so on) in a particular societal/national context. This is the reason why in different societies the same type of social policies can have a different effect (Jo, 2011; Brandth et al, 2017).

Welfare culture is hard to detect and it is firmly embedded within structural conditions. However, there are some indicators, such as measures of gender inequality and intergenerational solidarity (Dykstra, 2010).

Comparison of leave systems between countries: case selection

There have been a few previous efforts to take social and cultural factors into account in devising ideal type models of parenting leave, such as those proposed by Wall and Escobedo (2013). In their comparative study, using data for 22 European countries on leave systems, gender equality of leaves, ECEC services and maternal employment patterns, they proposed seven empirically based ideal types to describe leave policy. In the light of the reflections made so far, as well as building upon the Escobedo and Wall classifications of parenting leaves, we propose an analytical model that attempts to insert this classification into a broader framework capable of taking into account the structural and cultural dimensions summarised in Table 14.1.

In a comparative perspective, we focus in particular on four countries as examples for our argument, namely Germany, Italy, Sweden and the UK. They are countries for which comparable data are available and they also represent welfare regime types as established in the literature; 'conservative' regimes in the cases of Germany and Italy, 'social democratic' for Sweden, and 'liberal' for the UK. Such countries provide interesting variations in terms of both the broad societal context (Table 14.2) and leave systems (Table 14.3).

In Germany, the duration of Maternity Leave is 14 weeks (six weeks before the birth and eight mandatory weeks following the birth); it is paid at 100 per cent of earnings. While there is no Paternity Leave entitlement, three years of Parental Leave is provided as an individual, non-transferable entitlement. An employment protection right is provided during this leave and payment is set at an income replacement rate of 65 per cent of earnings for up to 14 months per family.

In Italy, 20 weeks (five months) of compulsory Maternity Leave are provided (at least four weeks before the birth) paid at 80 per cent of earnings for salaried workers (100 per cent for public sector workers). Fathers (employed or self-employed) take two days compulsory Paternity Leave. In addition, Parental Leave consists of six months

Table 14.1: The proposed analytical model for cross-national comparison of leave systems

Structural dimensions	Cultural dimensions
• Parental leave models • Gap between leave and ECEC • Occupational welfare • Family structures	• Gender inequality • Intergenerational solidarity orientation

Table 14.2: Contextual data for the exemplar countries

	Population (2014) millions	Total fertility rate (2015)	Income and equality		Maternal employment rate (2014)	
			GDP/capita (2011 PPS$) (2013)	Gini coefficient (2005–13)	Youngest child aged 0–2 years	Youngest child aged 3–5 years
Germany	82.7	1.5	43,207	30.6	51	70
Italy	61.1	1.4	34,167	35.5	52	54
Sweden	9.6	1.9	43,741	26.1	82	
UK	63.5	1.8	37,017	38.0	58	62
OECD average (2014)		1.7			53	66

Note: Maternal employment rate for Sweden is for 2014, children aged between 0–18 years.

Sources: Eurostat, http://ec.europa.eu/eurostat/data/database; OECD, https://data.oecd.org/pop/fertility-rates.htm; www.leavenetwork.org/fileadmin/Leavenetwork/Annual_reviews/2016_Full_draft_20_July.pdf, p.8.

Table 14.3: Summary of Parental Leave systems

	Germany	Italy	Sweden	UK
Maternity Leave	Statutory non-transferable entitlement.	Statutory non-transferable entitlement.	Statutory non-transferable entitlement.	Statutory non-transferable entitlement.
	Medium (14 weeks) and very well paid (100% earnings, no ceiling)	Medium length (20 weeks) and well paid (80% earnings, no ceiling)	Very short (two weeks). Well paid (77.6% of earnings, up to a ceiling)	Long (up to 52 weeks), but low flat rate payment (or unpaid) apart from first 6 weeks, which is very well paid (90% earnings with no ceiling).
				Fathers may take up to 50 weeks or the Maternity Leave instead of the mother (Shared Parental Leave), but they receive only the low flat-rate payment
Paternity Leave	No statutory entitlement	Statutory entitlement.	Statutory entitlement.	Statutory entitlement.
		Very short (2 days) and well paid (100% earnings)	Short (two weeks) and well paid (77.6% of earnings, up to a ceiling)	Short (one or two weeks) and low flat rate payment
Parental Leave	Statutory individual non-transferable entitlement.	Statutory individual non-transferable entitlement.	Statutory family and individual entitlement.	Statutory individual non-transferable entitlement.
	Flexible (part-time or full-time).	Father bonus.	Long (480 days) and well paid (77.6% earnings) for 390 days; 90 days with low flat rate	Medium length (18 weeks per child), unpaid
	Very long (up to three years), well paid (65% of earnings) for up to 14 months per family	Medium length (6 months), low payment (30% earnings if child under 6)		

Source: Blum et al, 2017

per parent, although the maximum total length of leave per family is ten months unless the father takes at least three months of leave; in which case the total length of leave can be extended to 11 months and the father can extend his leave to seven months (that is, there is a one-month father bonus). This leave can be taken on an hourly or other part-time basis, and is paid at 30 per cent of earnings when leave is taken for a child under six years old, unpaid if taken when a child is six to 12 years old.

In Sweden, each parent is entitled to Parental Leave until the child is 18 months old, but mothers have to take two weeks leave before or after birth. Payment is separately regulated, each parent can take 240 days of paid leave until a child is 12 years old, mostly paid at 77.6 per cent of earnings (the remaining period is at a flat rate); 90 days of this individual entitlement is not transferrable to the other parent. Leave can be taken in various part-time options.

In the UK, Maternity Leave consists of a maximum of 52 weeks, potentially starting from 11 weeks before the childbirth, including two mandatory weeks after childbirth. The first six weeks of leave are paid at 90 per cent of earnings, followed by a low flat rate for the next 33 weeks and no payment for the remaining 13 weeks. Mothers can transfer all Maternity Leave to the father, except for two weeks. Fathers are also entitled to two weeks of Paternity Leave, paid at a low flat rate. Each parent is further entitled to 18 weeks of non-transferable and unpaid Parental Leave.

Thus, it can be said that leave systems in these four countries vary considerably. They all offer some degree of individual, non-transferable rights, for each parent, but duration and payment vary considerably. We propose that it is analytically helpful to consider this variation of leave systems in conjunction with ECEC provision across these four countries (Tables 14.4 and 14.5). Indeed, a major theme

Table 14.4: Attendance rates for formal ECEC services, by age and hours of attendance (2015)

Children cared for as a percentage of all children in the same age group per week	Germany	Italy	Sweden	UK
0 to 2 years, 1 to 29 hours	10	10	21	26
0 to 2 years, 30 or more hours	16	17	43	4
Total 0 to 2 years receiving some care	26	27	64	30
Between 3 years and and compulsory school age, 1 to 29 hours	35	23	26	49
Between 3 years and compulsory school age, 30 or more hours	55	63	70	24
Total between 3 years and compulsory school age receiving some care	90	86	96	71

Source: Eurostat, http://ec.europa.eu/eurostat/tgm/refreshTableAction.do?tab=table&plugin=1&pcode=tps00185&language=en

of this chapter is that national leave systems need to be considered and discussed in relation to national ECEC systems. The availability of high quality, affordable services for young children from birth to compulsory school age is a priority for the European Union. For example, the 2002 European Council meeting in Barcelona set targets in this area: at least 33 per cent of children under three years of age should attend formal provision in each member state and at least 90 per cent of children between three years old and compulsory school age (European Commission, 2013). Data on formal attendance at these services shed some light on national work–life balance strategies, as far as such strategies can be said to exist, and the connection between leave entitlements for parents and ECEC services. The attendance rates presented here are calculated as the number of children cared for by formal ECEC arrangements as a percentage of all children of the same age group; they measure, therefore, the actual use (attendance) of existing formal provision for the two age groups, not the provision in terms of the actual number of places available (coverage).

Only Sweden meets the 'Barcelona targets' for both age groups of children. Although the UK nearly makes the target for the lower age group, the great majority of these children attend ECEC services for less than 30 hours per week, whereas in the other three countries, most attendance is for 30 hours or more; the same pattern of hours of attendance is found for older children. If we further look at the relationship between leave and ECEC entitlements (Table 14.5), while there is no gap between the end of well-paid leave and the beginning of an ECEC entitlement in Germany and Sweden, there is a considerable gap in the UK. In Italy, there is no formal entitlement

Table 14.5: Relationship between leave and ECEC entitlements

	Germany	Italy	Sweden	UK
Child's age (months) at:				
End of leave (total) (a)	36	14.8	36.5	13.9
End of well paid leave (b)	14	3.8	13	1.4
Start of ECEC entitlement (c)	1 year	No statutory entitlement	12 months	3 years (part time): for 20 hours a week or less
Gap between leave and ECEC:				
(c)–(a) months	No gap	No ECEC entitlement	No gap	22.1
(c)–(b) months	No gap		No gap	34.6

Source: Blum et al, 2017

to ECEC, although it is considered a social right enshrined in law (as of 2015).

As also noted in Chapter Nine, considering the situation of the United States, looking beyond statutory entitlements to voluntary occupational welfare sometimes provided by employers provides a more complete picture of the support available to parents (Table 14.6). Comparative analysis of voluntary occupational welfare in the EU is impeded by a lack of comparable statistical data. However, using data collected by the European Social Observatory, we can analyse the extent of a number of benefits and services in the work–life reconciliation area: working-time arrangements, leave, financial support (that is, child bonuses) and childcare provision. These are provided in different forms: at company-level or sector-level, and as bilateral funds at national or local levels. Such 'voluntary occupational welfare' (VOW) measures are mainly provided at the national bargaining level in Germany, Italy and Sweden, but with a growing amount at company level (in particular in Germany and Italy), which appears to be the prevalent level in the UK, consistent with its decentralised industrial relations model (Seeleib-Kaiser and Fleckenstein, 2009; OSE, 2014; Pesenti, 2016). In all countries considered here, these benefits are additional to the role of the state, with the exception of the UK where there is a partial substitution effect (in this case, occupational welfare at firm level partially compensates for a weak public welfare system). The analysis on VOW spending levels partially confirms the interplay between welfare regime and VOW: the highest levels are achieved in the UK, followed by Sweden and Germany, while the lowest are found in Italy. Again, we see considerable variation across countries.

Large changes in family structures across Europe in recent decades have added further complexity that needs to be taken into account (Table 14.7). In particular, increasing family instability and diversity

Table 14.6: Expenditure on work–life reconciliation as percentage of voluntary private expenditure

	% of voluntary private expenditure	VOW role in relation to welfare state	Form
Germany	6.4	Supplementary	Sectoral and company level
Italy	2.2	Supplementary	Bilateral funds (recently also company level)
Sweden	8.5	Supplementary	Sectoral level funds
UK	17.5	Partial substitute	Employers' plans

Source: OSE, 2014

Table 14.7: Family structures

	Crude divorce rate (Eurostat, 2015)	% of children living with two parents (OECD, 2014)	% of children living with a sole parent (OECD, 2014)	Births outside marriage (share of total births, %) (Eurostat, 2015)
Germany	2.0	83.1	15.6	35
Italy	1.4	86.6	12.8	30
Sweden	2.5	81.7	17.2	54.7
UK	1.9 (2014)	76.7	23.1	47.9

Note: The 'Crude Divorce Rate' is the number of divorces during a given year per 1,000 inhabitants.

Source: OECD, 2014; Eurostat, 2015

in family forms makes the issue of family and work reconciliation more complex.

In addition to the structural dimensions discussed previously, cultural dimensions broaden the frame, in particular, cultural ideas and expectations about family and care, and the extent to which people might feel themselves to be more or less embedded in an intergenerational network of care. By using data from the European Value Study (EVS), it is possible to evaluate attitudes to the exchange of care in family networks expressed through the presence of altruism in adult children towards their parents and vice-versa. This indicates cultural ideas about filial and parental obligations (Gans and Merril, 2006; Dykstra, 2010), but it also refers to more general cultural ideas about the care of family members.

The 'Index of family solidarity orientation' (Table 14.8) is a three-level measure (low, medium, high) of bi-directional intergenerational exchanges (that is, the presence of altruism and care exchange in children towards their parents and vice-versa) (Rossi, 2014). Italy, in contrast to the other three countries, has a high family solidarity orientation, which indicates care tasks are mainly expected to be delivered by family members (and in particular female family members). This is consistent with relatively low formal ECEC provision in a complex relationship: on one side, the lack of entitlement to ECEC is in line with cultural values that consider family as the best place to raise children; while on the other side, low ECEC provision reinforces traditional norm and slows change down.

In terms of gender equality, another important cultural dimension, we can use the Gender Inequality Index of the United Nations Development Programme, which includes indicators covering health, female employment and other labour market characteristics

Table 14.8: Family solidarity orientation

	Level on index of family solidarity orientation (%)		
	Low	Medium	High
Italy	10	38	52
Germany	38	36	26
Sweden	58	31	11
UK	43	38	19
EU28	24	35	41

Note: Variables in Index include agreement on the following statements: 'It is primarily the duty of adult children to take care of their severely ill or frail parents'; 'Children should love and respect their parents unconditionally/children do not have a duty to love and respect undeserving parents'; 'Parents have a duty to do the best for their children even at the cost of their own well-being/parents have their own life and should not be expected to sacrifice their own well-being for that of their children'; 'adult children have a duty to provide ongoing assistance to their parents, even at the cost of their own well-being/adult children have their own life and should not be expected to sacrifice their own well-being to help parents'.

Source: Authors' own calculation using European Values Study (EVS) data 4th wave 2008

(Table 14.9). According to this index, the UK seems less egalitarian than the other countries and in particular in comparison with Germany and Sweden.

In summary, when comparing leave systems in four countries (Germany, Italy, Sweden, the UK), we suggest that different aspects need to be considered: current leave models; ECEC provision and its relationship to statutory leave; voluntary occupational welfare; family stability, as well as intergenerational solidarity and gender inequality. How these aspects interact with and shape leave systems is discussed below.

Table 14.9: Gender inequality index (2015)

	Score	Ranking
Germany	0.066 (low)	9
Italy	0.085 (low–medium)	16
Sweden	0.048 (low)	4
UK	0.131 (medium–high)	28

Source: United Nations Development Programme, http://hdr.undp.org/en/composite/GII

Leave, structure and culture: interactions and effects

As mentioned before, the argument of this chapter is that analysis of Parental Leave policy must be conceptualised within a broader framework concerning care-work policies and cultural ideas with respect to care tasks. For example, the effects of Parental Leave schemes on gender equality are double-edged and need to consider the interplay between leave policies and other family policies: on the one hand, Parental Leave enables mothers and potentially fathers to combine caring with employment, thus potentially boosting the presence of women in the labour market and men as carers; on the other hand, long leave periods mostly taken by women reinforce the gendered division between paid and unpaid work, thus damaging women's career opportunities, which might also further increase gender differences in income (Ejrnæs, 2008; Escobedo and Wall, 2015). From this perspective, we can see the importance of considering leave policies within the structural and cultural context in each country (Table 14.10) to give a more complete understanding. Structural dimensions considered in the model include: different types of leave (Maternity, Paternity, Parental), ECEC services (for children under and over three-years-old), the relationship or gap between leave and ECEC entitlements, occupational welfare and family stability (for example, children living with two parents). Cultural dimensions include intergenerational solidarity orientation and levels of gender inequality.

When considering leave in this broader contextual framework, differences or similarities between countries emerge contributing to a more complex picture than conventional welfare regime types might suggest.

Germany is characterised by a medium level of intergenerational solidarity, a long-term and well-paid leave system including individual entitlements, a medium-high ECEC entitlement, and a medium level of occupational welfare expenditure. The leave system and care services are well connected, in a context of strong family bonds, quite low gender inequality and a well-developed occupational welfare system.

In Italy, a high level of intergenerational solidarity prevails, along with a more stable family structure. Leave policies provide a relatively short but well-paid leave for mothers, and a longer but less well-paid leave available to both parents. The lack of a formal entitlement to ECEC services means that these services do not completely meet demand, and in addition, occupational welfare expenditure is relatively low. This contributes to existing evidence that the family carries a lot of the weight of childcare.

Sweden is characterised by low gender inequality as well as low intergenerational solidarity, with relatively high levels of single parents (though also many separated parents with shared custody). A well-paid leave system, combining family and individual entitlements,

Table 14.10: Structural and cultural dimensions shaping care-work experiences

	Structural dimensions			Cultural dimensions		
Statutory parenting leave models	Gap between statutory leave and ECEC	Occupational Welfare	Prevalence of two-parent families	Gender Inequality	Intergenerational solidarity orientation
Germany	Individual, long duration entitlements for both parents, well paid	No gap	Medium	High–Medium	Low	Low–Medium
Italy	Individual entitlements for both parents, but low paid for fathers	No ECEC entitlement	Low	High	Low–Medium	High
Sweden	Individual and family entitlements, well paid	No gap	Medium	Low–Medium	Low	Low
UK	Limited individual entitlements, low paid, especially for fathers	1- or 2-year gap	High	Low	Medium–High	Low–Medium

is integrated with a high level of ECEC provision, providing the opportunity for families to care and work.

Finally, the UK perhaps has the biggest care-work 'crunch'. The leave system is not well paid, there is a long gap between leave and ECEC entitlements, children are likely to attend ECEC for fewer hours than in the other countries considered, there is a low/medium level of intergenerational solidarity, and medium-high gender inequality, all in a context of high family type plurality. The role of occupational welfare emerges as a substitute, to some extent, for statutory welfare.

From this analysis, we can see that Germany and Sweden follow a similar pattern, with a highly supportive care-work model for parents, in terms of leave and ECEC services allowing parents to balance care and work. Thus, care responsibilities are less reliant on the family and more shared between different social actors. In Italy, the pivotal role of family members in care responsibility is confirmed alongside a relatively higher level of gender inequality, with leave policies oriented to induce women to an early return into the labour market and sustain low fatherhood support; the weakest point in this picture appears to be the lack of a formal entitlement to ECEC services. The UK case can be said to be distant from the other country examples in terms of its overall lack of support for parents.

Conclusions

The original approach to 'welfare regimes', such as the theoretical model proposed by Esping-Andersen (1990), was built on the basis of a range of data collected in the mid-1980s and centred on the analysis of welfare systems in which the state exercised hegemonic functions. Subsequent changes introduced since the mid-1990s have led to a progressive pluralisation of the relevant actors, producing a complex configuration between these actors and a reduced and no longer hegemonic role of the state. To move beyond the welfare regime approach to cross-national comparisons of a given policy area, this chapter explores a theoretical link between the arena of welfare policies and some of the dimensions of wider socio-economic and institutional frameworks within which the different welfare regimes are placed. Thus, we aim to theoretically connect welfare models and the VoC analytical approach, looking in particular to include the concept of 'voluntary occupational welfare', namely the voluntary programmes introduced by social partners, bilaterally or through unilateral employers' actions (OSE, 2014).

This theoretical choice has been supported by some studies (Den Dulk et al, 2013) showing that the adoption of workplace work–life arrangements is only partially related to welfare regimes; it might be, for example, that better public provision helps to create a normative climate, which would encourage workplace work–life support or vice versa. In any case, there are important differences between countries in the same conventional welfare regime clusters. So, we can get a wider and more complex picture by analysing the wider voluntary occupational welfare context.

We suggest that analyses of Parental Leave could be better informed theoretically by including information about other related structural dimensions such as ECEC provision and entitlements, as well as cultural ideas over care tasks. In line with this conceptualisation, we have also considered a model based on structural and cultural dimensions: leaves (Maternity, Paternity, Parental), ECEC services and their relationship to leave entitlements, occupational welfare and family structures (children living with two parents) are considered structural dimensions, while gender inequality and intergenerational solidarity orientation are the proposed cultural dimensions. Considering these six dimensions, we focused on four countries, namely Germany, Italy, Sweden and the UK. These countries represent welfare regimes proposed by Esping-Anderson (1990), and have interesting variations across the dimensions. From our analysis Germany and Sweden seem more similar than conventional welfare regime models might suggest with regard to their support for employed parents, while Italy and UK both appear to be more difficult places for parents to combine work and care.

The proposed classification is certainly tentative, but nevertheless introduces a decisive question: what might be the causal nexus in relation to public policies, occupational welfare systems, cultural ideas about work and care, and family structures? The analysis suggests that the way in which statutory leave policies are experienced by parents is highly contingent on both structural and cultural dimensions in a given country at a given time. Naturally, the exploratory nature of our contribution does not allow us to define this relationship (between leave and structural/cultural dimensions) as causal in any way: including more quantitative methods, the use of more extensive datasets, and the extension of selected national cases could allow further insights into causal relationships in the future. However, we conclude that the extent to which Parental Leave enables parents (mothers and/or fathers) to stay in the labour market or encourages them to withdraw is strictly related not only to the design of leave policies, but also ECEC services and their relationship/gap with leave, occupational welfare, family in/ stability, gender inequality and intergenerational solidarity orientation. These structural and cultural elements are differently combined in each country, with different possible effects: for example, leave policies could help to make the transition from paid to care work more flexible and contribute to a resdistribution of the gendered division of care work in the home (that is, Nordic countries and Germany); while the lack of ECEC services could reinforce the role of family (Italy) and/ or the role of voluntary occupational welfare (UK).

References

Annesley, C. (2007) 'Lisbon and Social Europe: Towards a European "adult worker model" welfare system', *Journal of European Social Policy*, 17(4): 195–205.

Bertin, G. and Campostrini, S. (eds) (2015) *Equiwelfare and Social Innovation: A European Perspective.* Milano: Franco Angeli.

Blum, S., Koslowski, A. and Moss, P. (2017) *International Review of Leave Policies and Research 2017.* Available at www.leavenetwork.org/ lp_and_r_reports/

Brandth, B., Halrynjo, S. and Kvande, E. (eds) (2017) *Work–Family Dynamics: Competing Logics of Regulation, Economy and Morals.* London: Routledge.

Cardinali, V. (2013) 'Voucher per asili nido. Perché così non va' [Vouchers for nurseries: because it does not work) *Ingenere online.* Available at http: //ingenere.it/articoli/voucher-nidi-e-baby-sitter-perch-cos-non-va

Dallinger, U. (2001) 'Organisierte Solidaritat und Wohlfahrtskultur. Das Beispiel des "Generationenvertrages" [Organized solidarity and welfare culture. The example of the "Generation Contract"], *Sociologica Internationalis*, 39: 67–89.

Den Dulk, L., Peters, P. and Poutsma, E. (2012) 'Variations in adoption of workplace work–family arrangements in Europe: The influence of welfare-state regime and organizational characteristics', *The International Journal of Human Resources Management*, 23(13): 2785–2808.

Den Dulk, L., Groeneveld, S., Ollier-Malaterre, A. and Valcour, M. (2013) 'National context in work–life research: A multi-level cross-national analysis of the adoption of workplace work–life arrangements in Europe', *European Management Journal*, 31: 478–494.

Dykstra, P.A. (2010) *Intergenerational Family Relationships in Ageing Societies.* Available at www.unece.org/fileadmin/DAM/pau/_docs/ age/2010/Intergenerational-Relationships/ECE-WG.1-11.pdf

Ejrnæs, A. (2008) 'What is the role of Parental Leave policies in shaping work and care in the Enlarged EU?', in A. Ejrnæs, T. Boje, J. Lewis, A. Plumien (eds) *Workpackage 3: Labour Market and Social Policies*, Aberdeen: University of Aberdeen, pp 26–48.

Escobedo, A. and Wall, K. (2015) 'Leave policies in Southern Europe: Continuities and changes', *Community, Work and Family*, 18(2): 218–235.

Esping-Andersen, G. (1990) *Three Worlds of Welfare Capitalism*. Oxford: Polity Press.

European Commission (2013) *Barcelona Objectives*. Available at http://ec.europa.eu/justice/gender-equality/files/documents/130531_barcelona_en.pdf

Eurostat (2015) European statistics. Available at: https://ec.europa.eu/eurostat/web/population-demography-migration-projections/marriages-and-divorces-data/main-tables

Gans, D. and Merril, S. (2006) 'Norms of filial responsibility for aging parents across time and generations', *Journal of Marriage and Family*, 68(4): 961–976.

Hall, P. A. and Soskice, D. (eds) (2001) *Varieties of Capitalism: The Institutional Foundations of Comparative Advantage*, Oxford: Oxford University Press.

Hinrichs, K. (2000) 'Elephants on the move: Patterns of public pension reform in OECD countries', *European Review*, 8(3): 353–378.

Jo, N.K. (2011) 'Between the cultural foundations of welfare and welfare attitudes: The possibility of an in-between level conception of culture for the cultural analysis of welfare', *Journal of European Social Policy*, 21(1): 5–19.

Koslowski, A., Blum, S. and Moss, P. (eds) (2016) *12th International Review of Leave Policies and Related Research*. Available at www.leavenetwork.org/fileadmin/Leavenetwork/Annual_reviews/2016_Full_draft_20_July.pdf

Mazzucchelli, S. (2011) 'The impact of Law 53/00 (Regulation of Parental Leave) on fathers: A good law disregard in daily life', in M. Cortini, G. Tanucci and E. Morin (eds) *Boundaryless Careers and Occupational Well-Being*, Basingstoke: Palgrave Macmillan.

Mazzucchelli, S. and Rossi, G. (2015) '"I'd like to but I can't": The implementation of the Italian act on Parental Leave', *Families, Relationships and Societies*, 4(2): 295–308.

Natali, D. and Rago, M. (2010) 'L'analisi comparata delle politiche di welfare: una riflessione metodologica' [Comparative analysis of welfare policies: a methodological reflection] *Rivista Italiana di Politiche Pubbliche*, 1: 61–82.

Neidhard, F., Lepsius, R.M. and Weiss, J. (eds) (1986) *Kultur und Gesellschaft: Sonderheft 27 der Kolner Zeitschrift f'ur Soziologie und Sozialpsychologie* [*Culture and society. Special Issue 27 of the Kolner Zeitschrift für Soziologie und Sozialpsychologie*], Opladen: Westdeutscher Verlag.

OECD (Organisation for Economic Co-operation and Development) (2014) OECD family database. Available at: www.oecd.org/els/family/database.htm

OSE (Observatoire Social Européen) (2014) 'Comparing voluntary occupational welfare in the EU: Evidence from an international research study', *OSE Paper Series* 16. Available at www.ose.be/files/publication/OSEPaperSeries/Natali_Pavolini_2014_OseResearchPaper16.pdf

Ostner, I. (1998) 'The politics of care policies in Germany', in J. Lewis (ed) *Gender, Social Care and Welfare State Restructuring in Europe*, Aldershot: Ashgate, pp 111–137.

Pesenti, L. (2016) *Il welfare in azienda. Aziende smart e benessere dei lavoratori* [*The welfare in the company. Smart companies and workers' well-being*], Milano: Vita e Pensiero.

Pfau-Effinger, B. (2005) 'Culture and welfare state policies: Reflections on a complex interrelation', *Journal of Social Policy*, 34(1): 3–20.

Pfau-Effinger, B. and Geissler, B. (2002) 'Cultural change and family policies in East and West Germany', in A. Carling, S. Duncan and R. Edwards (eds) *Analysing Families: Morality and Rationality in Policy and Practice*, London: Routledge.

Rossi, G. (2014) 'The complex relationship between values and couple patterns', *Journal of Comparative Family Studies*, 45(1): 173–199.

Rostgaard, T. (2002) 'Caring for children and older people in Europe: A comparison of European policies and practices', *Policy Studies*, 23(1): 51–68.

Seeleib-Kaiser, M. and Fleckenstein, T. (2009) 'The political economy of occupational family policies: Comparing workplaces in Britain and Germany', *British Journal of Industrial Relations*, 47(4): 741–764.

Titmuss, R. (1958) *Essays on the Welfare State*, London: George Allen and Unwin.

Ullrich, C.G. (2000) 'Die soziale Akzeptanz des Wohlfahrtsstaates. Ergebnisse, Kritik und Perspektiven einer Forschungsrichtung' [Social acceptance of the welfare state: Results, criticism and perspectives on a research direction], *Soziale Welt*, 51: 131–151.

Wall, K. and Escobedo, A. (2013) 'Parental Leave policies, gender equity and family well-being in Europe: A comparative perspective', in A. Moreno Minguez (ed) *Family Well-being: European Perspectives*, Dordrecht: Springer, pp 103–129.

FIFTEEN

A social right? Access to leave and its relation to parents' labour market position

Ivana Dobrotić and Sonja Blum

Introduction

There are pronounced differences in eligibility for statutory leave, especially how countries grant leave rights in relation to parents' labour market position. This is highly relevant for the effects that various Parental Leave systems may have, as the interaction of policy design and inequalities in the labour market may lead to inequalities in access to leave rights. For instance, it seems that work–family policy measures tend to benefit primarily parents who already participate in the labour market, particularly dual-earner families with higher incomes (Cantillon, 2011; Ghysels and van Lancker, 2011). And yet, the comparative literature has been predominantly focused on leave duration and benefit levels (to a lesser extent, also leave transferability and flexibility), as well as the implications these may have for gender equality and parental employment (for reviews of the literature see for example, Dobrotić, 2015; McKay et al, 2016). Much less is known about leave eligibility in general, and particularly according to parents' employment histories (Javornik, 2014).

In some countries, access to leave rights is highly contingent on labour market attachment: in Belgium, for instance, eligibility to Parental Leave benefits is dependent on long, uninterrupted insurance periods with the same employer (Merla, 2018). While in other countries, such as Germany, there are at least some basic Parental Leave benefits available universally, that is, for all parents independent of labour market participation or the form it takes (Reimer et al, 2017). If stable employment is a principal condition of eligibility for leave rights, this could increase social inequalities in access. Furthermore, if access to leave rights differs between men and women, leave design may also result in gender inequalities. There is, however, a lack of research that would bring deeper understanding of the interaction of leave policy design and social inequalities (see also McKay et al, 2016).

It is thus important to understand how Parental Leave rights relate to the labour market participation of parents; particularly with a view to the position of parents atypically connected to or not participating in the labour market. This is the aim of the current chapter. Relying on the social rights literature, we develop a conceptual framework that allows us to distinguish approaches to how Parental Leave rights are granted (in)dependent of parents' labour market position, with four ideal types identified. We are *not* going to investigate the granting of leave rights for different family types (for example, single parents, adoptive parents, same-sex parents), which is a related but different topic. We conclude the chapter by illustrating the ideal types with country case examples of Parental Leave systems.

Conceptual framework: social rights and Parental Leave entitlements

As with other social policy areas, variations in leave policy design are related to variations in 'ideological notions on social citizenship' (Kvist, 2005, p.200), that is, prevalent ideas about the role of the state in providing individuals with opportunities and resources (Clasen and Clegg, 2007). Depending on the dominant social citizenship perspective that is taken in a particular period and country, leave policies may differently (dis)advantage various social groups, as well as men and women, since social citizenship is not gender-neutral (Orloff, 1993), but highly related to different conceptualisations about the division of paid and unpaid work and related essentialist assumptions (for example, Kurowska, 2016) that prevail in a country.

Three dimensions of social rights

The social citizenship rights literature can provide a basis for connecting the predominant focus on leave *benefits* with the question of who is *eligible* for these benefits (for example, Clasen and Clegg, 2007; Blank, 2011). A good starting point when considering social rights in the welfare state is Marshall (1964), who described social rights as the final stage of citizenship, developing after civil and political rights. Typically, social rights have an economic character, as they entail an entitlement to financial transfers, goods and services or, more generally, an entitlement in relation to the labour market (Blank, 2011). Esping-Andersen (1990) developed how social rights are granted in relation to capitalist labour markets, by introducing the concept of decommodification: 'If social rights are given the legal and practical status of property rights, if they are inviolable, and if they are granted on the basis of citizenship rather than performance, they will entail a de-commodification of the status of individuals vis-a-vis the market' (Esping-Andersen, 1990, p.21). Though social rights are not necessarily decommodifying (Blank, 2011), they can be defined by how much independence they give from labour market participation (for example, in the case of old age, unemployment or parenthood).

Social rights can be attached to gainful employment (for example, through social insurance), but they can also be attached to citizenship or 'need' (Esping-Andersen, 1990). 'Citizenship' as the basis for social rights is here used as a kind of umbrella term, as it *de facto* often also implies (equivalent) rights granted for (long-term) residency. Regulations may be different for asylum-seekers and refugees compared with other migrants, but significant differences exist here between EU countries (see for example, European Union, 2015). Generally speaking, the situation in the EU is special, as EU residents (and, under certain conditions, their families) living in other member states can, through worker status, gain equal access to social and tax benefits as the country's national citizens.

These different bases for social rights concern the first of three dimensions of social rights (Blank 2007; 2011; Clasen and Clegg, 2007), namely the *entitlement principle*. There are significant differences in the extent and ways in which countries build on different entitlement principles to grant social rights. Esping-Andersen (1990) argued that social democratic welfare states tend to grant social rights on the basis of citizenship and conservative welfare states on the basis of employment, whereas a 'need', identified through means-testing, serves as a dominant eligibility principle in liberal welfare states.

Furthermore, different principles are typically combined in granting social rights across the different areas of policy, and particularly so in family policies; Sainsbury (1996, p.44) states that entitlement is not necessarily bound solely to citizenship or employment, but also to parenthood or marriage; that is, in contrast to the decommodification concept, it may also include the social rights of the economically dependent, mostly women (Orloff, 1993; Lewis, 2001). A typical example is the combination of social insurance and marriage-based rights in conservative welfare states, the former traditionally directed at male employees and forming the basis of protection against 'old social risks' (see for example, Bonoli, 2005), while the latter is traditionally directed at female dependant spouses to reduce their risk of not participating in the labour market. Individual rights based on employment are more typical for defamilialising regimes, social rights based on marriage for familialising regimes. This gendered character of social rights is particularly important in leave policies, since their design significantly affects gender inequalities in both the household and the labour market (see for example, Dearing, 2016).

The second dimension of social rights focuses on the programme level, where it is important to include also the *eligibility criteria* behind the social rights (Clasen and Clegg, 2007). The historical focus on social rights based on employment, and on decommodification as one of the major indicators, can be critically discussed also from the perspective of social inequalities. Earnings-related benefits targeted at those in regular employment primarily benefit middle- and upper-income groups and can reinforce social inequalities. They can also reinforce social inequalities between different groups in the labour market, for example, between those with permanent or temporary contracts (Blofield and Martinez Franzoni, 2015). Hence, besides the effect of social provisions on the gender dimension, it is important to understand whether policies alter or reinforce existing labour market stratification; for instance, to what extent do policies extend protection to everyone active in the labour market or only to certain groups (for example, excluding the self-employed or those with less stable careers). Also, with the application of means-testing, the granting of social rights may depend on the need of the person. This second dimension of social rights thus allows inferences regarding social inequalities.

The third dimension of social rights concerns their actual content, that is, the *scope of the benefit*. As stated already by Marshall (cited in Orloff, 1993, pp.28–29), there is no universal principle determining the content of rights and obligations. Different entitlement principles may be followed by different benefit levels; for example, earnings-related rights are usually more generous than universal rights or derived rights based on marriage (Orloff, 1993). Still, comparative social policy analyses have often been based on benefit characteristics that are more easily quantified (for example, duration or amount) and there is a lack of knowledge of the so-called 'obligations' side of social rights relationships (Blank, 2007; Clasen and Clegg, 2007) – the preconditions determining access or exclusion as well as the scope of the benefit. This is particularly true for leave rights, where statutory entitlements and eligibility criteria are still underexplored (Javornik, 2014). Against that backdrop, a three-dimensional view on social rights (Figure 15.1) shows 'which kind and amount of support may be claimed under which conditions' (Blank, 2007, p.8).

Figure 15.1: Social rights: a three-dimensional conceptual framework

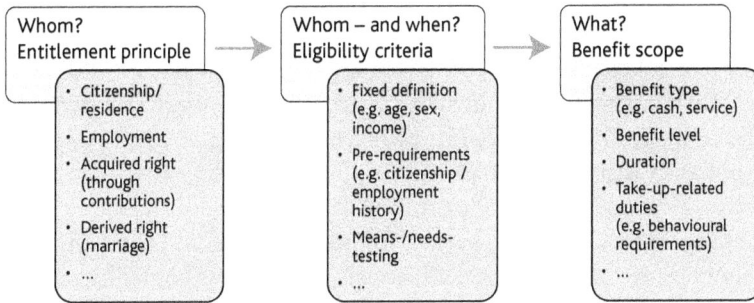

Whom? Entitlement principle	Whom – and when? Eligibility criteria	What? Benefit scope
• Citizenship/ residence • Employment • Acquired right (through contributions) • Derived right (marriage) • ...	• Fixed definition (e.g. age, sex, income) • Pre-requirements (e.g. citizenship / employment history) • Means-/needs-testing • ...	• Benefit type (e.g. cash, service) • Benefit level • Duration • Take-up-related duties (e.g. behavioural requirements) • ...

Source: Own figure based on Blank, 2011, p.55; see also Clasen and Clegg, 2007

The first two dimensions look at to whom and in what circumstances – or when – a social right is granted. This contains the entitlement principle and the eligibility criteria, that is, the conditions for the assertion of rights. They act as an important welfare state indicator that complements the rules that determine the character of provided benefits (Clasen and Clegg, 2007). These rules are captured under the third dimension, the 'what' of social rights, that is, the benefit scope. As Figure 15.1 shows, this typically contains also certain 'programme-related duties' (Blank, 2011), which have to be fulfilled to receive the (full) benefit, such as behavioural requirements (for example, not making use of public childcare facilities in order to receive benefits).

Leave policy: a typology of entitlements

The multidimensional character of leave policies brings additional complexity into the analysis. On the one hand, the scope of leave rights usually consists of several elements, which must be considered simultaneously in order to grasp their real character, such as duration, benefit level or flexibility (for example, Javornik, 2014; Blum et al, 2017). On the other hand, leave rights and their scope may also vary for different groups within a country (McKay et al, 2016). Leave benefit scope may particularly build on different entitlement principles and eligibility criteria.

As there has been much research already on the scope of Parental Leave rights (see for example, Ray et al, 2010; Ciccia and Verloo, 2012; Javornik, 2014), we focus on who is granted Parental Leave benefit and under which conditions, that is, the entitlement principle and eligibility criteria. Doing this, we can also indirectly shed light on whether these are related to differences in benefit scope. For example,

McKay et al (2016) show how in a country where Parental Leave rights are conditioned by strict employment-related requirements (Canada), access to these rights is highly dependent on the character and quality of parents' attachment to the labour market, and that parents in atypical employment are facing difficulties in accessing Parental Leave benefits. Blofield and Martinez (2015), primarily referring to Latin America, emphasise that this may particularly affect employed women from lower income quintiles who are usually less securely attached to the labour market and have less access to other resources to help them with care obligations. Thus, the entitlement principle and eligibility criteria here serve as crucial indicators of social and gender inequalities in accessing leave rights. In the following, we identify the main existing entitlement principles and eligibility criteria, based on the family policy and Parental Leave literature.

Entitlement principles for leave rights

There are two main entitlement principles for leave policies: citizenship (and/or residence), or employment. Leave rights based on *citizenship* typically follow a 'cash-for-care logic', with (low) flat-rate benefit payments (for example, Blum et al, 2017). Although they tend to be universal and thus more inclusive than employment-based rights, they are usually of a gendered character, that is, primarily aimed at mothers, so that even when defined in gender-neutral terms, women are the main users. Leave rights based on *employment* may contain flat-rate payments, but they may also contain income-related benefits that provide a wage replacement for the time on leave. For employment-based rights, residency may be additionally required for eligibility. Employment-based schemes aim to maintain leave takers' connection to the labour market, and tend to be of a more individualised character, that is, part of leave is granted explicitly to men and women or 'both parents' (see for example, Blum et al, 2017).

In practice, we also find *mixed* types, where different leave rights exist for different groups, for example, higher, income-related benefits for employed parents, and lower, flat-rate benefits for non-employed parents (for example, in Austria, see Rille-Pfeiffer et al, 2017). Income-related Parental Leave benefits are special in this regard, as they imply some 'hidden' eligibility criteria already in their benefit scope (or rather, benefit type): in other words, even if entitlement bases and eligibility criteria do not formally attach the right to employment, parents without employment income are not able to exercise the economic right. Therefore, we group income-related Parental Leave benefits as 'employment-based' by nature.

In this chapter, we primarily focus on the treatment of care work and social rights of the economically (in)dependent in policy design, which must be distinguished from the effect of leave policies on (de) gendered parenting practices. Rights that are gender-neutral 'on paper' (that is, granted as a 'family right') are less effective in shaping degendered parenting practices than individualised Parental Leave rights, that is, leaves explicitly granted to each parent or leaves that pay 'gender equality bonuses' (O'Brien, 2009; Ray et al, 2010; Dearing, 2016). The gendered effect on the division of paid and unpaid work and parental employment is particularly determined by the length of leave periods and the benefit scope (for reviews of the literature see, for example, Ray et al, 2010; Dobrotić, 2015); so, a degendered take-up of Parental Leave is strongly facilitated by well-paid Parental Leave benefits with a high earnings replacement rate (for example, Saxonberg, 2013).

Leave benefits based on citizenship differ from other family allowances (for example, child benefit) by their clear linkage to Parental Leave and employment. That is, they are typically linked to the duration of the leave right and to limits placed on employment while receiving benefits. Sometimes, the term parental *benefit* is used for employment-based benefits and the term parental *allowances* for citizenship-based benefits (see for example, Blum et al, 2017), but we will subsume both under 'Parental Leave benefit' throughout this chapter.

Eligibility criteria for leave rights

On the second dimension, the eligibility criteria come into focus, that is, the conditions under which leave rights may be exercised. These usually define the access to parental benefits. We can look at eligibility criteria subsequently for the two entitlement principles identified previously, that is, citizenship/residency or employment. These criteria can be more or less strict, tending towards a universal or a selective character. Universal rights entitle 'all citizens or residents to social services and income security, specified mainly by their position in the human life-cycle only' (Therborn, 1995, p.97); hence, within an approach of universal social citizenship, social rights cover all citizens or residents for a certain risk, regardless of their employment status. However, there are also alternative principles such as residualism, where social rights are primarily targeted towards the poor, and selectivism, where 'there are typically distinct programmes for different class and status groups' (Anttonen et al, 2012, pp.4–5). The latter principles tend towards segmented social citizenship, where the scope of leave rights depends, for example, on parents having a particular employment status. If employment-based policies are directed solely towards those in standard employment, then social inequalities between different employees on the labour market are further reinforced (for example, Blofield and Martinez Franzoni, 2015). Eligibility criteria are thus particularly important when it comes to the social equity of leave policies.

If we apply this perspective to citizenship-based leave rights (used here as an umbrella term including residency), these are typically further bound to criteria such as length and/or character of residency. Longer residency requirements may limit access to leave rights and thus produce more selective systems. In the EU, this particularly concerns non-EU migrants (see earlier). Furthermore, countries may apply means-testing (in terms of family income) to decide access or exclusion, in addition to the other eligibility criteria, which produces residual systems in which social rights are targeted towards the poorest citizens (Anttonen et al, 2012). Leave rights based on employment can be attached to criteria such as length of previous employment, number of hours worked in a given time period, or insurance period while with the same employer, and/or means-testing; the longer the qualifying period (particularly if needing to be uninterrupted or with the same employer), the less accessible employment-based benefits are, particularly for parents with less stable careers (for example, working on short-term or temporary contracts). Eligibility criteria can also regulate the benefit scope, for example, the benefit amount may increase with the duration of previous employment.

Other eligibility criteria in employment add yet more complexity to the analysis. Employment-based eligibility criteria can differ between public and private sectors, or across employment sectors due to different collective agreements and voluntary occupational welfare. Furthermore, the self-employed or marginally employed may be (partially) excluded from leave schemes, bringing additional inequalities in access to parental benefits (and their scope). Finally, there are differences between countries about whether students or the long-term unemployed have access to parental benefit payments (and, again, the scope of benefit may differ) (see for example, Blum et al, 2017). Once more we may talk of eligibility criteria stipulating a more universal or a more selective character of Parental Leave rights.

A typology of Parental Leave rights

Based on these distinctions we arrive at a classification of four different Parental Leave entitlement types (Figure 15.2). If Parental Leave rights follow the entitlement principle of citizenship, and the eligibility criteria are not strict (for example, residency is required only starting from the day of childbirth), there is a *universal parenthood model*. Universal here refers to the *coverage* of the social right. Correspondingly, if eligibility criteria are not strict, but the entitlement is based on employment (for example, any form of employment is needed on the day of childbirth), there is a *universal adult-worker model*; this follows Lewis (2001), who uses the term *adult-worker* for policies that assume all adults will be in the labour market, while care is commodified and defamilialised.

As described previously, eligibility criteria can also go in a selective (and possibly residual) direction, in which case there is a selective model, that is, benefits are targeted to certain socio-economic groups and social programmes differ between status groups. Within this, we identify a *selective parenthood model* if strict eligibility criteria are combined with a citizenship-based entitlement principle (for example, a residency of more than a year is required prior to childbirth); and a *selective adult-worker model* if strict eligibility criteria are combined with an employment-based entitlement principle (for example, uninterrupted employment of a certain duration is needed prior to childbirth). Countries inclining towards selective models will have higher social inequalities in leave rights, for example, parents with high attachment to the labour market or longer citizenship status will have access to (more generous) leave rights. Additionally, if means-testing is applied in addition to other eligibility criteria, the selective model will

Figure 15.2: Entitlements types for Parental Leave rights

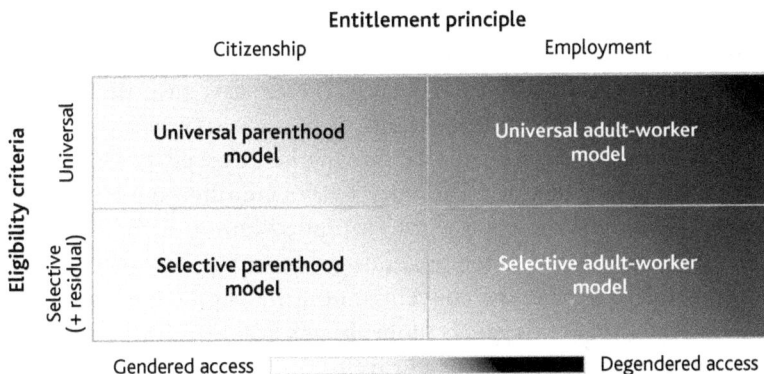

| | | Entitlement principle | |
		Citizenship	Employment
Eligibility criteria	Universal	Universal parenthood model	Universal adult-worker model
	Selective (+ residual)	Selective parenthood model	Selective adult-worker model

Gendered access ←——————→ Degendered access

become residual in its character, that is, leave rights will be targeted solely towards the poorest citizens/workers.

Access to leave rights may additionally differ for men and women. Different approaches in granting leave rights may be distinguished (Ray et al, 2010; Saxonberg, 2013; Dearing, 2016; Blum et al, 2017), ranging from gendered access (access to leave is primarily defined as solely a mother's right) to degendered access (leave is granted to both parents equally as an individual, non-transferable entitlement). The literature indicates that citizenship-based models usually have a gendered to gender-neutral access in their design, while employment-based models vary from gendered to degendered access (see Dobrotić and Blum, 2017).

As will be demonstrated when discussing concrete cases in the next section, the four ideal types of Parental Leave rights are rarely found in reality. One reason is that countries have increasingly moved towards mixed systems, which combine basic citizenship-based Parental Leave benefits with more generous employment-based Parental Leave benefits (Dobrotić and Blum, 2017). While pure employment-based models exist, this is not (or, rather, no longer) the case for citizenship-based models. Eligibility criteria vary from universal to residual, with different degrees in between, and we can also find within-country variations between public and private organisations, employed and self-employed, or different employment sectors.

National illustrative examples

To illustrate the Parental Leave entitlement types empirically, we draw on information provided by the international network's annual review (Blum et al, 2017), cross-checked with data provided by the OECD Family Database (OECD, 2018), the MISSOC Database for 2006 and 2016 (MISSOC, 2018) and national sources. To identify types, data on Parental Leave benefit entitlements have been analysed, that is, the entitlement to leave benefits available to mothers and fathers after Maternity and Paternity Leaves. These data provide the best way to capture access to leave rights of parents atypically connected to or not participating in the labour market, as well as the gender dimension; Maternity and Paternity Leaves are often directed solely towards employed parents (see for example, Blum et al, 2017), while Parental Leave more often extends to inactive and unemployed persons. Furthermore, we concentrate on the eligibility for parental benefit *payments*, as this speaks more about social inequalities in access to leave than access to a Parental Leave period as such, which is usually less conditioned and intended to provide employment protection. It should be noted that some countries have only unpaid Parental Leave (for example, Greece, Ireland, Spain, UK) (Blum et al, 2017).

Through the perspective of social rights, we focus on statutory entitlements regulated at the state level. However, these basic entitlements may be supplemented by collective agreements (for example, Denmark, Italy, Netherlands) or individual employers' provisions. While these additional entitlements may, in some countries, be significant, they do not qualify as social rights as long as they are not legal rights (see Blank, 2011).

We present three cases that illustrate the logic of the four identified ideal types or combinations, demonstrating the variety of entitlement principles and eligibility criteria identified in the previous discussion. They are Belgium, Croatia and Germany. Two of the three countries have experienced a shift towards a mixed system, starting from a citizenship-based model (Germany) and employment-based model (Croatia), and now leaning towards the more universal (Germany) and more selective (Croatia) type through their eligibility criteria. Belgium, on the other hand, comes quite close to the selective adult-worker model ideal type.

Belgium: a selective adult-worker model

Belgium offers only employment-based Parental Leave benefits. Maternity Leave is 15 weeks for employed mothers (12 weeks for self-employed) and there is also ten days Paternity Leave. Parental Leave consists of an individual, non-transferable entitlement to four months for both mother and father. Belgium thus exhibits a degendered model in access to Parental Leave. However, there is no well-paid, income-related benefit, but rather a flat-rate payment of €702 per month, which is reduced and paid pro-rata for workers taking part-time leave. There is also some regional variation: the Flemish community offers an additional payment, whose level varies between employment sectors (Merla, 2018).

Segmentation by employment is also typical of the Belgian case when it comes to Parental Leave entitlements. Eligibility in the private sector is restricted to persons who have been working for the same employer prior to leave for at least 12 months within the last 15 months; employers may grant leave to other workers, but only by agreement (Merla, 2018). But employees in the public sector do not need to fulfil this condition. Moreover, the self-employed are not eligible for Parental Leave or benefit. In all these respects, Belgium comes quite close to the ideal type of a selective and degendered adult-worker model.

Croatia: from a selective adult-worker model to a (selective) mixed system

Paid Parental Leave (so-called 'Additional Maternity Leave') was introduced in 1978 within an employment-based system. Citizenship-based, flat-rate benefits were introduced in the mid-1990s, first solely for parents of twins or of three or more children, and in the early 2000s for all parents. Croatia thus made an incremental transition towards a mixed system of more inclusive citizenship-based and employment-based Parental Leave rights via a series of smaller reforms. It also changed from a clearly gendered system towards a system which comprises some degendered elements: in 2009, an employment-based Parental Leave benefit, which used to be defined as the mother's right that might be transferred to the father under certain circumstances, was transformed into an individual, transferable right of both parents; while in 2013, a non-transferable Parental Leave benefit was introduced, though limited to dual-earner families with one or two children (see Dobrotić, 2012), so that after a seven months' Maternity Leave, each (self-)employed parent has the right to four months of earnings-related Parental Leave benefit, two of them non-transferable. However, the Parental Leave benefit remains fully transferable for parents of twins or of three or more children, who are entitled to 15 months of transferable leave; while the employed father is entitled to his right only if the mother is working, and as a low ceiling applies (€353.60 per month) the leave is mainly used by mothers.

The citizenship-based system grants a flat-rate Parental Leave benefit until the child turns one year (or three years of age in the case of multiple births or three or more children), in the first place to mothers. It may be transferred to the father only if the mother is entering the labour market or is not capable of caring for the child (Dobrotić, 2015). The system thus exhibits gendered access, especially for women with less attachment to the labour market, as the benefit may be transferred to the father only under certain conditions.

Since 2016, there are also regional variations. The city of Zagreb has introduced a so-called 'parent-caregiver' status, that is, the right to a generous allowance (€520 per month) for non-employed parents of three or more children with at least one child of pre-school age, and who have Croatian citizenship and uninterrupted five-year residency in the city of Zagreb before childbirth. It excludes the right of the child to a childcare place and it may be paid until the youngest child in the family reaches 15 years of age (Dobrotić, 2017).

Regarding the eligibility criteria, all (self-)employed parents with health insurance are entitled to the employment-based leave period; but parents who do not meet the condition of at least 12 months continual insurance or 18 months with interruptions in the previous two years are eligible for a lower flat-rate benefit available under a citizenship-based scheme. Parents without a regular employment contract (for example, freelance workers) are entitled only to citizenship-based benefits. These benefits are available to Croatian citizens or foreigners with permanent residence in Croatia who additionally fulfil a condition of uninterrupted residency before childbirth: either three years (parents without a regular working contract, registered unemployed parents, farmers) or five years (economically inactive parents, students). The residency period does not apply to persons granted asylum status or granted subsidiary protection. Unemployed persons must additionally fulfil the condition of being registered with the unemployment office for at least nine months or 12 months with interruptions within the two years before childbirth, or having at least six months of previous employment in this period (Dobrotić, 2017). Thus, Croatia represents a complex mixed system of selective employment- and citizenship-based Parental Leave benefits, still ambivalent in their gender character.

Germany: from a selective parenthood model to a universal mixed system

Parental Leave and the corresponding benefit payment were introduced in Germany in 1986 as a pure citizenship-based right. After various reforms, which mainly led to an increased duration, the benefit that existed in 2006 granted a flat-rate payment of €300 per month for two years, paid independent of any previous employment. It constituted a family right, which was thus gender-neutral in access, though not in effect, and it was means-tested, which could lead to a decreased payment or non-eligibility. Up to 2006, therefore, Germany had a selective parenthood model.

In 2007, the system was transformed fundamentally, with the introduction of an employment-based benefit (*Elterngeld*) offering earnings replacement of about 65 per cent (Reimer et al, 2017). However, the citizenship-based Parental Leave benefit was not abolished. There is still a minimum payment of €300, independent of previous employment (for example, to homemakers), but now only for one year. Although employment is not, therefore, a precondition to access rights as such, we may talk of a mixed system of employment- and citizenship-based Parental Leave benefits, since the income-dependent benefit is not accessible to parents who are non-employed.

The Parental Leave benefit is a family entitlement of 14 months, but two of these months are only available if both parents share leave; the system thus exhibits gender-sensitive access, as it includes an incentive to foster degenderisation. Such access has been strengthened further with the *ElterngeldPlus* available since 2015, under which parents of children under two years old can combine part-time leave and part-time work with some income replacement and also with an additional gender equality bonus if both parents work between 25 and 30 hours per week for at least four months (Reimer et al, 2017). There is some regional variation, as two federal states (Bavaria and Saxony) pay a means-tested benefit for two-year-old children (that is, extended to the third year of Parental Leave, as the individual right to absence from work is three years in Germany).

Regarding eligibility criteria, the system has become more universal with the 2007 reform, as means-testing is no longer conducted. Employment at the date of childbirth constitutes eligibility for employment-based benefits and no previous employment period is required. The self-employed are also included. Residency in Germany is required, but with exceptions (for example, for EU cross-border workers, adoptive parents). Non-EU residents are eligible if they have a permanent residence permit or working contract in Germany, but asylum seekers are only eligible after living in Germany for at least three years. Since 2011, the minimum payment is offset against social assistance payments, so that people who are long-term unemployed receive the minimum *Elterngeld* of €300 but their social assistance payments are reduced by the same amount; thus, the additional Parental Leave benefit has *de facto* been abolished for them since 2011, having been paid out from 2007 to 2010 (Reimer et al, 2017). This latter point makes less inclusive what is otherwise a rather universal mixed system of employment- and citizenship-based Parental Leave benefits.

Parental Leave rights: uses and limitations of the proposed typology

In this concluding section, we discuss how the typology of Parental Leave entitlement types can be applied, what it adds, what its limitations are and how it relates to existing typologies.

The analysis of citizenship-based and employment-based approaches in granting leave rights permits a deeper insight into social and gender inequalities in access to leave rights. It can, therefore, make an important contribution to the comparative literature on Parental Leave design, which has been predominantly focused on dimensions of the benefit scope. The social rights perspective throws light on which groups are left with fewer rights or are eventually excluded from leave benefits. It also shows how selective employment-based systems result in the different treatment of more secure employees, particularly in comparison with those who are less securely attached to the labour market or have less stable careers; access can also be limited with citizenship-based Parental Leave benefits. For example, some groups may be disadvantaged, such as the long-term unemployed (for example, Germany), or access to citizenship-based rights may be conditional on long residency requirements (for example, Croatia). The framework may also capture the gendered character of leave policy design, as it allows us to distinguish whether leave rights are granted solely to women, to both parents as a family right, or as an individual, non-transferable right.

The implications of different entitlement principles and eligibility criteria for social equity and gender equality are not unambiguous, though. So, while more inclusive citizenship-based rights may support social equity, they may be detrimental for gender equality, especially if these rights are of longer duration and directed solely to mothers or are 'gender-neutral' and low paid (Leitner, 2003; Javornik, 2014). Again, the social rights perspective may help to shed light on these lines of tension, and extend the analytical perspective also to groups not currently eligible for Parental Leave rights.

Regarding limitations, we have here only focused on who is eligible for Parental Leave benefits and on what basis, that is, the entitlement principle and eligibility criteria. Our typology can thus shed a light on 'hidden' inequalities in access to Parental Leave benefits within countries – differences between various socio-economic groups and for different levels of conditionality (types of employment, employment sectors, and so on). But it misses a systematic relation to the third dimension of social rights, the benefit scope. It does, however, give some indication of what consequences relying on different entitlement principles and eligibility criteria may have for the benefit scope; for instance, those with less stable careers are usually either entitled to lower, flat-rate leave benefits or they are left without entitlement (for example, Belgium). Also, as our focus was on labour market connectivity, we did not consider systematically other criteria which may also define access to leave rights, such as family status or number of children. Finally, there are many other socio-economic, cultural and institutional factors that may determine parents' 'sense of entitlement' and ability to exercise their rights, such as gendered norms at the workplace and in society (Hobson et al, 2011; see also Kurowska, 2016).

Finally, we conclude by discussing the status of the typology presented in this chapter vis-a-vis other typologies that have been applied to leave policies. As it goes beyond our scope and space limitations, we will solely highlight crucial points that may open the way for further investigation. We agree with Saxonberg's (2013, p.26) argument that 'typologies should concentrate on policies' and not include outcomes in their classifications. This separation becomes particularly relevant when aiming for an explanatory analysis, either focusing on the effects of certain policies or their determinants. The typology that is most often drawn upon when comparing family policies is the dichotomy of defamilialism and familalism (see Kurowska, 2016), which has been further refined especially by Leitner (2003), who introduced the distinction between explicit and implicit (de)familialisation. This typology has mainly been applied from a gender perspective, in particular the division of care work and waged work supported by (leave) policies.

The social rights perspective proposed in this chapter enables a more comprehensive look at the dimensions of leave policies. Specifically, gender-oriented classifications and comparisons tend to focus on the first and third of the three dimensions of social rights. Often stemming from the critique of Esping-Andersen's (de)commodification classification, the entitlement principle is regularly covered, albeit with a stronger focus on the benefit scope, such as duration and payment level (for example, Leitner, 2003; Ciccia and Verloo, 2012; Saxonberg, 2013; Dearing, 2016). The question of who is actually eligible is typically only extended to the rights of women versus men (family or individual right, transferability, and so on). The eligibility criteria are not systematically included, yet conditionality is decisive for understanding access to leave rights and social (in)equalities. This is the main strength of our typology. In the future, it may be interesting to combine it with the (de)familialisation classification, as only a more systematic connection between the first, second and third dimensions of leave rights can give the full picture of inequalities in leave rights between various groups (shorter benefit duration for the self-employed, higher benefits in the public sector, and so on). Finally, though leave rights are particularly important in this regard, the perspective of universal or selective, adult-worker- or parenthood-models can be extended to other family policies.

References

Anttonen, A., Haikio, L., Stefansson, K. and Sipila, J. (2012) 'Universalism and the challenge of diversity', in A. Anttonen, L. Haikio and K. Stefansson (eds) *Welfare State, Universalism and Diversity*, Cheltenham: Edward Elgar, pp 1–15.

Blank, F. (2007) 'Analyzing social rights in different contexts: A qualitative multi-dimensional approach', Paper presented at the ESPAnet Conference 2007, 20–22 September, Vienna.

Blank, F. (2011) *Soziale Rechte 1998–2005: Die Wohlfahrtsstaatsreformen der rot-grünen Bundesregierung* [*Social rights 1998–2005: The welfare state reforms of the red-green federal government*], Wiesbaden: VS.

Blofield, M. and Martinez Franzoni, J. (2015) 'Maternalism, co-responsibility, and social equity: A typology of work–family policies', *Social Politics*, 22(1): 38–59.

Blum, S., Koslowski, A. and Moss, P. (2017) *International Review on Leave Policies and Related Research 2017*. Available at www.leavenetwork.org/lp_and_r_reports/

Bonoli, G. (2005) 'The politics of new social policies: Providing coverage against new social risks in mature welfare states', *Policy and Politics*, 33(3): 431–449.

Cantillon, B. (2011) 'The paradox of the social investment state: Growth, employment and poverty in the Lisbon era', *Journal of European Social Policy*, 21(5): 432–449.

Ciccia, R. and Verloo, M. (2012) 'Parental Leave regulations and the persistence of the male breadwinner model: Using fuzzy-set ideal type analysis to assess gender equality in an enlarged Europe', *Journal of European Social Policy*, 22(5): 507–528.

Clasen, J. and Clegg, D. (2007) 'Levels and levers of conditionality: Measuring change within welfare states', in J. Clasen and N.A. Siegel (eds) *Investigating Welfare State Change: The 'Dependent Variable Problem' in Comparative Analysis*, Cheltenham: Edward Elgar, pp 166–197.

Dearing, H. (2016) 'Gender equality in the division of work: How to assess European leave policies regarding their compliance with an ideal leave model', *Journal of European Social Policy*, 26(3): 234–247.

Dobrotić, I. (2012) 'Dejavniki politik usklajevanja plačanega dela in družinskih obveznosti v posocialističnih državah' [Factors of reconciliation of paid work and family responsibilities in post-communist countries], *PhD thesis*, University of Ljubljana.

Dobrotić, I. (2015) 'Politike usklađivanja obiteljskih obaveza i plaćenog rada i položaj roditelja na tržištu rada' [Policies of harmonisation of family responsibilities and paid labour and parental position on the labour market], *Revija za socijalnu politiku*, 22(3): 353–374.

Dobrotić, I. (2017) 'Croatia country note', in S. Blum, A. Koslowski and P. Moss (eds) *International Review of Leave Policies and Related Research 2017*. Available at www.leavenetwork.org/lp_and_r_reports/

Dobrotić, I. and Blum, S. (2017) 'Parental Leave reforms and policy ideas: Are European countries heading towards an employment-led social-investment paradigm', Paper presented at the ESPAnet Conference 2017, 14–16 September, Lisbon.

Esping-Andersen, G. (1990) *The Three Worlds of Welfare Capitalism*, Princeton, NJ: Princeton University Press.

European Union (2015) *Work and Social Welfare for Asylum-Seekers and Refugees: Selected EU Member States*, European Parliamentary Research Service. Available at www.europarl.europa.eu/RegData/etudes/IDAN/2015/572784/EPRS_IDA(2015)572784_EN.pdf

Ghysels, J. and van Lancker, W. (2011) 'The unequal benefits of activation: An analysis of the social distribution of family policy among families with young children', *Journal of European Social Policy*, 21(5): 472–485.

Hobson, B., Fahlén, S. and Takács, J. (2011) 'Agency and capabilities to achieve a work–life balance: A comparison of Sweden and Hungary', *Social Politics*, 18(2): 168–198.

Javornik, J. (2014) 'Measuring state de-familialism: Contesting post-socialism exceptionalism', *Journal of European Social Policy*, 24(3): 240–257.

Kurowska, A. (2016) '(De)familization and (de)genderization: Competing or complementary perspectives in comparative policy analysis?', *Social Policy and Administration*, 47(1): 1–21.

Kvist, J. (2005) 'Exploring diversity: Measuring welfare state change with fuzzy-set methodology', in J. Clasen and N.A. Siegel (eds) *Investigating Welfare State Change: The 'Dependent Variable Problem' in Comparative Analysis*, Cheltenham: Edward Elgar.

Leitner, S. (2003) 'Varieties of familialism: The caring function of the family in comparative perspective', *European Societies*, 5(4): 353–375.

Lewis, J. (2001) 'The decline of the male breadwinner model: Implications for work and care', *Social Politics*, 8(2): 152–169.

Marshall, T.H. (1964) 'Citizenship and social class', in T.H. Marshall (ed) *Class, Citizenship, and Social Development, Essays*, Garden City, NY: Doubleday, pp 65–122.

McKay, L., Mathieu, S. and Doucet, A. (2016) 'Parental-leave rich and parental-leave poor: Inequality in Canadian labour market based policies', *Journal of Industrial Relations*, 58(4): 543–562

Merla, L. (2018) 'Belgium country note', in S. Blum, A. Koslowski and P. Moss (eds) *International Review of Leave Policies and Related Research 2017*. Available at www.leavenetwork.org/lp_and_r_reports/

MISSOC (Mutual Information System on Social Protection) (2018) *MISSOC Comparative Tables Database*. Available at www.missoc.org/INFORMATIONBASE/COMPARATIVETABLES/MISSOCDATABASE/comparativeTableSearch.jsp.

O'Brien, M. (2009) 'Fathers, parental leave policies, and infant quality of life: International perspectives and policy impact', *ANNALS of the American Academy of Political and Social Science 2009*, 624(1): 190–213.

OECD (2018) *OCED Family Database*. Available at www.oecd.org/els/family/database.htm

Orloff, A.S. (1993) 'Gender and the social rights of citizenship: The comparative analysis of gender relations and welfare states', *American Sociological Review*, 58(3): 303–328.

Ray, R., Gornick, J.C. and Schmitt, J. (2010) 'Who cares? Assessing generosity and gender equality in Parental Leave policy designs in 21 countries', *Journal of European Social Policy*, 20(3): 196–216.

Reimer, T., Erler, D. and Blum, S. (2017) 'Germany country note', in S. Blum, A. Koslowski and P. Moss (eds) *International Review on Leave Policies and Related Research 2017*. Available at www.leavenetwork.org/lp_and_r_reports/

Rille-Pfeiffer, C., Dearing, H. and Schmidt, A. (2017) 'Austria country note', in S. Blum, A. Koslowski and P. Moss (eds) *International Review of Leave Policies and Related Research 2017*. Available at www.leavenetwork.org/lp_and_r_reports/

Sainsbury, D. (ed) (1996) *Gender, Equality and Welfare States*, Cambridge: Cambridge University Press.

Saxonberg, S. (2013) 'From defamilialization to degenderization: Toward a new welfare typology', *Social Policy and Administration*, 47(1): 26–49.

Therborn, G. (1995) *European Modernity and Beyond: The Trajectory of European Societies 1945–2000*, London: Sage.

PART III

Future directions for leave policy

SIXTEEN

Universal Basic Income: what could it mean for gender equality in care work?

Alison Koslowski

Introduction

Support for the idea of a Basic Income (referred to henceforth as BI) paid to every eligible adult and child is gaining traction across the developed world, though it remains a controversial and largely untested proposal. It can be defined as 'an income paid by a political community to all its members on an individual basis, without means test or work requirement' (van Parijs, 2004, p.8). Such a BI would likely have significant implications for all socially valuable activities including those without direct economic benefit, and caring is one such activity.

This section of the book considers ways in which societies might aim to do things differently in the future. While not a new idea *per se*, BI as a policy proposal can be said to be one of the few truly radical shake-ups to welfare systems currently being mooted by actors across the political spectrum (Reed and Lansley, 2016). The proposal to introduce BI is, in part, a response to concerns about incoming technological changes, which may lead to revolutionary shifts in how we organise work, including care work, in our societies in coming decades. This could involve a rethink of how we support parents and other carers.

BI would replace many existing benefits, covering many income risks across the life course, similar to a state pension but not just post-retirement. By covering such needs for all members of a society, BI would potentially address income risks associated with disability, joblessness, parenting, childhood, illness and education. This abolishing of the *status quo*, which typically targets those considered to be in particular need at a specific point in their life, potentially raises some alarm bells, as it is possible that some vulnerable groups might be worse off if current benefits (for example, such as housing subsidies) are phased out. Furthermore, welfare benefits, including parenting leave policies, are frequently multi-dimensional in the way that they support citizens, going beyond financial provision and thus what a BI might offer.

This chapter explores to what extent a BI might be able to replace parenting leave payments and other aspects of parenting leave policies; the term 'parenting leave', as used here, covers all leave for parents, including Maternity Leave, Paternity Leave and Parental Leave. Many of the arguments explored are likely to apply to other forms of care and other forms of care leave. Indeed, a BI might lead to more support for carers than current systems, which tend to focus on early parenthood as if this were the only time that individuals have caring responsibilities. It is commonly argued that mothers and children would be particular winners under a BI scheme, but what the gendered implications might be of BI are contested, in particular what it might mean to be a parent responsible for childcare (McLean, 2016). While advocates argue that BI would alleviate child and maternal poverty, critics are concerned that it would further entrench a gendered domestic division of labour and exacerbate gender pay gaps and other aspects of gender inequality (McKay, 2007).

Political parties around the world are increasingly considering the potential merits of BI but it has yet to be introduced by any national government (De Wispelaere, 2016). The Swiss rejected the proposal in a referendum in 2016. At the time of writing, Finland has a small-scale experiment in the field (Kela, 2016), as does Canada (Macdonald, 2016). There have been small-scale versions of a BI in Brazil and in Alaska (De Wispelaere, 2016), but not in such a form that would provide empirical data to inform this chapter. Similarly, experiments in Canada in the 1970s were more about a guaranteed minimum income (thus means-tested) rather than a truly universal BI (Calnitsky, 2016). As such, this chapter is necessarily based on theoretical reflections as well as being informed by the empirical research base regarding parenting leave.

In what follows, there is a brief review of BI and what its proponents hope to achieve, as well as core objections. What the overlap might be between the aims of a BI and parenting leave policies is then explored, also considering the functions of parenting leave not covered by a BI scheme. The chapter then considers whether there might be any lessons learnt already from the implementation of parenting leave policies that might be helpful for those considering the implementation of BI, with respect to the distribution of benefits. The chapter concludes with the discussion of whether or not a BI could replace parenting leave or whether parenting leave would still be needed as a complement in so far as gender equality remains a concern.

Basic Income: a summary of the main arguments for and against

There are various definitions of a BI, but it generally refers to an unconditional payment to all members of a society. A key contrast between the BI model and most current social welfare models is that those considered of core working age, and fit to be actively seeking employment, would also receive such payments without means test or work requirement. This would include parents and other carers (van Parijs, 2004). Many welfare states currently have a restricted BI model for those over a certain age in the form of state pensions, and some for parents in the form of parenting leave payments and child benefits, and a BI might well seek to replace such benefits (Atkinson, 2015; Citizen's Income Trust, 2015).

There are variants on the name, and a BI is sometimes referred to as a 'universal basic income' and sometimes as a 'citizen's income' (Atkinson, 2015; Torry, 2016). How membership of a society would be defined would need to be carefully considered so as not to create a group within the community who fall outside the scope of BI. It would be for the individual political community to debate the particulars, such as the level of the payment. The recent Swiss Referendum suggested CHf2,500 (approximately €2,155) per month, which is much higher than the current suggestion by the UK Citizen's Income Trust of possibly £72 (€80) per week (Citizen's Income Trust, 2015; Torry, 2016).

Many claims are made about what a BI might achieve; for a summary of the main claims made for and against BI, see Table 16.1. Claims for a BI include reducing poverty and benefit traps, cutting bureaucracy, matching social security systems to better correspond with changes in working life, increasing wages, supporting creativity and entrepreneurship, reducing unhealthy dependencies within relationships, increasing well-being; and the list continues (Kela, 2016). Some also claim that a BI would reduce gender inequalities in society (Mckay, 2001).

BI is an idea that receives support from across the political spectrum; and while there are differences in some of the rationales for a BI made by those coming from different political backgrounds, what is perhaps particularly interesting is the potential for consensus. In part, this is

Table 16.1: A summary of the main claims made for and against a Basic Income

Issue/quality	Arguments for BI	Arguments against BI
Poverty reduction	✓	
Reduction of bureaucracy	✓	
Improved job quality	✓	
Unconditional payment to all	✓ (seen as a positive)	✓ (seen as a negative)
Support for carers	✓	✓ (concern that opposite might occur)
Reduced spectrum of benefits	✓ (seen as a positive)	✓ (seen as a negative)
Reducing unhealthy dependencies within personal relationships	✓	✓ (concern that opposite might occur – household income dynamics)
Gender equality	✓ (increased personal independence)	✓ (reinforcing current gender system)
Social inclusion	✓	✓ (what about non-eligible citizens)
Funding		✓ (how to fund)
Moral hazard		✓ (e.g., the lazy)

because both more left-wing and more right-wing parties favour a simplification in the administration of benefits and taxes. By providing a BI floor for all, the web of means tested and other benefits with their complex eligibilities could be swept away (Kela, 2016), although how far this would be so would presumably depend on the level of BI paid and other services provided by the state. A BI would also likely replace personal tax allowances (Citizen's Income Trust, 2015). As well as potential administrative efficiencies, the abolition of other benefits would probably be required in order to fund a BI (Reed and Lansley, 2016). BI can be seen as either an expansion or a reduction of the welfare state, depending on your standpoint.

Similarly, actors across the political spectrum seek the alleviation of the worst aspects of poverty in our societies. The difference that a BI could make to quality of life, certainly without accompanying reforms around housing provisions and, in some countries, around provisions for health and education, would likely be modest. As such, proponents of a BI argue that incentives for seeking income from employment would not significantly diminish, but there would be a more reliable and less complicated safety net for those more likely to be at risk of experiencing poverty. The unconditional and individual BI might also reduce unhealthy dependencies both within personal relationships and with employers.

At the same time there is much opposition to the idea of a BI from across the political spectrum. Perhaps the principal concern is how feasible it would be to fund a BI set at a useful amount. It is likely that a BI payment would indeed be quite low due to the demands even a guaranteed minimum income would make on any tax base (Tobin, 1970; Torry, 2016).

There is debate as to how a BI scheme might be funded, including ideas beyond a reliance on income tax (Henry, 2014; Cummine, 2016). However, funding models that draw on individual taxation as their source of income generation will particularly need to concern themselves with incentives and support for citizens to remain in employment, which would presumably be more problematic as the size of any payment increased. A higher level of BI could contribute to poverty alleviation and personal independence, but it might also reinforce withdrawal from the labour market and public life for certain groups, such as mothers of young children, in so far as financial decisions were still taken at household level (Fitzpatrick, 1999). Some point to the potential moral hazard (Piachaud, 2016): why would many go out to work and thus pay taxes to maintain the system if they could rather fill their time with other preferred leisure activities? Alternatively, this can be seen as a benefit, as there may be societal advantages to working fewer hours (Green Institute, 2016). Others might object to a universal benefit going to those not experiencing poverty.

Some point to the risk that a modest BI would not match the total payments from multiple benefits currently received by some under a means-tested system, leaving certain vulnerable groups worse off under a new system and a general retrenchment of the welfare state. On occasion, in recognition of this, something less than a full BI model has been mooted (for example, partial BI models (Kela, 2016; Reed and Lansley, 2016) such as guaranteed minimum income (Calnitsky, 2016) or a BI which retains means tested benefits (Torry, 2016)). There is debate around whether such partially implemented schemes might be necessary transitions to the full BI model (De Wispelaere, 2016).

One concern is how eligibility for a BI would be decided. Eligibility being linked to citizenship carries certain risks of social exclusion for the many non-citizens present in a society for various reasons at a given time. Partly in response to this, others make the case for a participation income, which would be paid not on the basis of membership or citizenship but rather on the basis of useful social participation, broadly defined, and which would complement existing social transfers rather than replacing them (Atkinson, 2015).

In so far as work can be seen as a site for integration into the broader community and into public life, a BI might be seen to reinforce barriers to the labour market for those who might most benefit from it. For example, there would be less pressure for politicians to worry about unemployment or job loss as those affected would have some financial security. Linked to this, there might also be less political pressure to safeguard routes into training essential for social mobility and integration (for example, of migrant workers) (Hassel, 2017). Gender income gaps related to the differential return to work of mothers following childbirth may also become less of a political concern. While a BI would provide women with unconditional income and thus recognise the social value of (gendered) caregiving (Fitzpatrick, 1999; McKay, 2001; 2005; Zelleke, 2011), it might also risk reinforcing gendered practices, and thus further entrench gender inequalities and maintain financial dependency within personal relationships (Robeyns, 2001; Gheaus, 2008).

The core enquiry of this chapter is how the experience of early parenthood might change (or not) following the introduction of a BI. Any reduction in poverty would be welcome for those parents, and in particular single parents, currently on very low incomes. Those involved in childcare would have some increased financial support and without conditionality or dependence on others. But it is not clear that a BI would create the conditions in which parental caregiving could become less gendered, which as we shall see in the next section, has been an explicit aim of some parenting leave policies.

What common ground is there between the aims of parenting leave policy and a Basic Income?

Although dependent on eligibility criteria, parenting leave has been seen as one of a group of measures (another, as previously mentioned, being a universal state pension) moving along the path to a BI (Robeyns, 2001). One aspect of parenting leave policy can be that it provides an income to parents while they are at home looking after a child. However, there is much variation across countries, from no payment (just leave) to near replacement wage rates (Blum et al, 2017). Also, payment is only one dimension of parenting leave policy. Other dimensions include duration of leave, whether leave is an individual or family entitlement and flexibility in how leave can be used, all of which are also extremely relevant to whether or not parenting leave can be seen to facilitate greater gender equality (Haas and Rostgaard, 2011; Castro-Garcia and Pazos-Moran, 2016).

A relatively well-established policy instrument, the aims of parenting leave policy vary according to time and place (Kamerman and Moss, 2009; ILO, 2014; Blum et al, 2017). A primary justification for the introduction of leave policies, and in particular Maternity Leave, has been concern for the health of the (employed) mother and child, including the concern that a mother could need protection from her place of work during pregnancy and while breastfeeding. The full range of aims of parenting leave might include: maternal, paternal and child health and well-being; the promotion of gender equality in domestic life; and the reduction of sexual discrimination in the workplace (Kamerman and Moss, 2009). Sometimes, this includes the explicit pledge to include fathers, but not always (Blum et al, 2017). Occasionally, parenting leave can also be seen as a pro-natalist policy instrument where the aim is to encourage citizens to have more children (Lalive and Zweimüller, 2009). In the following section, and in Table 16.2, the various potential aims of parenting leave are considered and the extent to which BI policy is compatible with each particular aim of parenting leave is discussed.

In some countries, parenting leave has the specific policy aim of increasing gender equality. It tries to achieve this in three main ways. First, it protects women's (and increasingly men's) position in the labour market, allowing them to return to their place of employment after a period of leave, and thus potentially helps to reduce labour market discrimination. Second, depending on policy design, it aims to support carers other than the birth mother, in particular fathers. Proponents of parenting leave policies typically support the idea

Table 16.2: Core aims of parenting leave policies and overlap with Basic Income

Potential core aims of parenting leave policy	Overlap and complementarity with Basic Income
Gender equality: labour market discrimination reduction	No
Gender equality: increase in men caring	No
Gender equality: individual income	Yes
Public health (primarily mother and child)	To some extent
Parental well-being: relationships	Potentially
Child well-being	Potentially
Pro-natalist	Potentially

that gender equality requires a change away from the assumption that mothers have primary responsibility for childcare. Third, again depending on policy design, it provides mothers (and fathers) with an income during early parenthood. A BI payment would probably tend towards the lower end of the current spectrum of parenting leave payments. Furthermore, while a BI would provide parents with an unconditional income, it would not provide employment protection, nor be designed to encourage increased care by fathers.

Parental Leave itself, an important component in parenting leave, can be seen as a political project, deliberately named so as to encourage a more even distribution of leave-taking between men and women. BI can also be described as a political project, which would be a gender-neutral policy in terms of its implementation. However, in order for a gender-neutral label to translate into non-gendered practice, the design of the policy and its implementation have to be carefully considered – at least this has been shown to be the case for parenting leave (for example, Brandth and Kvande, 2009).

Scholars and policy makers with an interest in how gender equality might be achieved have long observed that the social organisation of parenting (and other care) is the likely key (Koslowski, 2008). As long as a majority of mothers retain responsibility as a primary carer and a majority of fathers retain responsibility as a primary provider, this gendered split in the organisation of parenting is likely to spill over into gender inequalities across the life course. It is not clear how a BI payment, particularly if the payment was relatively modest, would challenge this *status quo* of mothers still taking most of the responsibility for early years childcare and fathers still taking most of the responsibility for financial provision for the family (Gerson, 2009). Indeed, it may reinforce a (male) breadwinner model. Single parents, most of whom are single mothers, would continue to be relatively disadvantaged as compared to dual-parent families, as they would remain without a source of income except for BI.

McLean (2015, p.2) notes that 'Basic Income is in some ways a microcosm of wider feminist controversies regarding how the state can recognise the unpaid work women largely do without reinforcing existing inequalities, also known as Wollstonecraft's Dilemma (Lister, 1995; Pateman, 1988)'. Indeed, feminists involved with policy sometimes find themselves falling into one of two camps: that of a more pragmatic approach and that of a more idealistic approach. The former aim to take the situation they see at a current time in front of them, such as mothers doing most of the childcare, and to support women in that situation. The latter might rather take issue with the root imbalance of this situation and aim to create a new situation where fathers are doing more childcare. Arguably, parenting leave is a more radically ambitious policy than BI in that it seeks change to this most gendered area of social life.

A BI would represent a new departure for any welfare state, but it would still be supporting a gender order, like preceding welfare states (Fraser, 1994). This observation is particularly pertinent for an understanding of the potential consequences of a BI policy for parenting leave policy.

If all mothers, fathers and children had a BI then it is possible that child poverty would be reduced or even eliminated, depending on the level of the BI. As the payment would be universal, there would be no complications, as there often is now with leave policy, regarding eligibility being conditional on having worked for an employer for a certain period prior to the birth of a child or linked to self-employment. In so far as the income safety net would reduce both maternal and paternal stress, this would also be beneficial to the health of the whole family in both the short and longer term. However, unless BI was paid at a much higher level than has been usually proposed, it would need to be topped up to match (a) levels of Maternity Leave pay found in most countries; and (b) levels of Parental Leave pay found in the minority of countries that have designed Parental Leave to actively promote gender equality (such as the Nordic countries (see Chapter Eleven), Germany, Slovenia, and Québec in Canada (see Chapter Thirteen)).

The two policies, parenting leave and BI, have a very different relationship to employment. The primary function of parenting leave is arguably not to provide an income to parents; rather, its primary function is to enable parents to have some leave (sometimes paid) from employment for the purpose of caring for their children while retaining the right to return to work at the end of the leave period. It is thus, at heart, an employment protection measure for parents in the dual sense that it allows parents to have some protected time away from the workplace, while also being assured of a return to equivalent employment, within a specified timeframe. Parenting leave can be seen as a mechanism for maintaining labour market participation and also income maintenance (often up to a ceiling amount) during early parenthood; it is not a policy that can be said to have redistributive effects between rich and poor. By contrast, BI provides a safety net to allow parents to potentially step back from the labour market or to engage with it on different terms, in such a way that it is particularly beneficial for those on the lowest wages and single parents. Where it exists, payment for parenting leave is often earnings-related and so more relevant to parents across a greater range of the income distribution than is the case for BI, which would be a flat-rate payment. Indeed, an aim of parenting leave might well be to keep higher earners (and higher rate taxpayers) in the labour market.

Historically, mothers have often been expected to withdraw from the labour market after the birth of a child, and indeed, many continue to experience discrimination during and after maternity (Equality and Human Rights Commission, 2015). Statistical discrimination refers to the more general discrimination applied to all women of childbearing age, regardless of their childbearing plans or status (for example, Konrad and Cannings, 1997). Leave for parents, particularly Maternity Leave, has been a key institution in the fight against discrimination, in that employers would now be warier of making a woman redundant during or before Maternity Leave than in the past; while it becomes a new norm that mothers return to the workplace after a period of Maternity Leave. It is less clear that a BI would necessarily be such an explicitly feminist policy (Fitzpatrick, 1999).

The relationship between a BI and employment protection might be fairly complex. There would arguably be less of a moral case to be made for the right to return to employment as income protection would be to some extent taken care of. Some argue that a BI would allow employees to walk away from employers more easily and that this would thus translate into an improvement in the occupational benefits offered by employers (van Parijs, 1991; Wright, 2006), perhaps including more generous leave provisions that went beyond the statutory entitlement. In general, an argument for an employer to offer parenting leave is that it improves the retention of valued staff and thus reduces training and other costs associated with high turnover. Staff retention may become increasingly important, both for employers and also for supporting a tax base, so in this sense parenting leave could be seen as a necessary complementary supplement to a BI policy.

BI is not particularly seen as an explicitly pro-natalist measure, though some argue it would increase fertility rates in developed countries (Brezis, 2014). While increasing fertility rates has not been a key aim of parenting leave policy in most countries, it has been influential in some (for example, Germany, Korea, Japan (see Chapter Six)). Furthermore, it has been argued that certain policy designs for parenting leave do support increasing fertility rates in a population (Lalive and Zweimüller, 2009).

One aspect of parent–child well-being is that the family is able to spend time together. A BI would support this aim in that it would provide a certain income floor to the parents without them feeling that they (both) had to rush back to employment in order to cover the basics. However, as discussed, it is not clear how gendered this arrangement might be and thus how far it would support relationships between all members of a family.

In summary, a BI policy would provide a reliable income to all parents and other care givers and thus render them less dependent on income from employment and each other during this period of the life course, though it would not be a wage replacement. The implementation of a BI would be gender neutral and so, in theory, fathers and mothers would have the same support. In practice, however, and especially given the likely low level of BI, this policy might have the (unintended) consequence of encouraging a return to the breadwinner model of parenting, with one parent better able to stay at home, but another parent still needing to remain firmly attached to the labour market.

Can we combine a Basic Income and parenting leave?

Perhaps the key lesson that scholarship offers parenting leave policy is that the aims of the policy need to be explicit and that specific measures to address these aims need to be incorporated into the design of the policy in order for them to be realised. For example, only in those countries where there has been an explicit goal of gender equality and shared parenting between mothers and fathers, combined with well-paid individual and non-transferable leave entitlements, have we seen any meaningful take-up by fathers of more than a few days of leave (Castro-García and Pazos-Moran, 2016). As with many things, the devil is in the detail and design matters.

While not an explicit parenting leave policy, the Belgium time credit system (see Chapter Seventeen) is an example of a seemingly gender-neutral scheme; in essence, this gives employees a 'time credit' that each can use over the life course to take time out from employment, for a variety of purposes. However, it has seen gendered use in practice. As discussed in Chapter Seventeen, mothers (but not fathers) in Belgium have overwhelmingly used their time credit account to care for children, in effect as an extension of parenting leave; it has, in practice, reinforced the gendered nature of childcare. This experience suggests that for a BI to have an egalitarian impact on the gendered practices of parenting, further thought would have to be given to how to achieve that specific goal.

Reflecting on the potentially gendered consequences of a BI, McLean (2016, p.284) reminds us of the importance of considering 'the position of women in all their diversity' and thus of intersectionality as an approach. As an individual entitlement, a BI helps to address the needs of those not following the nuclear family model, and those at the bottom end of the income distribution, but might be less relevant for those higher up the income distribution. Leave policies are certainly experienced differently by groups across a given population. Generally speaking, those with a higher level of education (and income) are more likely to be eligible for more generous parenting leave benefits, which is reflected in the socio-economic gradient in the take-up of leave, by both mothers and fathers, but in particular by fathers (Plantin, 2007; Koslowski and Kadar-Satat, 2018).

So, there is maybe a case for both a BI, which would be particularly supportive for parents and other caregivers at the lower end of the income distribution, and a parenting leave policy for those parents and caregivers engaged in the labour market and wanting to remain so. It is important to remember that in essence a BI is exactly what it says on the tin. As envisaged to date, it is essentially a bit more money for everyone – but probably not very much. Thus, if BI payment replaced parenting leave payment, it would not be enough to support most families in the manner to which they might have become accustomed. Indeed, it might well be similar to the kind of low level (nearly) universal child benefit in the UK.

One question is how much a BI over the life course might affect savings behaviour, if at all. At the moment, an advantage of carer's allowances and leave measures is that these types of benefits take account of specific needs at a given time (O'Reilly, 2008). It might be possible for individuals to save up their BI in advance of a life event such as parenthood, but this is shifting the risk to the individual, and assuming that there is disposable income available to save. Another option could be to consider a lifetime credit, a development of the time credit model discussed in Chapters Seventeen and Eighteen, which would give a quota of job-protected and high paid leave to each adult, available to be drawn on across the life course; this would also take policy beyond parenting leave and its narrow focus on early parenthood to other forms of care, including care for the self and care for others (not just children).

In summary, BI policies and parenting leave policies are likely to be appreciated differently across a given society. BI is likely to particularly benefit those mothers at risk of poverty and less attached to the labour market. Leave policies generally benefit those mothers in eligible employment, and parents with a higher socio-economic status enjoy the most generous policies. Furthermore, fathers with higher levels of education and occupational status more often use their entitlements to parenting leave. It would remain to be seen whether a BI would encourage or reduce the demand for different kinds of parental team work.

Conclusions

Leave policies are first and foremost a form of employment protection and potential tools to forward gender equality, above and beyond income maintenance assistance. If BI were seen as a replacement for parenting leave, it would risk these essential functions of parenting leave being left unaddressed. Parenting leave policy is much more than a device to ensure a minimum income to new parents, important as this is to some.

As such, this chapter concludes that were BI to be implemented, this should not be accompanied by any reduction in parenting leave entitlements. Thus, at least with regard to supporting early parenthood, there should not be an accompanying reduction in the range of support policies available; rather BI would represent a helpful boost to those most in need of support. Indeed, a BI would be most likely to support those who are not employed or otherwise not eligible for leave benefits. The same arguments might apply to other forms of care and other forms of care leave.

BI potentially facilitates people not having to be solely reliant on income from work, or at least not as much, for a certain period of time. In contrast, parenting leave helps people to remain attached to the labour market. In so far as it is seen as important, from a gender equality perspective, for women to participate in the labour market and for men to participate more in care, it is less certain that a BI would help to deliver on this. Whereas in principle BI would be gender neutral in implementation, the lessons of parenting leave policy suggest that to move towards gender equality requires specific emphasis on fathers caring if social norms are to shift. As such, there is a strong argument for the retention of incentives which support men with caring, as well as women.

The argument made here is that for a policy to have positive outcomes with regard to gender equality, it needs to have gender equality as an explicit policy aim. This is still no guarantee of general success, but without such explicitness gender equality is an unlikely unintended consequence. Thus, if BI was to have positive consequences for gender equality across the social spectrum, this goal would need to be explicitly considered in policy design in advance of implementation.

References

Atkinson, A.B. (2015) *Inequality: What Can be Done?*, Cambridge, MA: Harvard University Press.

Blum, S., Koslowski, A. and Moss, P. (2017) *International Review of Leave Policies and Research 2017*. Available at: www.leavenetwork.org/leave-policies-research/country-reports/

Brandth, B. and Kvande, E. (2009) 'Gendered or gender-neutral care politics for fathers?', *The Annals of the American Academy of Political and Social Science*, 624: 177–189.

Brezis, E. (2014) 'Paid BI, fertility rates and economic growth', *Homo Oeconomicus*, 31(1/2): 225–244.

Calnitsky, D. (2016) '"More normal than welfare": The Mincome Experiment, stigma, and community experience', *The Canadian Review of Sociology/La Revue canadienne de sociologie*, 53(1): 26–71.

Castro-García, C. and Pazos-Moran, M. (2016) 'Parental Leave policy and gender equality in Europe', *Feminist Economics*, 22 (3): 51–73.

Citizen's Income Trust (2015) *Citizen's Income: A Brief Introduction*. Available at www.citizensincome.org/wp-content/uploads/2016/03/Booklet2015.pdf

Cummine, A. (2016) *Citizens' Wealth: Why (and How) Sovereign Funds Should be Managed by the People for the People*, New Haven, CT: Yale University Press.

De Wispelaere, J. (2016) 'BI in our time: Improving political prospects through policy learning?', *Journal of Social Policy*, 45 (4): 617–634.

Equality and Human Rights Commission (2015) 'Pregnancy and maternity-related discrimination and disadvantage. First findings: Surveys of employers and mothers', *BIS Research Paper* 235. Available at www.equalityhumanrights.com/en/managing-pregnancy-and-maternity-workplace/pregnancy-and-maternity-discrimination-research-findings

Fitzpatrick, T. (1999) *Freedom and Security: An Introduction to the BI Debate*, Basingstoke: Macmillan.

Fraser, N. (1994) 'After the family wage: Gender equity and the welfare state', *Political Theory*, 22(4): 591–618.

Gerson, K. (2009) *The Unfinished Revolution: Coming of Age in a New Era of Gender, Work and Family*, Oxford: Oxford University Press.

Gheaus, A. (2008) 'Basic Income, Gender Justice and the Costs of Gender-Symmetrical Lifestyles', *Basic Income Studies*, 3(3). DOI: 10.2202/1932-0183.1134

Green Institute (eds) (2016) 'Can less work be more fair?', A discussion paper on Universal BI and shorter working week. Available at www. greeninstitute.org.au

Haas, L. and Rostgaard, T. (2011) 'Fathers' rights to paid parental leave in the Nordic countries: Consequences for the gendered division of leave', *Community, Work and Family*, 14 (2): 177–195.

Hassel, A. (2017) 'Unconditional BI is a dead end', *Süddeutsche Zeitung*, 7 February (English version courtesy of the Hertie School of Government). Available at www.socialeurope.eu/2017/03/ unconditional-basic-income-is-a-dead-end/

Henry, M. (2014) *How to Fund a Universal BI Without Scaring the Horses*, Centre for Welfare Reform. Available at www.centreforwelfarereform. org/library/by-az/how-to-fund-a-universal-basic-income.html

ILO (International Labour Office) (2014) *Maternity and Paternity at Work: Law and Practice Across the World*, Geneva: ILO.

Kamerman, S. and Moss, P. (eds) (2009) *The Politics of Parental Leave Policies: Children, Parenting, Gender and the Labour Market*, Bristol: Policy Press.

Kela (2016) 'From idea to experiment: Report on Universal BI experiment in Finland', *Kela Working Paper* 106, Helsinki: Kela.

Konrad, A. and Cannings, K. (1997) 'The effects of gender role congruence and statistical discrimination on managerial advancement', *Human Relations*, 50(10): 1305–1328.

Koslowski, A. (2008) *Who Cares? European Fathers and the Time they Spend Looking after their Children*, Saarbrücken: VDM Verlag.

Koslowski, A. and Kadar-Satat, G. (2018) 'Fathers at work: Explaining the gaps between entitlement to leave policies and uptake', *Community, Work and Family*. DOI: 10.1080/13668803.2018.1428174

Lalive, R. and Zweimüller, J. (2009) 'Does parental leave affect fertility and return to work? Evidence from two natural experiments', *The Quarterly Journal of Economics*, 124(3): 1363–1402.

Macdonald, D. (2016) *A Policymaker's Guide to BI*, Canadian Centre for Policy Alternatives. Available at www.policyalternatives.ca/ publications/reports/policymakers-guide-basic-income.

McKay, A. (2001) 'Rethinking work and income maintenance policy: Promoting gender equality through a Citizens' BI', *Feminist Economics*, 7(1): 97–118.

McKay, A. (2005) *The Future of Social Security Policy: Women, Work and a Citizens' BI*, Abingdon: Routledge.

McKay, A. (2007) 'Why a Citizens' BI? A question of gender equality or gender bias', *Work, Employment and Society*, 21(2): 337–348.

McLean, C. (2015) 'Beyond care: Expanding the feminist debate on Universal BI', *WiSE Working Paper Series* 1, WiSE Research Centre. Available at www.gcu.ac.uk/media/gcalwebv2/theuniversity/centresprojects/wise/90324WiSE_BriefingSheet.pdf

McLean, C. (2016) '…and justice for all?: BI and the principles of gender equity', *Juncture*, 22(4), pp 284–288.

O'Reilly, J. (2008) 'Can a BI lead to a more gender equal society?', *BI Studies*, 3(3): article 9.

Piachaud, D. (2016) 'Citizen's income: Rights and wrongs', *CASE/200 Working Paper*, London: LSE.

Plantin, L. (2007) 'Different classes, different fathers? On fatherhood, economic conditions and class in Sweden', *Community, Work and Family*, 10(1): 93–110.

Reed, H. and Lansley, S. (2016) *Universal BI: An idea whose time has come?*, London: Compass.

Robeyns, I. (2001) 'An income of one's own: A radical vision of welfare policies in Europe and beyond', *Gender and Development*, 9 (1): 82–89.

Robeyns, I. (2007) 'Some thoughts on BI from a feminist perspective', Paper presented at the Heinrich Böll Stiftung workshop, Berlin, 5 July.

Tobin, J. (1970) 'On limiting the domain of inequality', *Journal of Law and Economics*, 13: 263–277.

Torry, M. (2016) 'An evaluation of a strictly revenue neutral citizen's income scheme', *EUROMOD Working Paper Series*. Available at www.iser.essex.ac.uk/research/publications/working-papers/euromod/em5-16.pdf

van Parijs, P. (1991) 'Why surfers should be fed: The liberal case for an unconditional BI', *Philosophy and Public Affairs*, 20 (2): 101–131.

van Parijs, P. (2004) 'BI: A simple and powerful idea for the twenty-first century', *Politics and Society*, 32 (1): 7–39.

Wright, E.O. (2006) 'Two redistributive proposals: Universal BI and stakeholder grants', *Focus*, 24 (2): 5–7.

Zelleke, A. (2011) 'Feminist political theory and the argument for an unconditional BI', *Policy and Politics*, 39 (1): 27–42.

SEVENTEEN

The time credit system: the panacea for a life course approach?

Laura Merla and Fred Deven

Introduction

For more than 30 years, one European country has had a radical policy that goes beyond Parental Leave, not replacing Parental Leave but supplementing it with a leave system that spans the adult life course and has acknowledged a variety of reasons for taking a full or partial job-protected break from employment. That country is Belgium, and this chapter examines the innovative type of leave system that developed in Belgium from the mid-1980s onwards, and discusses in particular its developments since the year 2000. The 'career break' system (later relabelled as the 'time credit' system in the private sector) gradually extended and developed into an opportunity for employees to develop a kind of time management across their working lifetime.

We begin by looking into the introduction of this system in Belgium. We describe the political rhetoric and narratives legitimising the aims and objectives of the initial measure and its subsequent adaptations. We also give an indication of the use made of this new leave, which despite various constitutional reforms in Belgium devolving many powers to regional authorities remained the responsibility of the federal (national) government. We then consider various types of inequality that have emerged in the time credit system, with a specific focus on gender, age, region of residence, migrants and labour market positioning. We conclude with a reflection on current (and growing) inequalities in access to the time credit system due to changes in employment, in particular the growth of precarious forms of work, and the challenge of creating a more inclusive system, not only in terms of gender, but also class, employment status and ethnicity.

1985–1998: origins and philosophy of the Belgian time credit system

The dawning of the career break system in Belgium occurred in the dire socio-economic climate of the early 1980s, when Belgium witnessed almost unprecedented levels of unemployment and budget deficits, with soaring public debt. Following years of negotiation, a major constitutional reform was decided in 1980. The previous constitutional reform that took place in 1970 had created three cultural communities (Dutch-, French-, and German-language) in charge of cultural matters, and recognised the need to create three regions (Flanders, Wallonia, Brussels) mainly in charge of economic matters. The 1980 reform transferred a number of major policy areas from the federal government to those entities, adding health and social support at the Community level, and transferring economy-related policies such as trade and housing to the newly formed Flemish and Wallonia Regions. Flanders included all new responsibilities into a single entity (the Flemish government), whereas Wallonia developed a regional government alongside a government for the French-speaking Community of Belgium. (The Brussels Region was created during the 1988–1989 Constitutional reform.)

In February 1982, the federal government announced a devaluation of the Belgian Franc by 8.5 per cent, intended to boost a weak economy heavily reliant on exports. At that time, the federal government introduced various measures to make the labour market less rigid and to stimulate time management in the work organisation. In this context, Michel Hansenne, Minister of Labour, developed a number of creative measures, among which was the idea of a time credit system, then called 'career break' ('*loopbaanonderbreking*' in Flemish, '*interruption de carrière*' in French). First introduced on an experimental basis, and for two years, the initial take-up of career breaks proved to be successful enough for Miet Smet, the new Minister responsible for Employment, Labour and Equal Opportunities, to formally launch this measure on a permanent basis in 1985.

It appeared as a part of the Royal Decree (KB/AR – 22.01.1985), which implemented a federal-level Economic Recovery Law. The stated aims of the policy makers were twofold. First, to allow employees to spend more time on care, leisure or training during their life course without losing basic rights of social protection, that is, individual well-being. Second, to tackle an economic recession and rising unemployment rates, most clearly shown in the requirement that each employee taking a career break should be replaced by an unemployed person, that is, unemployment reduction. This measure was, therefore, not primarily developed with a rationale of equal opportunities or even work–life balance.

Initially, the career break system offered a break from employment for any reason for a minimum of three months and a maximum of one year, with the possibility of extending it for up to five years. There was a flat-rate payment of approximately €310 per month, but with additional payments in some cases (for example, a higher payment was made if leave was taken within six years of the birth or adoption of a second (plus €30) or a third child (plus €55)). In 1994, the Flemish Community government introduced a supplementary payment to members of its population (approximately an extra €110).

Career breaks were an individual entitlement for all employees, except for those at managerial level or working in companies with less than ten employees. The only condition attached was that the employer must be prepared to accept a previously unemployed worker as a replacement. Finally, the employer could also defer the employee taking a career break, and employers within the private sector could temporarily refuse to grant a career break if more than 3 per cent of employees were already using this entitlement at a given time. Overall, collective agreements could supplement the general legislation, enabling enhanced conditions to be negotiated for particular groups.

Once established, various periods in the evolution of the career break system can be distinguished (Deven and Nuelant, 1999). First, from 1986 to 1991 a number of modifications were introduced, which gradually improved the system from the perspective of employees. Second, in the early 1990s, there was first some retrenchment, in late 1992, mainly involving a cut in payments to some employees. This was followed in 1993 by some progress as the social partners negotiated a collective agreement in the National Labour Council (CAO/x No.56 – 13 July 1993). Third, the system received a further impetus by being broadened to permit career breaks to be taken on a half-time, third-time or quarter-time basis. Finally, in 1997, the Collective Convention 56 established the career break as a *right* for employees in the private sector, regardless of the existence or not of a specific collective convention at the company or sector level.

It should be noted that during the mid-1990s, in addition to the career break system, three additional types of leave were introduced in Belgium. First, to implement the EU's 1996 Directive on Parental Leave, Belgium introduced three months of leave per parent. In addition, provision was made for three months of palliative care leave as well as three months' leave to provide for medical assistance for relatives. Although these types of leave have not been widely taken up, they added overall to the idea that employment could be legitimately interrupted for the sake of care-giving.

These policy developments were closely linked to a specific feature of Belgium, which tends to be considered as a Belgian 'tradition', that is, early retirement from the labour market. As explained by Merla (2004), Belgium has had one of the lower employment rates in the EU among people over 50 years of age. This was in large part due to extremely low employment rates among women in this age category (below 20 per cent) and a general tendency of both male and female employees to retire early in order to make room for the young. The effective retirement age was already below 60 years during the 1960s, and early withdrawal from employment continued to increase during the 1990s, in spite of policy efforts to reverse this trend.

The career break system, which gave extra benefits to employees over 50 years old, represented one of three main ways by which this older age group could leave the labour market prematurely. In addition, there were conventional pensions available for empoyees taking early retirement and a special status for older unemployed people who received increased benefits and were exempted from the obligation to remain available on the labour market. Taken together, these three pathways out of the labour market, which were created during the 1970s and 1980s, contributed to ease the country's transition to a post-industrial society. They also had the convenient effect of (artificially) reducing Belgian unemployment rates, which was a key target in the context of the post-war 'full employment' policy.

A policy shift, however, occurred during the 1990s at EU and national levels, driven by growing concerns about population ageing and low female participation in the labour market. As the full employment policy of previous years, focused on keeping unemployment low, progressively gave way to the promotion of increased economic activity rates as a key target for labour market policies, it became clear that early withdrawal was no longer sustainable and should be curtailed. The various reforms of the career break system that took place during the first decade of the twenty-first century can be understood as part of this new plan to increase the activity rates of older (50+) employees, and women of all ages. Part-time career breaks in particular were seen as an important way to retain women in employment, while easing their working conditions and allowing them to meet their family obligations. Indeed, women accounted for the bulk of career break users by the end of the 1990s, while men continued to resort mainly to more conventional and better paid early retirement schemes.

1999–2011: the birth and rise of the 'time credit' system

An important policy shift occurred in Belgium at the turn of the millennium. In 1999, an unprecedented coalition government took command of the Federal government, pushing Christian Democrats into the opposition for the first time since the 1950s. This 'rainbow' coalition of Socialists, Liberals and Ecologists led by Prime Minister Guy Verhofstadt and surrounded by a young team of ministers (the majority being in their forties), with sometimes little or no government experience, broke with the austerity measures of previous governments. Laurette Onkelinx, the new federal Minister for Employment from the Socialist party launched a major review into the re-organisation and reduction of working time, which aimed at modernising and redistributing employment among larger numbers of people. Her main project was to implement a general reduction of working time – from 39 to 38 hours in a first phase, and down to 35 hours in a second phase.

In 2000, however, the General Federation of Belgian Labour (ABVV/FGTB), the Socialist national trade union federation, proposed to transform the career break system into a one-year 'time credit system' as part of a campaign called 'no democracy without balance', which aimed at combating gender inequalities at home and in the labour market (in particular, the pay gap) by encouraging men to take well-paid leave. This new form of leave was meant to offer workers the freedom to schedule periods of leave over their career to care for their children. The 'rainbow' federal government immediately supported this proposal. The Liberals saw the Swedish example as proof that well-paid leave was compatible with a flourishing economy. The Socialists emphasised the need for well-paid leave to encourage men to take time out and to support lone mothers, and insisted that such leave should not be restricted to care responsibilities but should also grant workers time to live, to rest, and to engage in leisure and citizenship activities. Finally, the Ecologists highlighted that such leave should be a right, that social rights should be maintained during leave and that benefits should offer a sufficient level of income to support life choices. The project was even supported by the Christian Democrats, in opposition at that time, who considered that the total period of leave to be available over a working lifetime should be raised to four years and with benefits at about 30,000 Belgian francs a month (approximately €750, the equivalent of unemployment benefits), and depending on the family situation of the employee (Vanoverbeke, 2000).

Laurette Onkelinx thus included this measure in her new 'Chosen time' plan, together with a series of other measures aiming at individually and collectively reducing working time, and making it more flexible and more compatible with an individualisation of the life course. In December 2000, work–life balance became one of the key themes of the inter-professional convention negotiated and adopted by the social partners for 2001–2002, covering two million employees from all sectors of activity in the private sector. They agreed on a new 'time credit' system to be implemented in January 2002, granting employees a right to take up to one year of full-time leave over their career for any reason, with a benefit of maximum 20,000 Belgian francs a month (approximately €500) – but which could be extended for up to five years by employers who wished to do so.

Those who had been employed for at least one year by the same employer in the private sector could choose a full- or a half-time leave (or a one-fifth leave for those with five years' seniority). The employer's agreement to leave-taking was only necessary for small companies with less than ten employees, whereas employers of larger companies were only allowed to postpone the leave if more than 5 per cent of their staff were simultaneously on leave. In addition, in an effort to reduce the use of pre-pension schemes and retain older employees in employment, extended rights were offered to employees aged 50 and over who had been working for more than 20 years. Time credit thus acted both as a work–life balance policy and an employment policy for (male) employees over 50; but at the same time, the previous link between career break and unemployment policy was broken by the withdrawal of the replacement rule, which had required career break users to be replaced by unemployed people (Vandeweyer and Glorieux, 2009).

The initial ambition to offer generous benefits, the only feature that really distinguished the new time credit from the former career break from the point of view of leave users, however, was abandoned for budgetary reasons, and the maximum payment for full-time leave (for all users who had worked at least five years for the same employer) was fixed at €516 per month. Only the one-fifth leave option actually compensated most of the income loss incurred by taking leave; indeed, a study based on the fiscal year 2004 estimated that the average income loss if taking a one-fifth time credit leave was relatively low (around 5.4 per cent) (ONEM, 2007). Otherwise income loss was relatively lower when, all other things being equal, the time credit user had: a) a low initial income; and/or b) a partner with a high level of income; and/or c) several dependent children, since income loss was partly compensated by tax advantages and family allowances that increased with the number of children. Lone time credit users (with no partner, and with or without dependent children) suffered the highest loss of income. For employers, the repeal of the requirement to substitute the leave taker by an unemployed worker was a major change compared to the career break scheme. From the perspective of the employees, more flexibility became a major asset.

This new scheme was an immediate success. By April 2002, 15,600 employees had made use of the time credit system, 6,000 of whom were men. But the age profiles of male and female users were strikingly different, and this difference still persists at the time of writing: whereas women taking leave were mainly in their mid-twenties to early forties and were most probably making use of the system for parenting reasons, two-thirds of the male users were aged 50 and over. Rather than improving gender equality in parenting, the time credit system actually continued to be a way for women to balance work and caring by temporarily staying at home or reducing their working time; and for an older age group of men to gradually prepare for retirement by remaining in employment while reducing their working time. The fact that extended rights for those aged over 50 to use the one-fifth leave option were limited to those who had 20 years of continuous employment excluded many older women, with a career interrupted by child-rearing, from this new opportunity.

In June 2002, the time credit system was extended to the 100,000 staff members of public companies in charge of the postal services, the railway system or the telecom business. The 'old' career break system continued as a label only for other services in the public sector. Between 2002 and 2012, the average number of users per year rose regularly, increasing from 23,165 by the end of 2002 to 136,391 in 2012. In 2009, users represented 2.5 per cent of the workforce, 3.4 per cent of women and 1.8 per cent of men (Merla and Deven, 2011).

Two reforms implemented in 2007 and 2010 reduced the length and scope of leave for employees under 50 years. In April 2007, the federal government's 'Solidarity between Generations' plan, which aimed at consolidating the financial viability of the social security system, affected the possibility to take more than one year of paid time credit through company agreements, by restricting paid leave beyond this one year period to training or care purposes (care for a child younger than eight years, for a seriously ill family member or for a disabled child). Time credit for 'personal purposes', also termed 'non-motivated' leave, (for example, to travel, renovate a house or simply take some rest), could still be taken, but with no pay. From March 2010, the number of years of previous work with the same employer to be eligible for time credit was raised from one to two years. Neither restriction, however, affected the growing use of this measure.

2012–2015: a system under pressure

This overall, quite flexible, system continued until a turning point was reached in 2012, in an effort by the federal government, under the leadership of Social Democrat Elio di Rupo, to cut down on ever rising public expenditure, with a plan to reduce public expenditure by €30 billion between 2012 and 2014. The new government, which finally took office in Autumn 2011 after more than 500 days of negotiations, scrapped the possibility of taking unpaid 'non-motivated' leave for more than one year (or an equivalent period if leave was taken using a part-time formula). This time, restrictions also applied to older employees; the age condition for the right to work reduced hours was increased from 50 to 55 years, after a minimum of 25 instead of 20 years of work, though some exceptions remained (for example, employees involved in physically demanding work or enrolled in companies undergoing a major restructuring). A third major change affected pensions; until now periods of time credit had been dealt with as equivalent to work for building up pension rights, but from 2012 onwards, periods of 'non-motivated' time credit were no longer counted. These measures halted the process of previous decades of gradually extending rights and possibilities, for example, by enhancing flexibility, doing so mainly by cutting back on some time credit options that employers had objected to because of their length, flexibility or the early age at which they could be used.

Additional measures, envisaged by the previous federal government of Prime Minister Di Rupo, have been implemented by the federal government in 2017, an unprecedented coalition of the two Liberal parties, the Flemish Christian Democrat party (CD&V) and the larger conservative Flemish nationalist party (NV-A). From 1 January 2015, it became impossible to take a one-year *paid* time credit for reasons other than training or care (for children, disabled children, severely ill relatives or palliative care for relatives). But *unpaid* leave for other reasons remained possible. In addition, the total duration of additional paid time credit as negotiated in sectoral or workplace collective agreements is now limited to 36 months (48 months if leave is taken to care for disabled or seriously ill children). Finally, the minimum age to become eligible for the 'end of career' time credit scheme will be progressively raised to 60 years (instead of 55).

The impact of the 2012 and 2015 reforms on the take-up of time credit leave is undeniable. Even though between 2007 and 2016, time credit payments increased by 16 per cent, the recently introduced restrictions have caused a decrease in the number of payments made in 2016, which fell back below the 2010 level. In addition, the removal of the right to payments for a 'non-motivated' time credit in particular caused a sharp increase in the number of people on unpaid leave (up six-fold between 2007 and 2016, and by a third just for 2015–2016).

In 2014, the majority of time credit users were female (62 per cent). The three main reasons for taking leave were end of career (58 per cent of users), 'no motivation' (24 per cent), and taking care of a child under eight years (16 per cent). The one-fifth leave option was the most popular (71 per cent), followed by half-time leave (25 per cent) (ONEM, 2014).

In sum, the career break system started mainly as a tool to increase the employment rate in response to the economic crisis of the early 1980s. But by the turn of the twenty-first century, the official aim had shifted, with a greater emphasis on increasing the well-being of employees by providing them with a possibility to ease the stress of combining work, care and social involvement over their life course, including towards the end of their working careers. This shift was symbolised by a semantic change, replacing 'career break' by 'time credit'. But the freedom offered by this system has been progressively reduced to a freedom to choose the timing and type of working time reduction, in a system that now only fully recognises the need to take time off from work for care, training and progressively retiring from the labour market as pension age nears.

Inequalities within the system

To develop a full picture of the Belgian career break/time credit system and its effects would require an analysis of all collective agreements covering various sectors and workplaces, in private as well as public enterprises, since the statutory entitlement is frequently supplemented by such agreements – a widespread social practice in Belgium. But although it is extremely difficult to evaluate the impact of the system, due to inadequate (mostly administrative) statistics and limited scientific research in this area, the available information points towards inequalities in how the system works, including by gender, age, region of residence, country of origin and labour market position.

It remains difficult to judge the gendered impact of the system. Until recently, it was clear that women predominantly used this policy tool to ease the burden of combining work and family life, in other words to give them more time for caring. Whereas a majority of men have used it to ease their transition from full-time employment to retirement, together with a limited number of younger somewhat atypical men using it to support their adoption of less traditional gender roles (for example, Vandeweyer, 2010). But by making leave an increasingly acceptable option for men, the time credit system most probably had a wider impact on male employees by encouraging them to take up at least the legal provision of Paternity Leave (two weeks) and, to a lesser extent, some part of Parental Leave.

Research in Flanders in 2004 on women and men aged 20–49 years compared a sample taking any kind of full-time or part-time career break (that is, both Parental Leave and/or time credit and/or career break) (Vandeweyer and Glorieux, 2009; Vandeweyer, 2010) with a sample of employees who took no leave. This study provided new insights into value structures, perceptions of time pressure and the importance allocated to leisure time and social contacts. Overall, it revealed that the most popular reason among men in this younger age group for taking full-time career break leave was to try out another job, whereas part-time male leave takers presented 'a strong image as caring fathers', taking leave to better balance work and family and increasing their share of household tasks and childcare while on leave (Vandeweyer and Glorieux, 2009, p.36). In contrast, the majority of women who took full-time or part-time leave reported that they did so primarily to spend 'more time with the children'. But the lack of longitudinal data limits the possibility to draw firm conclusions about what distinguishes over time those who took leave and those who did not.

Gender and age inequalities in leave use are closely linked. As shown previously, women who do not manage to accrue 20 years of continuous employment have been largely excluded from the possibility of using the extended leave opportunities for employees over 50 years of age. This has resulted in a division in the time credit system along gender and age lines, with women accounting for most leave users under 40 years of age, while being under-represented among those over 50.

There are also regional inequalities. Since its creation, the time credit system has predominantly been used by Flemish employees. In the north of the country, the Flemish Community government (making since 1994 a supplementary payment to its citizens of approximately €110 a month, at that time for two years) has certainly contributed to this (for example, Devisscher et al 2002; Devisscher and van Pelt,

2005). What is more important, Flanders counts a higher number of potentially eligible users than Brussels and Wallonia. In 2012, the Flemish region had 2,359,000 salaried employees, which is more than the Brussels and Wallonia regions combined (349,000 and 1,167,000 respectively).

A study of Parental Leave in Belgium provides some additional insight about regional variations (ONEM, 2014). Here again, the majority of Parental Leave users are in Flanders, which accounted for 70 per cent of all Belgian users in 2012. Both women and men are proportionately more likely to use Parental Leave in Flanders; in 2012, one employed woman out of 20 was on Parental Leave in Flanders, compared with one in 21 in Brussels and one in 25 in Wallonia. Flanders is also the region with the highest proportion of men taking Parental Leave, though there is still a large difference between male and female users with almost three times more women on leave then men. Moreover, public authorities in Flanders have developed a more comprehensive toolkit, included ECEC services, to ease the work–life balance of employed parents, certainly due in part to stronger public finances.

Finally, a recent study by Kil, Wood and Neels (2017) uses large-scale administrative data (N=10,976) to examine 'parental leave' uptake for all mothers legally residing in Belgium who had their first child between 2004 and 2010; 'parental leave' is used in this study to cover time credit, career break and statutory Parental Leave. To begin with they show that only 68 per cent of these mothers were eligible for leave. Among eligible Belgium-born mothers, 49 per cent used some form of 'parental leave', compared with 41 per cent among first-generation women originating from neighbouring countries, 43 per cent from other European countries, and 32 per cent among first-generation women originating from non-European countries other than Morocco and Turkey; first-generation women from Turkey show the lowest uptake rate, just 24 per cent.

These differences are mainly explained by labour force attachment and income before the transition to parenthood. In addition, mothers with a higher income are less likely to opt for full-time rather than part-time leave. The authors conclude that difficulty in accessing stable employment and eligibility conditions are major barriers to the use of the various 'parental leave' options, with leave uptake between migrant and native mothers being 'largely explained by the interaction between the more precarious employment trajectories and eligibility criteria governing access to parental leave schemes, suggesting that parental leave perpetuates labour market disadvantages by reserving work–family reconciliation mostly to those already firmly established in the labour force' (Kil et al, 2017). They call for a reconsideration of 'the design features of parental leave entitlements in relation to labour market disadvantages', an issue we also highlight in our conclusion.

Conclusion

The idea of granting all employees a right to take time 'off' work, in the form of a 'credit' that can be used over the course of working life, for any purpose of their choice, either in one block or during several shorter periods, was, and still largely is, quite revolutionary. The philosophy underpinning this kind of measure strongly supports a shift towards a 'multi-active society' (a concept explored in Chapter Eighteen), in which it is recognised that people have an equal right to participate in the various spheres of social life, such as paid work, family, leisure, political and civic activities. However, as we have tried to show in this chapter, the Belgian time credit system was from the very beginning conceived with other politico-economic purposes in mind, even if the rhetoric of 'freedom of choice', combined with increased gender equality, was clearly present in the debates surrounding the design of the system at the turn of the Millennium. Today, though, the successive austerity measures that have characterised the last decade have left Belgium with a time credit system that is a pale copy of the original proposal. It has never reached its full potential, due to budget restrictions, the reticence of employers to cope with this kind of flexibility among their employees, and the overall changes in the socio-economic climate. And future prospects are not very encouraging.

The waged society is under heavy stress (Castel, 2011). Waged work itself remains the predominant form of organisation of our societies; but the classical employment form of the full-time, permanent contract protected by labour law and offering social protection benefits, which characterised men's employment in the industrial era, is rapidly losing ground. According to Robert Castel, structural high unemployment rates and the rise of precarious forms of employment (such as short-term and zero hours contracts, temporary work, internships, part-time work), which do not offer adequate levels of social rights and protections, are leading to a recommodification of waged labour (that is, an increase in the market dependency of individuals).

Precarious forms of employment have always existed: the labour markets we inherited from the post-war boom are dual, divided between a 'core' made up of stable, full-time, permanent employment, mainly occupied by male breadwinners; and a periphery composed of precarious jobs mainly occupied by young people, migrants, the low-qualified and women. But what is new today is that, for many employees, precarious jobs are no longer a phase of transition to a stable contract: they are a permanent condition. According to trade unions, temporary work today accounts for 10 per cent of all waged employees in Belgium, and a third of young workers; while part-time work constitutes a third of all waged work, is mostly undertaken by women, and is only freely chosen in 7 to 8 per cent of cases. Such precariousness undermines the core labour market: 25 per cent of employees with a permanent contract say they are not sure that they will still have their employment in six months' time (FGTB, 2017).

In this context, the number of employees who are eligible for the time credit system is likely to be negatively affected, as it will become increasingly difficult to achieve the minimum number of years of work with the same employer (two years at the time of writing). The double process of dualisation and re-commodification of the labour market will most probably lead to a reinforcement of the various inequalities that we identified previously, with cumulative effects. Those who have traditionally occupied a weak position in the labour market (women and/or the young and/or migrants and/or the low qualified) are discriminated by a leave system based on labour-market based entitlements. In addition, the current climate of 'subjective precariousness' (Linhart, 2011) may lead those who are entitled to take leave to hesitate about making use of their rights. Beyond the question of work–family balance, these negative trends call for a large reflection on the future of social protection systems in countries increasingly characterised by stratified forms of citizenship.

Postscript

Since this chapter was written, the federal government in Belgium has introduced a further scheme with life course elements: the 'career savings account'. This measure will allow workers to accumulate and save 'vacation time' and/or 'remuneration', and then draw on these 'savings' during a temporary interruption of career, or to facilitate the transition between two jobs, or to top-up pension benefits. The scheme was specified in a Law of 5 March 2017, and entered into force on 1 February 2018; but in order to be activated and implemented, this measure still needs 'translation' by the social partners into sectoral collective agreements. The new system may not therefore be available to workers until later in 2018 or 2019.

References

Castel, R. (2011) 'Au-delà du salariat ou en-deçà de l'emploi? L'institutionnalisation du précariat' [Beyond the wage earner or beneath employment? The institutionalization of the precariat], in S. Paugam (ed) *Repenser la solidarité*, Paris: PUF, pp 415–433.

Deven, F. and Nuelant, T. (1999) 'Parental leave and career breaks in Belgium', in P. Moss and F. Deven (eds) *Parental Leave: Progress or Pitfall? Research and Policy Issues in Europe*, The Hague/Brussels: Netherlands Interdisciplinary Demographic Institute/Centrum voor Bevolkings – en Gezinsstudies, pp 141–154.

Devisscher, S. and van Pelt, A. (2005) *Impactanalyse van het systeem van loopbaanonderbreking/tijdskrediet in België* [*Impact analysis of the career break/time credit system in Belgium*], Brussel: IDEA Consult.

Devisscher, S., Peeters, A. and van der Beken, W. (2002) *Evaluatie Vlaamse premie loopbaanonderbreking en arbeidsduurvermindering I + II.* [*Evaluation of the Flemish premium for career breaks and working hours reduction I + II*], Brussels: IDEA Consult.

FGTB (Fédération Générale des Travailleurs de Belgique) (2017) 'La précarisation subjective des non précaires', *Syndicats* 12: 5.

Kil, T., Wood, J. and Neels, K. (2017) 'Parental leave uptake among migrant and native mothers: can precarious employment trajectories make a difference?', *Ethnicities*, DOI: https://doi.org/10.1177/1468796817715292

Linhart, D. (2011) 'Une précarisation subjective du travail?' [The subjective precariousness of the non-precarious], *Annales des Mines: Réalités industrielles*, 1 (February): 27–34.

Malderie, M. (1997) 'Oorsprong en ontwikkeling van de loopbaanonderbreking' [Origin and development of the career break], *Arbeidsblad*, 25: 7–15.

Merla, L. (2004) 'Belgium: From early to progressive retirement', in T. Maltby, B. De Vroom, M. Mirabile and E. Øverbye (eds) *Ageing and the Transition to Retirement: A Comparative Analysis of European Welfare States*, Aldershot: Ashgate, pp 154–164.

Merla, L. and Deven, F. (2011) 'Belgium country note', in P. Moss (ed) *International Review of Leave Policies and Research 2011*. Available at www.leavenetwork.org/fileadmin/Leavenetwork/Annual_reviews/2011_annual_review.pdf

ONEM (Office National de l'Emploi) (2007) *Quelle est l'influence d'une réduction des prestations d'1/5, via le credit-temps et l'interruption de carrière, sur le revenu du ménage?* [*What is the impact on household income of a 1/5 reduction in benefits, through time credit and career breaks?*]. Available at www.onem.be/sites/default/files/assets/publications/Etudes/2007/ReductionPrestations/ContentFR.pdf

ONEM (Office National de l'Emploi) (2014) *Congé parental: évolution de la part homme/femme 2002–2012* [*Parental leave: evolution of the male / female part 2002–2012*]. Available at www.onem.be/sites/default/files/assets/publications/Etudes/2014/Conge_Parental/FR.pdf

Vandeweyer, J. (2010) *Werkt loopbaanonderbreking? Arbeidsoriëntaties, tijdsbesteding en drukte bij loopbaanonderbrekers in Vlaanderen* [*Does career break work? Work orientation, time spent and activity of career breakers in Flanders*], Brussels: VUB Press.

Vandeweyer, J. and Glorieux, I. (2009) 'Belgium: Career breaks in Flanders', in P. Moss (ed) *International Review of Leave Policies and Related Research 2009 (BIS Employment Relations Research series*, 102*)*, London: Department for Business, Innovation and Skills, pp 32–49. Available at www.leavenetwork.org/fileadmin/Leavenetwork/Annual_reviews/2009_annual_report.pdf

Vanoverbeke, D. (2000) 'Joëlle Milquet: "Arrêtons de jouer"' [Joëlle Milquet Let's stop playing], *Le Soir*, 4 May.

EIGHTEEN

Towards a multi-active society: daring to imagine a new work–life regime

Bernard Fusulier and Chantal Nicole-Drancourt

> The so-called normal work situation was tailored to men who had a wife in the background to care for everything else – children, meals, washing and cleaning, emotional equilibrium, everyday therapy, and so on.
>
> (Beck, 2000, p.58)

Introduction

Multi-activity is a fact of daily life. However, there is a huge gap between daily life and the institutional organisation of society. Difficulties in reconciling working life and family life and persistent inequalities between men and women are two challenges (partially different, partially interdependent) with which our contemporary societies continue to struggle. We have to note that despite institutional responses and efforts by public authorities to develop certain support services for working parents, no comprehensive, satisfactory and durable solution has so far been found, even in Europe which may well be the most advanced region for equal opportunity and work/life balance policies. Many researchers have long accepted this fact but continue to work towards understanding how best to both pose the problem and open new paths to achieve social progress.

This chapter contributes to this collective task and seeks to deepen reflection on the work/family regime. Our hypothesis challenges the foundation on which, in the nineteenth century, the industrial labour society forged its coherence, namely a decoupling of productive functions (the production of goods and services needed for existence) from reproductive functions (the biological reproduction of human beings and of the labour force). That decoupling undermines any attempt to find an equilibrium and any scenario offering a more just and egalitarian future. First of all, we will justify our hypothesis; and second, we will try to show why the provisions of certain social policies seem to us to foster an alternative 'reconciliation' scenario, with the creation of a 'multi-active society' as the central goal (Fusulier and Nicole-Drancourt, 2015).

Traditional foundations of the work/family regime

Regardless of their cultural and regional identities, all the industrial labour societies that developed in the nineteenth century and all the welfare states that developed in the twentieth century were built upon common founding principles (Nicole-Drancourt, 2011). What concerns us here are the principles that mobilised the labour force in activities producing goods and services in public and private spheres. By attributing a place and a gender to moral sentiments (Théry and Bonnemère, 2008), modern societies *reified* sexual distinctions in their implicit social contracts, which naturalised differences and hierarchies in social relationships in the name of competencies seen as 'natural' to each sex (for example, Tilly and Scott, 1978; Lewis, 1992; Letablier and Lurol, 2000; Morel, 2007). Without claiming to be exhaustive, we can identify four fundamental characteristics of the work/family regime in these societies.

A bipolarisation of activities in distinct spheres

Embedded in one another in primary economies (agricultural or communitarian), activities linked to market production and those linked to reproducing the labour force become separated from one another following capitalism's concentration of production. The modern notion of 'work' introduced by political economy and its dominant representation in the social sciences completes the fiction of the separation between the place of production and the place of reproduction, each existing as a distinct spatial category (Kanter, 1977): there is the occupational/professional sphere (associated with public economic space) and the family sphere (associated with private, non-economic space).

Different values attached to production and reproduction activities

The value of activities carried out in each sphere is not the same. The value of activities in professional space is recognised as economic and productive of capital gains and for that reason legitimises paying the worker. On the other hand, the value of activities in the family space is not recognised beyond their affective content and the producer slips from the status of 'worker' to that of 'parent' (Vielle, 2001).

Types of 'producers' and a semantics adapted to the differences

Productive and reproductive spheres are traditionally opposed to one another by employing a specific rhetoric (work/outside work) and by referring to two distinct types of producer in each sphere of activity: that of *worker* applies to a producer in the so-called productive sphere and that of *carer* (*one who cares for*) is applied to the producer in the so-called reproductive sphere. In contrast, a common obligation is imposed on each type of producer, whatever the sphere of production: both the 'worker' and the 'carer' must be fully available on a full-time basis for the activities to which he/she devotes him- or herself. This results in two ideals: the ideal worker thought of as alone, freed from all relational constraints, marital or familial (Beck, 2001); and the ideal parent thought of as alone, freed from all professional constraints (Letablier, 2000).

Gendered assignments and hierarchical representations in various areas of activity

The naturalisation of male and female served to justify a strongly gendered allocation of activities in major areas of activity in the name of the principle of *unity of interests*: women were supposed to excel in relations of service and care (Tronto, 1993), men were supposed to excel in self-assertion, technique, rationality and force (Verjus, 2010); women were primarily assigned to the family sphere and unpaid work, and men primarily assigned to the productive sphere and paid work. Based on this gendered division of production and reproduction activities, all industrial labour societies developed a gendered division of socially useful activities with a hierarchy of recognition for these activities (Daune-Richard, 2004). The 'traditional' work–family relationship thus resulted from the *naturalisation* of a historically situated social construction, which based the coordination of socially useful activities (incidentally *atemporal* and *necessary*) on a *social* and *gendered division* of production and reproduction.

But to say that this situation is 'historically situated' and a 'social construction' presumes a permeability to social change.

Fissured pillars

Despite their democratic limitations (notably as regards women's place in society), the fundamentals of the 'traditional' work/family regime were long suited to a growing economy and the standardisation of practices: the model of the 'male breadwinner/female carer' (Crompton, 1999) resulting from it *ipso facto* allowed the reconciliation of productive and reproductive activities through the gendered complementarity of the investments of men and women in households. But that model has been in trouble for several decades, upset by a world in rapid evolution. Feminisation of the labour market and criticism of inequalities between men and women; increasingly precarious employment and the flexibilisation in professional working hours; human geographical mobility; diversification in family models, systems of kinship and parenting; ageing of the population; the contraction of intra-family and community mutual support networks; individualisation and the search for personal fulfilment; changed perceptions of the value of children's well-being; and the reconfiguration of space-time borders via information and communication technologies – all these are dimensions that attack the standardisation of practices, question the legitimacy of the gendered division of work, and undermine the coherence of the traditional work/family model. In other words, in an unprecedented manner, a 'silent revolution' has called into question the labour conditions of the 'first modernity' in terms of its principles of organisation (Ewald, 1986; Rosanvallon, 1992).

For this reason, the work/family relationship is not just a problem many families cope with on a daily basis, but also a structural problem for society as a whole. In many countries, we now hear about a crisis of care (Falquet et al, 2010), as they witness an increase in the demand for care and the emergence of a relative scarcity in the offer of care. This scarcity in the offer of care is induced by increasing and persistent development in the professional activity of women which, *de facto*, narrows their permanent availability to administer care and to take responsibility for their close relatives. The crisis of care, emerging from opposing movements of supply and demand, expresses itself in many ways, for instance:

* anxieties about collapsing birth rates in a number of developed countries, the poverty of single mothers, the difficulty among mothers of getting or maintaining a full-time job, or the abandonment of children by mothers who emigrate far from home

to care for other people's children in richer countries (Hochschild, 2003; Merla and Baldassar, 2010);

- dissatisfactions on the part of economically active or inactive women on whom responsibility for care giving essentially falls (Pailhé and Solaz, 2010);
- criticisms about the quality of care that users of services receive, and the professional identities and working and employment conditions of care providers (Molinier, 2005).

Societies are mobilising to restore coherence: the French example

Neither supranational institutions nor governments have remained indifferent to the problem posed by the work/family relationship. Both in countries with a tradition of delivering family policies and in countries that have few of them, innovative legal and other provisions have been put in place to overcome the obstacles to the inclusion of mothers into the labour force and to encourage fathers to participate in the responsibilities of domestic and family life (United Nations, 2011). While in former communist states or in developing countries where the welfare state is under construction, many provisions have also been put in place (Heinen et al, 2009). For its part, the European Commission has taken important initiatives; for example, in the area of supranational regulation there is the emblematic Directive on Parental Leave, first adopted in 1996 and enhanced in 2010 (Fusulier, 2009a).

In many welfare state regimes, a certain ambivalence has always existed vis-a-vis work/family relationships. In France, which we take as an illustrative example, a 'State feminism' protecting the working mother has always been matched by a strong valorisation of the gendered roles of 'a very traditional family' and the subsequent gendered division of productive and reproductive work (Revillard, 2007; 2009). This ambivalence continued in the 1980s and 1990s with the development of new tools for reconciling professional and family life (for example, paid Parental Leave, childcare and domestic services). This was accompanied by ambitious employment policies over the following two decades fostering a type of employment referred to as 'female', which included part-time professional work (Bouffartigue and Pendaries, 1990).

In contrast, the 2000s inaugurated a period of change in this area, in France and throughout Europe. Indeed, the European Strategy for Employment, launched in 2001 (European Council, 2000), recommended reinforcing public and company policies for promoting professional equality between men and women, and the right to exercise the parental role and the right to a 'possible work/family reconciliation' became priority goals. In other words, Europe now encourages equal opportunity between men and women through an improved reconciliation of employment and family obligations.

In France, this change has resulted in some major institutional steps being taken: for example, the so-called Genisson Law, from 2001, in which the question of the relationship between professional and family activities has been presented as a major issue for public authorities and for collective bargaining. This was followed by the Grésy Report in 2011 which, targeting 'the effectiveness of rights', envisaged sanctions in the event of non-compliance with obligations, and led to the law for 'real equality between men and women' which, in 2014, affirmed the intention 'to move from equality on paper to concrete equality'. From this perspective, it reaffirmed the political will 'to extend reconciliation practices to men'. It targeted them in the communication strategy and 'neutralised' the language of legal provisions (for example, France no longer refers to *Maternity* Leave, but to *birth* leave, and no longer speaks of a *Parental Leave for women*, but of a *shared Parental Leave* with periods that are not transferable between fathers and mothers).

This legislative activity led to a series of reforms and private initiatives. In fact, since 2001 France has witnessed a re-engagement of the state through the development of what might be called 'legal provisions', including the development of collective services for very young children (both crèches and family daycarers), the introduction of a voucher system for home-based or out-of-school services, and the extension of family leave (Maternity, Paternity and Parental Leave, and leave for sick or dependent close relatives) (Haut Conseil de la Famille, 2009). We are also witnessing the negotiated implementation of 'extra-legal' provisions in businesses favouring male/female equality in three areas:[1] 'gender mixed work' (with a requirement for better representation of women in all sectors of activity and professions), 'non-discrimination and homogenisation in employment trajectories' (with the requirement of closing the wage gap between men and women), and 'professional life and family life reconciliation' (with the requirement of developing provisions to support parenting). These guidelines have led to the development of various measures, including the managing of working time (full-time employment, part-time employment, flexible hours and 'family time' options), improved

---

[1] See the special issue of Politiques sociales et familiales, no 92 2008 on the theme *Work–family Reconciliation*. On the business side, see also Pailhé and Solaz, 2010.

compensation for loss of earnings (due to Maternity, Paternity and Parental Leave), and opening childcare services to the private sector (with 'childhood–youth contracts' or 'family tax credits' for enterprises participating in financing workplace childcare facilities).

The economic and financial crisis of the late 2000s did not call into question this general orientation nor policies for employment and family equality. France remained firm in its commitments. The law approved in 2014 by the Constitutional Council for real equality between women and men testifies to this and seeks to define the conditions for a *concrete* and *real* equality and 'an unprecedented effort to ensure the effectiveness of acquired rights'.[2]

In France, as elsewhere, society faces a paradox

Does the mobilisation of industrial labour societies to meet the challenge of emancipating women (at work and in other public spaces) and men (in the parental role and in private spaces) more satisfactorily lead to the declared objective of real equality between men and women? The answer is neither positive nor negative: it is paradoxical.

On the one hand, it is undeniable that more and more families are using these reconciliation provisions (COFACE, 2015) and, generally, 'conditions for women' have improved in France. Based on employment survey results conducted by the INSEE (Institut national de la statistique et des études économiques) or CEREQ (Centre d'études et de recherches sur les qualifications), the Lemière Report (2013) demonstrates that employment today (salaried and non-salaried) is continuing to become femininised, that the differential between male and female unemployment rates has shrunk,[3] that women no longer have higher job loss rates than men, and even that, until recently, female employment was more resistant or was decreasing less than male employment. Moreover, it is common knowledge that birth rates have been sustained in France despite the financial crisis (Pison, 2013) and that the pattern of discontinuous employment among women is disappearing (Djider, 2013). In other words, French women perform strongly both in relation to employment and childbearing. Carrying on professional activity is now an unexceptional and legitimate destiny for

---

[2] http://femmes.gouv.fr/wp-content/uploads/2014/07/20140731-Synthese-Loi-sur-lEgalite-reelle-femmes-hommes.pdf

[3] A female unemployment rate that was almost twice as high as the male rate in 1975 achieved parity (at 10.5 per cent) by the end of 2013.

the majority of contemporary women, indicating that the condition of women is improving.

On the other hand, it is impossible to deny the persistence of inequalities between men and women, and even an increase in certain gender inequalities over the last two decades (Morin-Chartier, 2013). Thus, many studies (and often the same ones as previously mentioned) show that, if we compare the situations of men and women in France (or in most developed countries), we find that women still suffer widespread inequality, for example: a low level of economic activity among women over 50; an over-representation among families in poverty of female-headed lone parent families; the under-representation of women in continuing education; and women assuming a disproportionate responsibility for parental, domestic and family tasks (Milewski, 2010; Cochard et al, 2011; Roy, 2012). In studying the interpretations proposed by these authors to explain differences between men and women, we can see that the majority blame certain developments in 'generalist' social policies, such as budgetary cuts in social protection and social services in response to recurring economic crises, the endless delays in the reform of social care (which lead to increased demands made of family carers), and inadequate compensation for lost income due to job loss in working families (which demands increased domestic production to compensate for these families no longer being able to purchase external services).

So, can we simultaneously talk about an improvement in women's condition and an increase in gender inequalities? We think that it is in understanding this paradox that we can open new research domains that will enable advances to be made about the question of inequalities between men and women.

Women winning, mothers losing or the resolution of a paradox

In fact, the situation of *women* has improved in modern societies, but that of *mothers* has been, and today remains, quite worrisome. What research basically tells us is that provisions to assist work/family reconciliation legitimise the entry of women into the labour market – but in no way prevent the reproduction of unequal male/female social relationships as soon as a child appears. In other words, we can simultaneously talk about improvement in women's conditions and an increase in gender inequalities once we decouple the category 'woman' from the category 'mother'.

Time-use surveys make that perfectly clear. We find no strong male/female difference in apportioning family time and professional time when neither are responsible for children. However, for women, the balance between professional and family time is structured by the quantity of family responsibilities that they have: the heavier they are, the more professional time decreases, but this is a phenomenon which is not observed among fathers. Finally, studies on social services show that parenthood threatens families' finances and obliges mothers themselves to take on extra burdens that had previously been externalised. In other words, what gets in the way of women's inclusion in the labour force and their autonomy is indeed what is called the 'double journée' in France (a day of both paid and unpaid work), and that women who have the identity of 'mothers of' are the most significantly affected (though women caring for dependent adult relatives are also badly affected).

Thus, the category 'woman' is much too broad for understanding the mechanisms reproducing gender inequalities: instead, talking about fathers or mothers, sons or daughters, or even women who win and mothers who lose out appears to us to be more useful in resolving the apparent paradox that reveals improvement and regression when analysing women's condition. Once we agree to adopt a father/mother distinction rather than man/woman we can then interpret this paradox as follows: France has long maintained a paradoxical welfare state regime combining, on the one hand, a familial image with a very traditional social division of labour, and on the other hand, an arsenal of 'woman friendly' provisions that support societal aspirations to individual autonomy for all.

The scenario of a multi-active society

Interpreting the paradox this way also allows us to open up new research areas fostering better relationships between professional life and family life and, more generally, equality between men and women.

Saying that the development of provisions to help the reconciliation of work and family has indeed facilitated change, but has not broken the reproduction of obstacles to true equality, is not neutral. It allows us to conclude that to be transformative, legislative choices must deconstruct the foundations of industrial labour societies. From this perspective, we think that only really disruptive policies can counter the decoupling of productive and reproductive functions.

Given the collective will to make serious progress on these questions (particularly in Europe), we would like to end this chapter by proposing a scenario that we have decided to call 'a scenario for a multi-active society'. This scenario is our interpretation of the best fit for many ongoing reforms aimed at modernising the labour market, rebuilding social protection systems, and reorganising socio-economic integration of all citizens. 'Multi-activity' is not understood here in a descriptive sense (practices) but rather in a paradigmatic sense (a frame): a 'multi-active' society defines itself by choosing a lifelong parity of participation for everyone, by its recognition of a wide range of productive, socially useful activities (education, care, community work, employment...), and by opposing a 'mono-active society', which is defined by its choice of a gendered participation in socially useful activities and by its recognition that the domain of productive activities consists only of employment.

Andre Gorz (1980), Ulrich Beck (2000) and other voices concerned with articulating a critical and forward-looking analysis have already outlined some of this multi-active society's contours, and have highlighted the need to rethink the work/family regime and the 'active status' at the scenario's centre. In this scenario, the structuring principle of societal organisation would not be 'employment' but rather 'contribution', and would no longer be centred on the figure of the free and available 'adult male worker'. It becomes a question then of recognising that everyone may be a 'contributor' by exerting her/his labour power to the full extent of her/his aspirations and capacities in *all* spheres of social exchange activities (whether personal, political, civic, professional or parental, for example), and doing so without being faced by gender or age discrimination. This scenario also values the importance of free time and leisure.

In return for such contributions, society should commit itself to supporting autonomy and protecting people's capacities over a lifelong basis. This scenario involves emancipating ourselves from the restrictive category of 'employment' (and its 'unemployment' corollary), fostering instead a broader understanding and concept of activity. In its multiple economic forms (reciprocal, commercial and redistributive), 'contributing' socially useful activities thus becomes the principal means of social integration, even if employment represents a key activity for acquiring social rights and resources.

Our development of this scenario involves situating every socially useful activity in terms of rights, thus providing those exercising them fully-fledged, active citizenship, which connects social contribution to status and protection. Perceived as value adders (according to new indicators of wealth) and income providers (in direct money payments or in units of account granting rights and/or income supplements), activities that are now thought of as being 'outside work' will gradually take their rightful place in social and economic relationships. Once achieved, this process of reconfiguring regimes of activity and social protection will end up pushing back the existing boundaries. It will recognise all types of multi-activity in individual biographies, recast periods of 'unemployment', and safeguard what will no longer be called 'non-working' periods but 'professional transitions'. In other words, by gradually erasing the stigmatising borders between employment and what is outside employment, between active and inactive, between the unemployed and those 'unable' to work, this societal scenario finally envisages, for both men and women, the possibility of rebalancing the time spent on a multiplicity of social activities (professional, family or civic, for example) and reconceptualising ways of undertaking these activities.

This scenario does not mean that the architecture of the industrial labour society is rendered obsolete, as employment would remain one important means of socio-economic integration and, above all, one of the central goals in policies of social investment in human capital. That said, in socially and economically validating forms of activity other than employment, this scenario opens up paths to a truly transformative progression towards a new type of society with a sustainable system of work. This will involve progressively developing a recognition of the plurality of activities contributing to the production of wealth, and neutralising the tendency to place productive and reproductive activities in competition. Of course, appropriately designed and well-funded policies would be needed to avoid turning multi-activity into a trap for women (and mothers in particular). For example, with respect to Parental Leave, studies have shown that to attract men to undertake this activity, caring for young children, the measures offered have to be well paid, flexible, not transferable between spouses, and avoid penalising professional careers.

The formula that already exists in Belgium of a paid time credit scheme (see Chapter Seventeen) may serve as an initial model for supporting a multi-active policy; others may follow. The time credit scheme is not revolutionary; it is a form of career break system, an individual entitlement for workers to spend more time on care or training (and to improve their work–life balance), while maintaining their social rights and ensuring job protection, and available across their whole adult life course (Fusulier, 2009b). This life course approach is a fundamental principle for structuring a multi-active society. At a semantic level, the term 'time credit' shows societal recognition of the importance of allocating time to a range of useful activities; and as such is different to the term 'leave', associated with employment only, that has become embedded in the old paradigm. For example, we might not give Parental Leave any longer, but rather offer a 'parental care time credit' (a public recognition of parental work). Of course, 'time credit' is just a reference model, and is not a panacea; in the scenario of a multi-active society, 'time credit' cannot be a substitute for supportive services (for example, ECEC and eldercare), and must be related to equal opportunity and family-friendly policies (existing or to be developed).

An example can help to further clarify the concept of the multi-activity society and its attendant policies. The following fictitious example underlines how over the course of a typical life, employment, 'time credit' (we imagine various types of time credit, so it is utopian but realistic) and training can alternate and be simultaneously combined with existing employment-related schemes (for instance, flexible working hours, telecommuting, and time savings accounts).

Fictitious example of a life course in a multi-active society

Following his master's degree in economics, Paul, an only child, obtains a job in an insurance company. At 27, he enters into a relationship with Laetitia, a full-time nurse. Two years later, they have a child. Paul takes an (obligatory) 'paternity time credit' of 15 days, and Laetitia an (obligatory) 'maternity time credit' of three months, which she extends with 12 months of full-time 'parental care time credit' combined with twice-weekly two-hour training sessions in nursing care, to maintain and further develop her professional skills. When she resumes her hospital work full time, Paul takes 18 months of half-time 'parental care time credit' (without a job training obligation, because his half-time presence in his job ensures that his professional skills and knowledge are maintained). One year later they have a second child, and in the same way, they use the time credit scheme once again. Following restructuring, Paul loses his job, and is unemployed for several months, which he takes advantage of to undertake a three-month financial statistics training course, at the end of which he begins a new job in a bank. To support him in this job, his father, 58, employed in a metalworking company, requests a 24-month half-time 'relative care time credit' to care for his grandchildren.

Paul and Laetitia then work for five years at 80 per cent time, combined with a 'parental care time credit' to cover the remaining 20 per cent. They resume their full-time professional work and, in accordance with company policy, Paul may telecommute one day per week from his home. Two years later, Laetitia's mother dies in a car crash, and her father has a serious heart attack, leaving him disabled. She decides to take a 'relative care time credit', 20 per cent for six months, at the end of which she returns full time to her nursing job.

A few years later, Paul and Laetitia separate. Following this traumatic event, Laetitia needs to take stock of her life, and uses three months of 'time credit for personal needs'. Paul uses a 25 per cent time 'parental care time credit' for a year, in order to support more closely the schooling of one of his children, of whom he has alternating custody and who is in danger of dropping out of school.

Their children become independent. Paul and Laetitia, each of whom have found partners once again, continue working full time in their professions. In her fifties, Laetitia takes a half-time 'education time credit' for one year, to complete a diploma in hospital management that will enable her to move to a coordinator position, in which she will finish her full-time professional career.

Paul and his second spouse, a teacher, decide at 56 and 54 years of age to temporarily reduce the time spent in their professions and devote one day per week to a social organisation supporting the integration of recent immigrants, through a renewable one year 'civic time credit'. Promoted to a management position in his bank, Paul does not renew his time credit, throwing himself into his new job.

Five years later, he resumes a 'relative care time credit' for three months at half time, which he extends by one month at full time thanks to his workplace time savings account, to support his mother, a widow for several years, in the last months of her life. He finishes his professional career at 80 per cent time as a trainer of young recruits in his bank, taking one day per week of 'relative care time credit' to support his children in their parental duties and professional lives.

Conclusion

The challenge of work–family relationships is to find a way of analysing the limits of our current societal organisation. Establishing corrective measures in response to the *status quo* is not enough; we must re-imagine the work–family regime by creating a scenario that offers quite different normative reference points: the scenario of a multi-active society. This scenario has yet to be refined and is a utopian ideal for now. However, it is not pure fantasy, as some movements and policies in this direction already exist.

Yet several questions of formidable complexity, to which we must respond, remain unanswered and open to debate. For example: how to determine the monetary 'value' of work outside employment, without at the same time damaging the 'value' of such paid labour? What would be the source of financing for the various types of 'time credit'? How to ensure 'social drawing rights' (social investments through time credit formulas in the aforementioned case) without destabilising the organisation of employment? Would a multi-active society be financially sustainable for the state (or even beneficial for public finances)? Would it be effective and efficient enough to maintain itself in the context of interdependencies between societies and international economic competition? Further questions exist. Having shown that an interdisciplinary approach to this scenario is essential, it would also be useful to discuss this type of scenario in the light of knowledge gained from studies on the social economy (Laville et al, 1994) and universal allowances such as Universal Basic Income (Vanderborght and van Parijs, 2005) (see also Chapter Sixteen). Last but not least, it may also be important to think about the scenario's relationship to some new forms of economy (collaborative economy, gig economy and so on).

Whatever the case, today it is necessary and even urgent to create an outline for a different society, with a view to defining the measures to be taken to overcome current impasses and, as a society, to contribute to the common good and the development of human well-being.

References

Barrère-Maurisson, M.-A. (2003) *Travail, famille: le nouveau contrat* [*Work, family: the new contract*], Paris: Gallimard, Folio actuel – Le Monde.

Beck, U. (2000) *The Brave New World of Work*, Cambridge: Polity Press.

Beck, U. (2001) *La société du risque: Sur la voie d'une autre modernité* [*The risk society: On track for another modernity*], Paris: Flammarion.

Bouffartigue, P. and Pendaries, R. (1990) 'Activité féminine et précarisation de l'emploi' [Female activity and job insecurity], *Travail et Emploi*, 46: 30-44.

Cochard, M., Milewski, F. and Périvier, H. (2011) 'Les hommes et les femmes face à la crise' [Men and women face the crisis], *Alternatives Economiques*, Hors-série, 088 (February).

COFACE (2015) *Concilier vie familiale et vie professionnelle: une vision pour l'Europe* [*Reconciling family and professional life: A vision for Europe*], Brussels: Confédération des organisations familiales de l'Union européenne. Available at www.cofaceeu.org/en/upload/ERP/ERP_FR.pdf

Crompton, R. (1999) *Restructuring Gender Relations and Employment: The Decline of the Male Bread Winner*, Oxford: Oxford University Press.

Daune-Richard, A.M. (2004) 'Les femmes et la société salariale: France, Royaume-Uni, Suède' [Women and the wage society: France, United Kingdom, Sweden], *Travail et Emploi*, 100: 69–84.

Djider, Z. (2013) 'Huit femmes au foyer sur dix ont eu un emploi par le passé' [Eight out of ten housewives have had a job in the past], *Insee Première*, 1463 (August).

European Council (2000) *Lisbon European Council 23 And 24 March 2000, Presidency Conclusions*. Available at www.europarl.europa.eu/summits/lis1_en.htm

Ewald, F. (1986) *L'État-providence* [*The Welfare State*], Paris: Grasset.

Falquet, J., Hirata, H., Kergoat, D., Labari, B., Le Feuvre, N. and Sow, F. (eds) (2010) *Le sexe de la mondialisation* [*The gendered nature of globalisation*], Paris: Presse de Sciences Po.

Fusulier, B. (2009a) 'The European Directive: Making supra-national parent leave policy', in S. Kamerman and P. Moss (eds) *The Politics of Parental Leave Policies: Children, Parenting, Gender and the Labour Market*, Bristol: The Policy Press, pp 243–258.

Fusulier, B. (2009b) *'Articulating work and family? The gendered use of institutional measures'*, in P. Moss (ed) *International Review of Leave Policies and Related Research 2009 (BIS Employment Relations Research series, 102)*, pp 14–31. Available at www.leavenetwork.org/fileadmin/Leavenetwork/Annual_reviews/2009_annual_report.pdf

Fusulier, B. and Nicole-Drancourt, C. (2015) *'Pursuing gender equality in a "multi-active society"'*, Global Dialogue, 5(1): 30–31.

Gorz, A. (1980) *Adieu au prolétariat: Au-delà du socialisme* [*Farewell to the proletariat: Beyond socialism*], Paris: Galilée.

Grésy, B. (2011) *Égal accès des femmes et des hommes aux responsabilités professionnelles et familiales dans le monde du travail'* [*Equal access of women and men to work and family responsibilities in the world of work*]. Rapport IGAS (Inspection générale des affaires sociales), Paris: La Documentation Française.

Haut Conseil de la Famille (2009) *Présentation générale des dispositifs en faveur des familles* [*General presentation of schemes for families*], Rapport préparatoire conférence annuelle 2009, www.hcfea.fr/IMG/pdf/HCF_Presentation_generale_des_dispositifs_en_faveur_des_familles_v20_10_09.pdf

Heinen, J., Hirata, H. and Pfefferkorn, R. (eds) (2009) 'État/Travail/Famille "conciliation" ou conflit?' [State/Labor/Family 'conciliation' or conflict?], *Cahiers du Genre*, 46, Paris: L'Harmattan.

Hochschild, A.R. (2003) *The Commercialization of Intimate Life: Notes from Home and Work*, San Francisco, CA: University of California Press.

Kanter, R.M. (1977) *Work and Family in the United States: A Critical Review and Agenda for Research and Policy*, New York, NY: Russell Sage Foundation.

Laville, J.L., Bélanger, P.R., Boucher, J. and Lévesque, B. (1994) *L'économie solidaire: une perspective internationale* [*The solidarity economy: an international perspective*], Paris: Desclée de Brouwer.

Lemière, S. (2013) *L'accès à l'emploi des femmes: une question de politiques* [*Access to Women's Employment: A Policy Issue*]. *Rapport pour le Ministère des droits des femmes*, Paris: La Documentation Française.

Letablier, M-T. (2000) 'Famille et emploi: une comparaison européenne' [Family and work: a European comparison], in M. Chauvière, M. Sassier, and B.M. Bouquet (eds) *Les implicites de la politique familiale*, Paris: Editions Dunod, pp 204–219.

Letablier, M.-T. and Lurol, M. (2000) 'Les femmes entre travail et famille dans les pays de l'Union européenne', *La Lettre du Centre d'Études de l'Emploi*, 63: 1–10.

Lewis, J. (1992) 'Gender and development of Welfare Regimes', *Journal of European Policy*, 2(3): 159–173.

Merla, L. and Baldassar, L. (eds) (2010) 'Les dynamiques de soin transnationales. Entre émotions et considérations économiques' [The transnational dynamics of care. Between emotions and economics], *Recherches sociologiques et anthropologiques*, 41(1).

Milewski, F. (2010) 'Chômage et emploi des femmes dans la crise en France' [Female unemployment and employment during the crisis in France], *Lettre de l'OFCE 318*, Paris: Presses de la Fondation nationale des sciences politiques, pp 1-8.

Molinier, P. (2005) 'Le *care* à l'épreuve du travail. Vulnérabilités croisées et savoir-faire discrets' [Care at the test of work. Crossed vulnerabilities and discrete know-how], in S. Laugier and P. Paperman (eds) *Le souci des autres: Éthique et politique du care* [*The concern of others: Ethics and politics of care*], Paris: Editions de l'EHESS, pp 299–316.

Morel, N. (2007) 'Le genre des politiques sociales: L'apport des *gender studies* à l'analyse des politiques sociales' [The nature of social policies: The contribution of gender studies to the analysis of social policies], *Sociologie du travail*, 49(3): 383–397.

Morin-Chartier, E. (2013) *Rapport sur les répercussions de la crise économique sur l'égalité entre les hommes et les femmes et les droits des femmes* [*Report on the impact of the economic crisis on gender equality and women's rights*], Paris: Commission des droits de la femme et de l'égalité des genres.

Nicole-Drancourt, C. (2011) *Donner du sens aux réformes. De l'équation sociale fordiste à la nouvelle équation sociale: L'enjeu des réformes dans l'ordre du genre* [*Give meaning to reforms. From the Fordist social equation to the new social equation: The challenge of gender reforms*], HDR, Paris: École des Hautes Études en Sciences Sociales.

Pailhé, A. and Solaz, A. (2010) 'L'implication des entreprises dans l'aide à la parentalité en France: Une initiative bienvenue, mais source d'inégalités entre salariés' [The involvement of companies in helping parents in France: A welcome initiative, but a source of inequality between employees], *Revue Interventions économiques*, 41. Available at: https://journals.openedition.org/interventionseconomiques/412

Pison, G. (2013) 'France 2012: Fécondité stable, mortalité infantile en baisse' [Stable fertility, falling infant mortality], *Populations et Sociétés*, 498: 1–4.

Revillard, A. (2007) *La cause des femmes dans l'Etat: une comparaison France-Québec (1965–2007)* [*The cause of women in the state: a comparison between France and Québec (1965–2007)*], Doctoral thesis in sociology. Available at http://halshs.archives-ouvertes.fr/view_by_stamp.php?

Revillard, A. (2009) 'Quelle politique pour les mères en emploi' [What policy for working mothers?], in C. Nicole-Drancourt (ed) *Conciliation Travail–Famille: attention travaux*, Paris: L'Harmattan, pp 89–99.

Rosanvallon, P. (1992) *La crise de l'État-providence* [*The crisis of the Welfare State*], Paris: Seuil.

Roy, D. (2012) *Le travail domestique, 60 milliards d'heures en 2010* [*Domestic work, 60 billion hours in 2010*], INSEE Première 1423, Paris: Institut national de la statistique et des études économiques.

Théry, I. and Bonnemère, P. (eds) (2008) *Ce que le genre fait aux personnes*, Paris: Editions EHESS.

Tilly, A.L. and Scott, J.W. (1978, French edn, 2002) *Les femmes le travail et la famille*, [*Women, work and family*], Paris: Petite Bibliothèque, Payot.

Tronto, J. (1993, French edn, 2009) *Un monde vulnérable: pour une politique du care* [*A vulnerable world: for a care policy*], Paris: La Découverte.

United Nations (2011) *Men in Families and Family Policy in a Changing World*, New York: DESA.

Vanderborght, Y. and van Parijs, P. (2005) *L'allocation universelle* [*The univeral allowance*], Paris: La Découverte (Repères 412).

Verjus, A. (2010) *Le bon mari: Une histoire politique des hommes et des femmes à l'époque révolutionnaire* [*The good husband: A political history of men and women in the revolutionary era*], Paris: Fayard.

Vielle, P. (2001) *La sécurité sociale et le coût indirect des responsabilités familiales* [*Social security and the indirect cost of family responsibilities*], Brussels: Bruylant.

NINETEEN

Re-imagining Parental Leave: a conceptual 'thought experiment'

Andrea Doucet, Lindsey McKay and Sophie Mathieu

Introduction

Over the past decade, the study of Parental Leave has burgeoned into a 'minor academic industry' that straddles many substantive and interconnected theoretical fields such as work/labour/industry, care, family policies, gender divisions of labour, mothering and fathering, welfare state regimes and comparative social policies. As a policy instrument, a set of practices and a potential facilitator of gender equality, Parental Leave is a complex and multi-layered object of investigation (Moss and Deven, 2015). Key studies have addressed, for example, the gendering of Parental Leave policy design (Escobedo and Wall, 2015; Eydal et al, 2015; Michoń, 2015), the facilitators and inhibitors of fathers' take-up of Parental Leave and their experiences while on leave (McKay and Doucet, 2010; Tremblay and Lazzari Dodeler, 2015; Wall and O'Brien, 2017), the relationship between fathers' take-up of leave and gender equality (Almqvist and Duvander, 2014; Meil, 2013; Romero-Balsas, 2015), and, more recently, class differences embedded in social policy design (McKay et al, 2016; see also Chapter Thirteen in this volume).

Across this thriving field, Gøsta Esping-Andersen's (1990) seminal work, *The Three Worlds of Welfare Capitalism*, his concept of stratification, and his tri-fold characterisation of welfare state regimes (social democratic, conservative and liberal) have been highly influential for social policy and welfare state researchers. This work has been simultaneously 'loved and debated' (Rice, 2013, p.93). The burgeoning literature on Esping-Andersen's (1990; 1999) welfare state typology and concepts of stratification and commodification/decommodification has attempted to refine his framework to address how the typology plays out at a 'more granulated level' (Baird and O'Brien, 2015, p.199), a scalar level (Mahon, 2006), and a policy level, rather than at a regime level (Saxonberg, 2013). Some scholars have identified the need for more than three welfare regime types in light of particular national policies (Abrahamson, 1999; Bambra, 2006; Escobedo and Wall, 2015; Rice, 2013), how some countries were 'misclassified' in his seminal text (Castles and Mitchell, 1993, p.106), and how these 'typology-based analyses…have probably reached the point of diminishing returns' (Orloff, 2009, p.330), especially given the varied ways that neoliberalism intersects with national policies (Deeming, 2017).

Esping-Andersen's conceptual framework was also revised (1999; 2000) in response to strong feminist demands to focus more on concepts of familialisation and defamilialisation, which recognise how 'countries organize the provision of welfare through *families* as well as through states and markets' (Orloff, 1993, p.303, emphasis added; see also Lewis, 1992; O'Connor et al, 1999). Yet with few exceptions (for example, Michoń, 2008; 2015; Rice, 2013; Saxonberg, 2013; Mathieu, 2016; Kurowska, 2018), there has been little study of how these concepts – commodification/decommodification and familialisation/defamilialisation – and their shifting meanings in changing neoliberal contexts might be useful for thinking about Parental Leave as a policy tool that could advance or impede gender and class equalities.

This chapter attempts to fill this gap by exploring the utility of commodification/decommodification and familialisation/defamilialisation for re-imagining more progressive futures through the '[development of] new conceptual and practical strategies for combating gender injustices of economy and culture' (Fraser, 2013, p.12) and other intersectional injustices. We argue that to fully appreciate the potential of Esping-Andersen's concepts of commodification/decommodification, we need to look to one of his greatest influences, the Hungarian economic historian Karl Polanyi, whose work has generated increasing attention in the last decade (see, for example, Bugra and Agartan, 2007; Dale, 2010; Fraser, 2013; Block and Somers, 2017). Here, we read Polanyi's work, including his seminal book *The Great Transformation* (1944), with and through the analytic lenses of Fred Block and Margaret Somers (2014), who argue that 'Karl Polanyi provides us with the most incisive intellectual apparatus available to understand the actual workings and consequences of market economies' (Block and Somers, 2014, p.218) and to challenge relations between current enhanced conditions of neoliberal restructuring and 'market fundamentalism'.

In a similar way, to appreciate the potential of the concepts of familialisation/defamilialisation, we draw on the feminist literature that inspired Esping-Andersen to consider how families play a central role in issues of social reproduction and social welfare. We work especially with Nancy Fraser's (2013) analysis of Polanyi's potential contributions to debates about social reproduction. While she maintains that 'Polanyi's framework harbors a major blind spot' in relation to gender, she also analyses his work from within 'a broader understanding of social justice... [that] would serve at once to honor Polanyi's insights and remedy his blind spots' (Fraser, 2013, pp.15, 241).

We approached writing this chapter as a conceptual, pragmatic and imaginative 'thought experiment' (Fraser, 2013, p.114). It builds theoretically and epistemologically on Doucet's previous and on-going work (2015; 2016; 2018) on Margaret Somers' (2008, p.172) 'historical sociology of concept formation', which is partly the 'work of turning social science back on itself to examine often taken-for-granted conceptual tools of research' and a view of concepts as 'words in their sites' (Hacking, 2002, p.24). This work is also influenced by, and resonates with, a rich transdisciplinary epistemological tradition of Foucauldian approaches to genealogies that views concepts and the theories they inform as necessarily provisional, contingent and relational, such that on any given theoretical terrain, 'even a slight change in the relations of these neighboring concepts begins a process of producing new concepts' (Grosz, 2011, p.66).

The chapter is organised in three sections. In the first two, we work selectively with a case study of Canada, a country characterised by Esping-Andersen (1999) and others (Béland et al, 2014; Baird and O'Brien, 2015) as a 'liberal welfare state regime'. The final section deepens and widens our 'thought experiment' by mapping new pathways for future imaginaries in leave-to-care policy making. Here, we work with both Fraser's and Somers and Block's reading of Polanyi. We follow the argument of Block and Somers (2014, p.28) that 'Polanyian ideas challenge familiar assumptions about how the world works' while also offering 'a powerful critique of existing social and economic arrangements and a vision of a real alternative'.

Concepts

Stratification, commodification, and decommodification

For Esping-Andersen (1990, p.23), each national 'welfare state...is, in its own right, a system of stratification. It is an active force in the ordering of social relations.' As Orloff writes (1993, pp.310–311), welfare states and their 'systems of social provision have stratifying effects: Some policies may promote equality, cross-class solidarity, or minimise economic differences, while others may promote social dualism or maintain or strengthen class, status, or occupational differentiation'. Through his study of 16 capitalist countries in the global North and their varied social policies (such as unemployment benefits, sickness allowances and public pensions), Esping-Andersen established his well-known tri-fold typology (or stratification index) of different welfare states: social democratic, liberal and conservative. While many contest the universal applicability of Esping-Andersen's framework, it is widely agreed that 'the welfare regime typology is here to stay as an analytical tool because there is clearly "something in it"' (Rice, 2013, p.94).

Esping-Andersen's concept of stratification is closely connected to his other core concepts, including commodification and decommodification. He drew on the work of Polanyi to argue that industrialism and capitalism had transformed workers into commodities whose 'survival was contingent upon the sale of their labor power' (Esping-Andersen, 1990, p.21). Initially, he described decommodification as 'the degree to which they [state policies] permit people to make their living standards independent from pure market forces' (Esping-Andersen, 1990, p.3). Commodification and decommodification, he explained, are concepts that '[capture] one important dimension of freedom and constraint in the everyday life of advanced capitalism' (Esping-Andersen, 2000, p.353). It is the state, as a stratifying actor, that Esping-Andersen views as the 'de-commodifier'. Through its varied insurance schemes and welfare state programmes that '[let] individuals lead their lives without relying entirely on the market' (Esping-Andersen, 1999, pp.21–22), decommodification is a process whereby 'citizens can freely, and without potential loss of job, income, or general welfare, opt out of work when they themselves consider it necessary' (Esping-Andersen, 1999, p.23).

Although it is important to note that the concept of commodification is rooted in the work of Karl Marx, it is Polanyi's influence that led Esping-Andersen to insert 'commodification' and 'de-commodification' into debates on relations between welfare states, markets and societies during the rise of neoliberalism, industrialisation and globalised capitalism. Building on Marx, Polanyi 'wrote about the tragic consequences of the Industrial Revolution's commodification of humans into labor during the nineteenth century's epoch of market fundamentalism' (Somers, 2008, p.116). Turning labour and land into commodities were, for him, processes of 'fictitious commodification'; that is, since 'true commodities...are things actually produced for the sole purpose of the market, what we call "labour" is actually a fictitious commodity, which is forced to behave and treated as if it is a real one' (Somers and Curtis, 2016, p.5). This led to 'a radical tearing apart of society, as this new fictitious commodity of labour [had to] be ripped from the totality of human social relations and social organization' (Somers and Curtis, 2016, p.5).

In recent years, Esping-Andersen's work, while still widely used in social policy debates, has been critiqued for holding on to a 'thin' version of Polanyi's concepts (Pintelon, 2012, p.6). Indeed, Esping-Andersen himself has acknowledged that his early attention to the concept of commodification was 'admittedly narrow' and that he is 'in basic agreement with the effort to make the concept more dynamic and multidimensional' (2000, p.533). Several authors (such as Room, 2000; Papadopoulos, 2005; Vail, 2010; Fraser, 2013; Block and Somers, 2014) have been working with broader versions that, for example, highlight how any focus on decommodification also attends to the 'political, social, or cultural process that reduces the scope and influence of the market in everyday life' (Vail, 2010, p.310).

These processes of social protection led to what Polanyi called 'the double movement' between market fundamentalism (and commodification) and social protectionism (and decommodification). In the case of the latter, the welfare state seeks to mitigate the 'perils of labor commodification through social protection via housing subsidies, unemployment benefits, health insurance, and pensions' (Vail, 2010, p.312). In other words, decommodification was 'necessary for system survival' and was a 'precondition for ensuring a tolerable level of individual welfare and security' (Esping-Andersen, 1990, p.37).

Familialisation and defamilialisation

Feminist scholars (Lewis, 1992; O'Connor, 1993; Orloff, 1993) critiqued Esping-Andersen's framework for being both family-blind and gender-blind, raising three key issues about his welfare state typology. First, they argued that the concept of commodification/decommodification only addressed states and markets, not adequately accounting for the role of families, and, more specifically, women, as sources and distributors of social welfare. Second, they contended that the concept of decommodification implicitly assumes a family wage provided by male breadwinners. As Orloff (1993, p.318) wrote: 'the decommodification dimension must be supplemented with a new analytic dimension that taps into the extent to which states promote or discourage women's paid employment – the right to be commodified, if you will' (see also Lister, 1995; Lewis, 1997;

Mathieu, 2016). Third, while Esping-Andersen focused on pensions and unemployment insurance, he did not consider specific family and care policies (Saxonberg, 2013).

Several scholars (for example Lister, 1994; McLaughlin and Glendinning, 1994) developed the concept of defamilialisation to parallel decommodification and draw attention to how paid and unpaid responsibilities are articulated differently for men and women. Defamilialisation highlights the links between women's family care responsibilities and their participation in gainful employment. Lister (1995, p.37) defines it as the 'capacity for individual adults to uphold a socially acceptable standard of living independently of family relationships, either through paid work, or social security provisions'.

Many welfare state researchers, including Esping Andersen himself (1999), have embraced these complementary concepts. As Saxonberg (2013, p.28) writes:

> One advantage of the familialization/defamilialization terminology is that it allows for a parallel to Esping-Andersen's scale of degrees of commodification and decommodification, thus providing feminists with a clear alternative to Esping-Andersen's manner of measuring welfare regimes. This parallel to degrees of decommodification probably accounts for much of the popularity of the term 'defamilialization'.

From families to gender: other concepts

It was again Orloff (1993; 2009) who laid the groundwork for thinking beyond families, about gender, aiming to 'develop a conceptual framework for analyzing the gender content of social provision' (Orloff, 1993, p.307). This shift in thinking led to different questions, such as 'Can the welfare state alter gender relations?' (Orloff, 1993, p.307; see also Cho, 2014; Mathieu, 2016). It also illuminated the need for concepts more relevant to understanding gendered differences in the provision of social welfare. Saxonberg (2013, p.32), for example, argued that '[i]f the main goal then is to eliminate gender roles and if the need to "genderize" welfare states has stood in the centre of the feminist discourse on social policies, then it makes more sense to talk about genderizing and degenderizing policies rather than familializing and defamilializing policies'. Similarly, Mathieu (2016, p.6) has argued for a new concept, the 'demotherization of care work' that focuses on how mothers can transfer part of their caregiving not only to male partners but also to the state, grand-parents or paid caregivers.

Our view is that concepts like degenderisation and demotherisation are crucial for articulating the critical shift to gender. At the same time, our theoretical and epistemological framework demands recognition of the relationality and specificity of concepts in particular sites and contexts, leading us to agree with Kurowska (2016, p.17), who 'acknowledge(s) the broader scope of (de)genderization, which does not reduce gender issues to familial relations', while also arguing that 'both concepts actually complement each other well'. We make this argument in relation to familialisation/defamilialisation, genderisation/degenderisation and Parental Leave.

Canadian Parental Leave: a conceptual case study

These conceptual issues can be explored through Canada's Parental Leave benefit system (for more information see Doucet et al, 2016; Doucet and McKay, 2017). Outside the province of Québec, Canada allows 15 to 17 weeks Maternity Leave (depending on the province) and 35 weeks Parental Leave, both paid at 55 per cent of earnings (with a low maximum payment ceiling); as of 1 December 2017, an option of 61 weeks 'extended Parental Leave' at 33 per cent of earnings is available. When used consecutively, a mother or two parents can take a total of up to 18 months of leave benefits. In addition, some employers top up the government's benefit payments; Marshall (2010) found that about one in five mothers received a top-up for 16 to 19 weeks (similar data was not collected for fathers). Since 2006, the province of Québec has had its own leave programme – the Québec Parental Insurance Programme. It differs significantly from the rest of the country in that it has lower eligibility criteria, higher benefit payments (and higher maximum ceilings), greater flexibility (offering either a shorter leave at a higher income replacement rate or a longer leave at a lower rate) and offers Paternity Leave (an individual three- to five-week entitlement for fathers) (for a fuller discussion of Québec Parental Insurance Programme, see Chapter Thirteen).

Outside Québec, the federal care benefit programme, comprised of six types of leave benefits – Sickness, Maternity, Parental, Compassionate Care, Sick-Child and a new family caregiver benefit – is a sub-programme of the (un)Employment Insurance (EI) system managed by the Department of Employment and Social Development Canada. Its location within EI is a defining feature of the care benefit programme; leave provisions for an anticipated post-natal leave and other forms of care are tacked onto a far larger programme designed for unanticipated individual unemployment, which assumes the standard employment situation of a breadwinner with a full-time job. Eligibility criteria for care benefits consequently vary only slightly from those for regular unemployment benefits. As self-employed workers must register a year prior to making a claim, like other non-standard workers, they are less often eligible for benefits. The same is true for non-standard births; for example, in a court case involving a multiple birth, it was determined that benefits should replace wages, not support caregiving, upholding the policy that awards the same benefit level regardless of the number of children born at one time.

Our recent research (McKay et al, 2016) demonstrated that Parental Leave policy design has considerable implications with regard to socioeconomic class differences. In Québec, a far greater proportion of low-income families receive benefits; in 2013, 85.4 per cent of families with an annual income of less than Can$30,000 received benefits, compared with only 44 per cent of families at the same income level in the rest of Canada. Nevertheless, with their labour market policy frameworks, both leave programmes use employment status as the basis for eligibility. Parental Leave, therefore, is both legally and politically conceptualised as 'leave from work' rather than as 'leave to care'.

Commodification/decommodification and Parental Leave

Canada exhibits qualities of a liberal welfare state in that it emphasises individualism, the primacy of the market and a low level of decommodification, leading citizens to rely largely on markets to meet their needs. Canadian society is thus stratified with 'a blend of a relative equality of poverty among state-welfare recipients [and a] market-differentiated welfare among the majorities, and a class-political dualism between the two' (Esping-Andersen, 1990, p.27). As Orloff (1993, pp.310–311) puts it, 'Liberal regimes do not greatly modify market-generated stratification or social mobility – any reductions of social inequalities occur over the life-span rather than across classes'. In our view, this characterisation applies to both federal and Québec Parental Leave regimes as entitlement to benefits depends on specific conditions of labour market participation and on financial contributions to leave insurance schemes, which limits decommodification.

Parental Leave can, however, be seen as a form of decommodification because it responds to workers' needs to 'opt out of work when they themselves consider it necessary' (Esping-Andersen, 1999, p.23). Yet, due to the use of outdated concepts of labour market relations and family structures (namely, the full-time breadwinner/stay-at-home-caregiver model), which are increasingly eroded by neoliberalism and the rise in dual-earner, separated and sole parent households, Parental Leave policies do not include all families and have unequal gender impacts, especially in liberal welfare regimes.

As already indicated, there are marked socioeconomic differences in access to Parental Leave benefits between Québec and other Canadian provinces and territories. In 2013, only 64 per cent of all mothers in Canada's nine provinces received maternity and/or parental benefits under EI (McKay et al, 2016), compared with 89 per cent in Québec (McKay et al, 2016). Thus, a large proportion of Canadian parents are excluded from government-sponsored benefits and the right to decommodification in order to care for their infants, and these exclusions are both class-, and, by extension, racially-based (McKay et al, 2016). In the final section of this chapter, working with Polanyian insights, we argue that these differences speak to questions about who has access to fundamental socio-economic citizen rights and, more broadly, to citizenship rights and human rights.

Familialisation/defamilialisation and genderisation/degenderisation

There are also stark differences in familialisation/defamilialisation between Québec and the rest of Canada. In Québec, the state plays a defamilialising role in social reproduction through its encompassing family policy consisting of low-cost state-regulated childcare, a universal child assistance payment, and a more inclusive system of Parental Leave (Noël, 2013). In the rest of Canada, there is an emphasis on 'choice' in childcare and an implicit assumption that social reproduction is a family responsibility, and even more centrally, the responsibility of mothers. Indeed, as we have argued previously (Doucet and McKay, 2017), a historical moment in 2001 saw the Canadian state shift from attempting to establish a national, universal childcare programme to, instead, extending Parental Leave by adding 25 more weeks. In 2017, this pattern was repeated with federal funding to provinces and territories for targeted state-funded childcare and up to 26 weeks' additional Parental Leave.

One of several explanations for this shift (see Evans, 2007; Dallaire and Anderson, 2009) is that caregiving continues to be viewed as a private responsibility in Canada and federal policies promote a traditional family policy paradigm (Bezanson, 2017). This approach is amplified by what we might call re-motherisation/re-genderisation, because a longer Parental Leave option without additional money is only affordable for families if a lower-earner uses it, most often a mother. Fathers are increasingly using leave benefits, but very unevenly. Outside Québec, only 9.4 per cent of Canadian fathers with insured employment took some leave in 2014, compared with 83 per cent of fathers in Québec (in 2013), with its three to five weeks of Paternity Leave (Statistics Canada, 2015).

It is important to link these concepts into a conceptual configuration that speaks to the complexities of Parental Leave and gender equality. Parental Leave can be viewed as defamilialising, but researchers should also maintain a focus on genderisation, as Parental Leave does not necessarily challenge the gendered division of care work within families and can even exacerbate gender inequalities (Mathieu, 2016). To shift towards degenderisation, and even towards what Mathieu (2016) calls the demotherisation of care work, Parental Leave benefits need to be substantial (so that families with higher-earning fathers can afford fathers' leave-taking) and include designated leave for fathers. In Canada, this has only occurred in Québec. Canada's recent decision to focus on family 'flexibility' by lengthening Parental Leave at a lower benefit payment represents a move that is both familialising and genderising. Further, this policy change deepens the class-based 'parental-leave rich and parental-leave poor' (O'Brien, 2009; McKay et al, 2016) divide between families, as long leaves are least affordable for lower earners.

In thinking about our national, Canadian context, we hold the view that all newborn children should have access to parental care and that all parents, both mothers and fathers, and regardless of labour force attachment, should be supported during the early period of children's lives. A broad social justice position would entirely detach paid support for parental care of newborns from employment to ensure equality of opportunity regardless of parents' relation to the labour market. This model would bring us closer to social democratic welfare states as it would foster 'solidarity by including all citizens in common programmes' and lead to a reduction in 'class differences through income redistribution' (Orloff, 1993, p.310).

New conceptual configurations and imaginaries

In this final section, we engage with creative and critical conceptual approaches to consider current issues and future directions for Parental Leave. We think about imaginative and slightly utopian conceptual configurations that bring together commodification/

decommodification, familialisation/defamilialisation, genderisation/ degenderisation and motherisation/demotherisation with shifting concepts of work, care and neoliberalism. We are guided by our case study of Canada's leave programmes, especially the federal programme, with its lower levels of decommodification and policies that are both familialising and genderising.

Shifting conceptual configurations

As times and contexts have changed, the concepts explored in this chapter have shifted, as have the concepts of care, work, social reproduction, social protection and even neoliberalism. For example, Fraser (2016, p.100) notes that care work is now defined and structured by the 'financialized neoliberal capitalism of our time' and that the 'care deficits we experience today are the form this contradiction takes' in what she names 'a third, most recent phase of capitalist development' (the previous two phases of 'social reproduction–cum–economic production in capitalism's history' being 'the 19th-century regime of liberal competitive capitalism' and 'the state-managed capitalism of the twentieth century').

Neoliberalism, as a contextual issue and as a concept, did not feature in Esping-Anderson's (1990) seminal text (Deeming, 2017), yet, it 'has come to dominate the policy direction of the Anglophone countries' both as 'a set of ideas' and as 'a series of political economic practices' (Baird and O'Brien, 2015, p.200). This shifting context calls for a reconfigured conceptual framework for understanding Parental Leave and neoliberalism.

A triple movement of commodification, decommodification and emancipation

Nancy Fraser (2013, p.16) argues that Polanyi's double movement needs to be widened to include what she calls a 'triple movement', as a shifting geopolitical terrain increasingly moves people out of the standard employment relationship. There is a 'a third pole of social struggle' and 'other forms of domination that need addressing', not only by feminists, she argues, but also by racialised, colonised and indigenous peoples (Fraser, 2013, p.16). Encroaching neoliberalism and the expanding commodification of 'nature, labor, and money', including 'burgeoning markets in carbon emissions and biotechnology and in child-care, schooling, and the care of the old' result in 'disintegrated communities, ruptured solidarities, and despoiled nature'

(Fraser, 2013, pp.228–229; see also Somers and Block, 2005; Vail, 2010; Block and Somers, 2014). What Fraser (2013) and Block and Somers (2005; 2014) agree is needed to counteract these effects are strategies, policies and movements 'to protect society and nature from the ravages of the market'.

With an explicit call for feminist theorising and strategies, Fraser (2013, p.2) writes that 'feminists should end, or be wary of, "dangerous liaisons" with neoliberalism and marketization' and instead work to 'forge a principled new alliance with social protection'. Specifically, she calls upon feminism to 'retrieve its insurrectionary spirit', including the rejection of 'androcentric valuations, especially the overvaluation of waged labor and the undervaluation of unwaged carework' (Fraser, 2013, p.1).

The important point for Parental Leave policies is that in addition to focusing on how to work with existing social policies, a critique must be developed that 'would work not to dissolve, but to *transform* social protections' (Fraser, 2013, p.239; emphasis added). In a similar way, Somers (2008, p.117) argues that 'in today's culture of market fundamentalism', a Polanyian focus attends to 'noncontractual relations of reciprocity, solidarity, and redistribution' as necessary characteristics of 'a robust and rights-centric civil society [as] necessary for the survival of democracy'. In short, Polanyi believed that 'while markets are necessary, they are also fundamentally threatening to human freedom and the collective good' and thus some dimensions of social life, including social reproduction, 'have to be protected from the market by social and political institutions and recognized as rights rather than commodities, or human freedom will be endangered' (Block and Somers, 2014, p.8).

'A battle for the soul of social protection'

Moving beyond the specifics of policy analysis, Fraser (2013, p.241) argues that there is a 'battle for the soul of social protection', and asks:

> Will the arrangements that re-embed markets in the post-neoliberal era be oppressive or emancipatory, hierarchical or egalitarian...? Will the emancipatory struggles of the twenty-first century serve to advance the disembedding and deregulation of markets? Or will they serve to extend and democratize social protections and to make them more just?

How can social protections, including Parental Leave, be made more just? In the face of the growing destandardisation of employment, Rubery (2016) and others (such as Vosko, 2006; 2010; Standing, 2011) argue for social protection measures to be disentangled from the labour market and, more broadly, from commodification. One way would be to reconfigure Parental Leave as benefits *to care* rather than as leave *from work*. To accomplish this in policy is not straightforward. Some countries have provisions for otherwise ineligible families embedded within Parental Leave programmes (Robson, 2017). This promising approach, however, requires more attention to ensure, for example, that newcomers and marginalised populations who do not file income taxes are included. Another possibility is the institution of a minimum basic income that would extend benefits to new parents who are out of the labour market (Fraser, 2013; see also Chapter Seventeen, this volume).

In Canada, Parental Leave benefits could be drawn (wholly or partially) from federal child benefit funds, which are supplemented in many provinces and are separate in Québec. These funds are universal and vary in amount according to family income. Québec's Child Assistance Payment takes variables such as the number of children in a household as well as the number of parents in shared custody households and, unlike leave benefits, these payments are guaranteed for every child. This policy mechanism levels the playing field by giving low-income parents proportionately more money. Blending Parental Leave and Child benefits could improve equity, decommodifying more families while defamilialising, degenderising and demotherising.

Citizenship rights rather than market place entitlements

Finally, we draw on Polanyian insights as articulated by theorists who link social protections to a vision of socio-economic rights that are conceptualised more broadly as citizenship rights and human rights as well as to children's rights to receive care (O'Brien, 2009; Tronto, 2013). As Somers argues in a recent interview (Somers and Curtis, 2016, p.15), 'Meaningful citizenship rights and full social inclusion, while always subject to the violence and violations of racial and gender exclusions, have now more than ever been converted from rights into a set of contingent privileges, ultimately dependent on one's economic means and market exchange value.' To envisage receiving benefits 'solely on the basis of citizenship' (Orloff, 1993, p.315) is rare. At the same time, such benefits can encourage degenderisation (Orloff, 1993) and help address social inequalities of race, ethnicity, age, sexuality and ability/disability.

Somers' (Somers and Curtis, 2016, p.7) reading of Polanyi's work further leads her to argue that citizenship rights are deeply entangled with socio-economic rights and human rights, concluding that

> it is difficult now to find a narrative that allows us to focus on building up socio-economic rights while at the same time not seeming to prioritize them over civil and political rights. This is a very serious difficulty, and one that is a distinct hangover from the early separation of these two sets of rights and their respective traditional associations.

Drawing on Hannah Arendt's (1951; cited in Somers, 2008, p.5) argument about 'the right to have rights', Somers maintains that citizenship rights 'emerge not from natural human nature but from inclusion in a political community', which leads to a more 'holistic realization of human rights' and a 'political economy of moral worth' (Somers and Curtis, 2016, p.16).

Conclusions

This chapter has attempted to reimagine Parental Leave as a set of policies and as a complex object of investigation through what Nancy Fraser (1994; 2013) calls a 'thought experiment'. We consider a range of concepts – commodification/decommodification, familialisation/ defamilialisation, genderisation/degenderisation, motherisation/ demotherisation – that could be useful in reimagining new pathways for Parental Leave policy design. We do so from within our own Canadian national context, broadly characterised as a liberal welfare state, considering how these concepts are applicable to our case study. We explore the radical potential of Polyani's contributions on market fundamentalism and social protection to the burgeoning field of scholarship on Parental Leave policies. We also engage in pragmatic, imaginative, utopian thinking as we participate in wider debates about Parental Leave as instruments of social stratification, decommodification, defamilialisation, degenderisation and demotherisation. We end by promoting Parental Leave as a complex set of rights (socio-economic, citizenship, parent and child) to both provide and receive care.

References

Abrahamson, P. (1999) 'The welfare modelling business', *Social Policy and Administration*, 33(4): 394–415.

Almqvist, A.-L. and Duvander, A.-Z. (2014) 'Changes in gender equality? Swedish fathers' Parental Leave, division of childcare and housework', *Journal of Family Studies*, 20(1): 19–27.

Arendt, H. (1951) *The Age of Totalitarianism*, New York: Harcourt Brace (1979).

Baird, M. and O'Brien, M. (2015) 'Dynamics of Parental Leave in Anglophone countries: The paradox of state expansion in the liberal welfare regime', *Community, Work and Family*, 18(2): 198–217.

Bambra, C. (2006) 'Decommodification and the worlds of welfare revisited', *Journal of European Social Policy*, 16(1): 73–80.

Béland, D., Blomqvist P., Andersen, J.G., Palme, J. and Waddan, A. (2014) 'The universal decline of universality? Social policy change in Canada, Denmark, Sweden and the UK', *Social Policy and Administration*, 48(7): 739–756.

Bezanson, K. (2017) 'Mad men social policy: Families, social reproduction, and childcare in a conservative Canada', in R. Langford, P. Albanese and S. Prentice (eds) *Caring for Children: Social Movements and Public Policy in Canada*, Vancouver: UBC Press, pp 19–36.

Block, F. (2003) 'Karl Polanyi and the writing of the great transformation', *Theory and Society* 32(3): 1–32.

Block, F. (2008) 'Polanyi's double movement and the reconstruction of critical theory', *Revue Interventions économiques*, 38: 1–17.

Block, F. and Somers, M. (1984) 'Beyond the economistic fallacy: The holistics social science of Karl Polanyi', in T. Skocpol (ed) *Vision and Method in Historical Sociology*, Cambridge: Cambridge University Press, pp 47–84.

Block, F. and Somers, M. (2014) *The Power of Market Fundamentalism: Karl Polanyi's Critique*, Cambridge, MA: Harvard University Press.

Block, F. and Somers, M. (2017) 'Karl Polanyi in an age of uncertainty', *Contemporary Sociology: A Journal of Reviews*, 46(4): 379–392.

Bugra, A. and Agartan, K. (2007) *Reading Karl Polanyi for the 21st century*, New York: Palgrave.

Castles, F.G. and Mitchell, D. (1993) 'Worlds of welfare and families of nations', in F.G. Castles (ed) *Families of Nations: Patterns of Public Policy in Western Democracies*, Aldershot: Dartmouth, pp 93–128.

Cho, E.Y.-N. (2014) 'Defamilization typology re-examined: Re-measuring the economic independence of women in welfare states', *Journal of European Social Policy*, 24: 442–454.

Dale, G. (2010) 'Social democracy, embeddedness, and decommodification: On the conceptual innovations and intellectual affiliations of Karl Polanyi', *New Political Economy*, 15(3): 369–393.

Dallaire, J. and Anderson, L. (2009) *The Fight for a Publicly-Funded Child Care System in Canada*, Ottawa: Canadian Centre for Policy Alternatives.

Deeming, C. (2017) 'The lost and the new "liberal world" of welfare capitalism: A critical assessment of Gøsta Esping-Andersen's the *Three Worlds of Welfare Capitalism* a quarter century later', *Social Policy and Society*, 16(3): 405–422.

Doucet, A. (2015) 'Parental responsibilities: Dilemmas of measurement and gender equality', *Journal of Marriage and Family*, 77(1): 224–242.

Doucet, A. (2016) 'Is the stay-at-home dad (SAHD) a feminist concept? A genealogical, relational, and feminist critique', *Sex Roles*, 75(1–2): 4–14.

Doucet, A. (2018) *Do Men Mother? Fathering, Care, Parental Responsibilities*, 2nd edn, Toronto: University of Toronto Press.

Doucet, A. and McKay, L. (2017) 'Parental Leave, class inequalities, and "caring with": An ethics of care approach to Canadian parental-leave policy', in R. Langford, S. Prentice and P. Albanese (eds) *Caring for Children: Social Movements and Public Policy in Canada*, Vancouver: UBC Press, pp 97–116.

Doucet, A., Lero, D.S., McKay, L. and Tremblay, D.-G. (2016) 'Canada country note', in A. Koslowski, S. Blum and P. Moss (eds) *International Review of Leave Policies and Research 2016*. Available at www.leavenetwork.org/lp_and_r_reports/

Escobedo, A. and Wall, K. (2015) 'Leave policies in Southern Europe: Continuities and changes', *Community, Work and Family*, 18(2): 218–235.

Esping-Andersen, G. (1990) *The Three Worlds of Welfare Capitalism*, Princeton, NJ: Princeton University Press.

Esping-Andersen, G. (1999) *Social Foundations of Postindustrial Economies*, New York: Oxford University Press.

Esping-Andersen, G. (2000) 'Multidimensional decommodification: A reply to Graham Room', *Policy and Politics*, 28(3): 353–359.

Evans, P.M. (2007) 'Comparative perspectives on changes to Canada's paid Parental Leave: Implications for class and gender', *International Journal of Social Welfare*, 16: 119–128.

Eydal, G.B., Gíslason, I.V., Rostgaard, T. et al (2015) 'Trends in Parental Leave in the Nordic countries: Has the forward march of gender equality halted?', *Community, Work and Family*, 18(2): 167–181.

Farstad, G.R. (2015) 'Difference and equality: Icelandic parents' division of Parental Leave within the context of a childcare gap', *Community, Work and Family*, 18(3): 351–367.

Fraser, N. (1994) 'After the family wage: Gender equity and the welfare state', *Political Theory*, 22(4): 591–618.

Fraser, N. (2013) *The Fortunes of Feminism: From State-Managed Capitalism to Neoliberal Crisis*, London: Verso.

Fraser N. (2016) 'Contradictions of capital and care', *New Left Review*, 100: 99–117.

Grosz, E. (2011) *Becoming Undone: Darwinian Reflections on Life, Politics, and Art*, Durham, NC: Duke University Press.

Haas, B. and Hartel, M. (2010) 'Towards the universal care course model', *European Societies*, 12(2): 139–162.

Hacking, I. (2002) *Historical Ontology*, Boston, MA: Harvard University Press.

Hull, J. (2013) 'Potential barriers to Aboriginal teenaged mothers' access to maternal and parental benefits', *The International Indigenous Policy Journal*, 4(1): 1–18.

Kurowska, A. (2018) '(De)familialization and (de)genderization: Competing or complementary perspectives in comparative policy analysis?', *Social Policy and Administration*, 52(1): 29–49.

Leitner, S. (2003) 'Varieties of familialism: The caring function of the family in comparative perspective', *European Societies*, 5(4): 353–375.

Lewis, J. (1992) 'Gender and the development of welfare regimes', *Journal of European Social Policy and Administration*, 2(3): 159–173.

Lewis, J. (1997) 'Gender and welfare regimes: Further thoughts', *Social Politics*, 4(2): 160–177.

Lister, R. (1995) 'Dilemmas in engendering citizenship', *Economy and Society*, 24: 35–40.

McKay, L. and Doucet, A. (2010) '"Without taking away her leave": A Canadian case study of couples' decisions on fathers' use of paid leave', *Fathering: A Journal of Theory, Research, and Practice About Men as Fathers*, 8(3): 300–320.

Mahon, R. (2006) 'Of scalar hierarchies and welfare redesign: Child care in three Canadian cities', *Transactions of the Institute of British Geographers*, 31(4): 452–466.

Marshall, K. (2010) Employer top-ups, *Perspectives on Labour and Income (Statistics Canada catalogue 75-001-XPE)*. Available at www.statcan.gc.ca/pub/75-001-x/2010102/pdf/11120-eng.pdf

Mathieu, S. (2016) 'From the defamilialization to the "demotherization" of care work', *Social Politics*, 23(4): 576–591.

McKay, L., Mathieu, S. and Doucet, A. (2016) 'Parental-leave rich and parental-leave poor: Inequality in Canadian labour market based leave policies', *Journal of Industrial Relations*, 58(4): 543–562.

McLaughlin, E. and Glendinning, C. (1994) 'Paying for care in Europe: Is there a feminist approach?', in L. Hantrais and S.P. Mangen (eds) *Family Policy and the Welfare of Women,* Loughborough: Loughborough University of Technology, pp 42–69.

Meil, G. (2013) 'European men's use of Parental Leave and their involvement in child care and housework', *Journal of Comparative Family Studies*, 44(5): 557–570.

Michoń, P. (2008) 'Familisation and defamilisation policy in 22 European countries', *Poznań University of Economics Review* 8(1): 34–54.

Michoń, P. (2015) 'Waiting for the incentives to work: Comparative analysis of the Parental Leave policies in the Visegrad countries', *Community, Work and Family*, 18(2): 182–197.

Moss, P. and Deven, F. (2015) 'Leave policies in challenging times: Reviewing the decade 2004–2014', *Community, Work and Family*, 18(2): 137–144.

Noël, A. (2013) 'Québec's new politics of redistribution', in K. Banting and J. Myles (eds) *Inequality and the Fading of Redistributive Politics*, Vancouver: UBC Press, pp 256–282.

O'Brien, M. (2009) 'Fathers, parental leave policies, and infant quality of life: International perspectives and policy impact', *The Annals of the American Academy of Political and Social Science*, 624(July): 190–213.

O'Connor, J.S. (1993) 'Gender, class and citizenship in the comparative analysis of welfare state regimes: Theoretical and methodological issues', *British Journal of Sociology*, 44(3): 501–518.

O'Connor, J.S., Orloff, A.S. and Shaver, S. (1999) *States, Markets, Families: Gender, Liberalism, and Social Policy in Australia, Canada, Great Britain and the United States*, Cambridge: Cambridge University Press.

Orloff, A.S. (1993) 'Gender and the social rights of citizenship: The comparative analysis of gender relations and welfare states', *American Sociological Review*, 58(3): 303–328.

Orloff, A.S. (2009) 'Gendering the comparative analysis of welfare states: An unfinished agenda', *Sociological Theory*, 27(3): 317–343.

Papadopoulos, T. (2005) 'The recommodification of European labour: Theoretical and empirical explorations', *ERI: The European Research Institute Working Paper Series* 3: 2–31.

Pintelon, O. (2012) 'Welfare state decommodification: Concepts, operationalizations and long-term trends', *CBS Working Paper* 12(20): 1–34.

Polanyi, K. (1944) *The Great Transformation: The Political and Economic Origins of our Time*, New York: Farrar and Rinehart (2001).

Rice, D. (2013) 'Beyond welfare regimes: From empirical typology to conceptual ideal types', *Social Policy and Administration*, 47(1): 93–110.

Robson, J. (2017) *Parental Benefits in Canada: Which Way Forward?*, Montreal, Québec: Institute for Research on Public Policy.

Romero-Balsas, P. (2015) 'Consequences of Paternity Leave on allocation of childcare and domestic tasks', *Revista Española de Investigaciones Sociológicas*, 149: 87–108.

Room, G. (2000) 'Commodification and decommodification: A developmental critique', *Policy and Politics*, 28(3): 331–351.

Rubery, J. (2016) 'Regulating for gender equality: A policy framework to support the universal caregiver vision', *Social Politics: International Studies in Gender, State and Society*, 22(4): 513–538.

Saxonberg, S. (2013) 'From defamilialization to degenderization: Toward a new welfare typology', *Social Policy and Administration*, 47(1): 26–49.

Somers, M.R. (1998) '"We're no angels": Rational choice, and relationality in social science', *Journal of Sociology*, 104(3): 722–784.

Somers, M.R. (2008) *Genealogies of Citizenship: Markets, Statelessness and the Right to Have Rights*, Cambridge: Cambridge University Press.

Somers, M.R. and Block F. (2005) 'From poverty to perversity: Ideas, markets, and institutions over 200 years of welfare debate', *American Sociological Review*, 70(2): 260–287.

Somers, M.R. and Curtis, J. (2016) *Socially Embedding the Market and the Role of Law: An Interview with Margaret Somers*, London: The Laboratory for Advanced Research on the Global Economy, LSE. Available at www.lse.ac.uk/humanRights/research/projects/theLab/Economics-and-Law-in-Conversation---Interview-with-Margaret-Somers-FINAL.pdf

Standing, G. (2011) *The Precariat: The New Dangerous Class*, London: Bloomsbury.

Statistics Canada (2015) 'Employment Insurance Coverage Survey, 2014', *The Daily*. Available at www.statcan.gc.ca/daily-quotidien/151123/dq151123b-eng.htm

Tremblay, D.-G. and Lazzari Dodeler, N. (2015) *Les pères et la prise du congé parental ou de paternité: une nouvelle réalité*, Québec: Presses de l'Université du Québec.

Tronto, J.C. (2013) *Caring Democracy: Markets, Equality, and Justice*. New York: New York University Press.

Vail, J. (2010) 'Decommodification and egalitarian political economy', *Politics and Society*, 38(3): 310–346.

Vosko, L. (2006) *Precarious Employment: Understanding Labour Market Insecurity in Canada*, Montreal: McGill-Queens University Press.

Vosko, L. (2010) *Managing the Margins Gender, Citizenship, and the International Regulation of Precarious Employment*, Oxford: Oxford University Press.

Wall, K. and O'Brien, M. (2017) *Comparative Perspectives on Work–Life Balance and Gender Equality: Fathers on Leave Alone*, New York: Springer.

TWENTY

Parental Leave and beyond: recent international developments, current issues and future directions

Alison Koslowski, Ann-Zofie Duvander and Peter Moss

Parental Leave and beyond

A book on Parental Leave policy sheds light on the situation of parents and young children in contemporary societies, but it cannot help but range into much broader questions: hence, the title of the book 'Parental Leave and beyond'. Indeed, as well as a detailed focus on Parental Leave, the chapters in this volume bring to the fore a debate around which activities we consider to be essential to human functioning and flourishing, including income generation and unpaid care work, as well as questions about how and to whom these activities are distributed. Essentially, our enquiry is into the kinds of societies in which we want to live, with particular attention to parents and children.

When considering Parental Leave and beyond, we reflect too on how we perceive our relationship to the future. Is it about adapting as best we can to economic and technological developments assumed inevitable, or should we attempt something bolder, seeking to shape these developments to meet ideas of a better life for all? This might include broadening the concept of care beyond parents and children, to adult care, and then beyond our households to our community and to the environment in which we find ourselves (Jamieson, 2016). We may extend into other 'time-use' categories than time in paid work, care and leisure; categories that may be altered by adopting a life course approach and by new entitlements to time and money. Our starting point is a commitment to the search for policies that enable a good life for all citizens.

Parental Leave policy typically presumes some pre-existing relationship to the labour market and aims to preserve this relationship for the parent. Paid work has been seen as a lynchpin for female empowerment and emancipation from unhealthy economic dependencies on male partners (for example, Hobson, 1990; Lewis, 2001). Paid work has also been seen as very important for full social inclusion with the universal or adult worker model, though this has taken a different turn with the 'activation' social policy paradigm (Lewis and Giullari, 2005; Perkins, 2010). There is starting to be some considerable backlash to this presumption that paid work is necessarily the best conduit for human flourishing (for example, Fraser, 2016; Bregman, 2017; van Parijs and Vanderborght, 2017). First, the labour market does not necessarily provide sufficiently high wages to alleviate poverty. Second, the quality of some paid work can be low and precarious, which in part is linked to changing technologies. Third, there are increasing tensions between how more people might reconcile paid work with caring relationships. Fourth, we are moving towards unsustainable environmental and community practices in the pursuit of such reconciliation (such as not cooking at home but depending on plastic-wrapped ready meals, or employing migrant domestic and care workers, which increases the number of us who work far from our families, perhaps in other cities or even countries). Thus, when thinking about future directions for how policies might best support parents, analysts should take into account these changing relationships to the labour market. Clearly, this is from an individual perspective, while a societal perspective will have to also include concerns for state budgets and other macro-economic factors. So an economy which relies on a constant and unquestioning expansion of its labour market is challenged for many reasons, ranging from the individual and familial, to the environmental and global.

The wealth of international experience and scholarship condensed into this volume points to a common tendency to compartmentalise different aspects of human activity, such as income generation and parental caregiving, as if they occur in isolation from one another, not carried out by the same actors. In so doing, we create many problems for ourselves. If we extend this observation to all care work and not just care for young children, this further highlights the unsustainability of organising these aspects of life as if the same people were not involved in simultaneous and multiple activities. Thus, we seek to focus on Parental Leave, but also on what must lie beyond it for broader aims to be realised.

In this concluding chapter, we summarise some of the main points raised by our authors. We turn to recent developments in individual countries and some of the current issues in Parental Leave, which are evident across a range of country contexts. We reflect, too, on future directions for Parental Leave policy and its attendant politics, but also go beyond Parental Leave. By so doing, we consider the empirical findings around what appears to work best (in a given time and place) for parents and children. This is where our volume can begin to offer practical suggestions to interested policy makers and employers as to how they might develop policy to better support parents and young children – and perhaps also other parties along the way. We also consider the methodological contributions, noting in particular the data that are and are not available, and the consequences this has for what we can know. Finally, we consider how scholars might most effectively frame future scholarship into Parental Leave.

Recent international developments and current issues

At the core of our enquiry into Parental Leave is a presumption that the state has a useful role to play in supporting the relationship between parents and children, so that fathers and mothers are able to continue labour market participation and working women and men can consider parenthood. The state plays this role because it wants people to work. Its support can be via institutional frameworks such as leave policy, but also via childcare and other related services. There are many political reasons why the state might choose to be involved in supporting parents, but whichever these are, it is generally the case that parenting is easier when there are structures in place to spread the work and costs of childrearing beyond the parents.

The importance of understanding the local politics of leave policies in order to better understand their formation was emphasised by the 2009 volume *The Politics of Parental Leave Policies: Children, Gender, Parenting and the Labour Market* (Kamerman and Moss, 2009). Following the continued international expansion of the International Network on Leave Policies and Research (to which contributors to this volume belong), our current enquiry is now able to range further afield than before, to include in Part I, recent developments not only in Europe, but in countries such as Israel (Chapter Five), Japan (Chapter Six), China (Chapter Seven), Mexico (Chapter Eight) and the United States (Chapter Nine). It has been often observed that care, as part of social reproduction 'comprising both affective and material labour, and often performed without pay, is indispensable to society' (Fraser, 2016, p.1). Why then, do state institutional structures often fail so spectacularly to create the ease of parenting and other care work that they have the capacity to bring about? This is a question guiding many contributions in Part I. Then, in Part II, a range of current issues in leave policy are considered. We highlight what we consider to be the key messages from Parts One and Two in the volume in the following sub-sections. We then go on to discuss the potential future directions that are brought up in Part III of the book, with the aim to point throughout to crucial issues for policy development.

Multiple rationales for leave

The contributions on the politics of Parental Leave in Part I confirm that leave policy continues to be advocated by governments for a variety of reasons. Countries differ in the importance they attach to these various reasons. The multiple rationales reported by authors in Part I include: gender equality, with regards to female labour market participation but also co-responsibility of parenting (Spain, Mexico), fertility (China, Japan, Poland) and social mobility (Mexico). A curious feature in some countries is the importance of a rhetoric around leave being available to fathers, which is then hardly used at all by fathers (for example, Japan, Poland, UK), in the context of a system which actually more or less explicitly supports maternalism. An underlying and less explicitly voiced concern is often the state budgetary need for more workers and tax payers, where parents (mothers) are an important stock from which to draw.

Typically, a country will focus on a particular set of rationales at a given point in time. However, these positions are often conflicting, for example, the goal to develop flexibility in the ways in which parents might organise themselves when they take leave, in the name of enhancing individual choice, appears at odds with gender equality, as demonstrated in Chapter Four on the UK and also in Chapter Twelve on the Norwegian situation. There are also, in some cases, rationales to not implement leave policy, such as a reluctance to impose further regulation on employers, most prominently in the case of the United States, which remains one of the few countries in the world without any paid statutory Maternity Leave (although, as Chapter Nine explains, some individual states now offer paid leave that includes maternity provision).

Cross-national comparison would sometimes seem to be a useful tool for influencing policy makers during government debates, but this is by no means always the case, and can change over time. In Chapter Five, we learn how Israel was once proud to consider itself ahead of the pack with regards to its Maternity Leave, but has since claimed lack of resource and rather fallen to the back of the pack with its leave policies. In other cases (for example, the UK), there is a reluctance to cross-reference its situation with other countries.

Policy design matters

In addition to multiple rationales for leave, there are large variations in the design of leave policies, even among high-income countries, a feature amply demonstrated by chapters in this book. Design of leave varies along dimensions such as overall length of leave, length of well-paid leave, eligibility, whether or not Maternity Leave is partially transferable to fathers, and whether Parental Leave is a family or individual entitlement. There are also varied forms of flexibility in how leave may be taken.

We learn as well that policy design matters with regard to a desired outcome. This is articulated particularly well in Chapter Eleven, which considers Parental Leave design and its effects on fathers' participation in the Nordic countries, drawing upon the variation in policy design within these countries. It seems from this experience, for example, that reserved months of well-paid leave for fathers promotes more equal use of leave between men and women, a stated aim of most Nordic countries. By contrast, a particular rhetoric around gender equality may be present in the leave policy debate in a given country at a given time, but it is not matched by an appropriate policy design for such an outcome to be realised. This is illustrated well by the situation in Poland, in Chapter Three: for while gender equality is part of the debate and the discourse around leave policy in Poland, the design of leave works against fathers using leave and embeds mothers into taking long if relatively well-paid leave. A further conclusion to draw is the need to monitor, evaluate and, if necessary, adapt leave policies to ensure the alignment of aims and design, and to continue to do so over time as effects may change.

Authors have presented considerable practical policy design advice for those involved in the development of leave policies across the world. Unfortunately, such development is generally more complex than to simply transfer a policy design from one country to another. As Korpi and colleagues note: 'Family policy institutions are always embedded in wider social, cultural and historical contexts, and result from different forces; policy configurations are alloys, not elements' (Korpi et al, 2013, p.9). Nonetheless, it is helpful to understand the consequences of a particular policy design at a given time, in a given place, as this knowledge can inform those involved in current policy development. Despite there being considerable scope for the development of Parental

Leave in most countries, there is nevertheless already a wealth of experience to draw upon. The combined knowledge from various contexts may help us understand what factors are important for successful policy implementation.

The contributions in this volume remind us that Parental Leave is not a uniform agenda, but rather that different governments are focused on particular outcomes and maybe less on others. It is important to remember that if a policy has not been designed to achieve a particular outcome, it is perhaps not surprising if it does not deliver such an outcome. Given the existence of a range of policy drivers across countries, there is possibly the (sometimes hopeful) projection that these might all be achieved, just by having some form of the policy in place. Experience demonstrates that this is unlikely. In some cases, much can be expected from Parental Leave policy, possibly too much for what is essentially very much a time limited intervention in the lives of parents and children. Parental Leave policy is not alone in this regard. Much of our ECEC provision is pitched at solving other societal problems (rather than education and care), such as social mobility, which is also possibly too much to ask of a single policy area. It is therefore important to consider policies in combination, for example to highlight potential care gaps between Parental Leave and the start of ECEC provision or the possible inconsistencies between Parental Leave and workplace practices and cultures.

The politics of flexibility and choice

There would seem to be a tension between realising gender equality, particularly with an emphasis on the role that fathers might play in care in addition to the role that mothers might play in the labour market, and the politics of flexibility and choice. Many chapters in the volume note that it is not sufficient to have gender neutral labelling of policy, as is often the case for transferable Maternity Leave or Parental Leave provided as a family rather than an individual entitlement, if the aim of a policy is gender equality with regard to co-responsibility for care. Where the politics of parental choice are cited as reasons to be content with the design of leave policy, this is generally correlated with what could be described as a maternalistic culture (for example, in the case of Israel, Poland and the UK).

Even where the explicit aim of policy is gender equality, such as in the Nordic countries or in Québec, flexibility may also cause problems. In this case, the flexibility in the design of Parental Leave has been heralded as a tool to help fathers, in particular to make fuller use of their entitlements. However, contributions to this volume suggest that flexibility in leave policy, with its assumed goal of increasing choice, should be approached with caution. Chapter Twelve on Norway and Chapter Thirteen on Québec both illustrate the stress that multi-tasking between the workplace and home, as well as not being able to settle into a particular pace, can bring to fathers on leave. In addition, fathers are not replaced by other employees while on leave (in contrast to mothers, for whom maternity cover is more frequently routinely found). While flexibility has been proposed as a positive solution to work–family reconciliation, it would appear to also have a potentially negative impact on well-being. Overall, then, such flexible provision of leave may not be helpful in truly supporting fathers to become equal caregivers as much as less flexible, more full-time leave-taking, a conclusion also drawn by the Leave Network publication on fathers on leave alone (O'Brien and Wall, 2017). Nevertheless, if the alternative is no leave at all by fathers, a flexible leave may be a stepping stone on the way towards realisation of gender equal parenthood.

Eligibility: employment related entitlement or social right?

As explored extensively in Chapter Fifteen, another theme to emerge is that we need to pay more attention to the eligibility conditions attached to leave policies; this can become particularly pertinent in response to changes to labour market structures. There is currently a close relationship between eligibility to leave policy and labour market and employment history. The conditioning of employment for access to Parental Leave is often based on the idea of Parental Leave as an employment right linked to social insurance, making possible a combination of work and children especially for women. The enablement of women to keep their jobs after becoming parents is a strong incentive to work before having children and a major mechanism by which Parental Leave contributes to women's economic independence and gender equality. Nevertheless, Parental Leave as an entitlement related to employment, or more particularly to a particular form of employment, excludes many people, for example, in China for its migrant workers (Chapter Seven); in Mexico for workers in its large informal economy (Chapter Eight); and in Canada with its many exclusions (Chapter Nineteen). For this and other reasons, there is a case to re-configure leave policy as a social right attached to citizenship or residence rather than an employment right attached to a paid work record (see Chapters Fifteen and Nineteen).

Often strongly correlated with labour market status and thus eligibility are socio-economic status indicators such as social class and level of education. It has been observed that family policies tend to be more beneficial for women with tertiary education across countries, and differ in the extent to which they improve the situation for women without higher levels of education (Korpi et al, 2013). We know too that fathers with a higher socio-economic status are more likely to take leave (for example, Koslowski and Kadar-Satat, 2018). It is important to recognise that Parental Leave policy is ambitious as it aims to support parents across the socio-economic spectrum, but that this ambition may well require a multi-pronged policy design for different groups (as highlighted in Chapter Sixteen which considers Basic Income and Parental Leave).

Do leave policies need to adapt to increasing diversity in employment and household type?

Several chapters illustrate how we should not assume that any particular policy is likely to serve all parents equally well (for example, Chapter Five on Israel and Chapter Ten, which considers leave policy preferences both within and between 27 countries). In the first instance, parents within a given country or region will exhibit multiple parenting practices and preferences (usually gendered to a certain degree); parents are not a homogenous group. In addition to sex and gender identity, education level, occupation, contract status (temporary versus permanent), income and wealth, among other socio-economic characteristics, are all correlated with parenting practices and preferences, including leave-taking. However, this is not so much an issue of having flexibility or choice with regard to leave-taking, but rather a restriction of access to leave for some groups of parents.

As we discuss in the previous section, eligibility to (and generosity of) Parental Leave is often premised on employment, rather than on being a universal right. As the nature of employment is changing and increasing numbers of parents are in more precarious work, increasing numbers of parents might find that they are not able to access benefits because of the conditions attached to eligibility. Parental Leave then runs the risk of increasingly serving a diminishing group that are also privileged by secure, stable employment often also associated with higher wages.

Much Parental Leave design assumes the birth mother as being a primary carer. In some cases, eligibility to leave for fathers is premised on the mother's eligibility to leave (for example, Chapter Four looking at the UK), as well as, in other cases, residence with the mother. It is likely that much Parental Leave legislation struggles to accommodate the increasing diversity in family forms, such as the co-parenting models found within the LGBT community (for example, Herbrand, 2017).

The impact of different levels of government on Parental Leave

Parental Leave legislation exists at multiple levels of government. At a regional level, the European Union has adopted Directives, which set minimum requirements with which member states must comply. Member state national governments are then free to implement and design Parental Leave as they wish, and most will exceed the minimum requirements, in terms of duration and other benefits (including payment levels). As with other policy areas, the European Union has been hugely influential as a pace setter.

We learn from Chapters Thirteen and Nineteen that there can be considerable variation in leave policy design within a country, as exemplified by the Canadian case, where the province of Québec is quite distinct from the rest of the country with its provision of leave. Similarly, in the US, as discussed in Chapter Nine, where there is no federal level statutory paid leave available, some states have taken a lead in establishing paid leave. Also, in Belgium, there is some regional variation (Chapter Seventeen). Alternatively, in other countries, such as the UK, leave policy is not a devolved area. This can play a role in how well integrated Parental Leave is with other related policies, such as ECEC, if, as in the case of the UK, one area is devolved across the four nations (that is, ECEC) and Parental Leave is not.

China is another country with much regional variation in the provisions available to parents. As noted in Chapter Seven, this also has the effect of amplifying rural and urban differences associated with the household registration system, in so far as many are not eligible for leave benefits due, in part, to a mismatch between their place of employment and their registration status.

Classic examples of 'path dependency' leading to sub-optimal policy versus 'tipping points' to change

Parental Leave policy can be an exciting exemplar for those interested in cases of policy which precedes, and thus perhaps can be attributed as a cause of behavioural change, as has been particularly clear with regard to fathers' increased take-up of leave in the Nordic countries, discussed in Chapter Eleven, but also in Québec (Chapter Thirteen). Parental Leave policy occasionally yields policy tipping points, when a newly implemented aspect of policy design can lead to a dramatic change in behaviour, in accordance with the policy's aims.

There are, however, also exemplars where Parental Leave policy serves to illustrate the phenomenon of 'path-dependency', where policy appears to be stuck in a rut. The particular aims that a government might have had can endure long after the event, for better or worse. Leave policy is sometimes developed in a piecemeal way, without clear long-term goals. The early 'pieces' can obstruct later attempts at reform to create a coherent and comprehensive policy, the path dependency problem (see Chapter Four on the UK). Similarly, the legacy of Communist-era leave policy design remains, with its maternalistic emphasis reflected in policy design encouraging a long leave duration for mothers (for example, see Chapters Three and Ten). Such path dependency in policy development is a particular hindrance to effective reform.

Other issues with implementation of policy have been related to the adverse effects of austerity, as we see in Spain (Chapter Two) and Israel (Chapter Five). In the case of Israel, the political debate has been explicit that lack of resources is the reason for not extending Parental Leave, rather than any particular ideological stance. In Spain, it has rather been the case of lost opportunity, as it would seem likely that there was the political will to move to more comprehensive leave policies, which may well have been implemented sooner if it had not been for a long period of austerity.

An awareness of these various stumbling blocks may help policy makers to better understand how to make the major turns in policy that we have seen earlier in countries such as Iceland and Germany (described in detail in Kamerman and Moss, 2009).

The relationship between Parental Leave, workplace culture and other policy areas

Statutory Parental Leave provision is sometimes enhanced by extra-statutory benefits provided by employers. These are also referred to as occupational benefits and sometimes as voluntary occupational welfare (see Chapter Fourteen). Such enhanced benefits can be offered by employers as a result of collective agreements, or simply as part of the benefits package offered to employees (such as salary, pension contributions and health insurances, to name a few other common benefits). Such 'top up' provision can be seen as part of the workplace culture, and is a key part of the context in which parents plan their leave taking (or not) (Moran and Koslowski, 2018). Chapter Fourteen reminds us of the importance of conceptualising leave within a broader framework, including workplace provision. In order to understand the reasons behind the variations that exist, there is much to take into consideration, including central gender-based institutions and outcomes (Orloff, 2009).

Leave policy strategy in developing countries

A motivation for this volume has been the observation that leave is high on the policy agenda internationally (ILO, 2014), including in lower income countries. Chapter Eight on Mexico highlights the particular challenges for leave policy in a country where many people are in informal employment, which is more prevalent in developing countries. The challenge is at least two-fold: the tax base is reduced and people are unlikely to be eligible for employment-related benefits. Many countries have Maternity Leave, but Parental Leave is much less common (ILO, 2014). More research is needed on leave policy in developing countries, as well as agreed international standards, which is yet another task.

Future directions for politics and policy

If our starting point is a commitment to the search for social and economic flourishing for all citizens, what might be potential future directions for politics and policy? While acknowledging that different political perspectives will take this starting point in different directions, we first consider potential future directions for Parental Leave policy, narrowly defined, before looking beyond Parental Leave, casting the net to other future scenarios for parenting and care.

For Parental Leave

Need for clarity on aims...then matching aims to design

A central recommendation from the empirical findings is that it is imperative to clearly identify the aims of leave policy and match them to appropriate policy design. It is unusual for a policy aim to be achieved without it being explicit. A good example is how few countries have gender equality as a clear aim of leave policy, accompanied by the appropriate gender equality policy design. Despite much rhetoric suggesting governmental support for gender equality, and perhaps even a hope that gender equality might emerge as a result of the implementation of a particular policy design, mothers remain predominantly as the primary carers of infants. Whether fathers are more involved is very much correlated with a certain policy design, as we see in Chapter Eleven on gender equality in the Nordic countries. What constitutes gender equality must also be clearly defined, not least so that the effectiveness of policy can be monitored and assessed, leading, if necessary, to policy changes to improve results.

Setting targets (perhaps)

In much the same way as the EU directives set minimum requirements for Parental Leave, we should perhaps revisit what it is we want to achieve with leave and become more outcome focused, rather than only concentrating on the existence of policy. For example, what use is a policy which technically allows for fathers to take leave, but is used by fewer than 1 per cent of fathers, as in the case of Japan and Poland? Perhaps targets for outcomes, such as leave uptake by fathers, would be another way to realise aims such as gender equality. Target setting is to be approached with caution, however, as such positive discrimination tools can also be prone to unintended and potentially unwelcome consequences.

Evaluation: development of indicators

A related issue is that we need good indicators to achieve meaningful statistics so that we can know if policies are working. This would include the cross-national harmonisation of indicators and data collection for the purposes of comparison by bodies such as the European Commission and international organisations such as the ILO, the OECD and the World Bank. Many of the chapters draw upon the annual review produced by the International Network on Leave Policies and Research. The review highlights the extreme variation across countries in routine administrative data collection around key indicators such as the take-up of leave and who is doing so. We urgently need to increase awareness regarding data, what information is available and what is lacking. The international community needs to approach the question of harmonisation of data in a sensible way. We need to be able to compare between countries, but also preserve data so that country-specific details are not lost in translation.

Coherence across policy areas

Perhaps the most important note for policy makers is that Parental Leave policies need to dovetail with other policies, in particular with early childhood education and care services. Leave policy needs to be seen as just one constituent part of a comprehensive package of measures, including: changes to workplace culture and organisation (in a move to a 'dual-carer dual-worker' model); development of ECEC and other formal services; and a wide range of measures to promote more equal sharing of care by men (both in the family and in services, where the workforce for young children and old people remains overwhelmingly female). This is not a new conclusion: the European Council of Ministers Recommendation on Childcare (92/241/EEC) in 1992 made just this point decades ago, but it is echoed again by our authors.

Finding ways of giving voice to children

The emphasis in our volume is on parents rather than children, reflecting the emphasis in Parental Leave politics and policy. While child welfare and well-being may be a consideration in leave policy, it is not apparent in most cases that the test of the best interests of the child – which according to Article 3 of the UN Convention of the Rights of the Child must be the primary concern in making decisions that may affect children – is applied and that the voice of the child is given a hearing. How that test might be applied and how that voice might be heard in formulating leave policy is currently unclear and little considered. It has particular relevance for whether leave policy is to be treated as an employment benefit or a social right, for the former approach would seem to be in contradiction to one that ensured that all children could benefit from parents having more time to devote to them. As it is, not only parents but children are disadvantaged where leave policies exclude many of the most insecure and vulnerable families in our societies.

Beyond Parental Leave

Future proofing or future building?

Parental Leave development can potentially be part of broader discussions about what sort of world we desire to live in, for ourselves and future generations. Future directions raise political and ethical issues about the kind of society and relationships we want. Is policy to be part of future proofing (that is, readying people to an inevitable future) or future building (helping to shape a desirable future)? The underlying issue here is stark: can our societies regain some political and social control over economic and technological development, so as to build better futures for all?

In terms of 'broader' reform, the authors of Part III propose some options for future directions to move beyond Parental Leave to (a) a life course approach; (b) a broad approach to care covering self, others and the environment (as in a broadly conceived ethics of care); and (c) universal coverage. These options might include: building up a range of leave, for example, to include leave for adult care; introducing a universal basic income, perhaps with a supplement of Parental Leave entitlements (Chapter Sixteen); and/or turning to a 'time credit' system, that is, a quota of time that can be drawn down over a lifetime for either any or a wide range of reasons (Chapters Seventeen and Eighteen), which might then need some mechanism to give additional time credit to those who have more caring to do because of more children, family members with illnesses/disabilities and so on. In all cases, a specific and constant focus on gender equality would be necessary, to avoid regression following new policy directions.

Workplace culture and practice

Public policy is not enough. It needs to be accompanied by change in workplace culture and practice commensurate with a dual carer model and a multi-activity society (as suggested in Chapter Eighteen). Welfare states are not the only providers of welfare, often employers play a role, also with leave benefits, but generally, the consensus remains that statutory benefits are a necessary foundation. Nonetheless, Boling (2015) has pointed to the importance of gaining the buy-in of business in order to provide backing to a statutory system, contrasting the cases of recent policy reform in Japan and Germany and the stark difference between the countries in subsequent behavioural change by parents. This often relates to the funding system in place in a country and the extent to which employers are supported, but also regulated, by the state in recognition of the impact leave taking has on them, both to the positive and in terms of the more challenging issues, especially for small- and medium-sized enterprises. Design of leave policy matters, but effects of good design can be undermined by the absence of parallel cultural change, for example, Japan with a well-designed Parental Leave, but very low take-up by fathers as workplace culture is generally not supportive of fathers using the leave.

Future directions for academia

Such a collection of scholarship as is to be found in this volume gives us pause to consider different approaches to the analysis of Parental Leave policy, and whether there have been, and perhaps continue to be, some lacunae in our conceptual frameworks. In the volume, authors present single country case studies and comparative analyses. In both instances, they are looking for patterns to aid our understanding and explanations; some authors seek a narrow focus on the details of Parental Leave policy design, while others aim for a broad focus, emphasising the context in which Parental Leave policies sit as important for a full analysis. It seems obvious to us that both approaches are needed to give further understanding, including obstacles and facilitators of leave-taking both at individual and structural levels.

As mentioned, there is much work to be done regarding the collection and harmonisation of data on leave and its use. Once the data are available, scholars will be better able to develop various methods and combinations of methods for analysis. In addition, there is work to be done to better understand the effects of combinations of the various dimensions of leave policy (for example, eligibility, length, generosity), as well as the combinations of leave with other policy areas.

Units of analysis

As well as considering the division of labour across groups in a society, we might also consider the division of labour within a household. Should we conceive of a parental team delivering care for small children in the household, or rather a primary carer, typically the mother supported by a father or other household or family members? This draws us to reflect upon the unit of analysis when considering Parental Leave: should it be the individual parent, the individual child, the parental team and/or household, the extended family and friends network, the local community? Herring (2013) considers whether the caring relationship, which brings two persons (in this case parent and child) into interdependency, rather than individual persons, might be a more appropriate unit of analysis in matters of care.

We also need to acknowledge, however, that there are not always two persons caring for a child, there may be one and there may be more than two of equal importance. This leads into an exciting new field of changing family forms and caring behaviour. Researchers need to reflect on and follow this development to avoid being confined by an ideal of dual-carers of different genders, which may soon be one among many caring choices to be made.

Conclusions

In summary, there is much research, policy development and discussion remaining to be done in the arena of Parental Leave. There is still the need to consider the basics around the current situation in the great majority of countries. This volume achieves a wider geographical spread than previous publications on Parental Leave; but as already acknowledged in the introductory chapter, there is more to know about many parts of the world not considered in this volume.

There are multiple rationales for the introduction and development of Parental Leave. These rationales may lead to various forms of path dependencies and incoherent or coherent designs of policy that need to be understood in order to appreciate how both to avoid pitfalls and how to progress towards successful policy development. The chapters in the book give examples of less successful path dependencies and developments halted because of economic austerity and other obstacles that we may learn from. Different starting points and different prioritisation of aims with the policy, however, will also lead to different outcomes. Examples are flexible leave policies that end up prioritising choice over gender equality, and eligibility conditions that incentivise certain forms of employment leading to economic independence for some women in preference to leave as a social right that encompasses those with a marginal relationship to the labour market. In addition to the development of a new labour market with more precarious employments, diversity in family forms needs to be considered when developing policy. It can be argued that much of the *status quo* can be linked to conflict over resource allocation, but there is also clear evidence that preferences are often strongly linked to what people know and that there is often reluctance towards change.

There will always be diversity in policy, as politicians make political choices, but as researchers, we may aim for informed diversity, supplying the analysis of what works for different aims. We can also propose and explore alternative normative frameworks. The book addresses issues of desirability and viability, but also of achievability across the whole population, all three being necessary conditions for what Erik Olin Wright (2007) terms 'real utopias'. Many questions remain, not least the question of gender equality and the dominance of the mother as primary carer. Linked to this question, we look beyond Parental Leave: could it be wiser to move beyond the current focus on early parenthood to consider our societies' overall social requirements for care across the life course? To this aim, we might continue to build on Nancy Fraser's 'universal caregiving' model of life (2016) and Joan Tronto's 'ethics of care', which expand our gaze beyond the individual towards the wider community and environment in which we live.

References

Boling, P. (2015) *The Politics of Work–Family Policies: Comparing Japan, France, Germany and the United States*, Cambridge: Cambridge University Press.

Bregman, R. (2017) *Utopia for Realists and How We Can Get There*, Bloomsbury: London.

Fraser, N. (2016) 'Contradictions of capital and care', *New Left Review*, 100 (July–August).

Herbrand, C. (2017), 'Co-parenting arrangements in lesbian and gay families: When the 'mum and dad' ideal generates innovative family forms', *Families, Relationships and Societies*. DOI: 10.1332/2046743 17x14888886530269

Herring, J. (2013) *Caring and the Law*, Oxford: Hart Publishing.

Hobson, B. (1990) 'No exit, no voice: Women's economic dependency and the welfare state', *Acta Sociologica*, 33(3): 235–250.

ILO (International Labour Office) (2014) *Maternity and Paternity at Work: Law and Practice Across the World*, Geneva: ILO.

Jamieson, L. (2016) 'Families, relationships and "environment": (Un)sustainability, climate change and biodiversity loss', *Families, Relationships and Societies*, 5(3): 335–355.

Kamerman, S. and Moss, P. (eds) (2009) *The Politics of Parental Leave Policies: Children, Gender, Parenting and the Labour Market*, Bristol: Policy Press.

Koch, M. and Mont, O. (eds) (2016) *Sustainability and the Political Economy of Welfare*, Routledge Studies in Ecological Economics, London: Routledge.

Korpi, W., Ferrarini, T. and Englund, S. (2013) 'Women's opportunities under different family policy constellations: Gender, class, and inequality tradeoffs in Western countries re-examined', *Social Politics*, 20(1): 1–40.

Koslowski, A. and Kadar-Satat, G. (2018) 'Fathers at work: Explaining the gaps between entitlement to leave and uptake', *Community, Work and Family*. DOI: 10.1080/13668803.2018.1428174

Lewis, J. (2001) 'The decline of the male breadwinner model: Implications for work and care', *Social Politics*, 8(2): 152–169.

Lewis, J. and Giullari, S. (2005) 'The adult worker model family, gender equality and care: The search for new policy principles and the possibilities and problems of a capabilities approach', *Economy and Society*, 34(1): 76–104.

Moran, J. and Koslowski, A. (2019) 'Making use of work–family balance entitlements: How to support fathers with combining employment and caregiving', *Community, Work and Family*, 22(1): 111–128. DOI: https://doi.org/10.1080/13668803.2018.1470966

O'Brien, M. and Wall, K. (eds) (2017) *Comparative Perspectives on Work–Life Balance and Gender Equality: Fathers on Leave Alone*, London: Springer.

Orloff, A. (2009) 'Gendering the comparative analysis of welfare states: An unfinished agenda.' *Sociological Theory*, 27(3): 317–343.

Perkins, D. (2010) 'Activation and social inclusion: Challenges and possibilities', *Australian Journal of Social Issues*, 45(2): 267–287.

van Parijs, P. and Vanderborght, Y. (2017) *Basic Income: A Radical Proposal for a Free Society and a Sane Economy*, Cambridge, MA: Harvard University Press.

Wright, E.O. (2007) 'Guidelines for envisioning real utopias', *Soundings*, 36(Summer): 26–39.

Index

www.ingramcontent.com/pod-product-compliance
Lightning Source LLC
Chambersburg PA
CBHW070901030426
42336CB00014BA/2276